Virtue Capitalists

Virtue Capitalists explores the rise of the professional middle class across the Anglophone world from *c.*1870 to 2008. With a focus on British settler colonies – Canada, Australia, New Zealand, and the United States – Hannah Forsyth argues that the British middle class structured old forms of virtue into rapidly expanding white-collar professional work, needed to drive both economic and civilizational expansion across their settler colonies. They invested that virtue to produce social and economic profit. This virtue became embedded in the networked Anglophone economy so that, by the mid-twentieth century, the professional class ruled the world in alliance with managers whose resources enabled the implementation of virtuous strategies. Since morality and capital had become materially entangled, the 1970s economic crisis also presented a moral crisis for all professions, beginning a process whereby the interests of expert and managerial workers separated and began to actively compete.

Hannah Forsyth is a historian at the Australian Catholic University, Sydney. She was President of the Australian and New Zealand History of Education Society 2020–2021. Her first book was *A History of the Modern Australian University* (2014).

Virtue Capitalists

The Rise and Fall of the Professional Class in the Anglophone World, 1870–2008

Hannah Forsyth

Australian Catholic University

CAMBRIDGE
UNIVERSITY PRESS

CAMBRIDGE
UNIVERSITY PRESS

Shaftesbury Road, Cambridge CB2 8EA, United Kingdom

One Liberty Plaza, 20th Floor, New York, NY 10006, USA

477 Williamstown Road, Port Melbourne, VIC 3207, Australia

314–321, 3rd Floor, Plot 3, Splendor Forum, Jasola District Centre, New Delhi – 110025, India

103 Penang Road, #05-06/07, Visioncrest Commercial, Singapore 238467

Cambridge University Press is part of Cambridge University Press & Assessment, a department of the University of Cambridge.

We share the University's mission to contribute to society through the pursuit of education, learning and research at the highest international levels of excellence.

www.cambridge.org
Information on this title: www.cambridge.org/9781009206488

DOI: 10.1017/9781009206471

First published 2023

A catalogue record for this publication is available from the British Library

Library of Congress Cataloging-in-Publication Data
Names: Forsyth, Hannah, author.
Title: Virtue capitalists : the rise and fall of the professional class in the Anglophone world, 1870–2008 / Hannah Forsyth, Australian Catholic University, Sydney.
Description: New York, NY : Cambridge University Press, 2023. | Includes bibliographical references.
Identifiers: LCCN 2022062164 (print) | LCCN 2022062165 (ebook) | ISBN 9781009206488 (hardback) | ISBN 9781009206457 (paperback) | ISBN 9781009206471 (epub)
Subjects: LCSH: Professional employees–History. | Capitalism–History.
Classification: LCC HD8038.A1 F65 2023 (print) | LCC HD8038.A1 (ebook) | DDC 658.3/044–dc23/eng/20230221
LC record available at https://lccn.loc.gov/2022062164
LC ebook record available at https://lccn.loc.gov/2022062165

ISBN 978-1-009-20648-8 Hardback

To all who have taught me. And to teachers, everywhere.

Contents

Figures

Acknowledgements

Even before I finished my first book on universities, I knew that the next historical question I was reaching for was embodied in professional work. To tackle this significant labour transformation shaping class, inequality, and hierarchy in the twentieth century, I began my research with a pilot study in the most unpromising of places: the Australian outback town of Broken Hill and nearby Wilcannia. This far-flung region was about as far from the core of Empire as one could imagine. Yet it was also the home of the mining company Broken Hill Proprietary, making it a cradle of settler-colonial capitalism and working-class consciousness.

It was a preposterous way to start, and I thank those who supported it with conversations, including Raewyn Connell, Stephen Garton, Julia Horne, Stuart Macintyre (now sadly deceased), and Tamson Pietsch. Sincere thanks are owed to Annette Cairnduff and Mike McDonnell, who supported a postdoctoral position at the University of Sydney, and to the Australian Catholic University (ACU), who followed this up with project seed funding. Many thanks to the wonderful team of volunteer archivists who were led by the extremely knowledgeable Brian Tonkin at the Broken Hill City Library and to the First Nations friends and informers who shared their stories. I am grateful to Leon Fink and two anonymous reviewers of the journal *Labor*, as well as Lorenzo Veracini and anonymous reviewers for *Settler Colonial Studies*, whose engagement with this pilot work was crucial to the larger project that followed.

This larger project was then enabled by a Discovery Early Career Researcher Award granted by the Australian Research Council (ARC). This grant is an extraordinary privilege and I appreciate everything it has offered. I am also grateful to anonymous ARC reviewers as well as those who diligently provided feedback on my application and much of the work that followed, including Melissa Bellanta, Nick Carter, Peter Hobbins, Nell Musgrove, Maggie Nolan, Michael Ondaatje, and Shurlee Swain. Scholars at ACU have continued to provide generous and critical readings of draft work, including Michael Champion,

Lorinda Cramer, Meggie Hutchison, Ben Mountford, and Jon Piccini. I am deeply grateful to Noah Riseman, who patiently read several drafts of my book proposal and most chapters, always helping me build clearer arguments. Mike Thompson read less than Noah, but made crucial suggestions as I structured the argument, transforming the book's breadth and shaping my understanding of virtue. I am so grateful.

Staff at the ACU also supported me in other ways. Annelisa Sipos gave library support that went far beyond expectations, and Duane Cabasal ensured my laptop worked, even after hours while I was on the other side of the world. Peter Vear in the School of Arts and Kely Kirwan and other staff in the Research Office ensured I managed my budget to best effect. I was further privileged to be hosted by the history faculty at the University of Cambridge, with valuable support from Peter Mandler but also from their library and IT staff. Thank you all.

I am grateful to staff at archives and libraries, especially the State Library of New South Wales, which was a second home for much of the project. Thanks also to the Noel Butlin Archives Centre in Canberra, the National Library of Australia, the National Archives of Australia, the Public Records Office of Victoria, State Library of Victoria, University of Melbourne Archives, and University of Queensland Fryer Library. Thanks too are owed to staff at the British Library, the Arthur and Elizabeth Schlesinger Library on the History of Women in America, and the Royal College of Nursing Archive. Many thanks to Chris Poullaos, who gave me access to his material on the history of accountancy, and Ann Curthoys, who sent me her wonderful archive box on equal pay.

Quantitative data was supplied, discussed, and understood with permission and assistance from the Australian Data Archive, the Australian Bureau of Statistics (with particular thanks to Paul Murrin), the Cambridge Group for the History of Population and Social Structure (especially Leigh Shaw-Taylor). Evan Roberts generously sent digitized New Zealand data that he had painstakingly entered into Excel – thank you. Lauren Vogel helped me initially compile and understand Australia's census data, for which I am most grateful. Other research assistance was provided by Davida Ivey, Aden Knaap, and Leah McGarrity – thank you all.

Some of the project was completed during the Covid-19 pandemic, which would have been impossible except for the digital collections maintained by diligent archivists. I am particularly grateful for online Canadian archives, especially the Saskatchewan collection, but also digitized professional journals for many societies. Thanks also to Newspapers.com,

NZ Papers Past, and one of our most valued repositories of Australian primary sources, Trove Australia. Digital and material archives are central to the historical storytelling we can do. Certainly, this project would have been impossible without them.

I was privileged to receive feedback on my progress at events hosted by the Australia and New Zealand History of Education Society, Australian Historical Association, American Historical Association, Sydney Feminist History Group, Women's History Network, Cambridge Cultural History Seminar, University of Tasmania Law Seminar (with special thanks to Susan Bartie), Penny Russell as Australian Studies Chair at Harvard, especially for her symposium on Class, the DC Labor History Group, University of Technology Sydney and History Now, and the ReWomen group on women's business history. Thanks are owed to Diane Kirkby and anonymous reviewers at *Labour History*, Andrew Seltzer and reviewers at *Australian Economic History Review*, and to Jess Gerrard and Steve Threadgold and reviewers for *Class in Australia*. Many historians graciously offered ideas, readings, advice, and, in one important Covid-induced emergency, a place to live. Thanks especially to Sven Beckert, Cath Bishop, Ann Curthoys, Desley Deacon, Barrie Dyster, Frances Flanaghan, Peter Hobbins, Di Kelly, Sophie Loy Wilson, Peter Mandler, Fallon Mody, Naomi Parry, Anat Rosenberg, Julianne Schultz, Ellie Shermer, Kylie Smith, and Claire Wright. Many thanks to students of the course Money and Power in 2021 and 2022, as well as my co-teachers Michael Pearson, Jon Piccini, and Joshua Black.

While I am grateful to all (and apologize to those I have inadvertently missed), if gratitude comes in pies to be divided into portions, the largest piece must go to Altin Gavranović. Love, collaborator, ay, husband, friend! Altin was a sometimes-paid research assistant who not only pored through records but also prepared thermoses of soup for us to take to archives together. Later, he acted as the harshest 'reviewer two' (and was irritatingly always right) and then comforted me as I faced my present shortcomings. We discussed ideas at dinner, and he reminded me of primary sources at breakfast. And then, in the final darkest months, he carried all household responsibility and topped this off by also formatting my footnotes. This book owes much to his labour, keen memory, generous love, and intellectual brilliance. *Virtue Capitalists* is not the book he would have written, but he supported my version anyway. I am eternally grateful.

My spectacular son, Cooper Forsyth, was thirteen when I started thinking about this project and is now a grown man. His ideas, activism, and life experiences have been important to my thinking throughout. In this, as in all things, Cooper is my constant inspiration.

Finally, many thanks to Cambridge University Press, to Michael Watson, Emily Plater, Stephanie Taylor, Nagalakshmi Karunanithi and the team as well as the very generous, insightful anonymous readers. The book literally would not exist without you.

1 Introduction
Capitalism, Class, and Virtue

In the last quarter of the nineteenth century, members of an established, English-speaking middle class built and consolidated a new category of work for themselves. Self-consciously upright men and women opened schools or took jobs as teachers in a rapidly expanding education sector. Respectable women, embodying ideas about middle-class femininity, took over healthcare, pushing out working-class midwives and nurses, just as the growing male-dominated medical establishment sidelined 'quacks'. Journalism grew into a major political force and developed new norms and techniques. Engineering, boosted by the expansion of railways, industrial mining, and manufacturing, drew on shop-floor knowledge to grow a distinguished, but also self-consciously practical, masculine elite. Lawyers joined with politicians on one hand and accountants on the other to design a legislative environment conducive to the flow of capital and knowledge, arrange for the transfer of property, including shares, and boost burgeoning political, literary, and scientific organizations with their lively sense that ideas could shape the world. Such ideas were also energizing charity organizations. Soon enough, charity workers professionalized into trained social work. These professions formed societies to set boundaries and manage standards, broadening earlier definitions of professional or learned vocation. No longer bounded so closely to religion, medicine, and law, professionals now embodied a broader faith that rationality – which they linked to race, class, and gender attributes – gave them moral standing. This belief was informed by the deep connection between the rise of the professional class and the growth of English-speaking settler colonial societies.

By doing this work and pursuing the social and collegial interests that went with it, members of what came to be 'white-collar', educated professions made themselves into a class. They became 'virtue capitalists' in that they invested a combination of virtue and money into society and the economy for the purpose of moral and financial profit. This placed them in a special relationship with those they deemed 'below' them. Morally, this was nearly everyone, even the aristocracy, though the social

1

circumstances produced by settler colonization gave their work a pioneering quality. The British middle class who became settler colonial elites sought a social order on frontiers where race, class, and gender uncertainties disrupted smooth commercial and governmental operations.[1] Resolving the social order, according to their values, demanded a kind of expertise that they made into professions.

The professional class, which in the Anglo world grew fastest in the settler colonies and then later in Britain, emerged in relationship to the world they helped colonize. As historian Achille Mbembe has argued, colonizers and colonized co-constructed a mirrored relationship with one another.[2] The moral goals that the professional class attached to their work were built on the selves they saw in this colonial mirror. For them, education was especially crucial. It was the foundation for moral uplift, raising the level of 'civilization' in settler colonies consisting of First Nations peoples as well as Anglo and Celtic immigrants whose manners, norms, and hierarchies were often more dislocated than their ethnic identities.[3] Education was also important for elites, who grew ideals for a rational settler society founded on merit-based opportunity. The same merit structured the professions. It became the 'currency' in which professionals traded, rewarding and signifying hierarchies of class achievement. Often enough, however, 'rational' techniques were also used to exclude people whose race, class, or gender characteristics labelled them deviants and undesirables.

In this context, virtue was materially important. It made the work professionals did socially valuable. Accuracy, probity, efficiency, and discipline made business and share trading more reliable, allowed railways to function, and prevented mines from caving in. Patience, duty, and hygiene made nursing and social work more efficacious. Truthfulness and sometimes objectivity made journalism an effective, reliable conduit for information, while sobriety and discipline were core to good teaching. By the embodied performance of virtue as work, the professional class made the moral material, converting it into economic

---

[1] See Desley Deacon, *Managing Gender: The State, the New Middle Class and Women Workers 1830–1930* (Oxford: Oxford University Press, 1989). On everyday colonial uncertainties, see, of many, Catherine Hall and Sonya Rose (eds), *At Home with the Empire: Metropolitan Culture and the Imperial World* (Cambridge: Cambridge University Press, 2006); Antoinette Burton, *The Trouble with Empire: Challenges to Modern British Imperialism* (Oxford: Oxford University Press, 2017); Penny Russell, *A Wish of Distinction: Colonial Gentility and Femininity* (Melbourne: Melbourne University Press, 1994).

[2] Achille Mbembe, *On the Postcolony* (Berkeley: University of California Press, 2001).

[3] See Penny Russell, *Savage or Civilised?* (Sydney: NewSouth, 2010).

stuff.[4] As the twentieth century unfolded, the moral and the economic became inextricably entangled. The professional class, as the owners of this moral matter, profited enormously by this, though their investment of virtue as capital was not wholly self-serving. Indeed, being virtue, it could not be. This was one reason the settler colonial project gave rise to the opportunity, though it hardly stopped at colonial borders.

By the mid-twentieth century, just as the world needed morality and money to recover from war and economic shock, these virtue capitalists ruled the world. Presiding over post-war reconstruction, the professional class redesigned the modern economy. They set about extending virtue into every corner of the world, establishing institutions and programs that they believed would end world hunger and disease, educate children everywhere, and assist decolonizing nations to 'develop'.[5] Decolonization, however, was not quite what they thought it would be. The global hierarchies established during the age of empire mirrored the merit-based hierarchies that structured the professional class. When decolonization turned hierarchies upside down, including those based on race, gender, and sexuality, this caused a moral crisis.[6]

After three decades, a combination of moral and economic crises in the 1970s precipitated the long fall of the professional-managerial class. A split between the expert and the managerial sides of this class was epistemological and economic. Dividing *knowing* from *doing*, new divisions over virtue have become battles for economic and political power. Real problems requiring expert judgment and action – some, like climate change, with potentially catastrophic consequences – have become sites of what amounts to a new class conflict.

This book uses US, British, Canadian, Australian, and Aotearoa/New Zealand occupation statistics *c.* 1870–2008 to give a transnational, bottom-up reconsideration of familiar events like progressivism, the

---

[4] A similar process is described in connection to international relations in Valeska Huber, Tamson Pietsch, and Katherine Rietzler, 'Women's International Thought and the New Professions, 1900–1940', *Modern Intellectual History* 18 (2021), 121–145.

[5] Among many, see Michael Barnett, *The Empire of Humanity: A History of Humanitarianism* (Ithaca: Cornell University Press, 2011); Glenda Sluga, *Internationalism in the Age of Nationalism* (Philadelphia: University of Pennsylvania Press, 2013); Jordanna Bailkin, *The Afterlife of Empire* (Berkeley: University of California Press, 2012); Agnieszka Sobicinska, *Saving the World? Western Volunteers and the Rise of the Humanitarian-Development Complex* (Cambridge: Cambridge University Press, 2021); Joy Damousi, Trevor Burnard, and Alan Lester (eds), *Humanitarianism, Empire and Transnationalism, 1760–1995* (Manchester: Manchester University Press, 2022); Eileen Boris, *Making the Woman Worker: Precarious Labor and the Fight for Global Standards, 1919–2019* (Oxford: Oxford University Press, 2019), 89–121.

[6] See Adom Getachew, *Worldmaking After Empire: The Rise and Fall of Self-Determination* (Princeton: Princeton University Press, 2019).

growth of the welfare state, and the New Deal.[7] As well as statistics, it is grounded in archival sources for a sample of educated, white-collar professions in the Anglo world, including records, reports, and newspaper commentary concerning law, medicine, engineering, teaching, accountancy, nursing, social work, and journalism. These were selected for the opportunity they present to explore gendered distinctions between occupations and to cover the various fields of professional work. Occupations that are regrettably missing, such as pharmacy and surveying, were excluded to avoid imbalances towards medical science on one hand or technology on the other, for instance. Through the history of this collection of occupations, *Virtue Capitalists* shows that the professionalization of the economy was no mere transformation in occupation structure. Rather, it was deeply entangled with the history and structure of capitalism in the 'long twentieth century' (*c.* 1870–2008) in ways that expose the centrality of virtue to the global economy.[8]

The remainder of this introductory chapter provides historiographical and philosophical background to the book; if you are here for the history and want to skip to Chapter 2 to find out what happened, I will understand completely. Theory junkies: there are three key frames through which *Virtue Capitalists* needs to be understood, each with historical, philosophical, and sociological traditions. The first is about the political geography of twentieth-century capitalism, including imperialism, the emergence of world-systems, and tensions between the free market and what might be characterized as more 'protectionist' moral purpose. This section on professionals and capitalism explains, among other things, my focus on the Anglo world. The second frame is about virtue. From Aristotle, through Max Weber's Protestant ethic to R. H. Tawney's theology of capitalism, this section defines and historicizes virtue.

The third frame explored in this chapter is class. While historians and sociologists have recognized something 'classy' (so to speak) about the professions, exactly what this means for twentieth-century class formation has been deeply disputed.[9] Giving an overview of this historiography of the professions, from British social historian Harold Perkin through

---

[7] On transnational history, see, of many, Akira Iriye, *Global and Transnational History: The Past, Present and Future* (London: Palgrave Macmillan, 2012); Fiona Paisley and Pamela Scully, *Writing Transnational History* (London: Bloomsbury, 2019); Ann Curthoys and Marilyn Lake (eds), *Connected Worlds: History in Transnational Perspective* (Canberra: ANU Press, 2005); Pierre-Yves Saunier, *Transnational History* (London: Bloomsbury, 2013).

[8] This date range is adapted from Giovanni Arrighi, *The Long Twentieth Century: Money, Power and the Origins of Our Times* (London: Verso, 1994).

[9] For an overview of some of these disputes, see Geoff Eley and Kieth Nield, *The Future of Class in History* (Ann Arbor: University of Michigan Press, 2007).

Marxists like Eliot Friedson and Margali Safatti Larson to Barbara Ehrenreich and John Ehrenreich on the professional-managerial class, I show why this book considers the professionals to be a class in and for itself in a Marxist-ish sense.[10] Doing so requires a small adjustment in the way we understand capitalism itself. By drawing virtue together with the processes that Marx first observed as conducive to class conflict, old forms of materialism meet the kinds of entanglements that are now sought by 'new' materialists who have come to prominence in the environmental humanities. The political implications of this reconsideration of class and capitalism, I hope, will help us resolve some of our most urgent problems.

Professionals and Capitalism in the Anglo World

In the late nineteenth century, a far-flung network of English speakers was consolidating into a global economic force. It was formed by a change in habits of British colonization, triggered by the American War of Independence around a century earlier. Historian James Belich calls this the 'settler revolution'.[11] European capitalism, which was growing through a combination of industrialization and colonial expansion, morphed – for the British at least – into settler colonialism. British settlers built new homes, enterprises, and identities westward from the American colonies, across the continent to the Pacific. Britons moved north and west, establishing what would become the provinces of Canada. While the United States was formally independent from the British global system, it remained deeply intertwined with the Anglo world, nevertheless. Economically, America was still connected by trade with Britain, and its enterprises, especially railways, were a key target of British investment. Socially, the United States was part of the same migration patterns that continued to shape Canada and the Antipodes. Culturally and politically America also shared ideas with the other settler colonies about progressive reform, rational government, and human capital investment.[12]

[10] Harold Perkin, *The Rise of Professional Society: England since 1880* (London: Routledge, 1989); Eliot Friedson, *Professional Dominance: The Social Structure of Medical Care* (Chicago: Atherton Press, 1970); Magali Larson, *The Rise of Professionalism* (Berkeley: University of California Press, 1977); Barbara Ehrenreich and John Ehrenreich, 'The Professional-Managerial Class', *Radical America* 11.2 (1976), 7–32.

[11] James Belich, *Replenishing the Earth: The Settler Revolution and the Rise of the Angloworld* (Oxford: Oxford University Press, 2009).

[12] Emily Rosenberg, *Spreading the American Dream: American Economic and Cultural Expansion, 1890–1945* (New York: Macmillan, 1982); Daniel Rogers, *Atlantic*

In the Southern Hemisphere, the same British emigration patterns established what would become Australia and Aotearoa/New Zealand.[13] These places were not part of a unified Britain, exactly, but were a consequence of the same historical push and, thereafter, deeply connected. Settlers, institutional and governmental planners in each place looked to the others to see how they organized themselves and which values they would bring to self-government.[14] Later, when professionals began forming fledgling societies, often their first task was to write for details of what their colleagues were doing in the other Anglo colonies.[15] The colonies were so entangled in British minds that when Florence Nightingale sent one of her protégés, Lucy Osburn, to Australia at the government's request, Osburn took a book to orient herself. In 1867 she wrote to Nightingale that she 'was afraid' the stories, while entertaining, were about a different colony. It was so easy to get the colonies mixed up.[16]

Following the colonists as they spread from Britain to the periphery, historians also typically thought about settler colonialism as unidirectional: the 'whole periphery', Patrick Wolfe once noted, was significantly 'singular'.[17] Nevertheless, understanding capitalism as a 'world-system', as Immanuel Wallerstein put it, helps to see the Anglo world as an organism, or network, rather than as a set of economic comparators fulfilling some unidirectional model of capitalist progress. Wallerstein and other world-systems economists, especially Giovanni Arrighi, are important in this book. Their work, which extended Marx's

---

Crossings: Social Politics in a Progressive Age (Cambridge, MA: Harvard University Press, 1998); Marilyn Lake, *Progressive New World: How Settler Colonialism and Transpacific Exchange Shaped American Reform* (Cambridge, MA: Harvard University Press, 2019); see also Huber, Pietsch and Rietzler, 'Women's International Thought and the New Professions'.

[13] There was also, as Belich points out, a slightly more tentative tie to South Africa.

[14] Kris Manjapra, 'The Semi-peripheral Hand: Middle-class Service Professionals of Imperial Capitalism', in Christof Dejung, David Motadel and Jürgen Osterhammel (eds), *The Global Bourgeoisie: The Rise of the Middle Classes in the Age of Empire* (Princeton: Princeton University Press, 2019); see also David Lambert and Alan Lester, *Colonial Lives across the British Empire: Imperial Careering in the Long Nineteenth Century* (Cambridge: Cambridge University Press, 2006).

[15] For a discussion of how this worked in medicine, and why we ought to look more transnationally rather than account for the rise of national systems, see Peter Hobbins and Kathryn Hillier, 'Isolated Cases? The History and Historiography of Australian Medical Research', *Health and History* 12.2 (2010), 1–17.

[16] Lucy Osburn to Florence Nightingale, 19 November 1867, Correspondence relating to nursing in Australia, Nightingale Papers, British Library, Vol.CLV/FF298.

[17] Patrick Wolfe, 'History and Imperialism: A Century of Theory, from Marx to Postcolonialism', *The American Historical Review* 102.2 (1997), 388–420. Quote from p. 397.

understanding of the relations of production, labour, and dependence to empirical work on long-wave patterns of global capitalism, helps show why the settler revolution produced a professional class; this is central to Chapter 2.[18] For this reason, *Virtue Capitalists* does not see Aotearoa/ New Zealand, Australia, Canada or even the United States as comparative 'case studies'. Rather, they are each a member of English-speaking 'webs of empire', working horizontally together, and often vertically with the British metropole to forge, despite their manifold differences, a systemic whole.[19] It is this whole that is the subject of *Virtue Capitalists*.

This Anglo world was founded on violent dispossession, where land theft in the settler colonies was the precondition to property ownership.[20] Black and Indigenous intellectual traditions, political theorist Robert Nichols shows, often frame this dispossession expansively to include dispossessed bodies, and dispossessed reproductive and sexual selfhood. Colonialism expropriated personhood, as well as property, and the interconnected society that was built from this theft was an economy that similarly consisted of economic and human matter.[21] Such a combination was not limited to the experiences of the colonized. Settler gains in property also consisted of both acreage and the construction of their own personhood. Whiteness, as Cheryl Harris famously claimed, became property, which settler colonists leveraged, like the land, for profit.[22] This was the grounding of the professional class. The world of ideas, techniques, discoveries, and legislative structures that the professional class shared across the Anglo world was constructed on the foundation of this property.

Colonialism forged hierarchical structures that continued to be important even when the British Empire was dismantled. Former colonies, dominated by people whose skin was not white, came to the fore in international discussions about inequality, welfare, and the global

---

[18] Immanuel Wallerstein, *The Modern World-System III: The Second Era of Great Expansion of the Capitalist World-Economy, 1730s–1840s* (Berkeley: University of California Press, 2011); Arrighi, *Long Twentieth Century.*
[19] John Darwin, *The Empire Project: The Rise and Fall of the British World-System 1830–1970* (Cambridge: Cambridge University Press, 2009); Tony Ballantyne, *Webs of Empire: Locating New Zealand's Colonial Past* (Wellington: Bridget Williams Books, 2012); Tony Ballantyne and Antoinette Burton, *Empires and the Reach of the Global 1870–1945* (Cambridge, MA: Harvard University Press, 2012); Alan Lester, *Imperial Networks: Creating Identities in Nineteenth Century South Africa and Britain* (London: Routledge, 2001).
[20] Glen Sean Coulthard, *Red Skin, White Masks: Rejecting the Colonial Politics of Recognition* (Minneapolis: University of Minnesota Press, 2014).
[21] Robert Nichols, *Theft Is Property! Dispossession and Critical Theory* (Durham, NC: Duke University Press, 2020).
[22] Cheryl Harris, 'Whiteness as Property', *Harvard Law Review* 106.8 (1993), 1707–1791.

economic order, inspiring new ideas that would reverse long-held global hierarchies.[23] Their thinking influenced civil rights movements in the Anglo world and held up a decolonizing mirror to the professional class's own hierarchies, which this book discusses in Chapter 7. The history of colonialism, however, continued to define the Anglo world geopolitically. One cannot fail to notice the dominance of the Anglo settler colonies at the core of Wallerstein's world-system, where peripheral dependencies and 'semi-peripheral' countries (those with both core and dependent sectors) offer a large-scale facsimile of the class relations capitalism produced in factories, towns, and cities.[24] While the rest of Wallerstein's core was constituted by Europe and Japan, those regions are not included in *Virtue Capitalists*.

This is to do with the place of the settler revolution in the professionalization of the global economy.[25] As I will show in Chapter 2, while capital in the late nineteenth century emanated from Europe, the massive investment in human capital that generated the professional class was fastest and firmest in the English-speaking settler colonies. US-based economic historians have typically seen this as uniquely American, though, as we will see later, Canada, Aotearoa/ New Zealand, and Australia were near-equal participants in the process. As time passed, this professional class came to dominate the world, including Europe, triggering massive global growth in higher education. From about the mid-twentieth century, European distinction from the Anglo settler colonies diminished, as I show in discussions about Britain. So, while other scholars may wish to extrapolate the changes that this book describes to Germany, Japan, or Scandinavia, I have not done so here.

The traditional centrality of Europe and the United States to studies of 'real' capitalism has kept the settler colonial world to a kind of scholarly periphery, despite its place at the core of Wallerstein's model. In past decades this tended to marginalize scholarly understanding of racial capitalism. Newer studies have reversed traditional imperial 'dependency theories' to show that colonial capitalism historically depended on two race-based forms of exploitation: slavery and settler colonialism. New histories of capitalism, emerging as the Great Recession exacerbated long-standing inequalities, have focused on the history of slavery to

---

[23] Getachew, *Worldmaking After Empire*.   [24] Wallerstein, *Modern World-System III*.
[25] It is also arguably related to the great divergence; see Kenneth Pomeranz, *The Great Divergence: China, Europe, and the Making of the Modern World Economy* (Princeton, NJ: Princeton University Press, 2000).

understand the racism systemically embedded in American capitalism.[26] This work has been expanded to demonstrate the legacies of slavery in Britain, South Africa, and the Antipodes.[27] Recognizing that slavery has 'afterlives' has been an important lens for understanding aspects of the history of professions, such as the historical exclusion of black nurses from healthcare work.[28] These legacies of slavery and colonial oppression also inform a long-standing alignment of racial exclusion with the system of merit, which is a key theme of this book, especially in Chapters 3 and 7.

The other way scholars have sought to understand racial capitalism is via a set of institutional, policy, and settlement patterns that Patrick Wolfe summarized as the 'logic of elimination'. This logic was central to his characterization of settler colonialism as a 'structure, not an event'. The logic of elimination is not – or, at least, not only – about the genocide of First Nations people and culture. Rather, building on Marxist critiques of imperialism, Wolfe argued that settlers were moved, by the logics of settler capitalism, to deploy a changing, flexible set of laws, policies, and cultural norms that would eliminate Indigenous claims to land and resources.[29] This logic continues to infuse First Nations and settler experience.[30] It means that we implicitly know that none of Nurse Osburn's reading on her ship to Australia recognized the sovereignty of those whose land and waterways were being permanently altered by the

[26] Of many, see Edward Baptist, *The Half Has Never Been Told: Slavery and the Making of American Capitalism* (New York: Basic Books, 2014); Walter Johnson, *River of Dark Dreams* (Cambridge, MA: Harvard University Press, 2013); Sven Beckert, *Empire of Cotton: A Global History* (New York: Vintage, 2015); Caitlin Rosenthal, *Accounting for Slavery: Masters and Management* (Cambridge, MA: Harvard University Press, 2018).

[27] Catherine Hall, Nicholas Draper, Keith McClelland, Katie Donington, and Rachel Lang, *Legacies of British Slave-Ownership: Colonial Slavery and the Formation of Victorian Britain* (Cambridge: Cambridge University Press, 2014); Emma Christopher, *Freedom in White and Black: A Lost Story of the Illegal Slave Trade and Its Global Legacy* (Madison: University of Wisconsin Press, 1988); Jane Lydon, *Anti-slavery and Australia: No Slavery in a Free Land?* (London: Routledge, 2021).

[28] Of many, see particularly Darlene Hine, *Black Women in White: Racial Conflict and Cooperation in the Nursing Profession, 1890–1950* (Bloomington: Indiana University Press, 2020).

[29] Patrick Wolfe, *Settler Colonialism and the Transformation of Anthropology: The Politics and Poetics of an Ethnographic Event* (London: Cassell, 1999); Patrick Wolfe, 'Settler Colonialism and the Elimination of the Native', *Journal of Genocide Research* 8.4 (2006), 387–409; Patrick Wolfe, 'Land, Labor, and Difference: Elementary Structures of Race', *The American Historical Review* 106.3 (2001), 866–905; Patrick Wolfe, 'Nation and Miscegenation: Discursive Continuity in the Post-Mabo Era', *Social Analysis: The International Journal of Social and Cultural Practice* 36 (1994), 93–152.

[30] Of many, see Chelsea Watego, *Another Day in the Colony* (Brisbane: University of Queensland Press, 2021), Emma Battell and Adam Barker, *Settler: Identity and Colonialism in Twenty-First Century Canada* (Halifax: Fernwood Publishing, 2015).

capitalist expansions that her book, like so many other accounts of colonization, depicted as 'adventure'.[31]

This matters deeply, for the logics of settler colonialism were often embodied in professional work. Lawyers made and prosecuted oppressive laws and policies.[32] Teachers actively suppressed Indigenous knowledge and imposed forms of education that were sometimes so brutal that, for example, Canadian residential schools became long-unacknowledged gravesites for hundreds of Indigenous children.[33] Healthcare and social workers also worked under the logic of elimination, imposing policies of assimilation and segregation that facilitated the catastrophe known as Australia's 'stolen generations'.[34] Professional virtue, as it was understood until the 1970s, was culturally genocidal in an important sense. That is, while they often sought emancipation, teachers, social workers, and other professionals actively set out to 'destroy' Indigenous 'savagery' because it was incompatible with their notions of virtue.[35]

The big picture provided by world-systems theory, and, by extension, settler colonial studies, disguises a great deal of complexity. In the 1970s and 1980s, Marxist scholars, drawing on Louis Althusser, began to consider the social, as well as economic, which revealed the ways that historically specific, local capitalist development often contained remnants of earlier modes of production.[36] Such frameworks, which in this book help expose relations between the moral values of middle-class Britain and settler capitalism, bear a relation to economist Karl Polanyi's notion of economic 'embeddedness'.[37] In his 1944 book *The Great Transformation*, Polanyi observed that markets do not tend to equilibrate on their own, and we need to see the economy as part of a historical, rather than ideal, capitalist system.[38] His description of the 'double movement' of laissez-faire market systems versus protectionist

---

[31] Lucy Osburn to Florence Nightingale, 19 November 1867, Correspondence relating to nursing in Australia, Nightingale Papers, British Library, Vol CLV/FF 298.

[32] Among many, see Lisa Ford, *Settler Sovereignty: Jurisdiction and Indigenous People in America and Australia, 1788–1836* (Cambridge, MA: Harvard University Press, 2010).

[33] John Milloy, *A National Crime: The Canadian Government and the Residential School System 1879 to 1986* (Winnipeg: University of Manitoba Press, 2017).

[34] Peter Read, *The Stolen Generations: The Removal of Aboriginal Children in New South Wales 1883 to 1969* (Sydney: Government Printer, 1981).

[35] See similarly David Lambert and Alan Lester, 'Geographies of Colonial Philanthropy', *Progress in Human Geography* 28.3 (2004), 320–341.

[36] Louis Althusser, *On the Reproduction of Capitalism: Ideology and Ideological State Apparatuses* (London: Verso Books, 2014).

[37] See Tim Rogan, *The Moral Economists: R.H. Tawney, Karl Polanyi, E.P. Thompson and the Critique of Capitalism* (Princeton, NJ: Princeton University Press, 2017).

[38] Karl Polanyi, *The Great Transformation* (Boston: Beacon Press, 1985).

counter-movements aligns in surprising ways with Barbara Ehrenreich's and John Ehrenreich's 1970s characterization of the 'professional-managerial class'. In their extremely influential essay (more on which in due course), the Ehrenreichs showed that since what American historians define as the 'Progressive Era' (*c.* 1890–1920), professionals have deployed moral and intellectual authority to *both* facilitate and oppose capitalism.[39] One thing that might explain this (but doesn't in fact, as I explain in the next couple of paragraphs) is via professionals' role on both sides of Polanyi's double movement.

From this perspective, Polanyian political economists Wolfgang Streeck and Colin Crouch offer, at least on the surface, one explanation for the 'fall' of the professional class, which I explore in Chapters 7 and 8 of this book. The 'rule of experts', which characterizes technocratic power in the *trente glorieuses* after the Second World War gives way, Streeck argues, to a strike back by capitalist interests after the 1970s. This reversal of Polanyi's double movement, fed at times by what Crouch defines as 'privatized Keynesianism', puts professional, technocratic interests on the back foot.[40] In the 1980s and 1990s, neoliberal reformers characterized the resulting changes as a matter of efficiency. They split ideal markets that were, at least in their imagination, naturally equilibrating away from what they characterized as inefficient, self-interested public services.[41] For Harold Perkin, this marked a class-like division in the society that was, by then, shaped by the 'professional ideal' – more on this in the section of this introduction on professionals as a class. As Third Way politics was then re-calibrating the British Labour Party, it seemed to Perkin that politics was now less informed by the economic divisions of *labour versus capital* than by those whose salaries were paid by *government versus the private sector.*[42]

Virtue Capitalists reconsiders this historiography by understanding the class consequences of acknowledging virtue – some virtue, at least – as an economic substance. Where Polanyi saw market logics embedded in society, this book sees professional virtue as *material*. This characterization enables a materialist exploration of its place in class formation.

---

[39] Ehrenreich and Ehrenreich, 'The Professional-Managerial Class'.
[40] See of many, Wolfgang Streeck, *Buying Time: The Delayed Crisis of Democratic Capitalism* (London: Verso, 2014); Colin Crouch, *The Strange Non-Death of Neo-Liberalism* (Cambridge: Polity Press, 2011); Colin Crouch, 'Privatized Keynesianism: An Unacknowledged Policy Regime', *The British Journal of Politics and International Relations* 11.3 (2009), 382–399.
[41] Among many, see Damien Cahill and Martijn Konings, *Neoliberalism* (Cambridge: Polity Press, 2017).
[42] Perkin, *Rise of Professional Society*, 472–519.

Before I explain my reasoning, let me first acknowledge that not all virtue is economic. Neither moral acts nor virtuous personhood are necessarily economic. Similarly, while all economies are built on a set of moral values, which may be implicit or explicit, not all have structured virtue into the manner in which work is performed. Even work, often characterized as inherently virtuous, does not necessarily turn all the virtue that a good worker may bring to their job into economic stuff. That is, a worker may accrue money in exchange for their labour, but their work may not in fact produce morally good outcomes. Rather, virtue as economically significant matter was made historically, under the specific conditions described in this book, especially in Chapter 2. It is to this virtue that we now turn.[43]

Professional Virtue

Most intellectual histories of virtue start with Aristotle, who argued in Ancient Greece that virtue was key to happiness or well-being, meaning *eudaimonia*, or acting in accordance with the highest good. Virtuous people live well by seeking the eudaimonia itself, and all other goods (money, power, health, friendships) are thought to be worthwhile because they lead to or enhance well-being. To act virtuously is to flourish, in this scheme. Such a view of Aristotelian virtue makes good character central, rather than merely adherence to rules. A person becomes virtuous by cultivating virtues like courage, wisdom, prudence, and temperance and comes to do the right thing, for the right reason, at the right time, and in the appropriate way on the basis of their virtuous character, rather than because they are following rules or seeking out some good other than virtue itself. Practice and habituation are therefore central to an Aristotelian account of virtue: one becomes virtuous by becoming habituated to it. The practices of a virtuous character, according to Aristotle, enabled people to become their true self perfectly aligned with virtue. This in turn produced observably good things for themselves and for others, though sometimes virtuous acts could impede others' flourishing – something that this book shows was true of the professional class, too.

In *After Virtue*, philosopher Alasdair MacIntyre makes a distinction between the way these 'goods' have been imagined historically, as either internal or external. While Thomas Aquinas and other pre-modern Christian interpreters in the Aristotelian tradition saw the practice of

---

[43] Many thanks to Michael Champion for helping me think this through.

virtue achieving and fulfilling natural morality at a spiritual, even super-natural level, this was internal to the self – though this too was an 'observable' good. At least, the well-being associated with virtue was internal to the virtuous person, even if it also resulted in the production of good things in the material world. For example, virtuous action could form friendships, result in better health, or increase one's resources; but since these external goods were not themselves the highest good, but only counted as good to the extent that they promoted well-being, it was 'internal' character and virtue that mattered.

By contrast, capitalist virtue produced something new. Here, happiness was not a matter of personal or spiritual becoming, but about success counted in economic terms. Moreover, the goods that virtue produced, now understood as material prosperity, were a matter of utility rather than the fulfilment of natural moral goods.[44] This kind of virtue nourished the professional class, at least in the first period described in this book, from around 1870 to 1945. Professional standards, as Chapters 2, 3 and 4 show, were primarily about good character. In the Anglo settler colonies, work performed by people of good character was not an Aristotelian end in itself but would, professionals believed, produce virtuous and prosperous outcomes for themselves and society.

This was a capitalist process. Chicago economist Deirdre McCloskey draws on the Aristotelian-Christian philosophical tradition to argue that the capitalist bourgeoisie – that middle, commercial class whose supposed superiority to aristocratic rule produced modern markets – is inherently virtuous.[45] McCloskey argues that bourgeois virtues, including love, faith, hope, and courage, are the foundation not only of commercial success but also of a good world, built from the kinds of capitalist accumulation that were forged on its basis. This positions bourgeois capitalism not as a historical structure but as a universal product of human becoming. She argues that undeniably horrific historical events, like slavery, are not a result of capitalism. Serving as an exemplar of the moral philosophy that political philosopher Jessica Whyte has shown underpins neoliberal conservatism, McCloskey says: 'No. Capitalism abolished slavery; early industrialism was an improvement on the idiocy of rural life; and imperialism and McDonaldization do not underlie the

---

[44] Alasdair MacIntyre, *After Virtue: A Study in Moral Theory* (Notre Dame, IN: University of Notre Dame Press, 1981).
[45] Deirdre McCloskey, *The Bourgeois Virtues: Ethics for an Age of Commerce* (Chicago: University of Chicago Press, 2006).

prosperity of the first world and have not undermined the prosperity of the third world.'[46]

By contrast to such empirically and morally questionable claims, this book does not argue that the professional class were in fact moral, as I discussed briefly previously. Their virtue was real, but as the hundreds of children buried in the gardens of Canadian residential schools attest, the products of their work were frequently immoral. This does not, on the other hand, turn the professional class into hypocritical villains. There is little evidence that the professional class were typically faking their virtue – 'virtue signalling' is a slur, not a structure. Instead, in *Virtue Capitalists* I seek to understand the quality of the substance that the professional class invested in themselves and in settler society, and thereafter global capitalism. This was capitalist not because McCloskey declares virtue to be bourgeois, but because it was, as the remainder of this book will show, a matter of seeking social and economic returns on a moral and financial investment.

Its historical and theological limitations notwithstanding, Max Weber's *Protestant Ethic and the Spirit of Capitalism* provides a useful framework with which to understand this. Starting with Martin Luther, Weber argued, Protestants translated Christian calling to worship into a vocation to work. This brought work to the centre of human virtue. When such industriousness was performed in embodied, material reality, that work began to structure the modern economy. Work, combined with a Puritan suspicion of spending its rewards on revelry and trifles, produced profit, which became the evidence of virtue. These surpluses produced by work were saved and then reinvested into the economy, producing a capitalist *habitus*.[47] The 'mighty cosmos' this produced became coercive:

The Puritans *wanted* to be men of calling – we, on the other hand, *must* be. For when asceticism moved out of the monastic cells and into working life, and began to dominate innerworldly morality, it helped to build that mighty cosmos of the modern economic order … Today this mighty cosmos determined, with overwhelming coercion, the style of life *not only* of those directly involved in business but of every individual who is born into this mechanism, and may well

[46] McCloskey, *The Bourgeois Virtues* a gloss on 'original accumulations, original sins', 512; see also Jessica Whyte, *The Morals of the Market: Human Rights and the Rise of Neoliberalism* (London: Verso, 2019).

[47] For discussion of 'habitus' as the word Weber used and what he really meant by the 'spirit' of capitalism, see Thomas Sokoll, 'The Moral Foundation of Modern Capitalism: Towards a Historical Reconsideration of Max Weber's 'Protestant Ethic', in Stefan Berger and Alexandra Przyrembel (eds), *Moralizing Capitalism: Agents, Discourses and Practices of Capitalism and Anti-Capitalism in the Modern Age* (London: Palgrave Macmillan, 2019), 79–110, habitus on p.94.

continue to do so until the day that the last ton of fossil fuel has been consumed.[48]

While the capitalist process of consuming fossil fuels to produce and consume goods was launched by Puritan asceticism, it ultimately undermined their rejection of consumerism. The 'light cloak' of worldly possessions became, under the weight of the mighty cosmos the Protestant ethic produced, a 'shell as hard as steel', more famously translated by Talcott Parsons as an iron cage.[49]

The notion of professional virtue, like that of a Protestant ethic guiding capitalism, came to shape both individual work and the moral norms of the wider society, now inflected not just by a general category of 'work' but also by particular virtues taken to be unique to different professions. As Chapter 2 will show, these virtues were distinctive to each occupation. The kind of virtues that Weber associated with the Protestant ethic, such as sobriety, discipline, and efficiency, were converted to the more specific virtues that shaped each profession. Accountancy valued probity, engineering accuracy, nursing patience, and teaching temperance. The performance of this work extended to the settler colonial world, first. The collapse of old village-sized communities into what historian Robert Wiebe described as a 'search for order' in late nineteenth- and early twentieth-century America, encouraged the same settlers who were committed to the end of children's factory work to also commit to their industriousness in school.[50] This use of education as the pathway to virtuous success was not uniquely American. Rather, such investment in human capital – a result of the shared Progressive values across the transpacific 'new world', as historian Marilyn Lake has shown – was a key characteristic of the settler revolution. In *Virtue Capitalists*, I argue it was the precondition to the professional class.[51]

British economic historian R. H. Tawney affirmed, in rather more theological detail than Weber, that Protestant ideas about virtue shaped the kind of capitalism that the professional class came to dominate. While prosperity – 'external' virtue in the Aristotelian sense – undermined good character, the Protestant ethic made prosperity the evidence of

---

[48] Max Weber, *The Protestant Ethic and the Spirit of Capitalism* (London: Penguin, 2002), 120–121, emphasis in the original translation.
[49] Weber, *Protestant Ethic*, 121.
[50] Robert Wiebe, *The Search for Order* (New York: Hill and Wang, 1967). Claudia Goldin, "The Human-Capital Century and American Leadership: Virtues of the Past', *The Journal of Economic History* 61.2 (2001), 263–292.
[51] Lake, *Progressive New World*.

salvation.[52] Like Weber, Tawney grounds this view in Calvinist predestination. In this theology, the identity of those destined for heaven was a mystery known only to God, but a hint of this celestial future was present in blessings on earth, including capitalist profitability. Tawney argued that this instilled in the Protestant middle class that first emerged, very little sympathy for the 'unworthy' poor who bore the consequences of the moral truism that 'if virtue is advantageous, vice is ruinous'.[53] This limited charity to a small proportion of the poor who were 'worthy', while the majority were merely living the consequences of vice. Soon, Protestants also resolved their initial Puritan aversion to consumption, which instead was now a good and necessary driver of virtuous industriousness. Profiteering too lost its suspiciousness. 'When duty was so profitable', mused Tawney, 'might not profit-making be a duty?'[54]

For the professional class, as this book argues, this relationship between virtue and success was subject to further historical change, though it continued to resemble many aspects of this Protestant ethic. As professional virtue emerged in the 1870s, there was no distinction between virtuous work and the good society that the professionals sought to build.[55] By the 1970s, as decolonization influenced international relations, many of the professional virtues were exposed for their complicity with unfair hierarchies. Traditional professional morality became the subject of vociferous criticism by Left-wing reformers like Ivan Illich; this is the subject of Chapter 7. This did not kill the Protestant ethic, however. On the contrary, the values that would later be disparaged by conservatives as 'virtue signalling' originated in this moment. Professional standards that, as Chapter 3 shows, excluded quacks and others on a system of merit that veiled race, class, and gender characteristics were reversed in the 1970s. Then, race, class, and gender *inclusion* became virtues that proved that professional merit was working. Virtue, still needed to help the buildings stay up, patients recover, and students learn effectively, was performed but was increasingly disaggregated from the self. No longer grounded in good *character*, virtue was externalized and became measurable and explicit. Crucially, for what happened next, this also made virtue subject to managerial audit.

---

[52] This is not to say that all Protestants were committed to prosperity theologies, nor that the phenomenon was in fact confined to Protestant believers.

[53] Richard Tawney, *Religion and the Rise of Capitalism* (London: Penguin, 1926), 244.

[54] Tawney, *Religion and the Rise of Capitalism*, 244; Rogan, *The Moral Economists*.

[55] See Stefan Collini, *Public Moralists: Political Thought and Intellectual Life in Britain 1850–1930* (Oxford: Clarendon Press, 1991); Richard Overy, *The Morbid Age: Britain and the Crisis of Civilisation 1919–1939* (London: Penguin, 2009).

The Protestant ethic was not only reversed, in the latter part of the twentieth century, by those aligned to the political Left. Conservative neoliberals, especially Milton Friedman, argued virtue veiled rent-seeking in ways that impeded the natural flow of profit. Additionally, amidst the massive growth of managers tasked with leading business to work 'smarter, not harder', success became the only virtue that mattered. In the age of managerialism, this ethic was not confined to capitalists (defined as those seeking return on investment, now dominated by shareholders rather than Rockefeller-like captains of industry) Rather, it also infused the behaviour of a growing managerial class.

The managerial side of the professional-managerial class – those responsible for strategy and resource allocation – began to split away from the application of professional expertise in the 1980s. In place of the long, respectable alliance between professionals and managers, a flamboyant, hyper-masculine, entrepreneurial style of manager acquired a new set of ethics that resembled nothing so much as the late Puritanism that Tawney described. This not only discarded the traditional virtues that had built the professional class but also narrowed their focus to economic, rather than moral, success. The rise of prosperity gospels, forging evangelical faith traditions deeply connected to this style of capitalist personhood, seems on the surface a barely recognizable inheritance of Puritan asceticism.[56] And yet observe the similarity between Gordon Gecko's 'greed is good' speech in the 1987 film *Wall Street* where 'greed clarifies, cuts through and captures the essence of the evolutionary spirit … [and] has marked the upward surge of mankind' and Tawney's description of late Puritans:

> The qualities which less enlightened ages had denounced as social vices emerged as economic virtues. They emerged as moral virtues as well. For the world exists not to be enjoyed but to be conquered … For such a philosophy, the question, 'What shall it profit a man?' carries no sting. In winning the world, he wins the salvation of his own soul as well.[57]

As Chapter 8 discusses, this professional-managerial split had economic as well as ideological drivers. The resulting two versions of the Protestant ethic, one based on virtuous inclusion and the other on success as the only virtue, define many aspects of class conflict today.

Before we get to this new class conflict, we need to first consider the aggregate effect of the Protestant ethic on the ideal of a rational society.

---

[56] See Kate Bowler, *Blessed: A History of American Prosperity Gospel* (Oxford: Oxford University Press, 2018), 9.
[57] Tawney, *Religion and the Rise of Capitalism*, 247; Oliver Stone (director), *Wall Street*, Twentieth Century Fox, 1987.

The constellation of virtues that the professional class embodied sought the kind of rational society that Weber associated with the European Enlightenment. This rationality translated, in the Anglo settler revolution, to a merit-based system of governmentality that favoured professional expertise. By governmentality I mean something close to that defined by Michel Foucault: institutions and knowledge systems that asserted expert authority in such a way as to encourage people to internalize its discipline.[58]

In the mid-twentieth century, this enabled the professional class to rule the world. In Chapter 5, I draw on Giorgio Agamben's theological characterization of the capitalist economy. In his *The Kingdom and the Glory*, Agamben extends Foucault's governmentality to consider the reasons this constellation of practices was translated into economy. This enables my analysis to go beyond Weber's characterization of the bureaucratic iron cage of rationality. Rather, it shows that bureaucratic government was the means, not the end, of the 'angelic' role which sought to 'glorify', to use Agamben's theological terms, expert rationality asserted in *both* business and government.[59] This is important. It underpins one of this book's key contributions, which is that regardless of public or private sector, enterprise structure, or even the profit motive – that is, without recourse to any of the ways that Marxist scholars have traditionally understood the capitalist 'means of production' – the professionals nevertheless constituted a class in capitalist terms.[60]

The Professional Class

Much scholarly literature on the history and sociology of the professions, and the middle class that housed them, argues that they do not, in fact, constitute a class. British social historian Harold Perkin, for example, argued that a 'professional society' emerged just as English 'class society', at its zenith between around 1880 and the Great War, was in decline. After the war, Perkin argued, a new 'social ideal' based on the utility of service to society, restructured English hierarchies into a system based on merit rather than an older sense of class that was frequently seen to be

---

[58] Among others, Michel Foucault, *The Birth of Biopolitics: Lectures at the College de France, 1978–1979* (London: Palgrave Macmillan, 2008).
[59] Giorgio Agamben, *The Kingdom and the Glory: For a Theological Genealogy of Economy and Government* (Stanford, CA: Stanford University Press, 2011).
[60] This is contrary to Jürgen Kocka's claim that the European middle classes were never a class in the Marxist sense due to this diversity in their relations to the means of production; see Jürgen Kocka, 'The Middle Classes in Europe', *The Journal of Modern History* 67.4 (1995), 783–806, specifically p.785.

'natural', or even God-given.[61] Hierarchy was not class, Perkin correctly said, and it applied far beyond the professions themselves. Professionals ruled the system of merit, which was increasingly used to educate and value people and occupations 'much farther down the social pyramid than ever landlordship or even business capital did'.[62]

While this system supplanted a caste system with roots that were much older than capitalism, merit-based hierarchy did not eradicate class, though Perkin was a little vague on how it now worked. Industrialism produced a capitalist class, he said, and the working class also continued to exist, though both were increasingly influenced by the professional ideal. Professionals themselves were also sometimes designated as a class in Perkin's work. Despite this class-like status and influence, the professionals were not 'just another ruling class', though Perkin feared that some would like to be.[63] In Perkin's estimation, a key characteristic of the professionals as a class was that they veiled their class interests, largely by denying the existence, or importance, of class at all. This was about their legitimacy, rather than their universality. Professional expertise leaned on objectivity and merit: admitting self-interest destabilized their claims and undermined their self-interest.[64] The economic crisis of the 1970s nevertheless exposed this, as Chapter 7 discusses.[65]

This allowed merit, which the professional ideal deemed to be objective, to structure a more rational society, focused on utility.[66] This all sounded good, except merit came with a sting in its tail: merit was not equally available to everyone, and it was often determined by pre-existing class status.[67] While some professionals continued to actively exclude people who were not already middle class, the logic of the professional ideal encouraged the expansion of merit until it nearly engulfed all people.[68] By the publication of *The Rise of Professional Society* in 1989, toward the end of the long reign of conservative neoliberal Prime Minister Margaret Thatcher, Perkin was persuaded that under the

---

[61] Perkin, *Rise of Professional Society*, 27–61.   [62] Ibid, 3.   [63] Ibid, 116–170.
[64] Lorraine Dalston and Peter Galison, *Objectivity* (New York: Zone Books, 2007).
[65] This was part of the 'legitimation crisis' that both Habermas and Lyotard saw; see Jürgen Habermas, *Legitimation Crisis* (Boston: Beacon Press, 1973); Jean-François Lyotard, *The Postmodern Condition: A Report on Knowledge* (Manchester: Manchester University Press, 1984).
[66] In this sense it was conceptually related to taxation, see Martin Daunton, *Trusting Leviathan: The Politics of Taxation in Britain, 1799–1914* (Cambridge: Cambridge University Press, 2001).
[67] In fact, as Peter Mandler points out, the idea that merit would be evenly spread through society at all is an interesting political question; see Peter Mandler, *The Crisis of the Meritocracy: Britain's Transition to Mass Education Since the Second World War* (Oxford: Oxford University Press, 2020), 73.
[68] Perkin, *Rise of Professional Society*, 1–26.

influence of the professional ideal, almost the only remnants of class conflict, expressed politically, were now to be found in whether one worked for the private, or public sector.[69] Perkin was not alone in wondering what the rise of a professional class might mean for class relations. In 1974, sociologist Anthony Giddens described a process he called 'class structuration', which saw classes as constantly in formation, subject to power and institutional domination. This confluence of structure and agency, he argued, was particularly apposite to the recent expansion of the professions. Like Perkin, Giddens suggested that class consciousness was not only about sharing an understanding of self-interest in relation to others but also, as in the case of the professional class, a shared belief that class did not exist or was irrelevant. This obfuscation of their own class interests served what he and others were starting to call the 'new' middle class.[70]

This in turn discouraged scholars from exploring any material foundations to professional class relations, in part because many believed the professionals did not have any material relations to speak of. What seemed extraordinary to Harold Perkin was held in common by many others: in capitalist society, professional experts achieved class and economic power without producing anything. It was this that led Perkin, mistakenly in my view, to believe that the power of the professional class was ideological, not material. Perkin was liberal, though there were plenty of Marxists who agreed. Political economist Nicos Poulantzas called their work 'unproductive', for they did not typically even *supervise* production. Poulantzas characterized the professionals as a 'new petty bourgeoisie'. He meant that the social conditions that gave rise to those who perform 'mental labour' were not the same as for the working class, even if their relation to the means of production was similar.[71] Ideological influences not only forged the type of work professionals did, it also underpinned their authority, their 'ideological domination over the working class'.[72]

Marxist sociologists and historians began to explore this ideological domination in more specific ways, usually in relation to particular

---

[69] Ibid, 472–519.
[70] Anthony Giddens, *The Class Structure of the Advanced Societies* (London: Hutchinson, 1980).
[71] Geoff Sharp, articulating in 1964 what would become known as the 'Arena Thesis', argued that this class was in fact *responsible* for these conditions, but by separating power from knowledge in universities they bore the potential for protest and resistance, see Raewyn Connell, 'Theorizing Intellectuals', *Arena Journal* 45/46 (2016), 12–27.
[72] Nicos Poulantzas, 'The New Petty Bourgeoisie', *The Insurgent Sociologist* 9.1 (1979), 56–60, quote p.60.

occupations, such as Eliot Friedson's study of medicine. Friedson argued that the organization of healthcare assured medicine's 'professional dominance', a kind of monopoly that gave doctors power over patients. This, he argued, was extended to other professions that relied on expertise. Terence Johnson's *Professions and Power* similarly argued that expert work was a matter of social control.[73] Margali Sarfatti Larson's 1977 *Rise of Professionalism* drew on Polanyi's double movement to argue that many occupations professionalized to shelter their market from competition, which also helped them retain their ideological authority.[74]

Andrew Abbott's *System of Professions*, published more than a decade after the spate of 1970s criticisms, reconsidered this sociological tradition to explore the professions through the lens of complex systems analysis. He saw professional power less as straightforward monopolies and more as a network of occupations that enclosed knowledge systems or used authority to claim jurisdiction over certain fields. The result was less *medical* dominance and more a specialized, competing market where fields like child behaviour, for example, might variously – over time, mostly – fall under the authority of education, law, psychology, or medicine.[75]

By considering the economic dominance of professional expertise, gained as a kind of social power, scholars foregrounded work on class-as-discourse that Patrick Joyce framed as 'vision', Gareth Stedman Jones and William Sewell saw as 'language' and a growing cohort of Foucauldian scholars saw as 'power'. These, like Giddens' earlier work, sought to expose the discursive, or ideological, purposes of knowledge, expertise, and objectivity in late capitalism.[76] Such attention to structures of meaning and agency turned scholarly attention from class as an economic phenomenon to inequality as a set of sociocultural meanings. Although Pierre Bourdieu's theories of cultural and social capital were markedly different to Foucauldian forms of power, understanding class via 'taste' offered a framework that seemed to make better sense to many

---

[73] Terence Johnson, *Professions and Power* (London: Mcmillian, 1972).

[74] Larson, *Rise of Professionalism*.

[75] Andrew Abbott, *The System of Professions: An Essay on the Division of Expert Labor* (Chicago: University of Chicago Press, 1988).

[76] Patrick Joyce, *Visions of the People: Industrial England and the Question of Class* (Cambridge: Cambridge University Press, 1994); Gareth Jones, *Languages of Class: Studies in English Working-Class History 1832–1982* (Cambridge: Cambridge University Press, 1983); William Sewell, *Work and Revolution in France: the Language of Labor from the Old Regime to 1848* (Cambridge: Cambridge University Press, 1980); of many, see Colin Jones and Roy Porter (eds), *Reassessing Foucault: Power, Medicine and the Body* (London: Routledge, 1994).

scholars.[77] For scholars of the middle class, Bourdieu's framework offers a way of understanding the centrality of consumer norms to class identity.[78] In this book, all these systems of authority, language, power, jurisdiction, and taste are at work. This is not just a matter of theoretical promiscuity on my part. Rather, all of these operate as important signifiers and operators of the professional class. None of them, however, are causal or material in the way that I am concerned with here. While the professional class signalled their membership by distinct consumption patterns, cultural practices, and discursive deployments of expert authority and power, I argue that it was constituted more fundamentally through its relation to a set of material conditions that I describe earlier as virtue capitalism.

To consider the materiality of the professional class, this book draws on Barbara and John Ehrenreich's classic work on the professional-managerial class.[79] This was a product of the New Left moment. The Ehrenreichs argued that the professional-managerial class had an 'antagonistic relationship' to wage earners, which excluded them from the working class. Nor were they a 'residual' class, the last remnant of the older petty bourgeoisie as Poulantzas had defined them, since they emerged on their own terms at the turn of the twentieth century. This historically specific understanding of the professional-managerial class was grounded in class 'as a relationship not a thing', to use E. P. Thompson's phrase, which arose out of the 'social division of labour'.[80] The Ehrenreichs' descriptor, 'professional-managerial', was evocative of professional expertise as a knowledge system and as management as a mechanism of authority, control, and action, in colonial settings but also in class, race, and gender-based superiority. It combined knowing and doing: 'professionals usually have administrative responsibilities', clarified Barbara Ehrenreich in *Fear of Falling*, 'making them part of management'.[81] In this book, the combination of knowing and doing, and an alliance between the professional and managerial, was key to the rise of the professionals as a class.

---

[77] For a contemporary example, see Mike Savage, *Social Class in the Twenty-first Century* (London: Penguin, 2015).

[78] Pierre Bourdieu, *Distinction: A Social Critique of the Judgement of Taste* (Cambridge, MA: Harvard University Press, 1984); for example, Mike Savage, *Identities and Social Change in Britain since 1940: The Politics of Method* (Oxford: Oxford University Press, 2010).

[79] Ehrenreich and Ehrenreich, 'The Professional-Managerial Class'; Barbara Ehrenreich and John Ehrenreich, 'The New Left and the Professional-Managerial Class', *Radical America* 11.3 (1976), 7–24.

[80] Ehrenreich and Ehrenreich, 'The Professional-Managerial Class', 12.

[81] Ehrenreich, Barbara, *Fear of Falling: The Inner Life of the Middle Class* (New York: Pantheon Books, 1989), 12.

Barbara Ehrenreich and John Ehrenreich further explained in class terms the ways that professionals asserted expert power over both the working class and at the same time expressed moral opposition to capitalist elites.[82] Both observations were central to the moral crisis of the 1970s, though the Ehrenreichs saw this as part of the intellectual milieu of the New Left, not as a product of a materialist history itself. It is at this point that *Virtue Capitalists* departs from the Ehrenreichs' theory of the professional-managerial class. They described the objective social and historical existence of the class (for itself, as it were) but they did not see it as participating in the production of anything. Building on their insightful characterization of professional class ideology, I extend this further to consider the moral as a material mirror to colonialism. This will help show why, among other things, the professional and the managerial sides of the middle class split up, so very soon after they were discovered, by the Ehrenreichs, in bed together.

Material Virtue

Here is where we must bring the discussion on class and virtue together to consider the economic materiality of professional virtue, which has been made historically. This historicity matters (both as a pun on matter, but also as the causal trigger) because morality is not automatically grounded in the material production of economic value. When busy work in general was deemed the solution to the devil's influence on idle hands, this did not make the virtue of that work material. Nor were the virtues valued by Aristotle in themselves material stuff, for virtue was realized in contemplation rather than politics. Prudence and temperance might indeed have helped a person become their best self, but neither necessarily became entangled in the economy as a result. Professional virtues, by contrast, did become material – both in the sense of becoming tangible, embodied matter and also by being subject to economic exchange. This was not just because the professional class wanted them to, which they did. Rather, professional virtue made a material difference, producing economic value.

This was related to the performance of work. When philosopher Judith Butler drew on Merleau-Ponty to consider the body as 'a set of possibilities', she sought to understand how ideas about gender were materialized.[83] By performing gender, it became, as Simone de Beauvoir had

---

[82] Ehrenreich and Ehrenreich, 'The Professional-Managerial Class'.
[83] Judith Butler, 'Performative Acts and Gender Constitution: An Essay in Phenomenology and Feminist Theory', *Theatre Journal* 40.4 (1988), 519–531, quote from 521.

phrased it, a 'historical situation'.[84] As we will see in the remainder of this book, professional virtue was also performed in this sense. Virtues were declared, enumerated as standards, and formalized into a system of merit as the professional class brought themselves into being. By performing these virtues, professionals spread across every town and city in the Anglo world and brought those virtues into the world in which they worked. As occupations professionalized, they imagined these virtuous attributes inhered in a person's character, as if the class of people from whom the professions were built were fundamentally pure, dutiful, and temperate. As Chapter 3 of this book will show, this helped the professions select for class, gender, and race characteristics that built merit on the basis of exclusion, and structured hierarchies that mirrored the colonial order.

In this sense, professional virtue also extended beyond the 'internal' good that Alasdair MacIntyre described in his discussion of the Aristotelian virtues. When doctors, accountants, and teachers performed virtue, they did much more than build their own character. Another philosopher, Karen Barad, helps here. Barad extends Judith Butler's characterization of gender performativity as a set of embodied acts to describe the entanglements of nature and culture that are required to make matter into a social and scientifically study-able substance. 'Matter, like meaning', she says, 'is not an individually articulated or static entity. Matter is not ... passively awaiting signification ... It does not require the mark of an external force like culture or history to complete it. Matter is always already an ongoing historicity'.[85] This is all very well for matter, perhaps, but how does this make *virtue* into economic stuff?

If patience and purity remained mere declarations, nurses would not have been as successful in caring for the sick and injured. Similarly, other professions performed their virtue in ways that made a material difference to the efficacy of engineered work, the accuracy of financial reporting, and the information available to the democratizing public. Virtue was not only an idea, or an inner possession, but also was, to use Barad's phrase, 'material-discursive'; brought into being by performance and then capitalized – invested – for social and economic profit. This helps connect the material world understood as matter, to materiality understood as economic activity. 'The chief defect of all hitherto existing materialism', Marx argued in his *Theses on Feuerbach*, 'is that

---

[84] Butler, 'Performative Acts', 519.
[85] Karen Barad, 'Posthumanist Performativity: Toward an Understanding of How Matter Comes to Matter', *Signs: Journal of Women in Culture and Society*, 28.3 (2003), 801–831, 821.

the thing, reality ... is conceived only in the form of the *object* ... not as *sensuous human activity, practice*.[86] Human practice, or activity, was central to Marx's politics: Thesis XI famously states that 'philosophers have only interpreted the world ... the point is to change it'. Human activity also underpinned Marx's economics, where work was the foundation of capitalist value.[87]

In *Virtue Capitalists*, the rise of the professional class was accomplished through the performance of virtue in this embodied, and then material, sense. Performing professional virtue as work created value, which the professional class saw – and made – into a kind of profit that they saw as both economic and moral. 'What shall it profit?', they saw, was simultaneously a moral and economic question. The profitable answer that they sought combined the types. Investing the work of their virtuous selves – not just the effort of a generic Protestant ethic, but the specific virtues of the Anglo professional class – would bring moral and economic profit to themselves and to capitalist society. Though this value was created by work, this did not make them, typically, workers, in the sense that Marx sought to capture.[88] As a class, the professionals became virtue capitalists. At least, at first.

I have already mentioned the relationship between expert knowing and doing. There is, as philosopher Jean-François Lyotard pithily described it in his 1979 essay *The Postmodern Condition*, an epistemological distinction between the observation that 'the door is closed' and the imperative to 'open the door'.[89] Lyotard thought that undermining this distinction threatened (which was mostly a good thing) the legitimacy of the present regime, grounded in rational objectivity. An instinct about this legitimacy may underpin the professional class's tendency, as Harold Perkin and others observed, to obfuscate their class interests. Acknowledging even their existence as a class endangered professional authority, based on their 'objective' expertise, which seemed less reliably objective when connected with class interest. This legitimation crisis, as Jürgen Habermas defined it, emerged from the inflationary conditions of the 1970s, as I discuss in Chapter 7 of this book.[90] The economic shocks of

---

[86] Karl Marx, *Theses on Feuerbach* Thesis I. www.marxists.org/archive/marx/works/1845/theses/theses.htm Accessed 27 September 2021.

[87] Marx, *Theses on Feuerbach*, thesis XI; Karl Marx, *Capital Vol. 1* (Harmondsworth: Penguin Books, 1976).

[88] Later chapters will discuss the ways that the value that they produced was extractive – extracting value from those they saw as 'below' them – and only sometimes properly generative, by producing human capital, though this too was achieved on the back of the free labour of children and others via schooling: Chapter 5 explores this.

[89] Lyotard, *Postmodern Condition*.   [90] Habermas, *Legitimation Crisis*.

the 1970s were inseparable from the moral shocks that rocked the professions, mostly because the moral and the material were entangled components of the same economic system.

While this transformed the structure of virtue, the fall of the professional class, which commenced in the 1970s and accelerated in the subsequent decades, was not really a result of the legitimation crisis. Rather, the rift between professionals and managers was historical. A shift in virtue where professions now sought to re-legitimize merit based on inclusion rather than exclusion, clashed with the new ethical paradigm embraced by managers, for whom success became the only virtue that mattered. With the professions growing rapidly, but not as rapidly as management, a tried-and-tested managerial technique ultimately assured the fall of the professional class: deskilling.

Deskilling is one of the consequences of the specialization of labour. In a factory, for example, reducing task size and complexity was a common method for reducing wages. A similar process applied to white-collar workers, as C. Wright Mills showed in his 1950s study of office work.[91] This 'lumpen bourgeoisie', Mills perspicaciously argued, borrowed from the old prestige of medicine and law but were swindled into roles with little power or material reward.[92] Their exploitation worsened as the professions expanded.[93] Having rejected the idea that professional virtue inhered in the person, the old virtues that once manifested as individual character were turned into auditable lists of ethics and skills. Paperwork assuring 'transparency' meant that professionals of all types found themselves filling in forms where they would once have performed their virtue. Such transparency made the system of merit, resource allocation, and work autonomy open to managerial control and moral deskilling. The resulting audit culture, with metrics for everything, kept the ascendant managerial class in power.

However, there was only so much control that the managerial class could assert over professional expertise, which still relied on virtue and therefore unavoidably retained an ever-diminishing autonomy. This book concludes by showing the ongoing conflict between the managerial and the professional classes. Each class wants and believes it has a moral responsibility to run the world. Though they once did this together, they sometimes behave as if excluding the other is more important than the

---

[91] C. Wright Mills, *White Collar: The American Middle Classes* (Oxford: Oxford University Press, 2002).

[92] 'Lumpen bourgeoisie' is from Mills, *White Collar*, 32.

[93] Nicholas Abercrombie and John Urry, *Capital, Labour and the Middle Classes* (London: Routledge, 2015).

things at stake, like preventing climate change. This is class conflict, driven by irresolvable divergent values and systems of accumulation. Unlike the kind of class conflict Marx believed would inevitably bring about social and economic transformation, this 'intra-bourgeois' conflict over who gets to be prime technocrat presents a truly critical problem.

The Structure of This Book

My argument is presented chronologically, in three parts. Part I – c.1870–1945, encompassing Chapters 2–4 – shows the making of the professional class and the ways they built a 'currency' with which to value their work. It also shows how professionals actively industrialized some aspects of professional activity to expand its influence in the Anglo economic sphere.

In this part, Chapter 2 explores the patterns of late nineteenth-century global capitalism through which a progressive, moral middle class built a system of professions. It uses the 1880s Melbourne land boom to show the sustained effect of the 'great heaves' of investment from the City of London into Australia, Canada, and the United States. This financializing economy, unlike earlier, short-term bubbles like Chicago's in the 1830s, stimulated the global expansion of professional occupations. Older moral values infused the professions across the Anglo world as they grew and institutionalized. Retaining capitalism's model of return on investment, the professional class made investment in humans the central professional ideal. Their class status was often concealed beneath layers of rationality and claims to expertise, but in the settler colonies they transformed capitalism into a form of moral investment for social return in ways that served their own interests first. As part of a global bourgeoisie, these transformations at the periphery of the Anglo world were soon also felt in the British metropole.

Chapter 3 describes the emergence of merit as a store of value. For professionals, merit was first earned and demonstrated in educational contexts, then 'cashed in' for access to professional pathways. There, further merit was accumulated doing virtuous work, and rapidly reinvested in advancement upwards. Each step on the career ladder was 'earned' by demonstrating one's increasing merit, and directly translated into material and social benefits. Across the Anglo world, the professional class expected that merit would help them avoid some of the 'old corruption' that many attached to British aristocratic traditions. Merit, however, was not the result of overblown settler claims to egalitarianism. Instead, merit was built from conceptions of virtue that were already deeply gendered and which were becoming entangled with emerging ideas about race. As merit became the currency with which the professional class purchased and managed their influence, this systematized multiple, intersecting forms of inequality. As they structured career ladders into their respective occupations, the professional class also built a ladder through society, so that each person's class and financial status, from the wealthy and influential to the poorest and most marginalized, seemed to be earned. This opened the opportunity for the professional class to extract moral and financial value from women, people of colour, and the working class, bolstering their own status and solidifying their class identity.

Scholars have often considered salary-earning professionals as workers since they did not own the means of production and, from the 1920s onwards, were subject to increasingly 'scientific' management. Professionals were not always salary earners, however. In the late nineteenth and early twentieth centuries, professionals tended to own small businesses. Some still do, though, as Chapter 4 shows, over the course of the twentieth century, professionals moved into ever-larger enterprises where they more often occupied the role of salaried employees than business owners. Early professional businesses included individual medical and accountancy practices, small legal partnerships, independent local newspapers, and engineering consultancies. Women, too, owned small schools and nursing homes or home-based private hospitals where they cared for the sick, or they worked on their own account. The transformation of the professional class from small, bourgeois business owners to a large salaried workforce has been poorly documented and theorized. This chapter remedies that, reconsidering the trajectory of professional work towards ever-larger, even industrializing, institutions. I argue that, even when salaried, the professional class retained the model of moral capitalization they had built – using merit – into their original bourgeois businesses. They supported the expansion of the enterprises in which they worked, even their industrialization, because it expanded their influence. This not only presented little threat to class identity; it extended virtue capitalism into every corner of the Anglo world.

Part II of this book – c. 1945–1975, including Chapters 4 and 5 – considers the professional class at the height of their power. Chapter 4 considers the alliance of the professions with the state and their role in building universal industriousness, or a modern Protestant ethic, into the global economy, while Chapter 5 explores the 'classy' nature of professional work and organization.

By the end of the Second World War, the professional class presided over a massive alignment of national and global institutions with virtue capitalism. This global 'welfare state' moment makes it seem that virtue capitalism went hand in hand with state control. However, professionals were often ambivalent about their connection to the state. When Canada first ventured into nationalized healthcare, for example, doctors in Saskatchewan went on strike to avoid it. Despite such examples of rejecting government interference, which many professionals feared might impede the integrity of their work, Chapter 5 shows that professionals were nevertheless central planners at heart. Central planning expressed an epistemology grounded in a moral relationship between knowing and doing, where they sought to use expertise to effect material change in the world and in individual lives. Such technocratic planning was fundamentally moral, embedding into mid-twentieth century capitalism the internalized, disciplining practices known as governmentality. Professionals were, to use Giorgio Agamben's theological framing of the governmental economy, *angels of the state*. The massive investment in human capital entangled industry, military, and higher education but, perhaps most importantly, led to an internalized, universal industriousness. The material effects of this 'angelic' work were sometimes deeply damaging, building social and economic 'dependencies' through the economy that mirrored, in individual lives, the hierarchies constructed by the colonial world writ large.

Chapter 6 considers the professionals' class behaviour. Labour movements deployed well-known strategies for collective action, but how did the professional class collectivize their interests? The mechanisms by which the professionals achieved and maintained their status in the mid-twentieth century are laid bare by records of an institution unique to Australasia: formal conciliation and arbitration courts. This chapter focuses on a particular event, the *Professional Engineers Case*, which was brought before the Australian Conciliation and Arbitration Commission between 1957 and 1961. The *Professional Engineers Case* established engineering as a national industry (even though most engineers worked for the state), setting a precedent that enabled other white-collar professions to do similarly, including social workers and university teachers. The *Professional Engineers Case* shows professionals articulating their class status to argue, in arbitration, for the value of their work to the nation's collective economic and moral good. This good was linked, for the judges who elevated their salaries, to the individual professional's investment in 'the drudgery of study' but also to the prospective worth of their virtuous work to the nation. The risk to the nation if unvirtuous people performed professional work was too high to let them fall behind in material terms. To belong to the professional class, it was not enough to be qualified – they also had to perform their belonging in their standard of living. Assuring consumption standards, then, was also a way to assure quality work – and the rationale that enabled the professional class to monetize their virtue.

Part III – *c*.1975–2008 – recounts in Chapters 7 and 8 the 'fall' of the professional class. Chapter 7 focuses on the 1970s, when anti-colonial movements sought to turn global hierarchies upside down. Their efforts moved from the US civil rights movement to expose the racism and sexism embedded in professional work, as in education, social work, and medicine. Teachers observed their 'hidden curriculum', which excluded those they long claimed to help. Lawyers noted their close alliance to capital and sought, for the less powerful, alternative routes to legal service. Engineers, who up to this point claimed that they had literally built civilization, began to ask whether they had in fact condemned society to live in concrete boxes and breathe polluted air. Even accountants were not immune. The high and fluctuating inflation that characterized the end of the moral-economic order established after the Second World War produced a legitimation crisis that required, in Britain, a Royal Commission on something as fundamental to capitalism as the calculation of profit.

From the 1980s, globalization produced conditions that demanded tough decisions in a complex set of fluctuating economic circumstances. This required more decision-makers, who discarded almost all virtue but success. Chapter 8 shows that to this new managerial elite, the moral character of the professionals was at best an old-fashioned affectation, at worst the sanctimonious preaching of the old establishment, bleating over their loss of prestige. Managers began to treat those merely applying their expertise as plug-and-play professionals, able to be manoeuvred in and out of place according to flexible strategies. These were applied under a new cliché: 'work smarter, not harder', where the 'smarter' referred mainly to managerial innovation. Under this managerial regime, success was the only virtue that mattered, while traditional aspects of professional virtue, still needed for professional work to succeed, were embedded into systems for quality and risk management, launching a process of moral deskilling. In this context, professionals turned to a more generic 'effectiveness' into which they could pour their personal professional values. This kept them investing relentlessly in their own human capital, reducing the kind of virtue that sought a better world into a category of virtuous consumption.

In the Epilogue I consider the ways that the rise and fall of the professional class has left the world in thrall to a conflict between *managerial capitalism and professional technocracy*. Unlike *labour versus capital*, this intra-bourgeois conflict is not productive of change. Rather, self-perpetuating cycles seeking material and moral authority have infected workplaces and global politics, impeding reform. Much is at stake, including climate change. Professionals, whose work remains necessary to a good society, need to separate virtue from capitalism, disaggregating their moral goals from their own class interests – even to the point of turning the hierarchy that they made on its head.

Part I

Professionalizing the Anglo Economy, *c.* 1870–1945

2 Civilizing Capitalism

In the late nineteenth century, London's professionals seemed deeply etched into the city's social and economic landscape. Harley Street housed England's most esteemed medical professionals; bewigged lawyers threaded their way between the Temple area and Lincoln's and Gray's Inns of Court; 'The London' and other hospitals shared the city's growing network of elite 'Nightingale' nurses; several universities and colleges clustered around Bloomsbury, marshalling educators and their professionals-in-training; and Lombard Street was the focus of 'the City', the world's most powerful financial centre, which was also a metropole for the emerging, if still rather Scottish, discipline of accountancy and other financial services.[1] It was finance that was most important at this stage, driving the growth of professions in England (see Figure 2.1). The other professions were growing much faster on the periphery of the Anglo world. While London's professional cartography often provided them with an ideal model, across North America and Australasia a network of middle-class, English-speaking women and men worked in their educated, expert way to civilize global capitalism.

They turned up in some unlikely locations. When the Australian outback town of Broken Hill was little more than a row of tents and shacks, professionals were already plentiful. The town was settled on Indigenous Wilyakali land in 1883 after station workers stumbled across the world's largest silver-lead-zinc lode, founding Broken Hill Proprietary, now the global mining giant, BHP Group Limited. It was an extremely inconvenient place. Prone to deadly dust storms, Broken Hill had no natural water supply. In fact, Jeremiah Boyle, the town's first schoolteacher, had a salary package that helped cover his £3 per month

---

[1] David Kynaston and David Milner, *City of London: The History* (London: Chatto & Windus, 2011), 146–147; Stephen Walker and Thomas Lee, *Studies in Early Professionalism: Scottish Chartered Accountants, 1853–1918* (New York: Garland, 1999); Ernest Morris, *A History of the London Hospital* (London: Edward Arnold, 1926); Alain Wijffels and Jonathan Bush, *Learning the Law: Teaching and the Transmission of Law in England, 1150–1900* (London: Hambledon, 1999).

water deliveries, which arrived by cart.[2] Lawyers settled there immediately and managed disputes between small businesses and big mines. Journalists reported on ore hauls, avidly read by share traders in London and Melbourne. Nurses and medical doctors treated the inevitable injuries resulting from industrialized mining. Engineers worldwide, whose expertise had blossomed on the gold fields of California, turned their focus to Broken Hill. Finance mattered there, too. Indeed, accountants were so plentiful that by 1905, they formed their own Broken Hill professional association.[3] Economic historians have often assumed that the professionalization of the global economy was a kind of specialization that emerged with urban complexity. Broken Hill shows it was not.[4]

The growth of professions in the outback did, however, have everything to do with financial activity in the City of London, where finance professionals were having a busy time. After a century of capitalist expansion, British businesses accumulated cash surpluses in such quantities that reinvesting them in the business was no longer useful or profitable. They looked to Lombard Street to help them.[5] With so much cash to offload, finance professionals found themselves jostling for investment opportunities to sell on to clients. Those looking for a safer bet invested within Britain – often rightly, as it turned out.[6] Still, many were prepared to risk money on colonial ventures. Finance professionals from across the Anglo world set up shop in London, selling shares in enterprises on the other side of the world. In what economic historian Sidney Pollard called 'great heaves', massive City investment went to overseas railways, public works, mining and agriculture, particularly in Australia (1877–1886), Argentina (1886–1890) and Canada (1900–1914).[7]

This chapter argues that the professionalization of the global economy emerged from the settler revolution, which, as historian James Belich described it, allowed English speakers across North America,

---

[2] Jeremiah Boyle to School Inspector, 6 May 1889, Broken Hill School File 5/15099 Bundle A, State Records of NSW.
[3] Hannah Forsyth, 'Class, Professional Work, and the History of Capitalism in Broken Hill, c. 1880–1910', *Labor* 15.2 (2018), 21–47.
[4] See, for example, Marc Law and Sukkoo Kim, 'Specialization and Regulation: The Rise of Professionals and the Emergence of Occupational Licensing Regulation', *The Journal of Economic History* 65.3 (2005), 723–756.
[5] Arrighi, *The Long Twentieth Century*, 166–171.
[6] Sidney Pollard, 'Capital Exports, 1870–1914: Harmful or Beneficial?', *The Economic History Review* 38.4 (1985), 489–514; Lance Davis and Robert Gallman, *Evolving Financial Markets and International Capital Flows: Britain, the Americas, and Australia, 1865–1914* (New York: Cambridge University Press, 2001), 232; Belich, *Replenishing the Earth*, 114–120.
[7] Arrighi, *The Long Twentieth Century*; Pollard 'Capital Exports', 499.

Australasia, and Britain to dominate the global economy.[8] Key to the expansion of professions was the relationship between the great heaves of investment from Lombard Street and colonial peripheries like Broken Hill. This financialization is explored first, in this chapter. A key intermediary in this case was the city of Melbourne, which linked London finance to what was just coming to be known as the Australian 'outback'. British credit and cash, which followed settler development, produced a speculative bubble in 1880s Melbourne, where the emerging professional class soon became prominent. This chapter uses land boom Melbourne and BHP's Broken Hill – as well as settler-colonial Canada, Aotearoa/New Zealand, and the United States – to show the ways professions like law, accountancy, architecture, and engineering grew in response to this financializing global economy. It is perhaps less intuitively obvious, but the same forces grew education and healthcare even more spectacularly, as this chapter will demonstrate. As the second part of this chapter argues, this was because the cash flowing from London enabled the global middle class to build the virtue that defined them as a class, into economic structures. Since business and professional elite alike 'saw themselves as the moral centre of the community', it was an investment that produced moral as well as economic profit.[9] This gave professional occupations, as the third section of the chapter shows, a framework for understanding themselves as a class, not just a marker of occupational change.

The Melbourne land boom, as the bubble was known, followed a similar pattern to a Chicago property bubble forty years earlier. Comparing them helps show the difference the 'great heaves' of London money made, though they were both a result of the same kind of process. In the mid-1830s, reports from Chicago's boosters reached London, persuading investors that Chicago would reap considerable returns. The result of British capital flows was that Chicago land sold at prices well beyond expectation, attracting speculators who bought property with a view to selling it at a massive profit again in the near future.[10] Chicago's streets became crowded, as English author Harriet Martineau wrote, 'with land speculators, hurrying from one sale to another' so that 'it seemed as if some prevalent mania infected the whole people'.[11] The information allowing long-distance investment was in

[8] Belich, *Replenishing the Earth.*
[9] Sven Beckert, *The Monied Metropolis: New York City and the Consolidation of the American Bourgeoisie* (Cambridge: Cambridge University Press, 2001), 35.
[10] Patrick McLear, 'Speculation, Promotion, and the Panic of 1837 in Chicago', *Journal of the Illinois State Historical Society* 62.2 (1969), 135–146.
[11] Harriet Martineau, *Society in America* (New York: Saunders and Otle, 1837), 261.

part a result of a new 'flow of business data' produced by armies of white-collar clerks, as historian Michael Zakim has shown.[12] Other white-collar work made more temporary gains during Chicago's boom. Martineau wrote that 'a young lawyer, of my acquaintance there, had realised five hundred dollars per day ... by merely making out titles to land'.[13] In contrast to the decades of British capital flow which produced the Melbourne land boom, investment in 1830s Chicago was a short-term fad, a bubble that burst when British credit dried up.[14] The massive City investment from around 1865 to the First World War, by contrast, not only produced a property bubble in Melbourne but also transformed the global economy, growing white-collar, expert work.

Finance Capital and the Global Spread of the Professions

Small settler populations in Australia, Argentina, and Canada meant British investment had dramatic effects, as we will see. We should note, though, that between 1865 and 1914, the United States received almost as much investment as Australia, Argentina, and Canada put together. City investment is also America's railway story: more than half of the massive US$5.2 billion worth of British money was invested in transport, mostly railways.[15] Canadian railways, both the legendary Canadian Pacific and the Grand Trunk, were also objects of the City of London's rapacious cash. Railways were rarely a good investment, but they captured imaginations, so the money flowed anyway.[16] Journalists spread with the railways, enthusiastically reporting the words of boosters and planners establishing towns and businesses. Reporters printed their words among the business news in London papers, ensuring potential investors were apprised of building proposals, rate wars between lines seeking access to mining areas and the civilizing, nation-building, trade-enabling benefits that would flow.[17] The complex task of building and running railways helped management to grow, as Alfred Chandler showed – though logistics in general, the domain of American

---

[12] Michael Zakim, *Accounting for Capitalism: The World the Clerk Made* (Chicago: University of Chicago Press, 2018), 10.
[13] Martineau, *Society in America*, 261.
[14] William Cronon, *Nature's Metropolis: Chicago and the Great West* (New York: W.W. Norton, 1991), 30.
[15] Davis and Gallman, *Evolving Financial Markets*, 251–255.
[16] Richard White, *Railroaded: The Transcontinentals and the Making of Modern America* (New York, Norton, 2011); Davis and Gallman, *Evolving Financial Markets*, 50–233; Pollard, 'Capital Exports', 489–514.
[17] White, *Railroaded*.

engineering, did a good deal to promote the growth of what became known as managerial capitalism.[18] Lombard Street's financial professionals also looked to Canadian expansion, contributing to settlement in the prairies, on the back of treaties that made First Nations people wards of the state.[19] Canadian industrialization proved tempting for British investors, who saw Canadian industrial expansion as the latest stage in Britain's industrial revolution.[20] In the following decades, the City of London funded industries, including mining and manufacturing, establishing a growing working class across the Anglo world. This ensured that a white – and sometimes Chinese, often subjected to significant racism – colonial working class reinforced the settler-colonial 'logic of elimination' whereby First Nations legal, religious, and economic structures were expected to disappear. Sometimes so too were Native peoples themselves expected to die out, or else eliminate ancient cultures by assimilating into Anglo society.[21]

Professional occupations grew in this context. This was no short-term bubble, like that which produced the Chicago land boom in the 1830s.[22] Rather, the heaves of British money funding the settler revolution transformed the global economy and remade labour markets across the Anglo world. Unlike Chicago's earlier boom, this massive investment was sufficiently sustained that the global bourgeoisie, already spread throughout the world administering empire, grew into a professional class whose moral efforts to civilize capitalist expansion also helped justify Indigenous dispossession. It still resulted, as we will see, in a land boom in Melbourne, where the behaviour of professionals shows that they became a self-conscious and self-interested class, not just an occupation category.

Perperson, the rate of City investment between 1865 and the First World War was US$8.36 per Argentinian, US$7.15 per Canadian, but only US$1.77 per person in the United States.[23] Only 15.5 per cent of British foreign investment between 1865 and 1914 went to Australia, but it was such a late settler colony that this amounted to US$11.33 per capita – more than six times that of the United States. More than the

[18] Alfred Chandler, *The Visible Hand: The Managerial Revolution in American Business* (Cambridge, MA: Harvard University Press, 1977); Yehouda Shenhav, *Manufacturing Rationality the Engineering Foundations of the Managerial Revolution* (Oxford: Oxford University Press, 2002).

[19] Margaret Conrad, *A Concise History of Canada* (Cambridge: Cambridge University Press, 2012), 134–163.

[20] Davis and Gallman, *Evolving Financial Markets*, 345–470.

[21] Wolfe, 'Settler Colonialism and the Elimination of the Native'.

[22] Cronon, *Nature's Metropolis*.   [23] Davis and Gallman, *Evolving Financial Markets*, 27.

equivalent of US$945 million British investment entered Australia between *c*.1880 and 1899.[24] It had dramatic effects, in part because Australia's stock exchanges were brand new, but also because that US $11.33 was not distributed very evenly. It was concentrated in Melbourne, whose capitalist entrepreneurs numbered as few as 250 or so people.[25]

In the 1880s, Melbourne was the most prosperous city in the global economy.[26] Situated on Kulin land that a century earlier Britain did not even know existed, the place was born out of professional vision. As they did across the Anglo world, experts, bringing with them older forms of middle-class morality, industriously planned, surveyed, built, managed, audited, reported, legislated, implemented, disputed, and enforced industrial and imperial activity.[27] Professional surveyor Robert Hoddle designed the grid in which Melbourne ordered commercial activity. The 'Hoddle grid', with its commercial centre on Collins Street, was built at about the time that local Indigenous greenstone mining, which had long supplied Aboriginal Australians with a kind of stone widely used as tools, stopped all production.[28] Without this suppression of Indigenous economies to make way for cities like Melbourne, the City of London would have had no financial infrastructure by which to invest in any of the settler colonies.[29]

On the basis of the Victorian gold rush, the Melbourne Stock Exchange was formed in the 1850s. It was twenty years before Sydney's exchange, establishing Melbourne as a preferred Antipodean destination for City investment. Indeed, the Victorian census typically reported more than double the number of share brokers than in Sydney to the

---

[24] Ibid.
[25] 250 individuals is from Graeme Davison, 'The Rise and Fall of Marvellous Melbourne, 1880–1895', unpublished PhD thesis, Australian National University, Canberra, 1969, 1. I am using 'capitalist entrepreneur' contra Richard White, who argued that American railways were established by entrepreneurs, but the capitalists were their distant creditors. This might technically comply with Marx's 'M-C-M' formula in a narrow sense, but it is obvious from the Melbourne land boom – and probably from American railways as well – that entrepreneurs sought profitable return from investment, even when their initial investment was based on credit. See White, *Railroaded*.
[26] Belich, *Replenishing the Earth*, 356–378.
[27] Kris Manjapra, 'The Semi-peripheral Hand: Middle-class service professionals of Imperial Capitalism', in Christof Dejung, David Motadel, and Jürgen Osterhammel (eds), *The Global Bourgeoisie: The Rise of the Middle Classes in the Age of Empire* (Princeton: Princeton University Press, 2019), 184–204.
[28] 'Hoddle grid' – see Susan Lawrence and Peter Davies, 'Melbourne: The Archaeology of a World City', *International Journal of Historical Archaeology* 22.1 (2018), 117–130.
[29] See Ian Mclean, *Why Australia Prospered: The Shifting Sources of Economic Growth* (Princeton: Princeton University Press, 2012).

north.[30] Still, until the 1880s Melbourne's economy grew at a similar rate to Sydney's. Then the place went mad. The Melbourne Stock Exchange facilitated extensive investment in mining in Broken Hill, banking across Victoria and Aotearoa/New Zealand and, notoriously, in Melbourne property.[31] The Melbourne land boom helped to expose the opportunity financialization presented for the middle class. No longer needed to administer empire straightforwardly, the children of the colonial middle class began to look to the professions.

One of these individuals, and a central figure in the Melbourne boom, was a young lawyer, Theodore Fink. A decade before the land boom, Fink was eighteen years old and in his second year of an articled clerkship for the Melbourne solicitor Henry J. Farmer, training to become a lawyer. We might think that this would have kept him busy enough, but in the same year he published an essay deriding the quality, of all things, of American journalism. 'Nowhere in the world', young Fink declared, 'are to be found such evidence of education combined with ignorance, morality and depravity, political acuteness and personal blackguardism, than are to be seen side by side in an United States newspaper'.[32] His sense of authority over the matter is striking. Fink was one of the up-and-coming young men of his generation. Son of a respected family in the sleepy coastal town of Geelong, Fink had attended school with Alfred Deakin, who, like Fink, was also studying law part-time at Melbourne University. Beyond their studies, they shared similar interests in journalism, literature, and the law. Both later entered politics, though Fink nowhere near as successfully as Deakin, who became Australia's second prime minister.[33] Fink outdid Deakin in newspapers, though: by the end of his life, Fink was mainly known as proprietor of the *Herald and Weekly Times* newspaper empire.[34]

[30] On average between the 1891, 1901, and 1911 censuses when stock broking is recorded, Victoria reported 123 per cent more brokers than New South Wales. The Melbourne Stock Exchange formed in 1852 but was disbanded and reconstituted at the Stock Exchange of Melbourne in 1884 to facilitate a fairly minor amendment in the rules regarding advertising and trade; see Alan Hall, *The Stock Exchange of Melbourne and the Victorian Economy 1852–1900* (Canberra: Australian National University Press, 1968).

[31] Michael Cannon, *The Land Boomers* (Melbourne: Melbourne University Press, 1966), 83–116, 165–177; Hall, *The Stock Exchange of Melbourne*, 192–196. Geoffrey Serle, *The Rush to be Rich: A History of the Colony of Victoria, 1883–1889* (Melbourne: Melbourne University Press, 1971), 247–294; Graeme Davison, *The Rise and Fall of Marvellous Melbourne* (Melbourne: Melbourne University Press, 1979), 72–94; Judith Brett, *The Enigmatic Mr Deakin* (Melbourne: Text Publishing, 2018).

[32] *Gympie Times and Mary River Mining Gazette*, 14 May 1873, 4.

[33] Brett, *Enigmatic Mr Deakin*.

[34] Sally Young, *Paper Emperors: The Rise of Australia's Newspaper Empire* (Sydney: NewSouth, 2019), 91–229.

The moral tone and international vision of Fink's youthful article was typical of the well-educated upper middle-class world both Fink and Deakin aspired to join. This rising set of middle-class professionals were self-consciously connected to the British metropole by empire, but also to North America via emerging reform movements.[35] It was a changing and transnational scene, bubbling with new ideas about society, religion, economy, and culture.[36] A whole moral world was in flux: Deakin dabbled in spiritualism, while other members of his class opposed it as superstition.[37] Artists, novelists, poets, and journalists dipped their toes in bohemia.[38] Temperance was a key preoccupation, as were democracy and the franchise, particularly for women.[39] Questions surrounded race and immigration – unsurprising, perhaps, in the settler colonies. Some put their intellects to work considering new modern forms of development, like agriculture and irrigation.[40]

In the United States, these ideas coalesced into the progressive movement of the 1900s–1910s, which was always an international phenomenon, though the effect on institutions shaped national economies.[41] Most importantly, however, the values at stake – which would be taken up by progressives in the United States, Canada, New Zealand, and Australia – were not abstract. It was not just that they went to questions of equality, citizenship, taxation, schooling, suffrage, and alcohol consumption, but they were becoming embodied and performed in the work people did as journalists, lawyers, teachers, clergy, and politicians. It was not a world that separated commerce from the state, nor morality from speculative profit – as we can see by the fact that the world that Deakin and Fink were entering was soon gripped by wild financial speculation.

The Melbourne land boom of the 1880s, once a favoured subject for Australian historians who saw in it one of the nation's founding toxins, was a consequence of global financialization.[42] British money poured into banks, building societies, colonial and municipal governments,

---

[35] Rogers, *Atlantic Crossings*; Lake, *Progressive New World*.
[36] Brett, *Enigmatic Mr Deakin*; Lake, *Progressive New World*, 22–44.
[37] Brett, *Enigmatic Mr Deakin*.
[38] John Docker, *The Nervous Nineties: Australian Cultural Life in the 1890s* (Oxford: Oxford University Press, 1991).
[39] Ellen Warne, *Agitate, Educate, Organise, Legislate: Protestant Women's Social Action in Post-Suffrage Australia* (Melbourne: Melbourne University Press, 2017).
[40] Marilyn Lake and Henry Reynolds, *Drawing the Global Colour Line: White Men's Countries and the International Challenge of Racial Inequality* (Cambridge, Cambridge University Press, 2008).
[41] Rogers, *Atlantic Crossings*; Lake, *Progressive New World*.
[42] Hall, *Stock Exchange of Melbourne*, 129.

syndicates laying out tramways, and a multiplicity of Australian companies that sent agents to Lombard Street to trade on the London Stock Exchange.[43] Mining and banking were the most popular stocks in Melbourne. Early colonial banks were built on Collins Street as soon as the original street was lain, owned in England but mainly operating in Victoria. The Victorian gold rush, however, encouraged locals to open many more, since miners sold their gold to banks who then sold it on to banks in England or leveraged it themselves to offer credit. In the 1870s and 1880s, on a per-person basis, the colony of Victoria had four times as many banks as England.[44]

In mining, the smart money was in Broken Hill Proprietary, which formed amidst this expansion in share trading, built on legislation that limited the liability of owners and partners of the corporations – like BHP – that blossomed as a result.[45] Stock markets were not just urban affairs. Several stock exchanges operated in the street in Broken Hill, but the founders of BHP registered their company in Melbourne. They had difficulties selling the initial batch of £9 shares on the Melbourne Exchange – £9 in 1883 was the equivalent of around US$1400 in 2020 terms. 'All of the people I have been speaking to about our Company think the payments stiff', complained their Melbourne agent.[46] The share brokers he used thought so too: '[T]he price asked of your property was generally speaking thought too high … intending purchasers … think they can purchase the shares cheaper by & bye.'[47] Those purchasers were wrong. Capitalist Melbourne came around, and, by 1888, BHP shares were worth nearly thirty times the original allotment, at £268 per share.[48]

BHP's initial problem with offloading their first shares was their unwillingness, according to share brokers Moore & MacLeod, to pay for advertising.[49] Soon there was little need, since journalists reported for them. Accounts of the quantities of ore mined and smelted were reprinted in newspapers across Australia and in London. Mine managers

---

[43] Ibid., 129–130; Belich, *Replenishing the Earth*, 356–372.
[44] Serle, *Rush to be Rich*, 66–69.
[45] Hall, *Stock Exchange of Melbourne*, 1–12; McLean, *Why Australia Prospered*, 75–76; Robert Parker, *Accounting in Australia: Historical Essays* (New York: Routledge, 2014), 242.
[46] Harvey Patterson to William Jamieson 29 June 1885, William Jamieson papers, University of Melbourne Archives MUA/1982.0065.0001, 1884–1885.
[47] H. Byron Moore & MacLeod, Financial & General Agents, The Exchange, Memorandum to William Jamieson Melbourne 8 July 1885, William Jamieson papers, University of Melbourne Archives, MUA/1982.0065.0001, 1884–1885.
[48] Stephen Salsbury and Kay Sweeney, *The Bull, the Bear, and the Kangaroo: The History of the Sydney Stock Exchange* (Sydney: Allen & Unwin, 1988), 134–135.
[49] H. Byron Moore & MacLeod to William Jamieson 8 July 1885, William Jamieson papers, University of Melbourne Archives, MUA/1982.0065.0001, 1884–1885.

were a key source of information, though they were not always forthcoming.[50] They sometimes fed journalists false information to fiddle the share price, inspiring journalists like 'Smiler' Hales – an early professional in the emerging investigative genre that became known in the United States as 'muckrakers' – to go undercover and expose their false reports.[51] Journalism in Australia, in fact, was built on this sort of reportage on mining activity. An outcome of the 'rush that never ended', mining journalism was a pathway to the more esteemed and lucrative city presses.[52] This was not because the public, apart from share traders, found mining all that interesting. Journalism in the outback, as it was along those North American railways, was a symptom of financialization.

British investment also grew engineering and, by extension, management. The kind of large, industrialized mines that attracted shareholders required vastly more managerial and engineering expertise than the simpler mining on earlier gold fields.[53] The new professional association for mining engineers, which grew in Broken Hill, was to pair mine management with engineering expertise. They had a moral task – mine safety – with which they sought to rehabilitate mining's reputation, tarnished by the many accidents that had killed workers as mining industrialized. Safety was paired, though, with mining efficiency and productivity and so ore profit and the share price. As with all aspects of settler capitalism, in mining, profit and morality were entangled. With new machinery and innovative techniques, engineers became crucial to success. At the top of the profession's hierarchy, they were inseparable from the capitalist class and deeply connected to finance. Two decades after BHP began operations, another engineer – future US president Herbert Hoover – established the Broken Hill company that solved the problem of extracting zinc from the mine tailings BHP was leaving lying around. Zinc Corporation's success depended on their relationship with financiers in London and Melbourne. Hoover's company helped launch one of Australia's most lucrative financial investment empires, Collins House.[54]

[50] Samuel Sleep to William Jamieson 5 September 1885, William Jamieson papers, University of Melbourne Archives, MUA/1982.0065.0001, 1884–1885.
[51] Forsyth, 'Class, Professional Work'; Donald Grant, 'Hales, Alfred Arthur Greenwood (1860–1936)', *Australian Dictionary of Biography, Volume 9* (Melbourne: Melbourne University Press, 1983).
[52] Denis Cryle, *The Press in Colonial Queensland: A Social and Political History, 1845–1875* (Brisbane: University of Queensland Press, 1989); Geoffrey Blainey, *The Rush That Never Ended: A History of Australian Mining* (Melbourne: Melbourne University Press, 1964).
[53] Geoffrey Blainey, *The Rise of Broken Hill* (Melbourne: Macmillan 1968).
[54] Geoffrey Blainey, 'Herbert Hoover's Forgotten Years', *Business Archives and History* 3.1 (1963), 53–70.

While globally networked engineers set their eyes on Broken Hill, in Melbourne, the local legal profession was most important, though accountancy benefited too. Lawyers held responsibility for the transfer of property – so all that buying and selling of Melbourne land was keeping them busy. The legal profession has tended to offer heroic accounts of their profession, centred on justice, equality under the law and the operation of the 'third arm' of the state.[55] This comes with a significant sense of dignity. Exemplifying this, the archives of the Law Institute of Victoria contain a sequence of portraits starting with a much-reproduced engraving of the fifteenth-century 'Judge Littleton', through the likes of sixteenth-century jurist Sir Edward Coke, nineteenth-century abolitionist Henry Brougham to Isaac Isaacs, who was Chief Justice of Australia early in the twentieth century, and later a governor general.[56]

This venerable, if somewhat forced, lineage does little to indicate the reality of most Melbourne lawyers' workday in the late nineteenth century. The average Melbourne lawyer spent the day gathering signatures, collecting and banking funds held in trust, preparing contracts and depositing documentation with the Land Titles Office. The Law Institute of Victoria archives shows much wrangling with the Land Titles Office over the procedural requirements that shaped their days. Why can't we collect proxy signatures, they whined, why must the office require *everyone* sign? Why does the Land Titles Office have such restrictive office hours? Why are the transfer fees so high? Melbourne was founded in a modern state, which by now accrued enormous administrative records. The record-keeping world the clerk was just starting to build during the land boom of 1830s Chicago culminated by the 1870s in the expansion of legal work. During the land boom, lawyers administered Melbourne.[57] Legal activities were mundane to be sure, but they kept the profession intimately connected with the whole network of well-heeled Melburnians trading in land, stocks, shares and bonds, and companies, and administering family estates.[58]

The network alone was invaluable. Theodore Fink was well placed, partly because his brother was one of the 'most dashing speculators of

---

[55] Morton Horwitz, *The Transformation of American Law, 1780–1860* (Cambridge, MA: Harvard University Press, 1977).
[56] Engravings and photographs, Law Institute of Victoria, Melbourne University Archives MUA/LIV/1978.0123/4.
[57] Zakim, *Accounting for Capitalism*, 9–10.
[58] Stationer's Letter Book 1842–1843 Law Institute of Victoria, Melbourne University Archives MUA/LIV LIV1978.0123/5; Memorandum Transfer Fees, Titles office, Fees Council Rulings 1897–1908 Law Institute of Victoria, Melbourne University Archives MUA/LIV/1978.0123/1.

1888'.[59] Benjamin Fink had founded a bank on the old Ballarat gold field in 1880, which later merged with the Collins Street City of Melbourne Bank. His bank was the biggest buyer of gold in Victoria, which gave him the backing to offer vast amounts of credit, including more than £300,000 he loaned to himself.[60] During the land boom, Benjamin Fink built one of Melbourne's tallest office blocks (which he named after himself), a leading, richly decorated shopping arcade called 'the block', a major book arcade and other shops and offices. He owned a furniture store and several hotels, brokered the float of a major brewery on the Melbourne Stock Exchange, and persuaded the Exchange to build on his land.[61] With such a brother, Theodore Fink's network was unsurpassed. He was further considered particularly gifted in connecting his friends and clients to investment opportunities and locating or constructing financial instruments that best suited their needs. Fink became known in Melbourne circles as the man to turn to for legal advice on financial matters.[62]

Financial speculation during Melbourne's land boom required a group of share brokers, managers, lawyers, accountants, and journalists, ideally as personal friends. Those roles overlapped considerably in the 1880s and 1890s; the Law Institute recorded many instances of lawyers also acting as real estate agents, stockbrokers, and accountants.[63] Theodore Fink held nearly all of those roles himself. They were needed because, as corporate and financial capitalism grew, there were some information asymmetries. These were as much about the distance from Melbourne to London, Auckland, or even the 500 miles to Broken Hill, as they were about the complexity of urban economies.[64] But professionals were evidently not only communicating expert advice to economic actors who needed information and advice from afar. They were active participants in the wealth-building that British finance enabled. During the Melbourne land boom, this was performed particularly melodramatically. Theodore Fink, like other professionals involved in making the system work, borrowed extensively to fund speculative investment.[65]

[59] Serle, *Rush to be Rich*, 262.
[60] The equivalent to more than US$51million in 2020 terms.
[61] Michael Cannon, 'Fink, Benjamin Josman (1874–1909), *Australian Dictionary of Biography, Volume 4* (Melbourne: Melbourne University Press, 1972).
[62] Cannon, *Land Boomers*; Peter Yule, *William Lawrence Baillieu: Founder of Australia's Greatest Business Empire* (Melbourne: Hardie Grant, 2012).
[63] Rulings related to advertising and practice of solicitors as accountants and stock agents and real estate agents; Council Rulings 1897–1908, Law Institute of Victoria, Melbourne University Archives MUA/LIV/1978.0123/1.
[64] See Geoffrey Blainey, *The Tyranny of Distance* (Melbourne, Sun Books, 1966).
[65] Cannon, *Land Boomers*.

All of the middle-class professions grew as British cash poured into the colony. This went well beyond lawyers exchanging contracts, account-ants preparing the books, financiers negotiating share trades, and engin-eers industrializing mining as a key object of investment. The numbers of self-styled 'professional men' expanded spectacularly. These were med-ical men, lawyers, clergy, architects, druggists, dentists, and accountants. In Melbourne, these occupations grew by more than 70 per cent in the decade after 1881.[66] It was not just middle-class men whose professional occupations became more important. Middle-class women similarly turned to healthcare and education in extraordinary numbers, often, as we will see in Chapter 4, starting their own businesses.[67] Understanding the logic of this expansion and its connection to the financialization of the global economy effected by these great heaves of British investment requires we step back from land boom Melbourne to consider the pat-terns of the growth of professions across the Anglo world. We will then return to Melbourne to see the ways the professionals behaved as a class, not just an occupation category. This was particularly obvious when things went wrong, which in Melbourne they did, spectacularly.

Growth Patterns in Professional Occupations across the Anglo World

Census data across the Anglo world in the decades after the 1870s show professions growing at extraordinary rates in North America and Australasia, but more slowly (except for finance professionals) in Britain. In the United States, between 1870 and 1940, population grew an average of 19 per cent per decade, while professional occupations grew an average of 56 per cent per decade.[68] This growth was not evenly spread across the professions. Over the whole period, engineering grew an average of 106 per cent, nursing 79 per cent, journalism 47 per cent, and teaching 38 per cent each decade. Medicine grew more slowly than average population growth, and law only exceeded it by 6 per cent. The fastest growth in the US professions was between 1880 and 1890, led by engineering, nursing, and journalism. That decade came hot on the heels of the previous one, where rapid growth was dominated by journalism, accountancy, teaching, and then engineering.

---

[66] Davison, 'Marvellous Melbourne', 203.
[67] Hannah Forsyth, 'Reconsidering Women's Role in the Professionalisation of the Economy: Evidence from the Australian Census 1881–1947', *Australian Economic History Review* 59(1) (2019): 55–79.
[68] Average decadal growth rate of teaching, nursing, accountancy, engineering, medicine, law, and journalism; includes social work after 1920. Data source: US Census.

Professions in the newer, still-British dominions were growing even faster. Population growth in Canada between 1881 and 1941 averaged 18 per cent per decade, while the professions grew at 118 per cent each decade on average over the same time period.[69] There, nursing and accountancy were consistently the fastest growing.[70] Engineering was very important too, particularly in the two decades between 1901 and 1921 – consistent with British investment in Canadian infrastructure. Law was the only profession not to keep pace with population growth. It grew rapidly with the first heave of British capital, increasing by 48 per cent of 1901 levels by 1911. Law grew relatively more slowly after that, however, and declined by 6 per cent during the 1920s.

The Australian census shows similar patterns. Growth of professional occupations on average between 1881 and 1947 was around double the rate of population growth. Relatively new professions, including engineering and accountancy, started from a low base but grew extremely rapidly, with growth rates for engineering peaking at 458 per cent in 1933 and accountants at 267 per cent in 1911. Nursing grew by more than 60 per cent each decade from the establishment of the professional association. Teaching, the most populous profession by far up to the 1930s Great Depression, grew by more than 30 per cent each decade from 1881 onwards. Pharmacy grew very rapidly in the late nineteenth century but declined in the 1920s as druggists were more regulated and the profession enclosed.[71]

Aotearoa/New Zealand's professionalization was on the surface even more rapid, though we need to be slightly wary of some of the data. On average, together the Pākehā and Māori population grew by 25 per cent each decade from 1881 to 1911, though this included a decline in Māori population by an average of 9 per cent between 1881 and 1896, but which was regained by 1901.[72] Over the same four decades, professions grew 192 per cent on average. This percentage is skewed by inflated growth reporting between 1891 and 1901, a symptom of changes to

---

[69] Average decadal growth rate of teaching, nursing, accountancy, engineering, medicine, law, and journalism. Data source: Canadian Census.

[70] Both nursing and accountancy were less reliable occupation categories than others in Canadian censuses in this period, as both professions were experiencing rapid changes in the nature of their professionalization. This is not to say that Canadian nursing and accountancy did not grow spectacularly in this time, for they did – but some of the growth in the census is also attributable to changes in classification.

[71] Average decadal growth rate of teaching, nursing, medicine, law, and the clergy; includes pharmacy from 1891; including nursing, accountancy, engineering, and charity and social work after 1901. Data source: Colonial Censuses 1881–1901, Australian Census 1911–1947.

[72] New Zealand Census 1881–1911. Many thanks to Evan Roberts for digitized data.

occupation category reporting.[73] Overall, the professions that grew the fastest in the Aotearoa/New Zealand economy were journalism, medicine, and engineering, though there also appears to have been a remarkable investment in the clergy at levels unusual elsewhere.

Importantly, the relative growth of occupations in the United States, Canada, Aotearoa/New Zealand, and Australia shows that the traditionally 'male' professions were not largely responsible for the professionalization of settler-colonial work. While engineering and accountancy grew very rapidly everywhere, teaching and nursing almost always dominated numerically – at least, until the 1930s economic depression, which stimulated rapid growth in accountancy. Teaching was a well-established profession by the late nineteenth century so that its growth, in this period, started from a relatively high base. Education was central to settler-colonial goals and the maintenance of middle-class values. The density of schoolteachers varied by population growth and training schemes, but rarely dipped below 40 teachers per 10,000 population (except for Australia in 1901), and in Canada and Aotearoa/New Zealand it often approached or exceeded 60 teachers per 10,000 population (see Figure 2.1). While Canada's school teaching workforce peaked at 74 teachers per 10,000 in 1901, the 1901 and 1911 New Zealand figures that show more than 80 per 10,000 are inflated, since the census aggregated schoolteachers with all other educators. Still, the majority of those would certainly have taught in schools.

Settler-colonial investment in education was not confined to schooling. Tutors and governesses regularly taught middle-class children at home. In Australia, where population was sparsely distributed and schools were often a long distance from home, there were around one quarter as many tutors and governesses as schoolteachers in the last two decades of the nineteenth century. The censuses of all four countries also showed a large number of music teachers; pianos especially provided, in the words of historian Humphrey McQueen, the 'accompaniment of colonial hopes and despairs'.[74] In Australia there were a similar number of music teachers to tutors and governesses, mostly (between 82 and

---

[73] In 1901 (and then again in 1911), New Zealand professions were reported as 'ministering to health', 'ministering to law and order' and so on, which aggregated several occupations in each category and inflated the overall figures. But while we need to take some of that growth with a grain of salt, it is telling that in the previous decade, which did not have the same classificatory disruption, the selected professions still grew by 131 per cent. For details of occupation classification and the effect on occupation statistics, see Erik Olssen and Maureen Hickey, *Class and Occupation: The New Zealand Reality* (Dunedin: Otago University Press, 2005).

[74] Humphrey McQueen, *A New Britannia* (Harmondsworth: Penguin, 1970), 117.

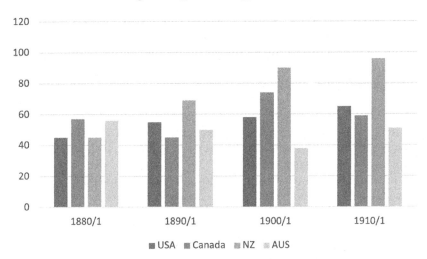

Figure 2.1   Teachers/10,000 in the United States, Canada, New
Zealand, and Australia 1880/1881–1910/1911.
Data sources: US Census, Canadian Census, NZ Census, Australian Census

95 per cent) women. While the numbers of governesses and tutors
declined from 1901 onwards, music teaching only began to decline in
the 1920s, presumably as gramophone sales increased.[75]

Nursing in this period was simultaneously an old profession and a new
one. Working-class women, particularly women of colour in North
America, who had long nursed new mothers and sick people for a living,
were being actively pushed out of this work by white, middle-class,
'professionalizing' nurses – I will explore this in more depth in
Chapter 3.[76] The category 'midwife', which carried implications of
'untrained' for some decades, covered many forms of nursing in most
earlier Australasian and North American colonial censuses – in
Australia's 1891 census, midwives still outnumbered all other type of
nurses. The Aotearoa/New Zealand census records sometimes separated
nurses, listed among professionals, from untrained nurses listed with
domestic servants. Their categories included 'sick' nurses (known as
'private duty' nurses in the United States, who assisted people in their
own homes) and a very old category of 'monthly' nurse, who assisted

---

[75] See Henry Reese, 'Shopgirls as Consumers: Selling Popular Music in 1920s Australia',
Labour History 121.1 (2021), 155–174.
[76] Hine, *Black Women in White.*

women with small babies, particularly in the first months after childbirth. The Australian census has an excellent record of the disparate types of nurses. There, hospital, sick, and monthly nurses grew through the first few decades of the twentieth century, while midwifery – now narrowed from general purpose healthcare to maternity care – declined. Growth in the nursing profession, however, was rapidly dominated by hospital nursing, which expanded into healthcare provision for the middle class from the late nineteenth century and, by the mid-twentieth century, constituted 98 per cent of all nursing in Australia, and similar everywhere else.

The United States had by far the highest density of nurses, which increased steadily each decade from 45 nurses per 10,000 population in 1880 to 65 nurses per 10,000 in 1910. Although nursing grew very fast in the other settler colonies, similar density was not achieved in this period. Australian nursing was in its infancy in 1881 when the census recorded 5 nurses per 10,000, increasing to 30 per 10,000 in 1911. Aotearoa/New Zealand nurses increased from 8 nurses per 10,000 to 54 in the same time frame, reflecting Aotearoa/New Zealand's general, very rapid professionalization.[77]

While the patterns across the settler colonies were broadly similar, showing high growth rates for engineering and accountancy, but where professionalization was dominated by teaching and nursing, Britain was very different. There finance professions increased by an average of 68 per cent each decade between 1851 and 1911 (see Figure 2.2) so that those working in finance grew from 9 per cent of all professionals in 1851 to 42 per cent of all professional work in 1911. Growth in the professions as a proportion of the total labour force was relatively sedate, however, increasing from 2.2 per cent of all workers in 1851 to 4.5 per cent in 1911.[78]

While the British professions did not grow at the pace of the settler colonies, there was nevertheless some significant movement. Medicine grew by 25 per cent between 1911 and 1921, but only 7 per cent in the following decade. Law declined by 15 per cent between 1911 and 1921, increasing by 5 per cent the 1920s. Writing, including journalism, grew

---

[77] Olssen and Hickey, *Class and Occupation*, 91.
[78] These figures are from the English and Welsh census. The Scottish census was conducted separately and was not included in Shaw-Taylor's figures; see Leigh Shaw-Taylor, England and Wales, supplied to the author with the following reference: Online Appendix Two, O. Saito and L. Shaw-Taylor (eds), *Occupational Structure, Industrialisation, and Economic Growth in a Comparative Perspective*, used with permission. Many thanks to Leigh Shaw-Taylor at the Cambridge Group for the History of Population and Social Structure for sharing this data.

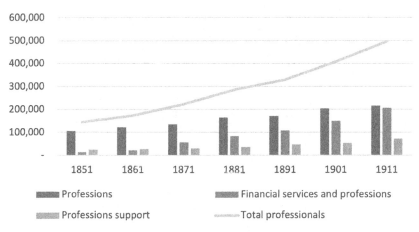

Figure 2.2 Professionals in England and Wales 1851–1911.
Data source: Leigh Shaw-Taylor, England and Wales, Online Appendix
Two, in Saito, O. and Shaw-Taylor, L. (eds) *Occupational Structure,
Industrialisation, and Economic Growth in a Comparative Perspective*, used
with permission

more quickly, by an average of 22 per cent over the period. Engineering
grew considerably, by more than 40 per cent per decade between
1911 and 1931. Accountancy declined between 1911 and 1921 but grew
by 78 per cent in the 1920s, a decade ahead of growth in the field in
North America but at a similar time to expansion in Australia. Routh's
figures for social work, nursing, and teaching only began in 1921. Social
work, and its antecedent charity work, barely registers, though it also had
very low numbers in the settler colonies. In Britain it was becoming
important in the delivery of healthcare for the poor.[79] This meant that
growth in social work was rapid, but it was a brand-new profession and
started from a very low base. Growth in teaching and nursing was
generally unspectacular in Britain, but commenced from a higher base
than most professions, so the professionalization of the economy in Great
Britain, as in the rest of the Anglo world, was still dominated by teaching
and nursing. Density was lower than the settler colonies but growing. By
the 1920s, Britain had 67 teachers per 10,000 population, only slightly

[79] Emily Abel, 'Medicine and Morality: The Health Care Program of the New York
Charity Organization Society', *The Social Service Review* 71.4 (1997), 634–651.

below Canada and the United States, but their 27 nurses per 10,000 represented a much lower density than in any of the settler colonies.

Entangling Moral with Economic Profit

The growth of the professions generally across the settler colonies, especially in teaching and healthcare, requires we complicate economist assumptions that professionalization was driven by a need for expert advice due to information asymmetry. Instead, the professionalization of the settler economies shows that while financialization in London was enabling growth across the Anglo world, that expansion consisted not only of investment in mining, railways, and agriculture but also of a growing investment in humans. This sense of humans as containers of value was central to the global economy envisaged – and ultimately ruled – by the Anglo middle class. Investment in health and education did little to make capitalist expansion more efficient, but it did mark a transfer of capitalist value from commodities to humans, grounded in merit (there will be much more to say about merit in Chapter 3). For the middle class, this began as an investment in themselves. They invested in their own education, medical treatment, private hospital, or home nursing, driving the growth of schooling, the expansion of hospitals beyond 'charity', and the professionalization of nursing.[80] Such a model of return on investment in human capital emerged as what Harold Perkin classified as the 'professional ideal', making humans vessels of economic and moral profit.[81] Despite the ways they appeared rational and objective in relation to late nineteenth-century society, the professional class was not outside capital. Instead, they *were* capital, in their very bodies.[82]

---

[80] Paul Axelrod, *The Promise of Canadian Schooling: Education in Canada 1800–1914* (Toronto: University of Toronto Press, 1997); Ian Cumming and Alan Cumming, *History of State Education in New Zealand 1840–1975* (Melbourne: Pitman Publishing, 1978); Craig Campbell and Helen Proctor, *A History of Australian Schooling* (Sydney: Allen & Unwin, 2014); John Rury, *Education and Social Change: Contours in the History of American Schooling* (New York: Routledge, 2012); David Labaree, 'Progressivism, Schools and Schools of Education: An American Romance', *Paedagogica Historica* 41.1–2 (2005), 275–288; James Gillespie, *The Price of Health: Australian Governments and Medical Politics 1910–1960* (Cambridge: Cambridge University Press, 1991); Paul Starr, *The Social Transformation of American Medicine* (New York: Basic Books, 1982); Dianne Dodd and Deborah Gorham, *Caring and Curing: Historical Perspectives on Women and Healing in Canada* (Ottawa: University of Ottawa Press, 1994); Derek Dow, *Safeguarding the Public Health: A History of New Zealand Department of Public Health* (Wellington: Victoria University Press, 1995); Gillian Sutherland, *In Search of the New Woman: Middle-Class Women and Work in Britain 1870–1914* (Cambridge: Cambridge University Press, 2015), 41–57.

[81] Perkin, *The Rise of Professional Society*, 1–26.

[82] See Goldin, 'The Human-Capital Century'.

This had everything to do with transformations in virtue. Middle-class morality was not new when Theodore Fink was young, but it was changing. Earlier in the nineteenth century, Protestants (often Evangelicals) reshaped public virtue through reforms like the anti-slavery movement, in the process, as Catherine Hall and others have shown, playing a 'mediating role' in the 'transition from an aristocratic and mercantile capitalist society ... to an industrial capitalist society with a large and influential bourgeoisie'.[83] Their influence was carried with the flows that empire created, their moral codes worked into middle-class industriousness. Such morality was never disconnected from middle-class work. Their literal and ideological 'civilizing missions' drew the lines – including the 'colour lines' that determined racialized structures of labour – of nineteenth-century global capitalism.[84] Middle-class morality, as historians of empire have long shown, helped to justify colonial violence and settler-colonial dispossession. They established, as hegemonic, European (and indeed, British) bourgeois ideologies.[85]

Towards the end of the nineteenth century, this middle class – defined, in many ways, as economist Deirdre McCloskey has suggested, by virtue – used this framework to reconsider the modernising world.[86] As middle-class progressives, rising politicians, artists, judges, barristers, and newspapermen gathered in Melbourne clubs, reading rooms and lecture halls they were as optimistic about the future they would build as they were anxious about violence among colonial youth, white manhood, and female suffrage.[87] They were barely separate from New Zealand's bourgeoisie, whose newspapers reported their every move, and they shared networks with British idealist reformers and North American progressives, who along with European reformers converged on

---

[83] Catherine Hall, *White, Male and Middle Class: Explorations in Feminism and History* (Cambridge: Polity Press, 1992), 75–123, quote from p. 79.

[84] Immanuel Wallerstein, *Historical Capitalism* (London: Verso, 1983) 75–93; Lake and Reynolds, *Drawing the Global Colour Line*; Patrick Wolfe, *Traces of History: Elementary Structures of Race* (London: Verso, 2016).

[85] Christof Dejung, 'From Global Civilizing Missions to Racial Warfare: Class Conflicts and the Representation of the Colonial World in European Middle-Class Thought' in Christof Dejung, David Motadel, and Jürgen Osterhammel (eds), *The Global Bourgeoisie: The Rise of the Middle Classes in the Age of Empire* (Princeton: Princeton University Press, 2019), 251–272; Marc Mulholland, *Bourgeois Liberty and the Politics of Fear: From Absolutism to Neo-conservatism* (Oxford: Oxford University Press, 2012), and Dipesh Chakrabarty, *Provincializing Europe: Postcolonial Thought and Historical Difference* (Princeton: Princeton University Press, 2000).

[86] McCloskey, *The Bourgeois Virtues*. See also Judith Brett, *Australian Liberals and the Moral Middle Class* (Cambridge: Cambridge University Press, 2003), 7–12; see also Collini, *Public Moralists*.

[87] Lake, *Progressive New World*; Warne, *Agitate, Educate, Organise*; Brett *Enigmatic Mr Deakin*.

Australasia as the world's 'social laboratory'.[88] Three spheres of activity particularly interested them: the modern state, the 'public sphere', and socio-economic progress.[89] These spheres were not separate. The youthful interests of Theodore Fink and Alfred Deakin show that in reconsidering the changing world, they saw little distinction between them. Their shared interest in the law, banking, politics, literature, and journalism was not dilettantism; it was part of the growing, cohesive middle-class vision for a capitalist system that was about financial profit connected in deep, structural ways to moral profit for individuals and society.

The transformation of individualized characteristics that middle-class men had once described as 'honourable' or 'gentlemanly' into a collective set of virtues could not be achieved in rarefied clubs, even if those clubs fostered robust discussions. Rather, systematizing morality and entrenching it into the global economy demanded institutions. Key among these institutions were the professional associations, which not only enshrined class-based virtue in associational life but also ensured virtue became embedded in the performance of work. These were modelled on early nineteenth-century institutions in Britain like the Institution of Civil Engineers (1918), the Law Society (1825), the British Medical Association (1832), the Royal Institute of British Architects (1834), and the Royal College of Veterinary Surgeons (1844). North American equivalents emerged in the mid-nineteenth century, especially the American Medical Association (1847), the National Teachers Association (1857), the American Veterinary Medical Association (1863), and the American Society for Civil Engineers (1867).[90] Nursing, accountancy, and journalism tended to form societies in the late nineteenth and early twentieth centuries, including the British Nurses Association (1887), American Association of Public Accountants (1887), Nurses' Associated Alumnae of the United States and Canada, later the American Nurses Association (1896).

In Australia and Aotearoa/New Zealand, British institutions often operated local branches, particularly in medicine. By the late nineteenth century, under increasing influence from North America, new Antipodean societies were being formed in a wider range of white-collar

---

[88] 'Social laboratory', see Stuart Macintyre, *Concise History of Australia* (Cambridge: Cambridge University Press, 2009), 122–155; Peter Coleman, 'New Zealand Liberalism and the Origin of the American Welfare State', *The Journal of American History* 69 (1982): 372–391.

[89] On the public sphere, see Jürgen Habermas, *The Structural Transformation of the Public Sphere: An Inquiry into a Category of Bourgeois Society* (Cambridge, MA: MIT Press, 1996).

[90] Larson, *Rise of Professionalism*, 246.

occupations. These include the Incorporated Institute of Accountants (1884), New Zealand Law Society (1869), the Australasian Trained Nurses Association (1899), Australian Institute of Journalism (1892), and the Teachers' Association of New South Wales (1892). The New Zealand Society of Civil Engineers was formed in 1914 and specialized engineering associations were amalgamated in Australia as the Institution of Engineers Australia in 1919.

In forming these professional associations, the Anglo middle class articulated morals that were not just abstract or ideal, but which also described the actual work people did. As I described in Chapter 1, historians have tended to depict middle-class virtue as either 'fake' – meaning sanctimonious, self-interested and patronising – or 'heroic', grounded in authentic concern for collective and individual well-being. However, when we look at professionals through the lens of their work, we can see that it is more accurate to consider this virtue as neither fake nor heroic, but rather as a rehearsed set of values that have been *performed*.[91] Unique virtues were associated with particular professions, but they were interrelated. For instance, the assemblage of values attached to nursing – courage, purity, patience, duty – articulated with the assemblage attached to accountancy – probity, honesty, orderliness, thrift. Together such professional moral assemblages formed a moral-economic system, all of which was only successful because it was performed as real, embodied work. Understandably, historians tend to write about morality from the pronouncements of the leadership of movements, organizations, and occupations. But moral declarations were not the actual vehicle by which the professions reshaped global capital. Rather, professional values became embedded throughout the economy via the work of many thousands of people.

Virtue expressed through work was deeply connected to civic responsibility. This was partly why professions and politics often overlapped. Take William Warren Lynch, for example. Called to the Canadian bar in 1868, Lynch was a conservative politician between 1871 and 1889, actively supporting railway development.[92] Although he was a lawyer, Lynch also served as president of the Provincial Association of Protestant Teachers. Teaching was a key channel for moral improvement among Protestant reformers, who connected literacy and then education more

---

[91] Judith Butler, 'Performative Acts'.
[92] Marie-Paule LaBrèque, 'Lynch, William Warren', in *Dictionary of Canadian Biography*, vol. 14 (Toronto: University of Toronto/Université Laval, 2003–).

broadly to morality, but also to national economic development.[93] In his presidential oration to the Association in 1884, Lynch lauded the 'national, moral and material blessings' that were to flow from education. By coming together, moreover, teachers were able to 'compare notes and deliberate intelligently and exhaustively for the public good'.[94]

With such moral values at stake, the upstanding character of individual teachers was obviously essential. One District Inspector's 1886 recommendation was typical: when Jeremiah Boyle was selected for the school in Broken Hill, the Inspector of Schools described him as 'a young, healthy, religious and strictly sober man'.[95] In their communities, teachers were expected to assert a moral authority that colonial leaders assumed was otherwise unavailable to working-class children. President of a new teachers' association, Albert Weigall, suggested that their central purpose was to provide support for individual teachers and thus, by their collective effort, 'strengthen the moral fibre of the community, for parental control and parental responsibility were too often neglected … [which] rendered the work of the [individual] teacher unnecessarily difficult'.[96]

Medical practitioners also saw moral threats in settler-colonial settings. The Anglo middle class in Winnipeg sought healthcare for the region's significant immigrant population and working-class poor. Eastern European immigration in the late nineteenth century bloated the population of what was soon to become a substantial west Canadian city. Canadians of English descent worked on a range of social reform projects. Key among these endeavours was public health nursing, which included a hygiene education program that guided family behaviour. This helped embed Canadian nursing in the project of assimilating

---

[93] Rebecca Swartz, *Education and Empire: Children, Race and Humanitarianism in the British Settler Colonies, 1833–1880* (Cham: Palgrave Macmillan, 2019), 199–233; Patricia Kmiec, '"Take This Normal Class Idea and Carry It Throughout the Land": Sunday School Teacher Training in Late Nineteenth-Century Ontario', *Historical Studies in Education/Revue d'histoire de l'éducation* 24.1 (2012), 195–211; Campbell and Proctor, *History of Australian Schooling*; Ann Allen, 'Gender, Professionalization, and the Child in the Progressive Era: Patty Smith Hill, 1868–1946', *Journal of Women's History* 23.2 (2011), 112–136; Anne Durst, *Women Educators in the Progressive Era: The Women Behind Dewey's Laboratory School* (New York: Palgrave Macmillan, 2010).

[94] 'Presidential Address, Provincial Association of Protestant Teachers', *The Gazette* (Montreal), 10 October 1884, 2.

[95] District Inspector to Chief Inspector, 10 August 1886, Broken Hill High School File, NSWSR/5/15099/Box 1/BundleA/1886–1891, State Records of New South Wales.

[96] *Sydney Morning Herald*, 7 September 1892, 9.

immigrants and the working class into an ideal of 'civilized', white Canada.[97]

In a similar spirit, in Aotearoa/New Zealand, doctors saw themselves like missionaries, bringing medicine and morality to the Māori.[98] 'Despite the gospel of health that has been preached zealously for years', lamented the *New Zealand Times*, 'superstition dies hard among the Maoris [sic]'. The high Indigenous mortality that was characteristic of settler colonization – and which some historians now consider to be genocide – was blamed, by medical practitioners, on Māori superstition. 'The native people cling to their old-time remedies', the *Times* reported, 'faith in charms, decoctions of herbs and immersion in cold water is still prevalent'.[99]

The move towards scientific rationality as the foundation of moral and medical authority made some medical men particularly vehement in their opposition to 'superstition' broadly. In the 1890s, Irish-born medical practitioner Samuel Knaggs published pamphlets opposing phrenology and spiritualism and gave satirical public exhibitions of levitation. His best-known publication was a novel exposing the irrationality of fortune telling, entitled *Dr. de Lion, Clairvoyant.*[100]

For the professional class, the kind of moral questions raised by the settler revolution consistently had a professional answer. Just as educators saw their profession as a solution to colonial immorality, so too did medicine. In Sydney, where violent behaviour among young men known as 'larrikins' was subject to middle-class moral consternation, members of the medical profession believed the problem within their jurisdiction:

Climate, cheap animal food, and the possession of too much money in the hands of the ignorant and brutish make Sydney a city where a large – I think an abnormally large – amount of coarse immorality exists. Witness the sexual relations of the larrikin class! Syphilis and gonorrhoea are constantly with them.[101]

[97] Marion McKay, 'Region, Faith and Health: The Development of Winnipeg's Visiting Nursing Agencies 1897–1926', in Jayne Elliott, Meryn Stuart, and Cynthia Toman (eds), *Place and Practice in Canadian Nursing History* (Vancouver: University of British Columbia Press, 2008), 70–90.

[98] Pratik Chakrabarti, *Medicine & Empire: 1600–1960* (Basingstoke: Palgrave Macmillan, 2014); Warwick Anderson, *The Cultivation of Whiteness: Science, Health and Racial Destiny in Australia* (Melbourne University Press, 2002).

[99] 'Enteric among Maoris', *New Zealand Times*, 6 September 1910, 1.

[100] Colin McDonald and Ruth Teale, 'Knaggs, Samuel Thomas (1842–1921)', *Australian Dictionary of Biography, Vol. 5* (Melbourne: Melbourne University Press, 1974).

[101] Robert Scot Skirving, 'Presidential Address', *The Australian Medical Gazette*, March 1892, 154–157; on larrikins see Melissa Bellanta, *Larrikins: A History* (Brisbane: University of Queensland Press, 2012).

The solution was medical supervision of prostitutes, according to the president of the local branch of the British Medical Association in 1892. Morality was thus deemed a medical problem, and medical authority was inextricable from the medical man's moral clout. This moral-expert nexus was significantly informed by older concepts of honour. Penny Russell's history of colonial manners describes a pair of medical practitioners who, in the 1840s, threatened pistols at dawn over a disputed diagnosis. A medical man's honour was impugned by another's opposing medical opinion.[102] By the late nineteenth century, this had shifted so that honourable conduct was increasingly paired with a more scientific, rational application of expertise, though it was still some years before such science made much difference to the efficacy of the work itself.[103]

An increasing equivalence of moral superiority with rational expertise spread across the professions. It radically transformed the field that was reclassifying itself as 'social work', but which was still described, in the Aotearoa/New Zealand and Australian censuses, as 'charity work' until the 1930s.[104] Charity work combined Victorian morality with emerging gendered forms of labour, contrasting the voluntary compassion of the 'domestic sphere' with the harsh, masculine values of industrial capitalism, which (not coincidentally) produced the problems that charity sought to address.[105] Charity workers organized working-class clubs, taught poor people to sing or sew, and advocated for better living conditions, especially improved sanitation, in poor areas.[106] In Britain and America, charity workers represented a remarkably well-educated women's movement, with the British charity societies and American settlement house movement led by university women, like Jane Addams, whose middle-class habits were considered to be an example to all.[107]

---

[102] Penny Russell, 'A Silly Quarrel About a Sore Knee? Defending Honour in a Professional Dispute, Sydney 1846', *Health and History* 14.2 (2012), 46–73.

[103] Starr, *Social Transformation of American Medicine.*

[104] Shurlee Swain, 'Do You Want Religion with That? Welfare History in a Secular Age', *History Australia* 2.3 (2005), 1–79.

[105] Mark Peel, *Miss Cutler & the Case of the Resurrected Horse: Social Work and the Story of Poverty in America, Australia, and Britain* (Chicago: University of Chicago Press, 2012); Graeme Davison and David Dunstan (eds), *The Outcasts of Melbourne* (Sydney: Allen & Unwin, 1985).

[106] Judith Trolander, *Professionalism and Social Change: From the Settlement House Movement to Neighborhood Centers 1886 to the Present* (New York: Colombia University Press, 1987); Philip Popple, *Social Work Practice and Social Welfare Policy in the United States: A History* (Oxford: Oxford University Press, 2018).

[107] Katharine Beauman, *Women and the Settlement Movement* (London: Radcliffe Press, 1996); Trolander, *Professionalism and Social Change*; Popple, *Social Work Practice and Social Welfare Policy.*

Historians of social work previously assumed that all New Zealand and Australian charity was an offshoot of British charity organizations. The close relationship of Antipodean social reformers to North American progressives, however, means that as it professionalized, social work in the Southern Hemisphere was American, rather than British, in influence and character.[108] This professionalizing process, as for medicine, used scientific reform, particularly social psychology, to bolster social work's moral status with professional expertise. In so doing, social workers adopted 'case work' as their preferred technique, bringing ideals about family and selfhood to their work with individuals.[109]

Other women's professions followed a similar pattern. About twenty years after Florence Nightingale selected Lucy Osburn to begin training professional nurses in Australia and Aotearoa/New Zealand, middle-class women describing themselves as 'trained' nurses established professional associations in both Australasia and North America. In 1896, the Nurses' Associated Alumnae of the United States and Canada was formed (later the American Nurses Association). In 1907 a Canadian National Association of Trained Nurses was forged from an amalgamation of several small organizations. The Australasian Trained Nurses' Association formed in 1899, uniting nurses in Australia and Aotearoa/New Zealand (though not Victoria, who established their own association in 1901). Each association formed for exactly the same purposes: they sought to enclose nursing via state-sanctioned registration, support their members (who were often single women) financially, and set educational and ethical standards. Professional nurses' associations were formed in alliance with the predominantly male medical establishment, which was important to the business of healthcare and to the social goals that middle-class men and women shared. It did not interfere with the gendered virtues that nursing embodied. Nursing paired moral ideals like duty, purity, and courage with professional activities like hygiene, neatness, and skill, in the process coupling Victorian gender norms to

---

[108] Jane Miller, 'The Predominance of American Influences on the Establishment of Social Work Education at the University of Melbourne 1920–1960', unpublished PhD dissertation, University of Melbourne (2015); Lake, *Progressive New World*, 169–192.

[109] Elizabeth Irvine, *Social Work and Human Problems: Casework, Consultation and Other Topics* (Oxford: Pergamon, 1979); Robert Lawrence, *Professional Social Work in Australia* (Canberra: Australian National University Press, 1965), 13; John Ehrenreich, *The Altruistic Imagination: A History of Social Work and Social Policy in the United States* (New York: Cornell University Press, 1985), 43–77; Daniel Walkowitz, *Working with Class: Social Workers and the Politics of Middle-Class Identity* (Chapel Hill, NC: University of North Carolina Press, 1999), 54–56.

professional competence.[110] As well as developing aptitude in invalid food preparation, patient care, pharmaceuticals, surgical skills, and a range of medical techniques, articles in nursing journals such as that entitled 'Nursing Discipline and Ethics' also instructed women to 'walk gracefully', to 'be ladies under all circumstances' and to avoid slang, gossip and 'practical jokes'.[111]

Teaching, medicine, nursing, and social work shared an obvious moral mission, but equally they served explicit economic purposes. While the network of British aristocratic women who arranged for Nightingale nurses in the colonies were no doubt comforted to know that healthcare was available to family members posted there, in publications like London's *Times*, this was in fact economic news.[112] It offered reassurance to London investors that the settler colonies were economically stable with good prospects for growth.[113] Census reports in the second half of the twentieth century began to report literacy levels as a key measure of economic progress.[114] Literacy and the expansion of primary education went together. The Anglo settler colonies expanded schooling faster than anyone else. Between 1860 and 1910, Aotearoa/New Zealand, Canada, and the United States had the highest rates of primary schooling in the world, well above British education rates and slightly higher than France, who led Europe's expansion into mass schooling. By 1910, almost 100 per cent of white children aged 5–14 were enrolled in primary schools in the United States, and around 90 per cent in Aotearoa/New Zealand and Canada.[115]

Professional associations for law, accountancy, journalism, and engineering were more obviously serving economic purposes and were thus less grounded in anxiety for the moral well-being of settler-colonial society than schooling and healthcare, but their legitimacy and efficacy nevertheless required virtue. Like teachers, nurses, and medical practitioners, engineers, who early in the twentieth century in North America and Australasia amalgamated several branches of engineering into national bodies representing all engineers, saw themselves as the engine

---

[110] Mary Poovey, *Uneven Developments: The Ideological Work of Gender in Mid-Victorian England* (Chicago: University of Chicago Press, 1988); Alison Bashford, *Purity and Pollution: Gender, Embodiment and Victorian Medicine* (London: Macmillan, 1998).

[111] 'Hospital Discipline and Ethics', *The Australasian Nurses' Journal*, June 1908, 15.

[112] Lady Harriet Mary Dowling to Florence Nightingale, 23 January 1863, Nightingale Papers. Vol. CLV (ff. 298), British Library.

[113] For example, 'Topics of the Moment in Australia', *The Times*, 6 August 1910, 5.

[114] Mclean, *Why Australia Prospered*, 200.

[115] Peter Lindert, *Growing Public: Social Spending and Economic Growth since the Eighteenth Century* (Cambridge: Cambridge University Press, 2004), 9.

of progress.[116] Engineering leaders argued that their professionals were characterized by modesty, hard work, an absorption in practical problem-solving and mathematically meticulous skills to apolitical, unemotional rationality, and upright character.[117]

When journalists began to form professional associations – starting in the United States in 1909, then in Australia in 1910 (though this was in fact a union) and Aotearoa/New Zealand in 1912 – they claimed that bold, honest reporting, strength of mind, and character as well as ethics were central to their collective responsibility to the 'progressive elements in public life, in science and in industrial activity'.[118] These associations were formed as journalists became conscious of the possibilities associated with exposing social ills. In the United States, practitioners of the 'New Journalism' conducted investigative and undercover reports, exposing ('muckraking') the nation's ills.[119] In Canada, Australia, and New Zealand, journalists used the same techniques to pursue similarly moral goals.[120]

Accountants, with their myriad professional societies commencing with the Institute for Chartered Accountants in Scotland in 1854, similarly claimed a relationship to capitalism that required meticulous attentiveness. By the 1920s, after very rapid growth in accountancy worldwide, their journals, like those of engineers, were prone to bold moral statements connecting beliefs about their virtue at work to a deeply moral sense of *business* activity itself. In 1925, accountant G. Montague Nettleship was moved to write his 'Business Creed', loosely modelled on the Nicene Creed:

---

[116] W. H. Warren, 'Inaugural Presidential Address', *Journal of the Institution of Engineers Australia* 1 (1920), 162–175.

[117] Sir John Henry Butters, 'Presidential Address', *Journal of the Institution of Engineers Australia* 8 (1927), xxxvii–lxii.

[118] Henry Gullett, 'Journalism as a Calling: A Half-Century's Impressions', *The Australian Journalist*, 25 April 1913, 1–2. The earlier 1892 Australian association did not last long.

[119] Louis Filler, *The Muckrakers* (Stanford: Stanford University Press, 1968); Geraldine Muhlmann, *A Political History of Journalism* (Cambridge: Polity, 2004); Ellen Fitzpatrick *Muckraking: Three Landmark Articles* (Boston: Bedford Books, 1994); Walter Brasch, *Forerunners of Revolution: Muckrakers and the American Social Conscience* (Lanham: University Press of America, 1990); Martin Oppenheimer, 'The Rise and Fall of the Muckrakers', *New Politics* 16.2 (2017), 87–96; John Thompson, 'American Muckrakers and Western Canadian Reform', *Journal of Popular Culture* 4.4 (1971), 1060–1070; Julianne Schultz, *Reviving the Fourth Estate: Democracy, Accountability, and the Media* (Cambridge: Cambridge University Press, 1998).

[120] Stephen Leccese, 'John D. Rockefeller, Standard Oil, and the Rise of Corporate Public Relations in Progressive America, 1902–1908', *The Journal of the Gilded Age and Progressive Era* 16.3 (2017), 245–263; Sally Young, *Paper Emperors*.

(1) I BELIEVE in the GOODS I am selling; In the FIRM I am working for; and in my ABILITY to get results.

(2) I BELIEVE that honest goods can be sold by honest men by honest methods.

(3) I BELIEVE in working, not waiting; in laughing not weeping; in boosting not knocking; and in the pleasure of honest toil.

(4) I BELIEVE THAT A MAN GETS WHAT HE GOES AFTER; that ONE application to-day is worth TWO to-morrow, and that no man is down and out until he has lost faith in himself.

(5) I BELIEVE in to-day and the work I am doing; in to-morrow and the work I hope to do, and in the sure reward which the future holds.

(6) I BELIEVE in COURTESY, in KINDNESS, in GENEROSITY in GOOD CHEER, in FRIENDSHIP, and honest competition.

(7) I BELIEVE there is an application some-where for every man ready to take one.

I BELIEVE I'M READY – RIGHT NOW.[121]

Moralizing went beyond progressive reading rooms and lecture halls, making its way through the swelling ranks of professionals into the conduct of capitalist enterprise.

Special among the professions, law developed a complex relationship to morality. The law was itself a moral structure, with a long-standing relationship to enlightenment ethics that linked a good society to natural justice and the rule of law. These underpinned lawyers' claims to 'dignity', which they expressed in ritualized courtroom performances and a set of ethics focused primarily on policing a rule forbidding advertising.[122] In the late nineteenth century, however, lawyers were already subject to ridicule over their reputation for swindling the public. Despite this dubious reputation, the law was nevertheless the exemplar profession for all of the others. When social workers, journalists, accountants, or engineers (for example) considered the purposes of associational life and the need for their profession to self-regulate ethics, conduct, and standards, they frequently looked to law.[123]

These male-dominated professionals – law, medicine, accountancy, engineering, and journalism – often articulated their moral standing as one of trust. For lawyers and accountants, for example, 'it was absolutely

---

[121] G. Montague Nettleship, 'My Business Creed', *Commonwealth Journal of Accountancy*, 1 November 1925, 61.

[122] Folio on Advertising, Law Institute of Victoria, University of Melbourne Archives MUA/LIV1960.008.14.

[123] Law Institute of Victoria Incorporation Group 2 Rules & by-laws, Melbourne University Archives Rules and By-Laws 1883 UMA/LIV1960.0008 Unit 1.

essential to the due performance of their duties that they should have the confidence of the public' – but there was more than trust at work too.[124] Again, this was neither fake nor heroic. Rather, it is important to see that for the professional class, virtue became materially necessary. The performance of professional work, auditing company records, preparing contracts, calculating bridge loads, and reporting on events required the virtues professional societies idealized. Audits needed to be correct, contracts had to be legal, bridges needed to bear weight, and the accuracy of newspaper reports, certainly at this stage in the history of communications, was essential for the conduct of business and government. The connection between moral character and professional expertise may sometimes have seemed fantastical, but it was also real and, through their professional associations, self-reinforcing.

The Making of the Professional Class

In 1889, the Melbourne property bubble burst, land prices dropped, shares were deemed worthless, and banks collapsed. David Munro, one of the most prominent sellers of land, 'was ruined by the land boom', according to newspapers. Ordered by the court to pay £3 a month, he declared himself unable to pay. 'This is a strange and awkward position', reported the paper, 'for a man who but a few months ago could scarcely count his wealth.' The *Argus* journalist was unable to resist moralizing: '[I]t serves as a wholesome commentary on the uncertainty which lies in the pathway of easy-going speculators'.[125] Other victims of the land boom also fell hard. Thomas Patrick Fallon, 'a well-known figure in commercial life', as a merchant and tramway investor, committed suicide in 1892.[126] His death was reported as 'Another Land Boom Victim', an oft-repeated headline in early 1890s Australian newspapers.[127] Speculators of every level were affected, including 'Maurice Franklin, a medical man', who was found drowned in Tasmania, his suicide being due to 'monetary troubles … arising from the land boom'.[128]

---

[124] 'Presidential Address', *Adelaide Advertiser*, 1 February 1894, 6.
[125] 'Land Boom Magic', *Singleton Argus*, 22 June 1892, 2; see also Michael Cannon, 'Munro, David (1844–1898)', *Australian Dictionary of Biography, Volume 5* (Melbourne: Melbourne University Press, 1974).
[126] Davison, 'Marvellous Melbourne', 514. 'Suicide of Mr. T.P. Fallon', *Argus*, 5 January 1892, 5.
[127] 'Another Land Boom Victim', *Advertiser*, 5 January 1892, 5; 'Another Land Boom Victim', *The Tasmanian*, 28 March 1891, 13.
[128] 'Suspected Suicide: A Victim to the Land Boom', *Australian Star*, 4 January 1890, 6.

In the winter of 1897, a few years after the collapse collided with the global depression, Theodore Fink and a fellow member of the legal profession, Judge Molesworth, attended the annual meeting of the Incorporated Institute of Accountants. According to the *Age*, Molesworth toasted the accountancy profession. 'What was an accountant?' he asked jovially. 'Some people would reply that an accountant was a very clever man who could prepare a rosy balance sheet (Laughter).'[129] This was extraordinary reporting by the *Age* which, like the other Melbourne newspapers, had narrated quite lightly the fate of the speculators who came to be known as 'land boomers' so that historians of journalism have smelled a conspiracy of sorts. Journalists, politicians, and lawyers, after all, were members of the same clubs.[130] Several of the key players in the property bubble were not only involved in a legal cover-up engineered by Theodore Fink, but they also owned an emerging newspaper empire through which, according to political scientist Sally Young, they sought to conceal their roles.[131] Land boomers did not own every newspaper, of course, and yet reports on how the boomers extricated themselves once the bubble burst were nevertheless notably scarce.[132] There is reason to believe that beyond a conspiracy of friends, the professionals were protecting themselves as a class.

Extricating themselves from the trouble that resulted meant the land boomers needed a plan. Theodore Fink masterminded this. Locating a little-used instrument called 'composition by arrangement', Fink represented many bankrupt speculators, including himself twice in one year, to come to a secret arrangement with creditors. The debtor – for example, architect Alfred Dunn, who owed £28,912 (around US$3M in 2020 terms) – called a meeting of creditors. If those present represented 75 per cent of the debt, they could agree to a composition whereby the debtor paid a certain amount in the pound and the whole arrangement was kept confidential. In Dunn's case, he repaid sixpence per pound (or one-fortieth of the debt) to his creditors. The next day, Dunn was free of debt and solvent, able to trade immediately with no smear on his reputation. In 1892, £803,658 of debt (around US$80M in 2020 terms) was resolved through these 'secret compositions', debtors often paying between a farthing (0.1 per cent) and five shillings (25 per cent) for every pound owed.[133]

[129] 'The Accountants' Institute. The Humors of Figures', *The Age*, 17 June 1897, 6.
[130] Cannon, *Land Boomers*, 55; Young, *Paper Emperors*, 124–129.
[131] Young, *Paper Emperors*, 119–142.
[132] Cannon, *Land Boomers*, 55; Young, *Paper Emperors*, 124–129.
[133] Figures from Cannon, *Land Boomers*, 211.

The secret compositions the following year were much more stagger-
ing. A total of £2,302,804 of debt (around US$248M in 2020 terms) was
dealt with secretly in 1893. Of this, £1,019,275 belonged solely to
Benjamin Fink.[134] Benjamin Fink paid just ½d per £1 (0.2 per cent of
the debt), and many paid between 1 and 7d per £1 of debt (0.4–3 per
cent of the debt). Some of the smaller debts for £1 to £2,000 (US
$1–200K in 2020) went for as much as 19s 11d per £1 (99.6 per cent).
Filling a room with a friendly 75 per cent of debtors was not difficult.
Since debtors owed the largest sums to banks and land companies who
were often themselves in need of debt relief, meetings of creditors were
stacked with friends today who would be applying for their own secret
composition tomorrow. Theodore Fink was 'masterful', historian Peter
Yule argued, at locating creditors whose own position made them 'amen-
able to a light composition'.[135]

The report of the Institute of Accountants annual meeting in the *Age* in
1897 was evidently intended for insiders to this process. We can hear, in
the report, their knowing laughter:

Well, he [Molesworth] presumed there were some who were adepts at the
preparation of balance sheets, warranted to mislead even very clever people
(Hear.) But of course such men were few in number. This was a peculiar
world. He had even heard aspersions cast on his own profession, and had heard
people ask – "Can you introduce me to an honest lawyer?" (Cries of Impossible
and laughter.) He believed the same answer suited both professions. (Laughter
and cries of Oh!) It was the man who made the profession noble and any man
who determined to do his work honestly ennobled his profession. He really
believed there were many honest lawyers – and accountants – (a laugh) – in
Melbourne. He knew at least one honest lawyer. (Loud laughter.)

As a judge, Molesworth opposed the secret compositions and actively
impeded some of the debtors' attempts to easily rescue themselves.[136]
Shrewd *Age* readers no doubt saw the significance of the subsequent toast
by Theodore Fink who said, 'Judge Molesworth ... had not been so
humorous that night as he was in another capacity. (Laughter).' Fink's
toast acknowledged, with faux self-deprecation, the faults recently displayed by professional men, many of whom were likely in the room,
suggesting:

A better class of professional men would ultimately arise ... and they might
content themselves with the reflection that there was to follow a generation far

---

[134] Ibid., 212–213.   [135] Yule, *Baillieu*, 46.
[136] Elise Histed, 'Molesworth, Hickman (1842–1907)', *Australian Dictionary of Biography*,
Volume 10 (Melbourne: Melbourne University Press 1986); Cannon, *Land Boomers*,
160–162, 206–209.

cleverer than their fathers. (Laughter.) So they should be. So they very easily could be. (Loud laughter.)

The secrecy of Fink's debt resolution meant that the reputations of law and accountancy were not as tarnished by the crash as they deserved. For accountants, the outcome was frankly advantageous. Molesworth's toast further congratulated the accountancy profession on the recent Company Act. This was the Victorian government's response to the land boom – more accurate, open accounts, prepared by recognized experts. This Act gave lots of extra work to professional accountants, whose integrity was now needed, the Victorian government believed, to protect capitalism from itself.

Fink had, in fact, vehemently opposed the Company Act. By then he was an elected representative of the people in Victoria's Legislative Assembly.[137] At the dinner he said, 'The Accountants' Society was the most successful instance of a rapidly developed legally constituted trades union he had ever heard of.' Fink continued: 'By a rapid stroke of the legislative pen it had been made compulsory for every company to be a customer of the institute. (Laughter.) The law was not so kind to lawyers. It did not compel clients to employ them.' Fink's banter then gestured to the sorts of reasoning professionals gave in order to conceal their self-interest, slyly suggesting, 'Of course, the Accountants Society was not one for the purpose of gain.'[138]

These professionals knew they were a class. To be sure, some of the professionals at the top of their hierarchy were also distinctly capitalist, Fink among them. Nevertheless, the men in the room were conscious that members of these white-collar societies – even if membership was still sometimes quite loose – were applying recognized expertise and shared a class interest. This interest was being constructed in the late nineteenth and early twentieth century in relation to capital. Their interests, indeed, their obligations, required them to help capitalist individuals and organizations, as Fink had during the boom, making connections, sharing profitable opportunity, and assuring the paperwork surrounding transactions was legal and accurate. Then, during the secret compositions, Fink was equally obliged to use his professional expertise to save capital from itself. In the Company Act that followed, the professional class assumed a regulatory obligation that was also bound up in their virtue, requiring them in future to inhibit capital's worst excesses.

---

[137] Cannon, *Land Boomers*, 142–147.
[138] 'The Accountants' Institute. The Humors of Figures', *The Age*, 17 June 1897, 6.

In this sense, the dice were loaded. Professionals acted on both sides of capital at once.[139]

Conclusion

This chapter has shown that a century of British industrialization gave Lombard Street extra cash to invest overseas. Great heaves of this investment went to the places where English-speaking colonists built new societies on stolen Indigenous land. This financializing economy, unlike earlier, short-term bubbles like Chicago's in the 1830s, impelled the global expansion of professional occupations. Middle-class colonists, already spread throughout the world administering empire, began settling into new societies and building new economies. Developing in each country, but also in relation to one another, they changed the world.

Older moral values, already rapidly changing through the nineteenth century, were converted into professionalizing occupations. New forms of virtue grew and institutionalized. Retaining capitalism's model of return on investment, the emerging professional class made investment in humans the central professional ideal. Their class status was often concealed beneath layers of rationality and claims to expertise, but across the Anglo world they transformed capitalism into a form of investment for moral profit.

This virtue served professionals' own interests. Each profession – including accountancy, medicine, and teaching – often held the answers to the problems emerging in the building of the settler-colonial world and then transferred their values back in the British metropole. Their own successful investment in themselves served as a model. On its foundation, the professional class persuaded Anglophone nations to build entangled economies that were centred on human capital. This was why professionalization was not confined to lawyers and accountants, whose services facilitated Lombard Street's profits. Rather, the logic of virtue guided capitalism across the Anglo world, its moral goals – virtue capitalism – consistent with the capitalist logic of return on investment more broadly. Professionals invested to acquire profit in American and Canadian dollars and British pounds, but they also developed a currency-like system that measured and proved their virtue. This 'currency' was merit, which is the subject of Chapter 3.

---

[139] The quote referenced here is, 'It is not a case of two interdependent forces working on each other. Les dés sont pipés [trans.: 'The dice are loaded'.]. Capital acts on both sides at once', Marx, *Capital Vol. 1*, 794.

3   Achieving Class

In 1918 when it was apparent that the Great War would mean a shortage of men for office work, one accountant, R. Adamson, advocated for equal pay for women. 'Merit, and merit alone', Adamson argued, 'should count, and women, as well as men, should be paid according to the quality of their work.'[1] Merit in this case was shorthand for 'objectively good at this', though it veiled many other qualities. In the twentieth century, merit became the method for evaluating candidates for work. In the process, merit valorized human capital – which, at least on the surface, was why Adamson connected it to the rate of pay. As this chapter will show, merit became the substance that made virtue capitalism function. Historians have often described the social and political role of merit over the long twentieth century.[2] This chapter reconsiders merit as a form of *economic* value (which does not mean it was only about money). Making merit central to twentieth-century

[1] R. Adamson, 'Women and Wages', *The Australasian Accountant and Secretary*, April 1918, 29–30.
[2] Joseph Kett, *Merit: The History of a Founding Ideal from the American Revolution to the Twenty-First Century* (Ithaca: Cornell University Press, 2012); Richard Sennett, *The Culture of the New Capitalism* (New Haven: Yale University Press, 2006), 83–130; Kenneth Arrow, Samuel Bowles, and Steven Durlauf (eds), *Meritocracy and Economic Inequality* (Princeton: Princeton University Press, 2000); Peter Saunders, 'Might Britain Be a Meritocracy?', *Sociology* 29.1 (1995), 23–41; Richard Breen and John Goldthorpe, 'Class Inequality and Meritocracy: A Critique of Saunders and an Alternative Analysis', *British Journal of Sociology* 50.1 (1999), 1–27; Richard Lampard, 'Might Britain Be a Meritocracy? A Comment on Saunders', *Sociology* 30.2 (1996), 387–393; Gordon Marshall and Adam Swift, 'Merit and Mobility: A Reply to Peter Saunders', *Sociology* 30.2 (1996), 375–386; Michelle Jackson, 'Meritocracy, Education and Occupational Attainment: What Do Employers Really See as Merit?', unpublished D.Phil. thesis, University of Oxford (2002); John Goldthorpe and Abigail McKnight, 'The Economic Basis of Social Class', in Stephen Morgan, David Grusky, and Gary Fields (eds), *Mobility and Inequality: Frontiers of Research in Sociology and Economics* (Stanford: Stanford University Press, 2006), 109–136; Tadeusz Krauze and Kazimierz Słomczyński, 'How Far to Meritocracy? Empirical Tests of a Controversial Thesis', *Social Forces* 63.3 (1985), 623–642; Christopher Whelan and Richard Layte, 'Late Industrialization and the Increased Merit Selection Hypothesis: Ireland as a Test Case', *European Sociological Review* 18.1 (2002), 35–50.

capitalism, as Adamson rather inadvertently predicted, had a particularly significant effect on middle-class women. Their role in building the professional class was more important than many historians have previously recognized.[3]

Historicizing merit is important. Although historians, sociologists, and educationalists have long debunked merit as a rather misleading label for the system of value at stake, we nevertheless inherit a very strong version of it in the present.[4] Our institutions, work structures, and social relations encourage us to conduct our work lives according to a system of merit, even to the point of using it to evaluate our self-worth. These experiences, often profoundly internalized, can make it seem as though merit was always the only right way to organize and value work. Considering merit historically helps us to see beyond this. More than an intellectual history of the concept of merit is needed, however, if we are to understand the ways merit became integral to twentieth-century capitalism.[5] We need to identify in its history the logic of merit as it came to permeate labour markets.

In Chapter 2, I argued that the performance of professional work required virtue. This was not just contrived; virtue was necessary to do the work. The products of that work, like trustworthy accounting and structurally sound bridges, reveal the 'use value' of professional morality and show that middle-class virtue had authentic utility. This chapter is about the ways this utility gained an 'exchange value'. Merit was an effect of equal citizenship under modern democracy, but it also became a way of understanding or measuring value. Each professional acquired more of this value through work, experience, and by study.[6] For the professional class collectively, merit became a 'socially recognized incarnation of human labour', as Marx once defined money.[7] This is an important definition; when considered historically, it exposes similarities between merit and money as a store of value. The comparison is imperfect, not

---

[3] See, for example, the role of women in what Julia Horne called the 'knowledge front' of the Great War: Julia Horne, 'The "Knowledge Front", Women, War and Peace', *History of Education Review* 45.2 (2016), 151–167.

[4] Benson Snyder, *The Hidden Curriculum* (New York: Knopf, 1971); Richard Teese, *Academic Success and Social Power: Examinations and Inequality* (Melbourne: Melbourne University Press, 2000); Sennett, *Culture of the New Capitalism*, 83–130.

[5] Though there have been some very good intellectual histories on merit, which are worth connecting to the behaviour of the historical economy. For example, Ben Jackson, *Equality and the British Left: A Study in Progressive Political Thought, 1900–1964* (Manchester: Manchester University Press, 2014); Martin Daunton, 'Michael Young and Meritocracy', *Contemporary British History* 19.3 (2005), 285–291; and for an intellectual and social history, Mandler, *Crisis of the Meritocracy*.

[6] Mandler, *Crisis of Meritocracy*, 3.   [7] Marx, *Capital*, 192.

least because, unlike money, merit did not put a price on exchange. As we will see, it still had some similar effects. The parallel between money and merit, while imperfect, is useful to understanding the shift in twentieth-century capitalism that positioned merit at the centre of much social and economic profitability.

This chapter begins with a brief overview of the history of merit as we understand it. I then describe the reasons that merit became so important to the professions. This section shows that excluding some people – in certain fields these were belittled as 'quacks' – established a monopoly for powerful interests in each profession. It did more than this too. Excluding certain people as 'unsuitable' established a moral barrier to each profession, which in turn centred virtue as the foundation for profit. This intersected with settler-colonial anxieties by excluding practitioners based on race. The subsequent section shows the ways that merit was 'earned' but nevertheless intersected with other attributes that were deemed 'natural'. This was a way that the professional class helped draw 'colour lines' and also embedded gender discrimination into the modern economy. The final section shows how merit structured the hierarchies each profession was establishing, making merit both evidence and reward for the performance of virtue.

What We Know about Merit

As a structure, merit developed with the modern state, to ensure public administration was performed by those most capable, rather than by those with the best family connections.[8] By the late nineteenth century, merit expanded to represent an expectation that both wealth and status were to be 'earned through accomplishment', a system that promised an economy that, while still unequal, at least seemed somehow fairer.[9] Merit undermined earlier views that class was natural and God-given.[10] Instead, class status now seemed to be earned. The professionals were an *achieving* class, in that class status was attained by the things that they did. Moreover, even for people who were born into middle-class families, with all the advantages this entailed, their very class status required ongoing achievement.

---

[8] Stafford Northcote and Charles Trevelyan, *Report on the Organization of the Permanent Civil Service* (London: Her Majesty's Stationary Office, 1854); Richard Willis, *Testing Times: A History of Vocational, Civil Service and Secondary Examinations in England since 1850* (Boston: Brill, 2013), 63–71.

[9] The phrase 'earned through accomplishment' is from Daniel Markovits, *The Meritocracy Trap* (London: Penguin, 2020), 1.

[10] On class status as God-given, see Perkin, *Rise of Professional Society*, 2–9.

While merit was supposed to be grounded in accomplishment, middle-class women and men had other attributes that were generally still deemed natural or God-given. This complicated the way that merit apportioned value. In the late nineteenth century, most people believed that men and women were naturally good at different things.[11] Following the massive colonial expansions of the previous century, many believed, too, that particular ethnicities were also naturally suited (or unsuited) to certain activities. Black men and women, for example, were supposed to be better at physical labour in hot conditions.[12] Paradoxically, since merit was supposed to ensure class was earned, class status – meaning the class into which one was born – also came with natural inclinations, though these differed from place to place.[13] In each case, merit's unequal distribution also seemed earned. This helps us see that class, race, and gender inequalities did not just 'intersect' as if they accidentally collided on their randomly different trajectories.[14] Rather, merit structured race and gender inequalities into early twentieth-century capitalism.

Boosters of merit like British economic historian and Christian socialist R. H. Tawney were conscious that merit harboured favourites, a problem they sought to overcome with universal secondary education. If only everyone could receive the same schooling, merit, they assumed – in deliberate opposition to eugenicist arguments then circulating – would be evenly distributed.[15] Education, however, did not stop at levelling the playing field (and it also failed to do that). With its grades and levels, education interacted with the system of professions to standardize

---

[11] John Tosh, *A Man's Place: Masculinity and the Middle-class Home in Victorian England* (New Haven: Yale University Press, 1999); Catherine Hall, 'Strains in the "Firm of Wife, Children and Friends"? Middle Class Women and Employment in Early Nineteenth-Century England', in Pat Hudson and William Lee (eds), *Women's Work and the Family Economy in Historical Perspective* (Manchester: Manchester University Press, 1990); Leonore Davidoff and Catherine Hall, *Family Fortunes: Men and Women of the English Middle Class, 1780–1850* (London: Routledge, 2002).

[12] Concomitantly, it was also 'widely believed that Europeans were unfit to labor in such harsh conditions'; this was also one of the ways that work aptitude was racially characterized. See Wolfe, 'Land, Labor and Difference', 870–871.

[13] In mid-twentieth-century Britain, for example, there was still a widely held belief that the middle class made better engineers than the aristocrats, who were naturally better at literature. Such a belief was impossible in the settler colonies which, by then at least, had no real aristocracy, but where other 'natural' characteristics were attributed along the lines of the class into which one was born; see Eric Ashby, *Technology and the Academics: An Essay on Universities and the Scientific Revolution* (London: Macmillan, 1958), 32.

[14] Anne Witz, *Professions and Patriarchy* (London: Routledge, 1992), 37–66. I am not suggesting that intersectionality theory does consider these to be random trajectories; rather, by situating these identities in the structure of merit, we can identify some of their systemic relationships; see Ange-Marie Hancock, *Intersectionality: An Intellectual History* (Oxford, Oxford University Press, 2016).

[15] See Jackson, *Equality and the British Left.*

measures of merit. Eventually, education fixed the weight of merit, just as metallic weights did for currencies, establishing a standard way to measure entry standards and facilitate progress along the professional ladder.[16] Merit emerged as a store of value in virtue capitalism at around the same time, worldwide. Historians, however, have tended to describe the emergence of merit as part of the social, economic, and educational histories of individual nations rather than as a phenomenon common to the world networked by global capitalism. For example, the history of merit in the United States was associated, according to Joseph Kett, with specifically American values that ensured monetary reward was structurally connected to personal productivity.[17] The American middle class conceived this as a contrast to the Old World, where reward was still based on birth and family connection.

In Canada, political and educational leaders were focused on a robust civil service that would be governed by merit, again in contrast to 'old-style patronage'.[18] The notorious corruption associated with one of confederated Canada's first governmental acts, the building of the Canadian Pacific Railway, was not permitted to become embedded in the nation's system of public administration. Designing and devising a system in 1918 that would ensure the independence of the administration of government responsibilities imagined merit as the foundation of modern government.[19] This extended to professional work so that 'professional' in nineteenth-century Canada soon supplanted 'gentlemen' as an ideal quality. Unlike being born a gentleman, this status was now earned by merit.[20]

Nineteenth-century Australian elites, like Canada's, also expected that merit would help them avoid some of the 'old corruption' that many attached to British aristocratic traditions. Emerging leaders in the Australian colonies similarly placed merit at the core of self-government and then nationhood.[21] This affected the composition of parliaments. At a time when only 7 per cent of the workforce were professional,

---

[16] Marx, *Capital*, 188–244.   [17] Kett, *Merit*, 250.

[18] Allison Prentice, *The School Promoters: Education and Social Class in Mid-Nineteenth Century Upper Canada* (Toronto: University of Toronto Press, 2004), 93–94.

[19] Luc Juillet, *Defending a Contested Ideal: Merit and the Public Service Commission, 1908–2008* (Ottawa: University of Ottawa Press, 2008), 48–73.

[20] R. D. Gidney and W. P. J. Millar, *Professional Gentlemen: The Professions in Nineteenth-Century Ontario* (Toronto: Toronto University Press, 1994).

[21] Terry Irving, 'The Idea of Responsible Government in New South Wales before 1856', *Historical Studies: Australia and New Zealand* 11.42 (1964), 192–205; Zoe Laidlaw, *Colonial Connections, 1815–1845: Patronage, the Information Revolution and Colonial Government* (Manchester, Manchester University Press, 2005).

36 per cent of Australia's first Federal House of Representatives in 1901 were professionals. These included fifteen lawyers, seven journalists, three surveyors, two members of the clergy, and a medical doctor. Such representation was largely confined to the non-labour parties: fifteen (of thirty-two) were protectionist, and ten (of twenty-four) were free traders. Only two of the nineteen labour representatives were professional.[22]

On the surface, Aotearoa/New Zealand went furthest of all. With an early reputation for social and political experimentation, including universal Pākehā and Māori women's suffrage, which became law in 1893, 'progressive policies were implemented for the western world to watch and emulate'.[23] Education – the structure most foundational to merit – was the cornerstone of Aotearoa/New Zealand egalitarian ideals. Universally available from 1877, free places were made available in secondary schools from 1903.[24]

While merit was foundational to settler-colonial states wishing to differentiate themselves from British class society, Harold Perkin showed merit also emerging in early twentieth-century England, arguably affecting the civil service first and then spreading across the economy.[25] The initial growth of professions in England, as we have seen, was primarily driven by finance, but it was merit more broadly that constituted Perkin's 'professional ideal'. Political characteristics within Britain at the height of class society, Perkin suggests, made it vulnerable to the kind of transformations in class relations that brought professionals to the fore.[26] This was initially achieved by excluding those deemed to be 'quacks'. In our present merit-soaked world, excluding quacks seems an obvious good. An 1889 article in the *St James Gazette* and republished across the Anglo world suggests this was more complicated than we might expect.

Merit, Class Status, and the Exclusion of 'Quacks'

The *St James's Gazette* was a London paper founded by the former governor of the Bank of England, Henry Hucks Gibbs. The story 'An Irregular Practitioner' playfully exposes connections among merit, professional advancement, and capitalism that are illuminating for the

---

[22] Compiled from documented membership of 1901 House of Representatives www.aph.gov.au/. Retrieved 23 February 2020.

[23] Melanie Nolan, 'The Reality and Myth of New Zealand Egalitarianism: Explaining the Pattern of a Labour Historiography at the Edge of Empires', *Labour History Review* 72.2 (2007), 113.

[24] Gregory Lee and Howard Lee, 'Comprehensive Post-primary Schooling in New Zealand 1935–75', *History of Education Review* 37.1 (2008), 56–76.

[25] Perkin, *Rise of Professional Society*, 90–91.   [26] Ibid., 116–170.

professions more broadly. The article opens by describing the narrator's friend from medical school, known as 'Sands'. Deploying a knowing, idiosyncratic language, the author says that Sands '"sapped" harder than any other six Triptolemus men put together'. Sands was not only 'a worker'; he 'had talent ... took all the hospital prizes [and] passed the "college" before he was one-and-twenty'.

The narrator, known as 'Jolly', contrasted Sands' authentic talent to 'Boffer', 'one of the senior surgeons now', who with the narrator passed their medical training with the assistance of 'Mugger, the grinder', a 'very artful fellow' whose 'boast was that he could get any man of ordinary intelligence through the college in three months for a £10-note'. If Boffer, who he knew intimately, was a man of even 'ordinary intelligence', the narrator says he 'never suspected it', though he's 'the great Boffer now'. Sands, by contrast to Boffer, had been unable to 'hang on' for the approximately five expected cash-strapped years establishing himself because 'the poor chap hadn't any coin'. Boffer, by contrast, was 'old Sir George's nephew' and subsequently 'married Slarker's second girl'. Family connections, not merit, were the foundation of professional success according to this story.[27] This is the opposite of what we would expect, for at this exact moment, the medical establishment, like other professions, was enthusiastically establishing its merit-based hierarchy.[28]

The reason for this article's divergence from standard opposition to quackery becomes clear in the next part of the story. Sands – due, we are given to suspect, to his lack of coin – had fallen out of the narrator's life and even the medical register by the events of the second half of the article, twenty years after their graduation. On a long train journey, the narrator encountered Sands again, now an obviously wealthy man:

> 'You seem to have got on Sands,' I said. 'You've made a good thing out of medicine, my boy,' I added.
> 'Yes,' he replied a little dryly, 'I have.'
> 'Lunacy, I suppose,' I said, and I dug him slyly in the ribs.
> 'Worse than that,' said Sands mournfully.
> 'Then you've married money,' I cried triumphantly.
> 'You'll never guess it,' said Sands in a piteous voice. 'I'm an irregular practitioner.'
> 'You're not a homeopath, Sands?' I cried in horror. 'I wouldn't ride in the same carriage as a homeopath!'[29]

27 'An Irregular Practitioner', St James's Gazette, 19 October 1889, 5; Reprinted in several, including Brisbane Courier, 19 December 1889, 7.
28 Evan Willis, Medical Dominance: The Division of Labour in Australian Health Care (Sydney: Allen & Unwin, 1983).
29 'An Irregular Practitioner'.

Here we need to pause to clarify these categories. 'Irregular practitioner' was the formal title, used in the census, for 'quacks'. They were not pariahs, though, and individuals and families often found that irregular practitioners provided exactly what was needed. Historian of medicine Paul Starr describes a protracted struggle between the 'regulars' and 'irregulars' in America. American doctors were part of a global profession, so it is unsurprising that the same struggle also took place in Britain, Aotearoa/New Zealand, Australia, and Canada. While the magical practice of 'cunning folk' continued despite the alleged disenchantment of modernity, homeopathy – treating like with like – made up the majority of the irregulars and was the philosophical opponent of what many medical historians have summarized as 'allopathic' medicine – combating the ailment with its opposite – which, by the late nineteenth century, was often known as 'regular' medicine.[30] At this point, the coexistence of homeopathic and allopathic medicine collapsed into an outright war, which the well-breeched 'regular' medical establishment was determined to win.[31]

The *St James's Gazette* story hints at this considerable effort that medical doctors took to push out 'irregulars'. Census figures would lead us to wonder why, however, for they operated in quite small numbers. In the New Zealand and Australian censuses for 1891, irregulars were just 12 and 13 per cent of medical practitioners, respectively. As we saw in Chapter 2, medicine was small too, compared to other professions, but still considerably larger than irregular medicine. While medical practitioners may have felt threatened by irregulars, they also needed 'quacks' for other reasons.[32] Sands and Jolly's story explained:

'Don't trample on a fallen man, hear what I've got to say … Don't judge me too harshly' … [said Sands].

There were tears in his voice as he said the words, and I hadn't the heart to refuse him. 'A quack!' I thought, 'and the enemy of mankind in general'; and

---

[30] Starr, *Social Transformation of American Medicine*; see Owen Davies, 'Cunning-Folk in the Medical Market-Place during the Nineteenth Century', *Medical History* 43 (1999), 55–73. On disenchantment, see Jason Ānanda Josephson Storm, *The Myth of Disenchantment: Magic, Modernity, and the Birth of the Human Sciences* (Chicago: University of Chicago Press, 2017).

[31] Friedson, *Professional Dominance*; Philippa Martyr, 'No Paradise for Quacks? Nineteenth Century Health Care in Tasmania', *Tasmanian Historical Studies* 5.2 (1997), 141–152; Roy Porter, *Quacks: Fakers & Charlatans in Medicine* (Charleston: Tempus, 2000).

[32] Note that these are census figures: the medical registers at this point vastly inflate the number of practitioners actually practising medicine in the colonies, for many were registered but actually lived in England or other British colonies. This gave them the right to practice in the colony if they were there, but the census figures offer a more realistic picture of the numbers actually offering medical services.

I looked at his great diamond ring and his huge watch chain, and I loathed, while I pitied my unfortunate friend.[33]

Middle-class attitudes towards money and merit were evidently complex, even sometimes contradictory. Jolly coveted Sands' wealth, but it was important that this wealth be a result of faithful work along the prescribed professional trajectory. Professional wrongdoing (like merit) came in grades. Specializing in 'lunacy' showed less moral character than more respectable medical specialties.[34] Descending into quackery, however, meant Sands had discarded professional respectability altogether. Jolly's pity for his friend made sense, since Sands' behaviour pushed him out of the professional class; but his loathing made sense too, for Sands was thus *unjustly* rewarded, making his conspicuous wealth particularly jarring.

Sands described how it came about:

'Jolly,' cried Sands, 'the profession very nearly killed me; I very nearly died of hard work and disappointment. My health was gone and my money: I was made a bankrupt, sir, and my butcher wanted to put me into prison.'[35]

From this we can see that the purpose of the article, was not, in fact, to undermine the infant system of merit in England with confessions of family connection and demagoguery, but rather to argue for the importance of a truly meritorious system. If Sands, with all his talent and hard work, could not make an adequate living from practising medicine, what were the consequences for the profession? The story went on to demonstrate the moral. Upon bankruptcy, Sands took a job as a dispensing assistant to a small chemist in London:

'My employer didn't live at the shop: he was a rich man, for even then the Methuselah Mixture was a property. I used to make the mixture and compose the testimonials. Like the industrious apprentice, Jolly, I married my master's daughter. I advertised, sir.'[36]

Advertising pushed Sands beyond the pale. A ban on advertising was forcefully policed by professional associations in medicine, law, and by some accountancy associations. It was not lifted, in some groups, until the 1980s. Banning advertising ensured that professionals working as sole traders did not compete commercially with one another. It was a gentlemanly agreement which, when broken, raised suspicions that one was not, after all, a gentleman. For professional gentlemen, profit needed

---

[33] 'An Irregular Practitioner'.   [34] Gillespie, *Price of Health*.
[35] 'An Irregular Practitioner'.   [36] Ibid.

the moral foundation that merit offered. Advertising endangered this moral superiority.[37] Sands confessed to Jolly that 'there's nothing but rhubarb and magnesia in Methuselah Mixture'. Sales of this innocuous medicine nevertheless made Sands 'rich beyond the dreams of avarice'. Historians of quackery have shown that many 'patent' medicines, as they came to be known, were innocuous or even, like eucalyptus oil, efficacious under the right circumstances.[38] But sometimes patent medicines were sold for conditions that only surgery could fix, causing extraordinary harm and even death.[39] Excluding quacks was an act of power, but it also protected people.[40] However, the *St James's Gazette* article was not about this. Instead, it showed that merit could only be guaranteed if professionals earned a good living. If merit really worked as the basis for a good income, Sands could have earned his living based on medical skill rather than by deceit. It would have made his profit moral.

Medicine invested considerable resources in anti-quack propaganda in the late nineteenth and early twentieth centuries. This was not merely about manipulating the social environment to unfairly extract income, or what economists call 'rent-seeking'.[41] Rather, it was a key structure of the professional moral economy. The professions could not afford to require birth and wealth, which underpinned Boffer's success in the *St James's Gazette* story, to be seen to govern professional advancement (though they often still did, in fact). If ungentlemanly, unethical, and even dangerous commercial behaviour could out-compete merit, this undermined professional virtue.

In some ways it sounds like the benefits of excluding quackery outweighed the risks, and maybe they did. It also functioned, though, as an instrument of racial exclusion. In Australasia and North America, the medical establishment regularly appropriated knowledge they derived from Indigenous medicine, but publicly denigrated native medical practice nevertheless as 'magic' and 'superstition'.[42] Chinese medical

---

[37] For example, in 1910, three members of the Australian Corporation of Public Accountants were excluded from association because they advertised Editorial, *The Public Accountant*, 25 June 1910, 82–83.

[38] Philippa Martyr, *Paradise of Quacks: An Alternative History of Medicine in Australia* (Paddington: Macleay Press, 2002).

[39] Starr, *Social Transformation American Medicine*, 127–140.

[40] See Frank Parkin, *Marxism and Class Theory* (London: Tavistock, 1979).

[41] Simon Kuznets and Milton Friedman, *Incomes from Independent Professional Practice* (New York: National Bureau of Economic Research, 1945), 72–73. For discussion, see Law and Kim, 'Specialization and Regulation'.

[42] Martyr, *Paradise of Quacks*, 21–22; Kristin Burnett, 'The Healing Work of Aboriginal Women in Indigenous and Newcomer Communities', in Jayne Elliot, Meryn Stuart, and

practitioners too were eventually excluded. The fact that Chinese medicine was relatively well accepted until the late nineteenth-century anti-quackery movements helps show the ways that the system of merit structured forms of inequality into the changing economy.

The mass migration from China to Australasia and North America in the nineteenth century included Chinese medical practitioners. For much of the nineteenth century, the practice of Chinese medicine was unrestricted. Chinese doctors, moreover, were often well respected, serving frontier populations throughout the American west and into Canada and in Melbourne and Sydney.[43] News of their work was reported across the Anglo world. In 1890, in Otago, on Aotearoa/New Zealand's south island, the local paper advertised that a Chinese doctor in San Francisco could earn £1,200 a month.[44] Chinese practitioners were regularly subjected to racism, but their services were sought frequently nevertheless.

Consumers of Chinese medicine were conscious that practitioners often had a similar amount of training as British doctors – whose training was still in the process of being regulated in the settler colonies. Many were impressed at the elite status they held in Chinese society.[45] In 1887, the *Victoria Daily Times* in Alberta, Canada, published an edited version of an interview with Dr Kwong Shang, which was originally printed in the *St Louis Globe-Democrat*. The Alberta paper removed the segments denigrating '8,000 years of ignorance' and focused on a positive section describing medical training in China:

He said that there were many government and private colleges in China in which pupils were instructed; that a course in surgery occupied about four years, and in medicine six years. Before entering a medical college there the pupil had to be well versed in the Chinese classics, and be well educated in all things pertaining to religion, as well as history, manners and customs. Only the most learned men are allowed to instruct in medicine.[46]

They did not publish the Orientalized line drawing of Dr Shang holding an opium pipe, included in the *Globe-Democrat* version.

In 1892, despite having practiced for some decades in several colonies and even on London's Harley Street, Dr George On Lee was fined £10 (and £5 5s in costs) for using the title 'doctor' in contravention of new

Cynthia Toman (eds), *Place and Practice in Canadian Nursing History* (Vancouver: UBC Press, 2008), 40–52.
[43] Peter Phillips, *Kill or Cure? Lotions, Potions, Characters and Quacks of Early Australia* (Richmond: Greenhouse Publications, 1984), 19.
[44] Advertisement, *Bruce Herald* 21 (2138), 7 February 1890, 1.
[45] Martyr, *Paradise of Quacks*, 73–75.
[46] 'The Chinese Doctor', *The Victoria Daily Times*, 20 May 1887, 3.

laws, lobbied for by the profession, reserving the term for members of British medical professional associations.[47] On Lee was exceptionally well known in Sydney as a businessman, as well as a practitioner of Chinese medicine who was called upon for medical services by members of Sydney's white, as well as Chinese, community. His practice was not always welcomed by the medical establishment, but it was not until the 1890s that it was legally impeded: he was probably previously protected before because he was an elite man married to an Englishwoman who socialized in exclusive circles. Emphasizing his class status in the 1892 case, On Lee faced his challengers in court wearing the spectacular purple, gold, and red robes of his Mandarin Fourth Rank – equivalent to a foreign diplomat – his hat adorned with the official blue button that was a privilege of his rank.[48] We know from other newspaper reports that Sydney society was impressed not only by On Lee's Mandarin status but also by his robes.[49] While, throughout his earlier career, On Lee's class status alone was adequate for entry to professional ranks, by 1892 this no longer sufficed. Formal qualifications increasingly mattered and, since professional bodies set the credentials, these were British in style and content.[50] The process of professionalization not only restricted Chinese people from practising medicine in the Anglo world but also established professional merit as distinctly Anglo.

The British medical establishment performed the class-based work of identifying forms of medicine that were to be excluded from the profession. Settler colonies like America, Canada, Aotearoa/New Zealand, and Australia, however, had more heterogenous healthcare fields than Europe. The settler colonies had some elite doctors, to be sure, but they also harboured many more medical practitioners whose class status was less secure.[51] As Paul Starr showed in the United States, the process of excluding quacks in those systems reinforced the shakier class status of medical practitioners, who were on uncertain ground, in terms of their respectability, in the settler colonies than they were in Britain. By the

[47] *The Age*, 25 November 1892, 6; Willis, *Medical Dominance*.

[48] Michelle Bootcov, 'Dr George On Lee (葉七秀): Not Just a Medical Practitioner in Colonial Australia', *Chinese Southern Diaspora Studies* 南方華裔研究雜誌, 第八卷 8 (2019), 82–101. Many thanks to Michelle Bootcov for pointing me to Dr On Lee's case.

[49] 'A Distinguished Chinese Doctor', *Portland Guardian*, 17 February 1893, 2; 'The Imperial Chinese Commissioners', *Sydney Morning Herald*, 9 May 1887, 8.

[50] Milton Lewis and Roy Macleod, 'Medical Politics and the Professionalization of Medicine in New South Wales, 1850–1901', *Journal of Australian Studies* 12.22 (1988), 69–82.

[51] Tony Pensabene, *The Rise of the Medical Practitioner in Victoria* (Canberra: ANU Press, 1980); Friedson, *Professional Dominance*; Willis, *Medical Dominance*.

1890s, 'regular' medical practitioners in the settler colonies were a more homogenous group in terms of their philosophy, educational background, and manners than they had been in earlier decades. For those seeking healthcare, this bolstering of medical status increased the distance between patient and doctor, a process by which medicine also increased its social power.[52]

The history of quackery exposes the complex task of class-making that the middle class encountered as their status began to turn on the professionalization of the economy. The moral claims that the professional class sought to make hinged on their claims to merit. As the professional class grew, they tried to make it clear that legitimate professionals had merit, while quacks did not. This either-or structure worked well for medicine and some of the other professions. It was complicated, though, by beliefs about other characteristics, like gender and race, that were seen to be a product not of achievement, but of nature.

Merit as 'Natural' but Also 'Achieved': Intersections with Gender, Class, and Race

The term 'quack' was associated with medicine, but most professions had equivalents. Nursing across the British Empire named their 'quack' after a character in the Charles Dickens novel *Martin Chuzzlewit*. Sarah Gamp – pronounced, in the accent Dickens sought to convey as 'Sairey' – was a working-class woman who took individual clients needing home-based care while they were sick or collected a fee to 'lay out' a person who had died, before burial. By the early twentieth century, it was common for older nurses and medical practitioners to recollect the Sairey Gamp–types that they encountered in the profession in decades past.[53] Dr Francis Shepherd, dean of McGill's Medical Faculty, described the old Sairey Gamp nurses as 'old, fat, red in the face' with '"langwidge" that was frequent and painful and free'. By contrast, the middle-class surgeon's wife who stepped in at Montreal General, he said, was still untrained but 'stately, with a notable resemblance to Queen Victoria' while 'her name stood for dignity, duty and discipline'.[54]

In a similar vein, Dr Robert Scot Skirving remembered:

Lots of you, whose memories go back as far as mine, know that Sairey Gamp was not wholly extinct as recently as thirty years ago … I remember one kindly

---

[52] Starr, *Transformation of American Medicine*, 79–144.
[53] Kathryn McPherson, *Bedside Matters: The Transformation of Canadian Nursing, 1900–1990* (Toronto: University of Toronto Press, 2012), 27–29.
[54] 'How They Were', *The Gazette*, 20 February 1988, 18.

incompetent old fool – ample-bosomed, whose quivering adiposity clung about her, even as a garment, with a kind of ponderous comeliness. She had a husband, a weakling, almost hairless, whom she always spoke of as 'my poor fool'. She dearly loved a dirty sponge and a nip of something hoy, but she had no use for the thermometer and 'she didn't 'old with epidermic medicines' ... But I liked this woman, and she could make tea or toddy to perfection.[55]

A nurse's class behaviour was inextricable from their competence. Medical denigration of the Sairey Gamps of the early days of the nursing profession seems indeed to focus on mocking 'comeliness' and accent.[56] As nursing established educational standards, the profession connected professional tasks like bedside care, medical procedures, and invalid cookery to respectable, white, middle-class manners. '"Nurses" did I say? Could you only see them, I should have to apologize to the nice-looking girls I see round me,' recalled Mrs Murray, inaugural matron at the Prince Alfred Hospital in Sydney. 'At first, many a time I sat up all night with an operation case or a bad typhoid, feeling uncertain whom to trust, and of course having to do all my day work as well.'[57] Eventually, so many girls from 'respectable' families sought to enter nursing that the hospital could have its pick. In the process, the profession not only excluded Sairey Gamp–types, but, like the anti-quack movement in medicine, also excluded people of colour – though in America, by the 1920s, black nurses provided vital labour for 'black hospitals'.[58]

The division of professional women from working-class women was no accident.[59] Selection into training schemes was a key method of exclusion.[60] Entrance examinations tested the class status of nurses, alongside their adherence to gender norms. Each year, the Australasian Trained Nurses' Association (ATNA) published their examinations. In 1910 the examination asked prospective nurses, usually around seventeen years old, to '[w]rite out sentences in which the following words shall be correctly employed: Luxuriantly, Respectively, Reparation, Prudence, Foresight, Tact' and to write an essay either on 'Duty' or 'Women's Work'. The following year, girls were asked to write essays on 'A stitch in time saves nine' or 'Charity' and to write 'a short account of any pleasure excursion you have just made, *or* a short description of any piece of

---

[55] Robert Scot Skirving, 'The Development of Modern Nursing', *Australasian Nurses' Journal*, 15 August 1923, 372–384.
[56] Skirving, 'The Development of Modern Nursing'.
[57] Mrs Murray, 'Notes of My Acquaintance with Prince Alfred Hospital', *Australasian Nurses Journal*, 15 May 1906, 154–159.
[58] Hine, *Black Women in White*.
[59] Joan Brumberg and Nancy Tomes argue that this 'hastened the demise of female culture', Brumberg and Tomes, 'Professional Women', 286.
[60] McPherson, *Bedside Matters*, 29.

scenery which pleased you'.[61] These essays did little to indicate young women's potential in any of the areas of work they would perform as a nurse. The questions also did more than test basic literacy, instead examining their class-based outlook on pleasure, responsibility, and femininity, evaluating each young woman's understanding of key middle-class values. Duty, charity, and prudence, for example, were part of the constellation of moral order outlined in Chapter 2, which were also deeply gendered.

These moral values were not just rhetorical. Early twentieth-century nurses worked long hours, and probationers usually lived in supervised accommodation according to disciplinary regimes deemed appropriate to their age and gender. Later feminists often described these aspects of the nursing profession through the lens of gender oppression.[62] Primary sources, however, suggest that middle-class women engaged eagerly in the task of professionalizing Victorian gender norms, as they built expressions of courage, cleanliness, discipline, and duty into the practice of modern nursing. As nurses transferred women's authority over the domestic sphere into the modern hospital, they also capitalized Victorian femininity: they turned white middle-class womanhood into an economic asset.[63] For many professional women, and nurses in particular, middle-class femininity itself became a form of merit, which was the foundation of moral and economic gain.

Take Muriel Knox Doherty, who was the daughter of a clerk. She was schooled by a governess at home and later, like many middle-class Australian girls in the period, attended a small private school.[64] Knox Doherty began her formal nursing training at the Prince Alfred Hospital in Sydney in 1921 at the age of 25, having volunteered during the Great War. Her account of her training described a camaraderie that included practical jokes or playfulness; a deep, passionate interest in learning; and a culture of gentle gossip about the personalities of senior nurses and doctors.

---

[61] 'Preliminary Educational Examination A.T.N.A.', *The Australian Nurses' Journal*, 13 October 1910, 345–346; 'Preliminary Examination', *The Australian Nurses' Journal*, 15 September 1911, 306.
[62] Lynette Russell, *From Nightingale to Now: Nurse Education in Australia*, (Sydney, Harcourt Brace Jovanovich, 1990); see also Correspondence, Education Task Force, Canberra, Noel Butlin Archive Centre, NBAC/RANF/AZ486.
[63] The professionalization of Victorian women's authority over the domestic sphere is from Mary Poovey, *Uneven Developments*; see also Harris, 'Whiteness as Property'.
[64] Lynette Russell, 'Doherty, Muriel Knox (1896–1988)', *Australian Dictionary of Biography, Volume 17* (Melbourne: Melbourne University Press, 2007); Marjorie Theobald, *Knowing Women: Origins of Women's Education in Nineteenth-Century Australia* (Cambridge, Cambridge University Press, 1996).

'If we did come off duty footsore and weary', Knox Doherty remembered of their three hours a day of leisure, 'we were compensated with unlimited hot baths, comfortable beds in single rooms and as much good food as we wanted'.[65] She recalled sitting on 'the step' – the one warmed by the hot water pipe beneath it – overlooking the quadrangle of the nurse's home, which was accommodation reserved for nurse trainees. This step was the 'focal point for female gossip and "*shop*" where experiences were exchanged ... and speculation as to whom would fall the coveted honour of "*being asked back*" after graduation'. Knox Doherty's autobiography described a world where young women were absorbed in their work:

There is no doubt that hard work brings the greatest happiness and fortunately I was endowed with boundless energy. Our life was full and satisfying in that hospital world of pain and suffering, patience and fortitude, where selfless service so often tipped the scales. Our greatest thrill was to see a patient rescued ... our saddest when we lost the fight and a life ebbed away.[66]

While their lives were subject to strict hours and disciplined work habits, the nurses' home also hosted dances, where the warm step was the site of 'many a romance'.

Their sexual and romantic lives were gently subject to the discipline of single women. After hours, Knox Doherty said 'the usual mode of dress was the Kimono', but as 1920s 'fashions changed, so the *dishabille* of some became less circumspect until one day a reprimand notice appeared over the Home Sister's signature concluding with – "*Nurses, is this fair to George?*"'.[67] There is no evidence from Muriel Knox Doherty's story that this discipline was resented. It became part of the hard work and femininity that nurses offered in the production of their own human capital and the investment of morality into society. Their work was gendered to be sure, and in ways that later feminists found problematic, but through that work they developed professional practices and institutions which, as historian Nancy Cott has shown, provided an institutional and even ideological scaffold for modern feminism.[68] Women professionals took that which was deemed natural – gender – and capitalized it to become the moral-economic value that was merit.

This is important because the ways that professional women used merit to valorize gender, converting it into human capital, not only helps

---

[65] Muriel Doherty, *Off the Record: The Life and Times of Muriel Knox Doherty 1896–1988: An Autobiography* (Sydney: New South Wales College of Nursing, 1996), 9.
[66] Doherty, *Off the Record*, 9.   [67] Ibid.
[68] Nancy Cott, *The Grounding of Modern Feminism* (New Haven: Yale University Press, 1987), 215–239.

to see the economic role of merit but also shows the reasons that merit never really delivered on its promise in promoting social and economic equality. The problem with merit was not confined to women professionals of course, but they help to illustrate it. Moreover, in the early decades of the twentieth century, professional women – nurses, teachers, dentists, accountants, lawyers, social workers, and medical practitioners – were more important than historians have traditionally acknowledged. When in 1918 Adamson advocated for equal pay in accountancy, he described the entry of women into the professional world, arguing that 'she is proving her ability to fill almost every conceivable position hitherto occupied exclusively by men' and in fact 'woman has established the right to enter into any sphere of business-life or profession'.[69] When we consider the proportions of professional women in the workforce, it appears Adamson was justified in his observations.

As the global economy professionalized, professional women were a much higher percentage of the female labour force than professional men. In the United States, women professionals were between 8 and 14 per cent of women's labour between 1890 and 1930, compared to a very stable 3 to 5 per cent of men who were professionals (see Figure 3.1). Even fewer Canadian men were professional, between 2 and 4 per cent as the economy began to professionalize, while professional women were between 10 and 19 per cent of the female workforce (see Figure 3.2). In the Australian census, professional women (as aggregated by the government statistician) increased from 5 per cent of the female labour force in 1881 to 25 per cent in 1933 (see Figure 3.3). Male professionals grew from 2 to 10 per cent of the male labour force in the same period. In Aotearoa/New Zealand, women professionals were already 13 per cent of the female labour force in 1891, compared to the 3 per cent that professional men made of the male labour force. Male professionals increased to 5 per cent of the male labour force by 1901, and female professionals increased to 14 per cent of the female labour force (see Figure 3.4).

The growth of the professions as a percentage of the workforce was slower in Britain in the first part of the twentieth century, but there too the role of women was marked (see Figure 3.5). Although total percentages of British professionals did not really increase significantly until after the Second World War, professional women were between 6.7 and 7.25 per cent of the female workforce, while professional men were around 3 to 3.5 per cent of male labour until the 1951 census. These

---

[69] Adamson, 'Women and Wages', 29–30.

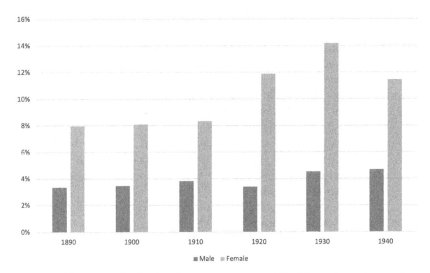

Figure 3.1 Professionals as a percentage of the labour force, by gender, the United States 1890–1940. *Data source*: US Census

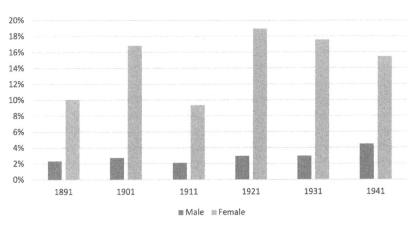

Figure 3.2 Professionals as a percentage of the labour force, by gender, Canada 1891–1941. *Data source*: Canadian Census

figures do not reflect the absolute numbers: there were in total more male professionals than female professionals, though in the United States this was only by a very slight margin and it was a diminishing margin in Australia and Canada. In Aotearoa/New Zealand, in 1891, 45 per cent of professionals were women. This proportion decreased to 40 per cent

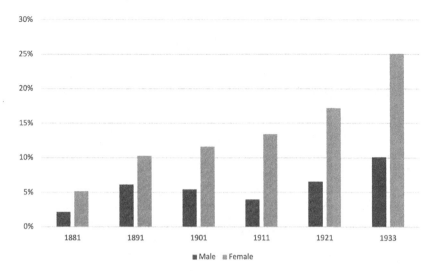

Figure 3.3 Professionals as a percentage of the labour force, by gender, Australia 1881–1933. Data sources: Australian Colonial Censuses 1881–1901 Australian Data Archive; Australian Census 1911–1933 Australian Bureau of Statistics

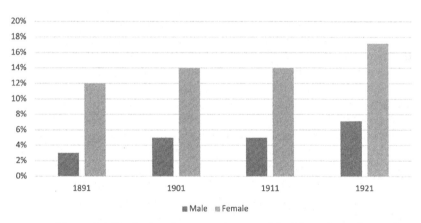

Figure 3.4 Professionals as a percentage of the labour force, by gender, New Zealand 1891–1921. *Data source*: New Zealand Census

when escalating numbers of male engineers entered the New Zealand workforce early in the twentieth century. In Great Britain, between 1911 and 1931, there was hardly any difference between the number of professional men and professional women. The numbers of professional

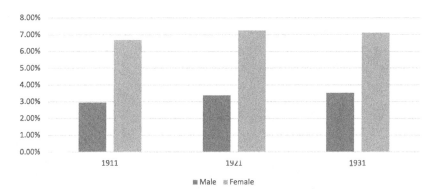

Figure 3.5 Professionals as a percentage of the labour force, by gender, Great Britain 1911–1931. *Data source*: A. H. Halsey (ed.), *British Social Trends since 1900* (Macmillan, 1988)

men increased, widening the gap over professional women, only from 1951 onwards.[70] This seems counterintuitive. The traditional account of women professionals describes their initial exclusion, followed by a 'charge of the parasols' as women fought for a place in professional work that was really only achieved late in the twentieth century (and still has a way to go in some fields, like engineering).[71] These figures require us to reconsider that narrative. They tell us that as the professions established their place in the global economy, it was in fact women who, in their daily work, drove much of the process. In considering the ways that merit was gendered, it is important to keep in mind that this gendering was not only about exclusion – or at least, it was not only about the exclusion of white middle-class women. Middle-class women leveraged their class, race, and gender norms in ways that help us see that merit, as the store of value by which class status was increasingly earned, was not about skills and talents that were evenly distributed throughout society. Rather, merit was defined by characteristics that the Anglo middle class often already held.[72]

This gendering of professional merit also underpinned the massive growth of women professionals as teachers. Teaching was by far the most

---

[70] Albert Halsey, *British Social Trends since 1900* (London: Macmillan, 1988).
[71] Catriona Blake, *The Charge of the Parasols: Women's Entry to the Medical Profession* (London: The Women's Press, 1990).
[72] Witz, *Professions and Patriarchy*.

populous profession in Australia and the United States, where we have good figures for the whole period. In Australia, women teachers increased from 58 per cent of teachers in 1871 to 69 per cent in 1921. The tightening of the marriage bar during the Great Depression contributed to a slight drop in women's share of teaching labour, declining from 63 per cent to 57 per cent between 1933 and 1961.[73] Women were an even higher percentage of teachers in the United States, where they constituted 69 per cent of teachers in 1870, increasing to 84 per cent in 1920 and 81 per cent in 1930.[74] Teaching, along with nursing, was work that women traditionally performed in an older household economy. Middle-class women professionalized this work to good effect, taking it out of the domestic world and into the professional sphere.[75]

While teaching, like nursing, allowed women to perform work that capitalized on both gender norms and traditional women's roles in household economies, middle-class women also considered their femininity to be merit in professions that were dominated by men. American sources are important here, where professional women's associations in medicine and law formed earlier (1893 and 1899 respectively) than elsewhere. These institutions focused on professional activity informed by womanhood, and which would benefit women in the profession and beyond. Medical women, for example, advocated for equal pay, for the promotion of women into senior medical positions and for women doctors who would provide medical services that women particularly needed, such as maternity care. They supported the establishment of women's hospitals where medical issues affecting women could be confronted by women professionals, a pattern women doctors replicated in Australasia.[76] 'We realize, as practical women,' argued Kate B. Karpeles in 1936, 'that there still exist a great many problems that are particularly the concern of medical women.'[77] Women medical practitioners were therefore particularly valuable in 'general family practice, as specialists in the fields of maternity and care of women and children,

---

[73] Helen Proctor and Ashleigh Driscoll, 'Bureaucratic Governance, Family Economies and the 1930s NSW Teachers' Marriage Bar, Australia', *Journal of Educational Administration and History* 49.2 (2017), 157–170; Marjorie Theobald and Donna Dwyer, 'An Episode in Feminist Politics: The Married Women (Lecturers and Teachers) Act, 1932–1947', *Labour History* 76, 1999, 59–77; Jennifer Redmond and Judith Harford, 'One Man One Job', *Paedagogica Historica* 46.5 (2010), 639–654.
[74] US Census Data. www.census.gov/prod/www/decennial.html. Retrieved 3 April 2020.
[75] Hannah Forsyth, 'Reconsidering Women's Role in the Professionalization of the Economy'.
[76] Leo Butler, *100 Years of Nurse Training at the Royal Women's Hospital* (Melbourne: Royal Women's Hospital, 1963).
[77] Kate Karpeles, 'The First Big Goal', *Women in Medicine*, April 1936, 11.

in laboratory teaching and research, in public health and institutional positions'.[78] In a keynote address to the Association, Dr Emily Dunning Barringer argued, 'There are many subjects which have only been studied from a masculine point of view', requiring women physicians to intervene. Like nurses, though, women medical practitioners were asked to retain gendered forms of comportment as well as develop skills that focused on the specific needs of women: 'Be temperate in your habits,' Barringer warned, which included alcohol, nicotine, and narcotics. She also suggested regular sports, being unafraid of hard work but finding rest, and to 'keep a good sense of humor'.[79]

Leaders of the National Association of Women Lawyers were even more determined to use their professional standing to advocate for legal reforms on grounds that were specifically feminine. These included issues that were of particular interest to women, like equal rights, uniform marriage and divorce law, and an investigation into potentially harmful ingredients in cosmetics, as well as some broader moral concerns. There were, for example, moves in the 1930s to crack down on the 'moving picture industry', with its depictions of excessive drinking, gambling, and organized crime.[80]

Women professionals were conscious that their merit was in part grounded in being a woman, a characteristic they perceived as a 'natural', not earned, advantage. They sought to use this for society's well-being as well as their own: this was the moral-economic pairing we saw in Chapter 2. Professional women, however, as Nancy Cott demonstrated, also sought equality with middle-class men on the basis of their achievement – merit as an 'earned' substance, in this case. Such equality was not as easy to come by as the concept seemed to promise. While women dominated teaching numerically, for example, as feminist educational historians have long shown, female teachers in industrialized schooling systems typically had less power, diminished working conditions and lower salaries than their male counterparts.[81] How did the system of merit, that dominant ideology of the professional class, permit such discrimination? In order to understand this, we need to recall that the professional class considered people by race and gender to be naturally better at certain tasks.

---

[78] Emily Barringer, 'Address Delivered at the Eighty-Seventh Opening of the W.M.C. of P.A.', *Women in Medicine*, January 1937, 15–17.

[79] Barringer, 'Address'.

[80] National Association of Women Lawyers, Records of Annual Meetings c.1935–1949. Cambridge, MA: Schlesinger Library SL/MC740/I/1.

[81] Marjorie Theobald, 'Imagining the Woman Teacher: An International Perspective', *Australian Educational Researcher* 22.3(1995), 87–111.

Dr Robert Scot Skirving, for example, betrayed his view about women's natural affinity for nursing care by discussing male nurses:

I do not propose to discuss the merits of training of male nurse. They are often admirable ... and for certain classes of cases they are most necessary. But for nursing generally, in private or on a vast scale, in hospitals and campaigns, of course women are far more suitable. I cannot conceive of a male matron being efficient! I have seen lots of male nurses who could do certain things as well as any woman, but for general fitness for tending the sick, a woman, in my judgment, is first every time.[82]

When Adamson, the accountant with whom this chapter opened, sought 'merit' applied equally to women as to men, this was because he believed that based on merit, men would win, but not if women had the 'unfair' advantage of being cheaper. Adamson's insistence on merit betrayed the mythic way that merit's level playing field made achievement seem fair, while establishing systems that privileged those around whom merit was designed. Equal pay, for Adamson, was not about fairness for women. Instead, merit would ensure preferential treatment for men according to the hierarchy in accountancy, which privileged masculine qualities. Adamson thus reassured readers of the *Australasian Accountant and Secretary*:

Men will undoubtedly have first preference in most instances, and thereby the male sex will be protected from the unfair competition of women who need to work only for pin money, and the cupidity of managers who have an eye only on the curtailment of expenses.[83]

Such characterizations went beyond gendered forms of closure, where men and women sought to protect their respective professions from the other.[84] Rather, while gender was 'natural' but achievement 'earned', merit consisted of both. This did not mean women had no chance in the accountancy profession; it was just that they would always be granted fewer opportunities than men. Others faced the same kind of barriers based on the 'natural' components of merit, including race, gender, or class.

The effect of merit's discrimination became obvious with the enclosure of professional fields. Professional closure was the process whereby professional groups claimed jurisdiction over certain areas of work and,

[82] Skirving, 'The Development of Modern Nursing'.
[83] Adamson, 'Women and Wages'.
[84] See Witz, *Professions and Patriarchy*, 10–66 (note that this is *professional*, not class-based closure; c.f. Jack Barbalet, 'Social Closure in Class Analysis: A Critique of Parkin', *Sociology* 16.4 (1982), 484–497).

through regulation or legislation succeeded in keeping people out, often by imposing new credentials as the basis of entry.[85] Enclosure thus helped to boost the 'market' value of merit and encouraged people to invest, ever-increasingly, in their education and other markers of their own human capital. In the process, education increasingly standardized merit, in the same way as metallic measures standardized currencies. This standardization made it easier for professional associations and employers to appraise individual professionals' relative value for entry to each profession and as the steps they took to progress up the career ladder.

These effects are evident in the statistics in the early period of the professionalization of the economy (i.e. before the Second World War) and had a disproportionate impact on women and people of colour. The professionalization of dentistry for example, meant that women dentists in Australia declined by 90 per cent between 1921 and 1933. By the 1947 census, only 77 women were described as dentists, down from 1,403 in 1921. Even prior to that peak, in 1911, 668 women were categorized as dentists in the census – and more than 100 as early as 1901.[86] In the same period, between the 1921 and 1933 Australian censuses, the number of women pharmacists more than halved, for the same reason. Accountancy in Australia enclosed twice: women declined from 17 per cent of accountants in the 1921 census to just 4 per cent in 1933; then women declined from 27 per cent of accountants in 1947 to just 3 per cent in 1961. They began to grow again in the 1980s so that by 2006, women constituted 46 per cent of Australian accountants.[87]

Enclosure sometimes 'grandfathered' in existing members of a profession, since they were already doing the work.[88] Most professions, however, took the opportunity that enclosure presented to increase the value of membership by excluding those who seemed to debase it. The exclusion of women dentists and pharmacists was not merely a result of increasing standards that educational norms meant women were unlikely to reach, but because excluding women practitioners enhanced the status

---

[85] Abbott, *The System of Professions*.

[86] Australian Census 1911, 1921, 1933, 1947; see also Tamson Pietsch, 'Universities, War and the Professionalization of Dentistry', *History of Education Review* 45.2 (2016), 168–182.

[87] Australian Census. www.abs.gov.au. Retrieved 6 December 2017; Colonial Census; US Census. Accountancy in the US Census was not recorded as a consistent category through the twentieth century, so while 2000 and 1920 figures are comparable, accurate long-run figures cannot be provided for the duration.

[88] The legal profession in Victoria did this, for example. Applications to Practice under the 1912 Act, Law Institute of Victoria, Melbourne University Archives, MUA/ LIV1968.0008.

of the profession. This is a recognizable process. Just as pushing out
Sairey Gamp–types enhanced the status of nursing and excluding
'quacks' helped elevate medicine, narrowing accountancy and dentistry
to men may have been intended to lift the status of those professions.
A long-standing debate in social work made the strategy explicit. Social
work, like nursing, was a women's profession. It was formed by women,
mostly, out of the nineteenth-century charity work that was largely the
responsibility of middle-class women. Women dominated the profession
throughout its history.[89] This, some members believed, pushed the
entire profession down an imagined hierarchy that not only governed
the internal structure of each profession but also structured their status
relative to one another.[90]

When social workers developed 'scientific' approaches and increasingly rigid educational standards, they also sought to elevate the status of
their profession. Many members believed that they would achieve
increased status if there were more men. Since the profession required
qualities that some women considered to be especially theirs, this was
controversial. This debate, which commenced in the early twentieth
century, continued into the 1960s. It was based on arguments about
skill, suggesting that men offered skills and insights that women did not
possess.[91] As a strategy, even a half-hearted one, recruiting more males
to social work was wholly unsuccessful. In fact, the reverse occurred.
While women constituted around 60 per cent of social workers in
Australia in 1891, they were almost 83 per cent of the profession in
2006; in the United States the percentage of women social workers
increased less dramatically but did so nevertheless, growing from
75 per cent of the profession in 1900 to 79 per cent in 2000.[92]

The high proportions of women responsible for the professionalization
of the global economy in the late nineteenth and early twentieth centuries
requires us to reconsider their role in the growth of the professions.[93] It
also offers an opportunity to observe the ways that attributes which
people considered to be natural, especially gender and race, became in

[89] Sutherland, *In Search of the New Woman*, 41–57.
[90] Sue Brown, 'A Woman's Profession', in Helen Marchant and Betsy Wearing (eds),
Gender Reclaimed: Women in Social Work (Sydney: Hale & Iremonger, 1986), 223–233.
[91] Davida Ivey, 'Becoming a Social Worker: A History of Women Social Workers in
Australia 1929–1965', unpublished Honours Thesis, Australian Catholic University
(2020), 32–34.
[92] Australian Census; United States Census.
[93] Joan Brumberg and Nancy Tomes, 'Women in the Professions: A Research Agenda for
American Historians', *Reviews in American History* 10.2 (1982), 275–296; Forsyth,
'Reconsidering Women's Role in the Professionalization of the Economy'.

themselves a kind of merit. This was the *coup* of the old middle class as economies professionalized: they took the traits they already possessed and converted them into a store of value. Such natural traits were not enough, however, to fulfil merit's role as the currency of virtue capitalism. Middle-class morality required industriousness. It was a 'Protestant ethic' that linked meritorious effort with reward.[94]

Circulating Merit, the Currency of Virtue Capitalism

Medicine's preoccupation with quacks made merit look like a person had it or they didn't, but this was not actually how it worked. Merit came in grades. Here we see the stocks and flows of merit, the way it circulated as a kind of moral-economic currency. First, for every professional, merit accumulated over time. No professional sat forever on the minimal merit that allowed them to enter the profession. Even just by doing their job, every professional accumulated more. This progressive amassing of experience was sometimes recognized via material signifiers. Across the United States, newspapers reported on ceremonies where, once a pupil nurse passed her initial examination, she entered as a probationer. She was recognizable by a 'universally becoming' probationer's cap.[95] Probationer's caps were common across the Anglo world, where from the 1890s, hospital nursing was rapidly superseding private duty nursing. In hospitals, hierarchies became more visible.[96] In Australia, a trainee nurse's probationer's cap was replaced by a first-year cap and finally a different fourth-year cap, marked by insignia. The seniority of nurses was reflected by their dress, usually combinations of caps and veils. Hospitals had varying norms for nurses' uniforms. Nurses travelling to different jurisdictions often noted them, particularly when the veil – long a sign of seniority among nurses – seemed to be granted prematurely. M. R. Turner, an English nurse who travelled to Sydney, wrote to the newspaper to say that in her day, a nurse on graduation gained 'the privilege of wearing strings and a bow' on her cap but did not take a veil until she

---

[94] Max Weber, *Protestant Ethic*.

[95] The phrase 'universally becoming' is from Pauline Pry: 'Pauline Pry has a chance at becoming a trained nurse', *Evening Star*, 7 December 1895, 19; see also, for example, 'Thirty to Receive Caps', *The Cincinnati Enquirer*, 31 January 1930, 16; 'Student Nurses Presented Caps', *The Decatur Daily Review*, 17 November 1927, 18; 'Fifteen Awarded Nurses' Caps' *Altoona Tribune*, 31 March 1934, 4.

[96] Jean Whelan, 'Too Many, Too Few: The Supply, Demand, and Distribution of Private Duty Nurses, 1910–1965', unpublished PhD dissertation, University of Pennsylvania (2000); Starr, *Social Transformation of American Medicine*; Witz, *Professions and Patriarchy*, 134–138.

gained more experience and responsibility. Turner could not, she said, 'get used to this idea of a trained nurse wearing a veil ... whether she is in charge of a ward or not', though the spirit of her preoccupation with hierarchy was embodied by distinctive veils that differentiated a junior sister from a senior sister.[97]

Similarly, with each year of work, engineers increased their standing and pay rate. There, as in many other professions, the number of years' experience was an indicator of merit. Such experience was accumulated but could also be specialized. An engineer even with many years of railway experience would be likely to continue to build skills in that specialization.[98] Their experience embedded merit in their selves.[99] Engineers had notably long hierarchies, both internal to the profession and relative to others. Some engineering overlapped with work that was definitely not 'white collar'. This encouraged some engineers to sharply distinguish themselves from boilermakers and other trades. Other engineering specialities, like mining engineering, deliberately kept foremen and fitters close, as this encouraged innovation.[100]

For journalists, hierarchical progression was also based on years of experience. A 'junior' learned the trade by performing menial and minor tasks for those with more experience. With each year, a journalist's increased experience led then to increases in responsibility in line with prior performance. In journalism, experience accumulated increased breadth of knowledge, which once gained, became merit. A typical pathway moved a journalist from copy boy through shipping news, to local news, crime reporting, and court 'beats' culminating, with sufficient merit, in political reporting. The highest levels of this ladder, usually Editor positions, were highly esteemed.[101]

Other professions asked their members to invest more continuously and deliberately in their own human capital. As professional associations became more established, their journals, the booklists available to purchase, reading rooms and conferences provided measures of merit.

---

[97] Turner had trained earlier in the century, but she was writing to the newspaper at the time where nurses were beginning to be ambivalent about caps and veils. See M. R. Turner, 'Nurses Caps and Veils', *Sydney Morning Herald*, 23 September 1963, 2.

[98] Brian Lloyd, *Engineers in Australia* (Melbourne: Macmillan, 1991).

[99] Lloyd, *Engineers in Australia*.

[100] See Hannah Forsyth and Michael Pearson, 'Engineers and Social Engineering: Professional/Trade Unions and Social Mobility', *Labour History* 120 (2021), 169–195.

[101] Bridget Griffen-Foley, 'Operating on "an Intelligent Level": Cadet Training at Consolidated Press in the 1940s', in Ann Curthoys and Julianne Schultz (eds), *Journalism: Print, Politics and Popular Culture* (Brisbane: University of Queensland Press, 1999), 142–154.

As each profession firmed up its ladder, they also developed merit-based mechanisms for climbing it, attaining ever-increasing professional status and financial reward. Teachers typically entered a hierarchical system that was based on examination. In systems where pupillage was still the norm, young pupil teachers, still teenagers, sometimes only began to receive payment after an initial examination, which was wholly dependent on the schedule of the District Inspector of Schools. A series of examinations conducted by the District Inspector, alongside their testing of students and inspection of attendance records, governed the relative levels of responsibility teachers might attain and their associated pay rates, though men always earned more than women teachers. In some rural schools, teachers were sometimes appointed as families, with the expectation that the male teacher's wife would instruct girls in sewing, cooking, and perhaps music. The height of the teacher's career path was headmaster or headmistress and between those, the age of the school-children made a difference: the older the students, the higher the teacher's perceived level of responsibility and pay.[102]

Accountants, in order to differentiate themselves from bookkeepers and clerks, also required aspirants invest in their own human capital to produce merit. Advertisements for accountancy courses in the early twentieth century made the return on investment explicit, connecting it moreover to personal satisfaction. In 1906, Hemingway & Robertson, who had offices on Collins Street, Melbourne; Moore Street, Sydney; and Customs Street, Auckland, were one of dozens of organizations offering accountancy training, advertising their course in the *Australasian Accountant and Secretary*. Under the heading 'Interesting Profitable Essential', Hemingway & Robertson promised:

You will find the study of our accountancy course intensely INTERESTING, because the lessons are clearly compiled – replete with illustrations – and full of sound practical business advice and information. Your studies soon become PROFITABLE, for your salary will increase with your knowledge, and it is quite a common thing for students to recoup the expense of the Course out [sic] increased earnings long before the studies are completed. And the study is ESSENTIAL, because every office man must nowadays be an expert – trained and qualified – holding his Accountancy Degree, and study with us will soon put you in possession of the Degree.[103]

Upon completion of the 'degree' (Hemingway & Robertson were not in fact offering a recognized qualification), accountants and other

---

[102] Campbell and Proctor, *History of Australian Schooling*, 64–105.
[103] Advertisement, *The Australasian Accountant and Secretary*, 1 October 1906, 338.

professionals would then be encouraged to continue to improve. By climbing the professional ladder, work was more interesting, and more profitable. The logic of return on investment in oneself became embedded in the hierarchical structure and educational apparatus of each profession.

As a structure governing class status, merit-based hierarchies minimized what might otherwise have been class conflict. Pupil teachers, for example, who started working at the age of thirteen, were often unpaid until the Inspector of Schools visited and conducted examinations. Spaces between visits could take months or even, in remote schools, years. One pupil teacher's clearly unionized parent withdrew their child from pupillage in the Broken Hill school, arguing that their child was being exploited. Correspondence between the headmaster, Jeremiah Boyle, and the District Inspector was haughty: these working-class parents clearly did not understand the system. Pupil teachers were not supposed to look upon those above them as 'bosses', but as the embodiment of their own aspiration.[104] Professionals, even those at the bottom of the ladder, even those plainly exploited – as later generations of educational reformers admitted of pupil teaching – were structured into a system whereby their desire was directed upwards.[105] This desire, directed into the accumulation of merit, would be rewarded with more work. The accumulation of more work was ongoing evidence of the kind of understanding the Broken Hill parents had failed to accept. Merit, as evidence of investment in one's own human capital was rewarded with work, which became the foundation of both status and pay.

The continuous nature of investment in merit became particularly strong in medicine. In an address to medical students in 1896, Samuel T. Knaggs – lecturer in clinical medicine and a noted surgeon at the Prince Alfred Hospital – argued that the 'noble sphere of the medical profession' was underpinned by 'patient and continued labour' and 'indominable perseverance':

Success is very pleasurable and gratifying … yet when success is assured, do not rest there … early success is in reality only putting the foot upon one rung of the ladder that leads upwards, and … the rung of the ladder is never meant to rest upon, but hold a man's foot long enough to enable him to put the other somewhat higher'.[106]

---

[104] District Inspector to Chief Inspector, 10 August 1886, Broken Hill High School File.
[105] Campbell and Proctor, *History of Australian Schooling*, 64–105.
[106] Samuel T. Knaggs, 'The Elements of Success in a Medical Career: An Address to the Members of the Sydney University Medical Society', *Australasian Medical Gazette*, 21 September 1896, 375.

Work, merit, and money circulated in the moral economy; they could not keep still. Industriousness, not class conflict, was the motor that produced hierarchical status in the professional class. Merit, earned through such industriousness, was the currency that demonstrated class status. Moreover, the value of merit could only be realized with ongoing exchange or circulation. The career ladder not only facilitated this exchange, it was also the tangible evidence that the 'achieving class' earned their status.

Like metallic currencies that were made consistent with a fixed weight, merit too was increasingly standardized. In the late nineteenth century, the Law Institute of Victoria was one of the earliest to confront the problem of standardization, though all other professions also faced it over the long twentieth century. Articled clerkships along an apprenticeship-style model remained crucial to preparation, combined with a Melbourne University course intended to help standardize training. Articled clerks provided important, cheap, and increasingly expert labour for the large number of small law partnerships that dotted Victoria. Although the university course moved the profession towards standardization, it was found inadequate. Law offices specialized further, so that articled clerks rarely developed the breadth of training that would give the public confidence in the consistency of expertise shared by lawyers. Continual movements that ensured the consistency of legal education characterized legal education reform over the following century.[107]

The need for standardized education to undergird public trust and expectations and to facilitate merit-based selection into legal practice fuelled tertiary education. In the United States, for-profit colleges in medicine, nursing, accountancy, and teaching often thrived, though there were such substantial differences in the quality, duration, and content of courses that standardization was usually only achieved when professional associations intervened.[108] Australasian professions generally followed British conventions regarding education, but increasingly moved training into colonial and state universities. Law and medicine moved into universities first.[109] Engineering also entered universities in

---

[107] Susan Bartie, *Free Hands and Minds: Pioneering Australian Legal Scholars* (Oxford: Bloomsbury, 2019), 1–42.

[108] Alex Angulo, *Diploma Mills: How For-Profit Colleges Stiffed Students, Taxpayers, and the American Dream* (Baltimore: Johns Hopkins University Press, 2016).

[109] Hannah Forsyth, *A History of the Modern Australian University* (Sydney: NewSouth, 2014), 20–45; see also Wesley Pue, 'Guild Training vs. Professional Education: The Committee on Legal Education and the Law Department of Queen's College, Birmingham in the 1850s', *The American Journal of Legal History* 33.3 (1989), 241–287; Thomas Bonner, *Becoming a Physician: Medical Education in Britain, France, Germany, and the United States, 1750–1945* (Oxford: Oxford University Press, 1995);

the late nineteenth century, but it was not the primary way of training engineers until after the Second World War.[110] Other professions became attached to higher education for the same reasons, but at different times. Accountancy in the Antipodes started in a haphazard manner, since it was a habit of senior accountants to form a new association, each with their own entry examination, as a profitable endeavour – or perhaps because they themselves were unsuccessful in entering one.[111] Education for all the professions moved into the universities within the twentieth century.[112]

Conclusion

Merit made the professionals an achieving class. Collectively, they valued work as a central ethic, believed that they deserved its rewards, and considered the status and authority that they accumulated to be just and fair. The moral superiority of achievement as the basis of class status, compared to older, irrational, and arbitrary rewards associated with inherited wealth and position, bolstered the moral relationship between work and profit.

In part, this relationship was necessary to make the professions function effectively. The kind of pure commerce that gave Sands, with his rhubarb-and-magnesia 'Methuselah Mixture', his spectacular success would undermine the moral authority that medical practitioners needed to ensure people listened to them and followed their advice. As the professional class emerged, they sought a structure that would reward Sands for his hard work and talent, not for his commercial acumen alone. This was not a morality separated from profit. Rather, profit would now be the just reward for virtuous effort, not merely a result of hardnosed investment.

Albert Harno, *Legal Education in the United States* (San Francisco: Bancroft-Whitney Company, 1953).

[110] Hannah Forsyth, 'Census Data on Universities, Professions and War', in Kate Darian-Smith and James Waghorne (eds), *The First World War, the Universities and the Professions in Australia 1913–1939* (Melbourne: Melbourne University Press, 2019), 10–28.

[111] Robert Linn, *Power, Progress & Profit: A History of the Australian Accounting Profession* (Melbourne: Australian Society of Certified Practicing Accountants, 1996); Glenn Van Wyhe, 'A History of US Higher Education in Accounting, Part 1: Situating Accounting within the Academy', *Issues in Accounting Education* 22.2 (2007), 165; Paul Miranti, *Accountancy Comes of Age: The Development of an American Profession 1886–1940* (Chapel Hill: University of North Carolina Press, 1990).

[112] Harold Perkin, 'History of Universities', in James Forest and Philip Altbach (eds), *International Handbook of Higher Education* (Dordrecht: Springer, 2007), 159–205.

The 'Protestant ethic' was structured into the economies that resulted from such professional labour.[113] This was achieved as each profession established a hierarchy. Each professional 'ladder' enabled achievement to be recognized and rewarded, systematizing the relationship between virtue and profit. For individual professionals, the hierarchy was internalized as evidence of their value. When Muriel Knox Doherty gossiped with her friends on the warm step of the nurses' quarters at the Prince Alfred Hospital, their anxiety, desire, and motivation were directed to which of them would be rewarded – with more work – for their talent and hard work. The privilege of accessing the ladder (perhaps modelled on Jacob's biblical vision, with heaven the goal) made 'ladder-climbing' effortful achievement – their 'way of life'.[114] Their continual accumulation of merit was to become the precondition for belonging in their chosen profession.

Merit also became the currency by which the value of human capital was calculated. As these measures were increasingly standardized, usually by regulating education, this helped facilitate the exchange of human capital. This seemed so rational, compared to older ways of evaluating class, that it became the foundation of the twentieth-century labour force. Race and gender, however, were not subject to a similar kind of rationalizing. Those were seen as natural, while merit was not, so that the work the professional class did helped embed global 'colour lines' and gender inequalities into changing the global economy. Generations of sociologists observing this subsequently warned that merit was never the objective substance it purported to be. Instead, it was shaped by parental advantage and preconceived class, race, and gender characteristics. Still, merit's beneficiaries promoted it. This was more than propaganda; it was a material structure shaped, as Chapter 4 explores, by changes in middle-class business organization.

---

[113] Weber, *Protestant Ethic.*
[114] See Stefan Collini's recent reflections of the poor correlation between a material ladder and its metaphorical function in the system of merit in Stefan Collini, 'Snakes and Ladders', *London Review of Books* 43(7), 2021, 15.

4   From Bourgeois to Professional

By the 1930s, the business world was changing, and the difference was obvious by a professional man's desk. 'Roll-top desks, partner desks and desks with rows of drawers on either side seem to be going out of fashion', advised accountant W. Brice Rainsford. This was not because of the growth of the typewriter, which few professional men used regularly, but because it was no longer appropriate for there to be 'hiding places for all sorts of papers'.[1] The kind of order that the new, flat modern desk represented contrasted to the individualized, personal desks of previous decades. Those desks suited their era, when the work was closely connected to the individual character of the professional man (and it was almost always a man) and his unique relationship to his network of business clients. Now, the businessman's work was subject to a universalizing form of order. 'Keep the desk clear', Rainsford further advised, 'an untidy desk is ... indicative of an unsystematic mind'.[2]

This was the era of systematization, scientific management, and specialization that transformed white-collar office processes.[3] Such changes were intended to increase efficiency: managers were becoming conscious of office productivity as the average size of American firms grew by 30 per cent in just fifteen years after 1904.[4] The move from the ornate desk, with nooks and crannies holding a professional man's myriad interests, to a flat desk clear of 'all papers except those on which one is working' symbolized the increased focus, even specialization, that white-collar professions now sought.[5] Unlike Theodore Fink, whose diverse

---

[1] W. Bruce Rainsford, 'The Office Desk and Its Importance to the Accountant', *The Commonwealth Journal of Accountancy*, 1 June 1935, 290.
[2] Rainsford, 'The Office Desk', 290.
[3] Gideon Haigh, *The Office: A Hardworking History* (Melbourne: Miegunyah Press, 2012), 58–137.
[4] John Quail, 'Becoming Fully Functional: The Conceptual Struggle for a New Structure for the Giant Corporation in the US and UK in the First Half of the Twentieth Century', *Business History* 50.2 (2008), 127–146.
[5] Rainsford, 'The Office Desk', 290.

professional career was on display in Chapter 2, no longer was a professional man likely to be journalist, lawyer, and politician all at the same time.

In fact, not only was a professional more likely to specialize within their vocation, but office work in general was also specializing. Smaller, more discrete tasks were being rationalized across a now-feminizing office, with women typists and secretaries taking on a range of activities that were previously the domain of mostly male clerks or apprentice professionals, like the young, articled clerks training in accountancy or law. Many Marxist scholars have argued that for most office workers, the calculated, task-based scientific management practices inspired by engineer and management expert, Frederick Taylor, 'deskilled' office work with smaller, less-skilled tasks and thus lower-paid jobs.[6]

Like the desk, scientific management also transformed the office itself. Such a contrast to the warm, cluttered 'club-like' workspaces of the late nineteenth century, modern offices became light, open areas with straight, neat rows of desks. The new scientific management thus also subjected work habits to the kind of surveillance that Foucauldian scholars have described, where office workers internalized efficiency and order as their professional selfhood.[7]

This chapter will show that other professional spaces were subjected to similar transformations. Home-based medical practices gave way to uniform and systematized enterprises. This allowed healthcare to expand still further: hospitals had more beds per institution and centralized medical practices saw more patients than when a local physician visited individuals in their homes.[8] Hospital wards with bed layouts remarkably like the new modern offices took over from individual sick rooms in private homes, genteel home-like hospitals, and cottage infirmaries. Hospitals were soon patronized by the middle class, who previously preferred a more domestic space for their healthcare needs, since traditional hospitals were charity institutions for the poor.[9] Increased

---

[6] Mills, *White Collar*, 112–141; Harry Braverman, *Labor and Monopoly Capital* (New York: Monthly Review Press, 1974); Rosemary Crompton and Gareth Jones, *White-Collar Proletariat* (London: Palgrave, 1984).

[7] Lee Parker and Ingrid Jeacle, 'The Construction of the Efficient Office: Scientific Management, Accountability, and the Neo-Liberal State', *Contemporary Accounting Research* 36.3 (2019), 1883–1926.

[8] Starr, *Social Transformation of American Medicine*, 60–78; Ann Digby, *The Evolution of British General Practice 1850–1948* (Oxford: Oxford University Press, 1999).

[9] Starr, *Social Transformation of American Medicine*, 145–179; Barry Carruthers and Lesley Carruthers, *A History of Britain's Hospitals* (Sussex: Book Guild Publishing, 2005), 57–104 and 219–249; Morris Vogel, *The Invention of the Modern Hospital: Boston 1870–1930* (Chicago: University of Chicago Press, 1980), 97–119; Robert Dingwall,

demand for healthcare, led by the middle class, was paradoxically responsible for the emergence of medical social work, still called hospital almonry in some places. These inheritors of nineteenth-century charity work were gatekeepers, employed to ensure middle-class patients capable of paying for medical services were not given free 'charity' healthcare. Soon social workers engaged actively with families to assist with recovery, childcare, and other effects of illness on working-class family life.[10]

Schooling systems too, began in earnest to displace governesses and tutors. Small private schools, which had often been run by women from homes or home-like buildings, further gave way to larger, more uniform schools. Pupils per school increased everywhere when the 'human capital century' began to mature, as parents saw the advantages education offered their children.[11] Schooling also grew, of course, because of compulsory education and government and community-run schooling systems.[12] Primary and secondary education in the United States grew faster than everywhere else. In 1900, there were 439,522 American teachers, growing to 1,062,615 by 1930.[13] While this expansion coincided with progressivist pedagogies that sought to undermine some of the factory-inspired teaching practices of the nineteenth century, this chapter will show that the massive expansion of schooling asserted a logic that still standardized educational enterprise, undermining the diverse system previously in place, included many schools that were owned by women.

Encompassing schools, hospitals, and offices, the industrialization of professional work attracted scholarly observers, armed with patterns of exploitation they knew from factories. Many anticipated the emergence of a white-collar working class. In 1951, for example, American

---

Anne Rafferty, and Charles Webster, *An Introduction to the Social History of Nursing* (London: Routledge, 1988), 79; Brian Abel-Smith, *The Hospitals 1800–1948* (London: Heinemann, 1964), 189, 339; Sutherland, *In Search of the New Woman*.

[10] Enid Bell, *The Story of Hospital Almoners: The Birth of a Profession* (London: Faber and Faber, 1961); Agnes Macintyre, 'The Hospital Almoner', *Medical Journal of Australia*, 8 February 1930, 159; Brian Abel-Smith, *A History of the Nursing Profession* (London: Heinemann, 1960), 36–60; Laurie O'Brien and Cynthia Turner, *Establishing Medical Social Work in Victoria* (Melbourne: University of Melbourne Press, 1979); Colleen Lundy and Therese Jennissen, *One Hundred Years of Social Work: A History of the Profession in English Canada, 1900–2000* (Waterloo: Wilfrid Laurier University Press, 2011), 31–32.

[11] Goldin, 'Human-Capital Century'; Mandler, *Crisis of Meritocracy*.

[12] Edward Janak, 'Education in the Progressive Period (Ca. 1890s–1920s)', in Edward Janak (ed), *A Brief History of Schooling in the United States: From Pre-Colonial Times to the Present* (Cham: Springer, 2019), 43–63; Campbell and Proctor, *History of Australian Schooling*; Axelrod, *Promise of Canadian Schooling*.

[13] US Census, 1920 and 1930.

sociologist C. Wright Mills saw large public and private bureaucracies managing a new division of labour in ways that contributed to white-collar alienation. Mills, and the many scholars since who have observed the exploitation of white-collar workers, were describing something real and important. As this chapter will explore, however, on the whole, professionals in the first half of the twentieth century tended to support the increased efficiencies associated with modern enterprise management. Mills believed that they were misled by their professional associations, who borrowed from the prestige of nineteenth-century elite doctors and lawyers, seducing them into less-skilled, less-rewarding work.[14]

Such claims to professional 'false consciousness', or in more Foucauldian terms, the internalization of the surveillance regime promoted by the modernizing workplace, fail to explain several consequences of the changes in enterprise structure in the first half of the twentieth century.[15] For example, there was evident cooperation between the professions and the managerial techniques and imperatives transforming offices, hospitals, and schools; this will be explored first in this chapter. Office work in this chapter is considered separately to healthcare and education. In part this is because office work was largely dominated by men, though this was slowly changing. Healthcare and education, by contrast, were dominated by women, though men mostly controlled medical science. Despite their differences, 'male' and 'female' businesses – as they were understood at the time – were subject to similar changes in scope and scale, as this chapter will show. Having considered both men's and women's business structures, this chapter then seeks to understand something of the coincidence of white-collar exploitation with their spectacular rise to power, which was achieved by the mid-twentieth century. This is explored here through changes to medicine, which also compelled new developments in medical social work. The purpose of this chapter is to reconcile the spread of professionals and their virtue through every town and city across the Anglo world with changes in their business structures. This will show that the transformation of professional workplaces shaped class relations for white-collar workers, though not always in the ways that parallels to factory work have led scholars to assume.

•

[14] Mills, *White Collar*.
[15] See Peter Miller and Ted O'Leary, 'Accounting and the Construction of the Governable Person', *Accounting, Organizations and Society* 12.3 (1987), 235–265; Peter Miller and Nikolas Rose, 'Governing Economic Life', *Economy and Society* 19.1 (1990), 1–31; Vaughan Radcliffe, 'Knowing Efficiency: The Enactment of Efficiency in Efficiency Auditing', *Accounting, Organizations and Society* 24.4 (1999), 333–362.

Rational and Efficient Office Work

Massive growth in firm sizes was not limited to America, though it was most spectacular there. Still, while business structures were changing in Britain and the southern Anglosphere too, in the 1930s lawyers and accountants mostly worked for themselves or in small partnerships. Partnerships were beginning to swell into significant enterprises, however, since accountancy was on the cusp of a 'long boom' worldwide that was boosted by increased auditing regulations in response to the Great Depression.[16] The same economic slump had the opposite effect on the legal profession, however. Melbourne firm Maddock & Partners, for example, grew to around thirty employees, including four partners, in the 1910s and 1920s. They provided legal services to stable clients among growing industrial giants like Carlton United Breweries as well as large civic organizations like the Deaf and Dumb Institute and the YMCA. The 'manufacturing, commercial and building boom' of the 1920s collapsed in the 1930s and Maddock & Partners shrank to around twelve staff members, including three partners.[17]

The struggling legal profession complained, in this context, that accountants often stole their business. As we saw in Chapter 2, there was considerable overlap between those professions in the early part of the twentieth century. The accountancy advantage was bolstered when lawyers suffered severe reputational damage – more than usual, that is – when individual practitioners, struggling to maintain middle-class lifestyles during the Depression, were discovered pilfering the money they held on behalf of clients, their (ironically named, in this moment) 'trust' accounts. In Victoria, this prompted legislative proposals requiring audits of solicitor trust accounts, which gave the accountancy profession a share of legal incomes and, as one Victorian lawyer put it, propelled 'the English practice of passing on to their clients the costs imposed ... by legislation requiring the audit of all trust funds'.[18]

Although Victorian lawyers rankled over the indignity of sharing client income with accountants, they nevertheless formed an alliance with them

[16] Ian Gow and Stuart Kells, *The Big Four: The Curious Past and Perilous Future of the Global Accounting Monopoly* (Melbourne: La Trobe University Press, 2018), 55.

[17] Helen Penrose, *To Build a Firm: The Maddocks Story* (Melbourne: Maddocks, 2010), 19–32.

[18] Charles Churchill Palmer, Henry Churchill Palmer, Commissioners for Affidavits for High Court all States & New Zealand to Secretary, Law Institute of Victoria, 12 November 1946, Professional Practice Act (drafts and correspondence), Law Institute of Victoria, Melbourne, University of Melbourne Archives, MUA/ LIV1960.008.10.

in opposition to independent auditors appointed by government. 'It seems monstrous that strangers ... should pry into the affairs of our clients', wrote H. E. De Gruchy of Ford, Aspinwall & De Gruchy. '[L]et the Act require compulsory Audit by all means, but by Auditors of a Solicitor's own selection'.[19] De Gruchy and his colleagues were evidently yet to embrace the principles of openness and scientific transparency associated with the flat, modern desk. Lawyers preferred club-like networks of business associates – we saw some of those during the Melbourne land boom, in Chapter 2 – whose confidentiality was assured by their individual relationship.

In contrast to lawyers, accountants, with their innovative commitment to modern office processes, became the answer to the economy's moral problems. Just as auditors were the apparently obvious rejoinder to the moral troubles faced by the legal profession, so too was accountancy seen to be the appropriate vehicle to heal the fractures in global capitalism made visible by the sequential shocks of the 1890s Depression, the First World War and the American stock market crash of 1929. Across the Anglo world, new government regulation on one hand and commercial innovation on the other strengthened the accountancy profession.[20]

With so much change afoot, accountants were rapidly defining new boundaries for their profession, emerging as it was from a loose collection of work that included administrative and secretarial tasks, book-keeping, auditing, office and workflow management as well as the growing field of cost accounting. In the specializing office, the first three tasks were increasingly left to the growing army of female secretaries.

[19] H. E. De Gruchy to Secretary Law Institute of Victoria, 7 November 1941, Professional Practice Act (drafts and correspondence), Law Institute of Victoria, Melbourne, University of Melbourne Archives, MUA/LIV1960.008.10.

[20] John Edwards, *Company Legislation and Changing Patterns of Disclosure in British Company Accounts 1900–1940* (London: Institute of Chartered Accountants in England and Wales, 1981); Garry Carnegie, 'The Development of Accounting Regulation, Education and Literature in Australia 1788–2005', *Australian Economic History Review* 49.3 (2009), 276–301; Linn, *Power, Progress & Profit*; Derek Matthews, Malcolm Anderson, and John Edwards, *The Priesthood of Industry: the Rise of the Professional Accountant in British Management* (Oxford : Oxford University Press, 1998); George Staubus, *Economic Influences on the Development of Accounting in Firms* (New York: Garland, 1996); Dominic Detzen, 'A "New Deal" for the Profession', *Accounting, Auditing and Accountability* 31.3 (2018), 970–992; Chris Poullaos, 'The Self-Governing Dominions of South Africa, Australia, and Canada and the Evolution of the Imperial Accountancy Arena during the 1920s', in Chris Poullaos and Suki (eds), *Accountancy and Empire the British Legacy of Professional Organization* (London: Routledge, 2010); Grietjie Verhoef and Grant Samkin, 'The Accounting Profession and Education', *Accounting, Auditing and Accountability* 30.6 (2017), 1370–1398; Alan Richardson, 'Merging the Profession: A Social Network Analysis of the Consolidation of the Accounting Profession in Canada', *Accounting Perspectives* 16.2 (2017), 83–104.

Auditing remained accountancy's bread and butter, resting on the moral distance from business activity, which they attached to their expertise (see Chapter 2). Workflow and cost accounting, however, propelled accountancy into the realm of scientific management. Cost accounting considered the value of the business based on projected costs (of, say, replacing machinery) rather than an evaluation of assets (which focused on the initial price of the machinery, minus depreciation). By its nature, cost accounting stressed business planning and helped accelerate the professionalization of business management. Cost accounting brought accountants into management consulting, especially in London and the United States, and was foundational to large multinational accountancy firms like Deloitte, Ernst & Young, and KPMG.[21] Management in general and scientific management in particular had in fact emerged out of engineering work, not accounting, since engineers worked on logistics and plant processes. While engineers brought scientific management to manufacturing, however, accountants arguably brought it to the office.[22]

In this environment, accountants began to reconsider the nature of their work and the moral codes by which they collectively professionalized. They asked new questions about relationships between labour and capital and began actively to capitalize on links between professional enterprise and the state. In 1935, G. S. Crimp wrote in the *Commonwealth Journal of Accountancy* that

[i]ndividualistic days may have gone beyond recall, and that the significant relations of the future will be between bodies of employers and employees, between numbers of interdependent businesses, between individuals and State, and later between nation and nation.[23]

The growing size and complexity of all forms of enterprise, according to US accountant W. J. Black a decade earlier, 'has reduced management to the consideration of masses of figures and made the man of figures the fittest to survive'.[24] This was more than a Darwinian survival of the fittest. The 'man of figures' carried the virtue associated with a new scientific approach to capitalist enterprise into all the businesses for whom he worked.

---

[21] See Louis Hyman, *Temp: How American Work, American Business and the American Dream Became Temporary* (New York: Viking, 2018); Gow and Kells, *Big Four*.
[22] Shenhav, *Manufacturing Rationality*.
[23] G. S. Crimp, 'Developments in Accounting Practice', *Commonwealth Journal of Accountancy*, 1 August 1935, 350–358.
[24] W. J. Black, 'The First Half-Century of "the Accountant"', *Commonwealth Journal of Accountancy*, 1 March 1926, 165. Reprinted from *The Economic Journal* 35.139 (September 1925), 493–495.

In professional journals, accountants displayed considerable interest in scientific management. They advocated it when advising others and developed scientific tools to manage themselves. The Dey Time Machine was popular – a device that recorded attendance and work type. Dey Time advertising in the 1920s ran with the tag line 'Time is your capital, so don't let it be wasted'.[25] This sense that professional time was capital requiring virtuous management began to permeate accountancy practice. F. Oswald Barnett advocated for detailed planning and costing of the accountant's time. 'The first thing [the accountant] must realise', Barnett argued, 'is that the only commodity he has to sell is time'.[26]

In the era of systematization, Barnett declared that an accountant 'must ... keep a rigid record of what he does with every minute of every day'. His surveillance of his own time was literally to keep account of time as the substance of capitalist exchange. Barnett's five-minute diary – he published a segment of his own as an example – presents a case study of a senior accountant's morning in 1936. He spent thirty minutes dealing with the mail, an hour and a half with clients regarding their shares and sales tax, and attended a director's meeting, which took one hour and forty-five minutes. This application of accountancy's long-standing connections between thrift, rectitude, and attention to detail applied, in Barnett's view, to the individual accountant, but it was important that it also scaled up. Barnett suggested that 'as his practice grows and he employs others to help him, a complete record must also be kept of their time'.[27]

Accountants were not only interested in timekeeping as a mere apparatus of managerial surveillance. Scientific, rational management was their moral responsibility, assuring the most prudent use of time as capital. Accountancy journals reveal a consistent enthusiasm for efficiencies obtained through detailed time management, including of their own time, but the same articles often also pondered the share of profit between capital and labour. Since both invested their time, a consistent moral argument would see both capital and labour rewarded.[28] As industrial relations historian Diana Kelly has shown, early twentieth-century members of a group of advocates for scientific management, called the

[25] Advertisement for Dey Time Recorder, *The Australian Accountant*, 1 April 1926, 179.
[26] F. Oswald Barnett, 'The Accountant's Time and Cost Records', *The Australian Accountant*, March 1936, 40.
[27] Barnett, 'Accountant's Time and Cost Records', 40–42.
[28] For example, Major E. A. Pells, 'The Benefit to the Workman of Scientific Management', *The Australasian Accountant and Secretary*, 1 January 1920, 25; Henry W. Allingham, 'The Determination of Standards in Scientific Management', *The Australasian Accountant and Secretary*, 1 February 1920, 52–53.

'Taylor Society', were not always capitalist overseers intent on deskilling the workforce in the sense famously critiqued by Marxist political economist, Harry Braverman.[29] In fact, Kelly argues that it is more accurate to consider the Taylor Society as part of the progressive movement, seeking systems that would enable technocratic planning towards a better society.[30] Accountancy's preoccupation with scientific management thus emerged as a furtherance of the profession's ethics, which grew out of a shared moral vision for a capitalist society whose profits were grounded in an investment in human integrity, as shown in Chapter 2.

Accountancy journals bear out Diana Kelly's call for a more complex interpretation of Taylorism. In the 1935 article cited earlier, G. S. Crimp – like many others in accounting journals in the 1920s and 1930s – argued for profit-sharing between capital and labour. He believed that planning the next phase of capitalism should result in cooperation between labour, capital, and the state. Accountancy between the world wars was closely connected to the discipline of economics, which commercial and academic professionals brought to bear on business and government – enterprises that they saw as part of the same system.[31] Contrary to Harold Perkin's account of this period, which imposed backwards 1980s debates about private and public sources of funding, these professionals did not see the state as a structure that competed with capitalism.[32] Rather, the professional class tended to equate the rational modern state with scientific business techniques as part of the same moral-economic order. F. Oswald Barnett's five-minute diary sheet was a pragmatic tool he developed for billing purposes, but it also represented the kind of orderly rationality the professional class sought for society at large. Pieces of time, along with merit as we saw in Chapter 3, were converted into discrete items, exchanged for profit. Aggregated, however, such professional work was an investment in an orderly, rational economy that included workers, commercial enterprise, and the state.

The universities were a growing part of this order, where economics and accountancy grew as academic fields, though each retained a focus on public engagement, offering business and policy advice. During the Great Depression, for example, the Wharton Institute, which was

---

[29] Braverman, *Labor and Monopoly Capital*.
[30] Diana Kelly, 'Perceptions of Taylorism and a Marxist scientific manager', *Journal of Management History* 22. 3 (2016), 298–319.
[31] Yves Rees, 'A War of Card Indexes: From Political Economy to Economic Science', in Kate Darian-Smith and James Waghorne (eds), *The First World War, the Universities and the Professions in Australia 1914–1939* (Melbourne: Melbourne University Press, 2019).
[32] Perkin, *Rise of Professional Society*, 11–16 and 390–402.

established as a business school at the University of Philadelphia in the late nineteenth century, held roundtable sessions that were 'open to all men interested in business and financial problems'. Topics included 'accounting; insolvency – legal and economic implications; future trends in the consumption of goods; real estate taxation and recent social changes: problems of the family'.[33] Similarly, in Brooklyn, New York, the Commerce Department of the Catholic St John's University gave free public lectures on double-entry bookkeeping and the essentials of a business contract.[34]

In the same spirit of public education, Sydney Accounting Professor Allan Clunies Ross prepared a pamphlet on *The People's Money and How They Control It*. Confronting the Australian labour movement's campaign against the 'money power', Clunies Ross sought to educate the public on money, cash, cheques, and credit, offering academic reassurance that 'banks will not refuse to lend without very good reason', because 'the interests of the banks and those of the community are closely connected'.[35] The following year, Clunies Ross published the book *Practical Business Economics for Australian Conditions*, aimed at accountants, lawyers, and others who worked in white-collar commercial enterprise. The book included instructions for bookkeeping and other aspects of accountancy but also read like an etiquette manual, or moral guide, for the business world:

The true business man recognises responsibility to customers, to employees, and to himself. If he is determined to make his occupation an honourable and dignified 'profession', he bases his actions on moral principles, guides them by knowledge acquired by study, and inspires them by the consciousness of good service rendered.[36]

Such morality did not contradict or moderate capitalist processes for Clunies Ross. On the contrary, the 'true' businessman's moral investment was intrinsically connected to bourgeois processes of investment of capital for profit. It was as if the businessman was investing his very self when Clunies Ross argued that 'the people we have called business men differ from the rest, because they use their own property and risk losing it in the process of giving their service'.[37]

---

[33] 'Wharton Institute to Discuss Banking', *The Philadelphia Inquirer*, 19 March 1933, 36.
[34] Advertisement St John's University, *Times Union*, 12 September 1933, 21.
[35] Allan Clunies Ross, *The People's Money and How They Control It* (Sydney: Sound Finance League of Australia, 1934); see Peter Love, *Labour and the Money Power: Australian Labour Populism 1890–1950* (Melbourne: Melbourne University Press, 1984).
[36] Clunies Ross, *People's Money*, 366   [37] Ibid., 17–18.

The businessman's preparedness to risk his own capital constituted a moral stamp, authorizing the value, to him, of the work he performed. This suggests that the small business structure that originally dominated professional work was not just a matter of investing money in the production of services for profit; it also capitalized time, virtue, and even professional selfhood. While this evidently validated capitalist processes of investment and return, like many Taylorists, Clunies Ross believed the resulting profit should be shared with labour, since through their work, labourers also invested *their* selves in the production of profit.[38] This position suggests that the profit extracted with the aid of tools like F. Oswald Barnett's five-minute diary was not a disinterested result of this scientific system. Rather, financial profit for the professional class was perceived to be the just and natural consequence of a rational, scientific, and moral order that permeated the modern self.

This evidence shows that professionals, particularly accountants, were not hapless victims of scientific management. Taylorism and other rational, scientific, or technical means of measuring and standardizing work time and business activity were a continuation of the moral order that the middle class embedded into the professions from the late nineteenth century onwards. Such techniques were still disruptive, imposing industrialized logics to the office in ways that changed work processes, office aesthetics, and the division of labour. The effect undeniably resulted in some deskilling in the male-dominated office, opening office jobs, albeit at reduced salaries, for women. However, accountants, alongside engineers, not only gave substantial intellectual consideration to the possibilities that new forms of management offered, but they also transferred this to office work more widely. If they noticed that the expansion of office work was leading to a labour force of white-collar salaried employees, supplanting the bourgeois men who, as Allan Clunies Ross put it, 'use their own property and risk losing it', they did not seem to believe the transformation posed any kind of moral threat.[39]

Accountants were particularly self-conscious about the changes underway, but it is worth briefly noting that newspapers too were changing. The thousands of journalists who dragged printers into every remote corner of the Anglo world to report on local news in ways that spread across nations and empires were becoming replaced with very large, influential newspaper empires. These had their roots in the financializing world described in Chapter 2. Theodore Fink, for example, had long led

---

[38] Allan Clunies Ross, *The Workers' Shares under the Companies Act, New South Wales* (Hamilton, NZ: Employee Partnership Institute, 1936).
[39] Clunies Ross, *People's Money*, 17–18.

one major news empire by the time he died in 1942.[40] Also in Melbourne, the Collins House finance group, whose wealth was derived from speculation starting in Broken Hill, used a paper empire built around the Melbourne *Herald* to influence politics in ways that benefited their financial interests. They also unwittingly shaped much of the twentieth century when, in 1927, they employed Keith Murdoch. Murdoch had already been an influential character in Australia since the Great War, though by the late twentieth century, his son Rupert Murdoch's media empire extended to *The Sun* and the *News of the World* in the United Kingdom and *The Wall Street Journal* and Fox News in the United States.[41] Influence aside, the industrialization of newspapers changed journalism, transforming the profession from one where many men (mostly) owned their own newspapers to much larger conglomerates. These big firms in turn standardized forms of journalism training, wages, and work processes.[42]

From Domestic Sphere to Professional Institution

It was not only men who traditionally risked their capital in the pursuit of professional goals, and who were now becoming a salaried workforce instead. Women had always worked and were entering offices in growing numbers. Women were also business owners, whose status was rapidly changing.[43] The business history of bourgeois women has often been overlooked in general, though interest is growing.[44] In addition, histories of institutions like hospitals and schools often describe antecedents and then skip straight to women's status as employees. Moreover, certain histories of hospitals have failed to discuss women or nurses at all.[45]

---

[40] Wilma Hannah, 'Fink, Theodore (1855–1942)', *Australian Dictionary of Biography, Volume 8* (Melbourne: Melbourne University Press, 1981).

[41] Geoffrey Serle, 'Murdoch, Sir Keith Arthur (1885–1952)', *Australian Dictionary of Biography, Volume 10* (Melbourne: Melbourne University Press, 1986); Young, *Paper Emperors*, 192–195.

[42] Bridget Griffen-Foley, 'Operating on "an Intelligent Level"', 142–154; Clem Lloyd, *Profession: Journalist: A History of the Australian Journalists' Association* (Sydney: Hale & Iremonger, 1985); Yung-Ho Im, 'Class, Culture, and Newsworkers: Theories of the Labor Process and the Labor History of the Newspaper', unpublished PhD dissertation, the University of Iowa (1990).

[43] Alice Kessler-Harris, *Women Have Always Worked*, 2nd ed. (Champaign, IL: University of Illinois Press, 2018); of many, see also Boris, *Making the Woman Worker*; Helen McCarthy, *Double Lives: A History of Working Motherhood* (London: Bloomsbury, 2020); Patricia Grimshaw, Ellen Warne, and Shurlee Swain, 'Constructing the Working Mother: Australian Perspectives 1920–1970', *Hecate* 31.2 (2005), 21–33.

[44] For example, Jennifer Aston and Catherine Bishop (eds), *Female Entrepreneurs in the Long Nineteenth Century: A Global Perspective* (Cham: Palgrave Macmillan, 2020).

[45] Vogel, *Invention of the Modern Hospital*, 1980.

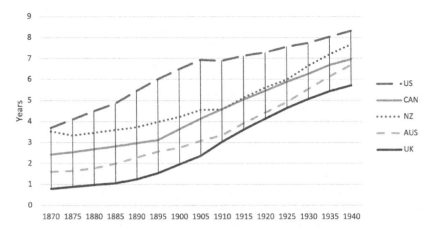

Figure 4.1 Mean years of schooling in the United States, Canada, New Zealand, Australia, and Great Britain 1870–1940. Data sources: Lee, Jong-Wha and Hanol Lee, 2016, "Human Capital in the Long Run," *Journal of Development Economics* 122, 147–169; Barro, Robert and Jong-Wha Lee, 2013, "A New Data Set of Educational Attainment in the World, 1950–2010." *Journal of Development Economics* 104, 184–198.

To solve this problem, we need to step back in this section of the chapter to the late nineteenth and early twentieth centuries to better appreciate the existing structure of women's professional businesses. This will help us understand the effect of modernized expansion for women professionals who, like men, traditionally invested their own capital for profit.

Across the Anglo world, in homes and home-like spaces, just as women asserted Victorian authority over the domestic sphere, professional women used their property – their own capital, time, and feminine authority – to provide services as teachers, nurses, and medical practitioners.[46] Teaching grew very quickly as average years of schooling increased (see Chapter 2), which meant twentieth-century growth started from a high base, especially in America (see Figure 4.1).[47]

Governments were increasingly interested in schooling. However, it was also middle-class women, and a smaller number of middle-class men, whose educational businesses ensured that by the twentieth

---

[46] Theobald, *Knowing Women*; Poovey, *Uneven Developments*.
[47] Goldin, 'Human-Capital Century'.

century, formal learning dominated the life of nearly every English-speaking child. Schooling businesses took remarkably diverse forms. By way of example, American novelist Louisa May Alcott's 1868 book *Little Women* portrayed the full spectrum of education available in the Anglo world in the second half of the nineteenth century. Alcott's tale of four sisters included Amy March, who attended a school. Stories of Amy's experiences of school discipline, humiliation, and tearful industry over less-favoured subjects are familiar fare in the school story genre established by Thomas Hughes' *Tom Brown's School Days*. *Little Women*'s Beth March, however, was 'too bashful to go to school' and 'did her lessons at home with her father'.[48] The eldest sister Meg was a governess, earning her living teaching the children of a wealthy family. The March's next-door neighbour, Laurie, was also from a wealthy family. He studied at home, under a paid university-educated tutor. Jo March, who later in the story also worked as a governess (which, she said, was 'as good as a clerk'), late in the novel inherited her aunt's large home, Plumfield, which she then turned into a school.[49] Jo's virtuous passion was in education for the poor, though as she proclaimed to Laurie:

Of course I shall have rich pupils, also – perhaps begin with such altogether. Then, when I've got a start, I can take in a ragamuffin or two, just for a relish. Rich people's children often need care and comfort, as well as poor.[50]

Alcott has her heroine Jo pursuing a moral agenda that would uplift society by educating the working class. However, her school was necessarily also a business.

Within literary history, schooling in *Little Women* and its sequels has been interpreted as 'domesticating' the school story. By moving education into a home-like space, Alcott 're-gendered' the *Tom Brown* genre, which was focused on masculine institutions, typically English boarding schools.[51] In the settler colonies, however, far from 're-gendering' education, teaching in the domestic sphere, like Jo's school at Plumfield, largely preceded mass schooling in standardized institutions. In Sydney, for example, Louisa Green (née Greenwood), eldest daughter of education reformer James Greenwood, saw her home as a business opportunity:

Towards the end of 1885 I conceived the idea of opening a school of my own. My sister (Pollie) was to leave school when it closed that year, and a school of our

---

[48] Louisa May Alcott, *Little Women*, Project Gutenberg https://gutenberg.org/files/514/514-h/514-h.htm, chapter 4.
[49] Ibid., chapter 33.   [50] Ibid., chapter 47.
[51] Beverly Clark, 'Domesticating the School Story, Regendering a Genre: Alcott's "Little Men"', *New Literary History* 26.2 (1995), 323–342; Theobald, *Knowing Women*.

own would afford a means of livelihood for all of us three girls. Our youngest sister Gertie would be leaving school too, before long ... and we spent the summer holidays 1885–1886, in preparation for our new venture.[52]

To build their school, the Misses Greenwood rearranged the family home. Their dining room became the school room, with desks, a blackboard, and a cupboard for slates. 'There was plenty of room for a play ground,' Louisa wrote, 'and a vestibule connecting the parts of our house – became a hat and cloak room'.[53]

'How thrilling it was when the room was ready for us to open our own school,' Green recalled. Recruiting students, though, was a nerve-wracking business, and Louisa went door to door in her neighbourhood inviting parents to enrol their children:

It was terribly hard to call on a stranger at all, and the idea of asking for pupils seemed to me to be rather effrontery. I have walked past a house once or twice before I could screw up the courage to go in. However I never was received with anything but friendliness and was often successful in getting one – or perhaps two pupils.[54]

Louisa Greenwood's school opened with six students in 1886, increasing to an average of forty pupils each year.

Music, French and Drawing were extras – and I gave these lessons after the usual school hours 9.30 to 12.30 and 2.0 [sic] to 3.30 ... Two music lessons were wedged in before school in the mornings; two others in the luncheon recess – and several after school in the afternoon. Drawing and Painting lessons came a good deal after I had learnt enough to tackle teaching those subjects ... Most of the evenings I prepared work for the next day, and was only free on Friday and Saturday evenings.[55]

The school consumed all female effort in the Greenwood household. Green recruited her sisters as teachers, and Green's mother did the cooking for pupils as well as for the family. With only one domestic servant and one laundress, 'hers was a very strenuous existence'.[56]

Small private schools that ran along the model of Louisa Greenwood's were common across the settler-colonial world. In Aotearoa/New Zealand, Miss Thornton and Miss Were-Aplin had a private school in suburban Wellington where Misses Mitchell also taught at their kindergarten and preparatory school. Miss C. Hayden had a school in nearby Lower Hutt.[57] Miss Harriet Stedman was 'proprietress of a private

---

[52] Papers of Annie Louisa Green, 1946–1947, National Library of Australia NLA/MS8574/ Recollections, 147–150.
[53] Green, Recollections, 149. [54] Ibid., 148–149. [55] Ibid., 147–150.
[56] Ibid., 149. [57] Advertisement, *Evening Post*, 8 February 1913, 2.

boarding school' in Whanganui.[58] In 1900 the Misses Parker announced that they would soon open a private school for boys on their property in another Wellington, this one in rural New South Wales.[59] In nearby Orange, the daughter of the local stationmaster, Miss Lovett, opened a school in 1908.[60] In North Queensland, the Misses Wright had a school in Mackay.[61] Miss Schroedinger owned a school in Adelaide and Mrs Bardon in Brisbane.[62]

Similar institutions dotted North America. Miss McLachlan had a private school in Alberta, Miss Gordon had one in Vancouver, and Miss Ermetrouts' private school was in Reading, Pennsylvania, where other women also ran schools, including Madame Ruenzler, Miss Benade, and the Misses Stewart.[63] In New York State, small private schools were owned by Miss Shannon in Rochester and Miss Hendrick in Middletown.[64] Women-run private schools also operated in Great Britain, like Miss Beale's Private School in Glasgow and Miss Chant's in Guernsey, but declined considerably after the 1902 Balfour Act, which – amidst bitter disputes between competing brands of Protestantism – established governmental authorities that helped standardize elementary and secondary schooling.[65] Some women-run schools did continue nevertheless, like Miss Lucy Reynolds' (whose advertising shows she held a BA with honours) and Miss Knight's private schools, both in London.[66]

Beginning from the late nineteenth century, women sometimes owned hospitals along a similar model to these schools. This 'home hospital' business structure was the brainchild of the man who became secretary of

[58] Obituary, *Manawatu Standard*, 7 March 1938, 11.
[59] *Wellington Times*, 26 March 1900, 2.
[60] *Glen Innes Examiner*, 5 April 1910, 2; *Leader*, 21 January 1908, 2.
[61] *Mackay Mercury*, 16 December 1905, 2.
[62] *South Australian Register*, 23 December 1899, 11; *Queensland Times, Ipswich Herald and General Advertiser*, 9 December 1899, 2.
[63] Advertising, *Calgary Herald*, 8 February 1913, 2; *Reading Times*, 2 September 1907, 7.
[64] *Vancouver Daily World*, 19 December 1902, 1; *Democrat and Chronicle*, 14 February 1914, 15; *Middletown Times-Press*, 24 March 1916, 10.
[65] *Glasgow Herald*, 9 June 1890, 7; *The Star* (*Guernsey*), 18 December 1890, 2; Annie Crombie, 'A Free Hand and Ready Help? The Supervision and Control of Elementary Education in Staffordshire *c.*1902–1914', *Oxford Review of Education* 28.2–3 (2002), 173–186; D. R. Pugh, 'English Nonconformity, Education and Passive Resistance 1903–1906', *History of Education* 19.4 (1990), 355–373; Roger Ottewill, 'Law Breaking in Hampshire as an Expression of Nonconformist Opposition to the Education Act 1902', *Family and Community History* 23.1 (2020), 42–54; Tony Taylor, 'Arthur Balfour and Educational Change: The Myth Revisited', *British Journal of Educational Studies* 42.2 (1994), 133–149.
[66] Advertisement, *The Guardian*, 13 July 1915, 1; The Hulme Grammar School, *The Guardian*, 27 June 1920, 6.

the share and loan department at the London Stock Exchange in 1880, Henry Burdett. Burdett's role is revealing of the social and financial networks which established the professional class. As a member of hospital boards and a prominent businessman, Burdett observed that professional care for wealthier patients in pleasant settings, where the stay was like being in an agreeable home, rather than institution, would relieve unwanted burdens on family members obliged to care for one another. Burdett's institutions became cottage hospitals, governed by local boards, but also home-style businesses that were quickly referred to as 'nursing homes'.[67] The latter evolved into facilities focused almost wholly to aged and sometimes disability care by the second half of the twentieth century.[68]

In considering the growing market for middle-class hospital care, Burdett further identified a new class of younger person who, in the case of illness, had no family on hand. These were the 'governesses and ... young men – clerks, students and the like – occupying lodgings often at a great distance from their homes'.[69] His observation applied across the Anglo world. As the global economy professionalized, cities worldwide were filling with single young people. Those who would once have worked in the family drapery business with a view to one day taking over, for instance, often now performed professional work. Young and single people converged on Boston, London, Vancouver, and Melbourne. They were not all lawyers and doctors: young men worked as clerks and, later, young women took employment as *typistes*.[70] Having left rural family homes, these young white-collar workers lived in lodgings like the ones Burdett alluded to in London. When they were injured or fell ill, their families were not nearby to help them.

American medical historian Morris Vogel described the emergence of small private hospitals in Boston, most of which he said were 'little more than boarding houses'. Vogel categorized in them in two groups: 'those run by nonprofessionals, mainly businesswomen, to profit on payments for room and board, and those owned by physicians, either as individuals or in groups'.[71] Vogel did not discuss nurses at all in his *Invention of the Modern Hospital*, but it is possible that, as was the case in Britain and Australia at least, some businesswomen were also nurses; it is likely that,

---

[67] Carruthers and Carruthers, *A History of Britain's Hospitals*, 219–249.
[68] Henry C. Burdett, 'Home Hospitals: Their Scope, Object and Management', *The British Medical Journal*, 25 August 1877, 243; on aged care, see Charlotte Greenhalgh, *Aging in Twentieth Century Britain* (Oakland, University of California Press, 2018).
[69] Burdett, 'Home Hospitals'.
[70] Zakim, *Accounting for Capitalism*, 85–121; Warne, *Agitate, Educate, Organize, Legislate*.
[71] Vogel, *Invention of the Modern Hospital*, 103.

at the very least, some performed nursing-type work in the care of boarders.

Advertising in US newspapers further shows an abundance of maternity hospitals and abortion clinics, many more than general home infirmaries. Ida von Schultz, for example, described herself as a licensed obstetrician in Chicago in 1906, with a 'fine private home'. She was just one of several. Mrs A. Becker also had a 'fine home', Mrs Swift's home was 'elegant', and a sanatorium was owned by a Mrs Dietrich who had '20 years' experience'. Mrs White's had a 'physician in attendance' and promised 'babies adopted'. Abortion was common, though usually described in euphemisms. Many spoke openly of the 'restoration' of 'monthly periods'. In Chicago, Dr Reed and Dr Martha Walker offered a $500 and $1000 'reward' respectively if their 'safe' and 'speedy relief' failed.[72]

In late nineteenth-century San Francisco, women ran similar businesses with advertisements that labelled themselves 'Mrs Dr'. While obstetrics and abortion were evidently core services, these women practitioners advertised other treatments as well. Mrs Dr Gwyer, for example, offered a 'safe and speedy cure for all monthly irregularities' but also a 'home in confinement', 'best treatment for rheumatism and paralysis', and a 'guaranteed cure for the morphine and liquor habit'. She was, the advertisement promised, 'a true friend to her sex'.[73] The American Medical Association, as historian Leslie Reagan has shown, was frequently embarrassed into anti-abortion action against medical practices offering women such 'friendship', often by the undercover reportage of the New Journalism. Eventually abortion was made illegal in most US states until 1973.[74]

Before the New Journalism pushed medicine into acting against abortion, such US businesses were advertised with seemingly few blushes. In Australia, by contrast, health practitioners went to considerable pains to stress that their women-owned private hospitals – including the approximately two-thirds that served as maternity homes – provided a respectable setting for those whose class status precluded them from being treated in public hospitals, but for whom healthcare at home was inconvenient or, for increasing numbers of the more-mobile middle-class, too far away.[75] Nurse Brandon's private hospital, for example,

---

[72] *The Inter Ocean (Chicago)*, 9 November 1906, 12.

[73] Advertisement, *The San Francisco Examiner*, 7 July 1893, 8.

[74] Leslie Reagan, *When Abortion was a Crime: Women, Medicine and the Law in the United States 1867–1973* (Berkley: University of California Press, 1997), 14 and 46–79.

[75] 'Private Hospitals', *Medical Journal of Australia*, 25 February 1918, 160.

was established in Sydney in 1899, where the sick and injured were 'kindly and skilfully treated', in 'well lighted rooms' with a view of Sydney Harbour. 'It is not run by doctors', the newspaper stressed, 'but by the nurse herself, though of course she occasionally receives patients from the doctors', several of whom were listed as supporters.[76]

In advertising Nurse Brandon's private hospital, the editors of the *Sydney Stock and Station Journal* were evidently conscious of the association between private hospitals and abortion, and sought to protect their own reputation:

This journal has always had the reputation of being clean, and containing none but straightforward, genuine advertisements. So it was only after careful investigation, and satisfying ourselves with the moral standing of Nurse Brandon's Private Hospital, that we consented to insert her advertisement – first as a matter of business, and, secondly, because it will be filling a longfelt [sic] want of a large number of our readers.[77]

The *Sydney Stock and Station Journal* was aimed at the 'squatter' class who owned sheep or cattle stations. These stations were and are extremely large: even with modern transport, those who live on the same stations today rarely see their neighbours, monitor their land holdings by helicopter, and school their children at the 'school of the air' or in faraway boarding schools.[78] Medical care on such stations was always difficult. In Sydney, Nurse Brandon employed nine nurses who were available to visit such homes in the country, although the advertisement specified that 'it is, of course, preferable to come to town'.[79] When visiting Sydney to see the doctor, it was, as another advertisement noted, 'awkward to have surgery in a hotel'.[80] Seeking medical assistance in Australia, dominated as it was by the 'tyranny of distance', often required a kind of travel that meant middle-class visitors to cities and towns augmented the demand from new middle-class young professionals.[81] Middle-class patients need not fear surgery in hospitals reserved for the poor, for Nurse Braddon, like many other private hospital owners, purchased the latest 'iron and glass' table for surgery in her home hospital, where trained nurses were on hand to assist in surgery and provide post-surgical care.[82]

[76] *Sydney Stock and Station Journal*, 10 January 1899, 2.
[77] *Sydney Stock and Station Journal*, 10 January 1899, 2.
[78] Phyllis Gibb, *Classrooms a World Apart: The Story of the Founding of the Broken Hill School of the Air* (Melbourne: Spectrum, 1986).
[79] *Sydney Stock and Station Journal*, 10 January 1899, 2.
[80] *Week* (Brisbane), 20 February 1891, 23.   [81] Blainey, *The Tyranny of Distance*.
[82] *Sydney Stock and Station Journal*, 10 January 1899, 2.

Hospitals like Nurse Braddon's spread throughout Australian cities and towns, almost all of them owned by women. Between around 1890 and 1939, women-owned private hospitals dominated healthcare in Australia.[83] They advertised in Australian newspapers and traded their businesses in the journal of the Australasian Nurses' Association. The prices for hospitals varied considerably, based on number of beds and location, though – unlike similar trade in medical practices in the *Medical Journal of Australia* – nurses typically gave few details of annual income or other indicators of profitability, instead inviting personal contact. In some towns, journalists regularly reported on the progress of patients, which helps give some idea of the breadth of medical services offered. In 1912, at Nurse Stokes' private hospital in Orange, Abe Baker 'passed through amputation successfully'; a little boy had a sore throat; Cecil Toms had pneumonia; and 'Mr Burton's son' suffered from blood poisoning; he was reportedly recovering well a week later.[84]

Similar private hospitals were less widespread in Britain, though for a few decades from the 1890s onwards, it was fashionable for respectable women to establish nursing homes. These were not always as profitable as such women hoped. A 1905 article in the British *Nursing Times* described the costs of establishing a private hospital and the preconditions to commercial success. The author gave details regarding bookkeeping, the timing of the purchase of consumables, recreation spaces for nursing and domestic staff, the kind of portable table to procure if a surgical theatre was unaffordable, and the ideal location in the home for medical and pharmaceutical supplies. These all offer a useful picture of the private home hospital. The key to success, however, was the nurse's relationship with local medical men. On the 'vital and inevitable question whether [the local medical doctor] will give her work', the author was firm:

> The doctor will not willfully mislead [but] the nurse's own buoyant hopefulness may – and take good heed that it is an *absolute* statement that he is making – that he *has* patients to send, and *will* send them, and not a mere polite intimation ... if [mere promises] form the chief basis of support on the doctor's side, don't start a home![85]

This alliance between medical men and middle-class nurses is evident throughout the records. Locally, medical men and women – both medical doctors and trained nurses – collaborated across their individual businesses to provide middle-class care, while physicians and surgeons

---

[83] 'Private Hospitals', *Medical Journal of Australia*, 25 February 1918, 160.
[84] *Leader* (*Orange*), 26 January 1912, 2; *Leader*, 3 January 1912, 4; *Leader*, 10 January 1912, 3.
[85] 'How to Start a Nursing Home', *The Nursing Times*, 29 May 1905, 46–47.

worked in honorary positions in hospitals as a gesture to their traditional charity status. Medical journals in the 1920s included memories of nearly lost days where the typical doctor worked from home as a solo practitioner for life, perhaps becoming a specialist 'consultant' late in their career, though even this was frequently only as a supplement to their general practice. Large hospitals played a rather marginal role in healthcare provision outside surgery, except in so far as providing free care to the poorer classes. Medical practitioners still performed most treatments themselves. Local private hospitals offered post-operative and other nursing care.[86]

The Australasian Trained Nurses Association, perhaps as an expression of their shared class status, expected the medical profession to support them. The implicit alliance between doctors and professional nurses, however, was sometimes breached. Members of the Association complained, for example, when local medical practitioners referred patients to hospitals run by untrained women. In one case, a medical practitioner who had been a patient in a registered private hospital wrote to the journal to suggest that nurses should object more resoundingly when a medical doctor, as his did, attended the private hospital charging 100 guineas (more than US$6,000 in 2020 terms) for a half hour of surgery, of which the attending nurse received 6s 8d – the equivalent of around US$20 in 2020.[87]

Such trained nurses working in women-owned private hospitals across Australasia performed a similar role to private duty nurses in North America. Young Canadian women completed their nursing training in hospitals, but on graduation most nurses went into private practice. These nurses advertised their services in local registries and were contracted to individual patients. Healthcare was often provided in the patient's home, though from 1900 onwards hospitals were increasing in popularity and some private nurses cared for their individual patient in the hospital. Canadian hospitals relied very heavily on student nurses, who in the first decades of the twentieth century were paid between CA $8 and CA$12 per month, compared to the graduate nurse rate of around CA$25 a week. As demand for hospital care increased, hospitals increased their student intake.[88] The dominance of private duty nursing in North America kept professional women close to the domestic

---

[86] A. C. F. Halford, 'Medical Practice of To-Day', *Medical Journal of Australia*, 15 October 1921, 303–306; 'A Retrospect', *Medical Journal of Australia*, 6 January 1923, 15–19; R. B. Wade, 'An Address', *Medical Journal of Australia*, 13 October 1923, 377–378.

[87] George Brown, 'Candid Critics', *The Australasian Nurses' Journal*, August 1924, 399–400.

[88] McPherson, *Bedside Matters*, 26–73.

sphere – just as private hospitals (and for that matter, private schools) did elsewhere. Even in the growing hospitals, private rooms and kitchens where nurses practised invalid cookery often resembled homes.[89]

Growth in demand for hospital care, particularly among the middle class, transformed medicine in the first half of the twentieth century. Historians of medicine usually see this as key to the modernization of healthcare, though the causes remain unclear. Some have posited that improvements in anaesthesia and other surgical technologies were responsible. Pain management surely made surgery more attractive, though historians have also pointed out that technological change did not make medicine terribly more efficacious, at least for some time. Other historians have suggested the boosterism of the medical establishment was responsible. Certainly, the expansion of hospital care coincides with their increased influence, and with the decline of 'quacks' (see Chapter 3).[90] No single explanation is really fulfilling, though with few exceptions most historians look to male-dominated medicine for explanations. Trained nursing is more rarely given as a key middle-class draw-card, nor indeed the decline in domestic service altogether, which previously dominated women's work in charity hospitals. Most nevertheless agree that trained nurses became necessary once middle-class people attended hospitals.[91]

The expansion of the large, modern hospital had the effect of moving most nursing care from this precarious private duty work to more stable employment in hospitals.[92] In Australia in 1891, only 16 per cent of nurses worked in hospitals. By 1911, 37 per cent of nurses worked in hospitals, a proportion that kept rising thereafter.[93] We cannot know for certain why middle-class people began to seek more healthcare in hospitals, but we do know that their presence expanded medical services. In the end, the smaller, more domestic-like spaces they initially preferred gave way to the efficiencies afforded by larger hospitals with more beds and, eventually, open 'industrialized' wards. The fact that the office became similarly more open in firms expanding in scale at the same time points to a growing preference for clean, flat, open, and scientific enterprises over older, more ornate, individualized spaces.

[89] Ibid., 38.

[90] Starr, *Social Transformation of American Medicine*, 60–78; Dingwall, Rafferty and Webster, *Social History of Nursing*, 71; Abel-Smith, *Hospitals*, 189, 339.

[91] Whelan, 'Private Duty Nursing'.   [92] Ibid., 414.

[93] Australian Colonial Censuses 1891, 1901; Australian Census 1911.

Spreading Virtue

The scale and scope of industrial enterprise was the subject of economic historian Alfred Chandler's classic exposition of the growth of modern capitalist businesses. Chandler argued that organizational capacity was the key to the relative competitiveness of German and American industrial enterprise, over the 'personal capitalism' that characterized British business in the early twentieth century. This expansive enterprise had a 'fundamental role', Chandler suggested, 'in the transformation of Western economies'.[94] Chandler's work helps here, to see that the transformation of professional life from a bourgeois system where people owned their own small business to salaried roles in larger organizations was a symptom, not of Taylorist surveillance, but of expansion itself. This helps explain why professionals supported a shift in pay structure that could have reduced their status and reward. Their support for this 'proletarianizing' change was not false consciousness, as political economists have sometimes claimed. Nor did it reduce their status, overall. Rather, professionals supported expansion out of a desire to extend the influence of each profession. For the professional class, more education, healthcare, auditing, business planning, and social services was obviously better than less – better for society and for them. Massive expansion, even industrialization, of professional work gave the professional class the opportunity to spread virtue into every corner of the Anglo world.

In this context, the expansion of schooling coincided, a little paradoxically, with the end of factory-like monitorial systems. The monitorial system was purposely modelled on the factory by Scottish Episcopalian Andrew Bell and English Quaker Joseph Lancaster and then spread throughout the Anglo world. In the monitorial schoolroom, rote learning was achieved by chanting and older children – monitors – each instructed a row of younger children, under the teacher's masterful surveillance.[95] Even before this widespread and highly efficient system for teaching basic literacy and mathematics, the orderly schoolroom was a tool for teaching

---

[94] Alfred Chandler, *Scale and Scope: The Dynamics of Industrial Capitalism* (Cambridge, MA: Harvard University Press, 1994), 3, 593–630.

[95] Michel Foucault, *Discipline and Punish: The Birth of the Prison* (Harmondsworth: Penguin, 1979), 212; Leopoldo Mesquita, 'The Lancasterian Monitorial System as an Education Industry with a Logic of Capitalist Valorisation', *Paedagogica Historica* 48.5 (2012), 661–675; Joakim Landahl, 'Learning to Listen and Look: The Shift from the Monitorial System of Education to Teacher-Lead Lessons', *The Senses & Society* 14.2 (2019), 194–206; Sue Middleton, 'Schooling the Labouring Classes: Children, Families, and Learning in Wellington, 1840–1845', *International Studies in Sociology of Education* 18.2 (2008), 133–146; Helen May, *School Beginnings: A Nineteenth Century Colonial Story* (Wellington, NZ: NZCER Press, 2005).

children industrialized work habits.[96] Theoretically, in the late nineteenth century, this was changing. A progressive movement known as the 'New Education' was increasingly influential across the Anglo world, influenced by European thinkers Friedrich Fröbel and Maria Montessori who argued that schooling needed to acknowledge children's uniqueness.[97] Utilizing the language of 'scientific education', schooling systems began – at least on paper – to encourage teachers to build relationships with their pupils.[98]

Rather than stressing such individual relationships with students, influential American progressive John Dewey argued for empirical foundations for student learning – workshops and practical classes – and for the professionalization of teaching. Dewey's timing was good. In the 1890s and 1900s, he gave moral and pedagogical justification for the professionalization that was already under way, worldwide. For teachers of Louisa Greenwood's ilk, who ran their own school as a small business, such professionalization entangled their future prospects with their acceptance by the educational establishment. This pushed would-be teachers towards compliance with and employment in the bigger institutions that governed the profession.

Larger schools enhanced each nation's capacity to grow education. The number of years children typically attended school grew very rapidly. Growth in the mean years of schooling increased across the Anglo world, led by the United States, which grew education from a mean of 3.7 years in 1870 to 8.3 years in 1940. They were followed closely by

[96] Goldin, 'The Human-Capital Century'; Clara Núñez, 'Literacy, Schooling and Economic Modernization: A Historian's Approach', *Paedagogica Historica* 39.5 (2003), 535–558; Raymond Williams, *Marx and Literature* (Oxford: Oxford University Press, 1977); Robert Davis, James Conroy, and Julie Clague, 'Schools as Factories: The Limits of a Metaphor', *Journal of Philosophy of Education* 54.5 (2020), 1471–1488.

[97] Lawrence Cremin, *The Transformation of the School: Progressivism in American Education, 1876–1957* (New York: Knopf, 1961); Larry Cuban, *How Teachers Taught: Constancy and Change in American Classrooms 1890–1980* (New York: Longman, 1984); Richard Selleck, *The New Education: The English Background* (London: Pitman, 1968); Helen May, Kristen Nawrotzki, and Larry Prochner (eds), *Kindergarten Narratives on Froebelian Education: Transnational Investigations* (London, Bloomsbury, 2018); Monica Van Aken, 'The History of Montessori Education in America, 1909–2004', unpublished Ed. D Dissertation, University of Virginia (2004); Alan Barcan, *A History of Australian Education* (Oxford: Oxford University Press, 1980), 274–283; Patricia Graham, *Progressive Education from Arcady to Academe: A History of the Progressive Education Association 1919–1955* (New York: Teachers College Press, 1967).

[98] Albert Austin, *Australian Education 1788–1900* (Melbourne: Pitman, 1972), 173–237; Celia Jenkins, 'New Education and Its Emancipatory Interests (1920–1950)', *History of Education (Tavistock)* 29.2 (2000), 139–151; Kevin Brehony, 'A New Education for a New Era: The Contribution of the Conferences of the New Education Fellowship to the Disciplinary Field of Education 1921–1938', *Paedagogica Historica* 40.5–6 (2004), 733–755.

Aotearoa/New Zealand. Great Britain was at the bottom, with an average of just 0.8 years in 1870, though the gap between this and the United States narrowed by 1940, when the mean years of education was 5.7; see Figure 4.1.[99]

Standardization affected schooling from high-school levels down to the newly emerging kindergartens. American progressive kindergarten reformer Patty Smith Hill – responsible for innovations like building blocks and singing 'happy birthday' – not only introduced Fröbel-inspired pedagogical reforms but also sought 'the integration of an originally woman-led institution into mainstream academic and governmental structures under male leadership'.[100] The professionalization of teaching, alongside the pressures of efficiency that the expanding schooling systems demanded, kept schooling on its industrializing pathway, even in the face of progressive reform. Classrooms remained uniform, student behaviour was still subjected to disciplining surveillance, syllabi were increasingly controlled by school boards and not the teacher, and industrial time-discipline continually imparted. Women continued to dominate teaching, but they did so far less often in schools that they also owned or controlled.[101]

Hospitals underwent the same change. In North America, Abraham Flexner's 1910 report for the Carnegie Foundation, prepared at the behest of the increasingly muscular medical establishment, standardized and constrained medical education and the registration of teaching hospitals.[102] Medical training was restricted to a smaller number of elite universities, now requiring six to eight years of education that included both theoretical and practical training.[103] Notoriously, this closed access to medical training for American women and restricted access for people of colour.[104] On the back of the moral panic the American Medical Association spread about abortion, women medical practitioners and,

[99] Jong-Wha Lee and Hanol Lee, 'Human Capital in the Long Run,' *Journal of Development Economics* 122 (2016), 147–169; Robert Barro and Jong-Wha Lee, 'A New Data Set of Educational Attainment in the World, 1950–2010', *Journal of Development Economics* 104 (2013), 184–198.

[100] Allen, 'Gender, Professionalization, and the Child in the Progressive Era'.

[101] Barbara Fedders, 'The Constant and Expanding Classroom: Surveillance in K-12 Public Schools', *North Carolina Law Review* 97.6 (2019), 1673–1725; Perpetua Kirby, 'Children's Agency in the Modern Primary Classroom', *Children & Society* 34.1 (2020), 17–30.

[102] Abraham Flexner, *Medical Education in the United States and Canada: A Report to the Carnegie Foundation for the Advancement of Teaching* (New York: Carnegie Foundation, 1910); Steven Wheatley, *The Politics of Philanthropy: Abraham Flexner and Medical Education* (Madison: University of Wisconsin Press, 1988).

[103] Flexner, *Medical Education in the United States and Canada*, 21–27.

[104] Hine, *Black Women in White*.

arguably, women's medicine were pushed out of medicine just as surely as bourgeois nursing eliminated Sairey Gamp (see Chapter 3).[105] The medical establishment credited Flexner with boosting healthcare standards, though similar transformations were under way in Britain as well as in Australia and Aotearoa/New Zealand.[106] Carnegie's tentacles, so influential in the Flexner changes, reached into the Pacific, but were focused to education, including libraries, not medical training.[107] Hospitals in New South Wales expanded after legislation required registration of hospitals for the purposes of nurse training, so that all nurses were educated in hospitals with a minimum of eight beds. This was a result of lobbying by the Australasian Trained Nurses' Association and was in part intended to enclose hospital services, restricting registration to their members.[108]

By the 1920s, Australian medical practitioners had fought off post–First World War plans to nationalize medicine and used union-derived strategies to undermine the Friendly Societies whose employment of doctors reduced the costs of medical care to working and lower-middle-class families, but also reduced some doctors' income.[109] Now doctors faced what they called the 'hospital problem'. Hospitals were increasingly high-tech centres of advanced medicine rather than places to provide charity to the poor. In response, the medical establishment squabbled over how to provide wider access to hospitals without hurting their own bottom line. This was a problem that they faced in tandem with state governments, whose royal commissions and inquiries formed the background for medicine's internal debates. As demand expanded and expectations grew for coherent, systemic, and affordable healthcare,

---

[105] Angel Kwollek-Folland, *Incorporating Women: A History of Women and Business in the United States* (New York: Palgrave, 2002), 96–106; Reagan, *When Abortion was a Crime*.

[106] Andrew Beck, 'The Flexner Report and the Standardization of American Medical Education', *The Journal of the American Medical Association* 291.17 (2004), 2139–2140.

[107] Mary Carroll, 'Republic of the Learned', *History of Education* 38.6 (2009), 809–823; Bill Green, 'Carnegie in Australia: Philanthropic Power and Public Education in the Early Twentieth Century', *History of Education Review* 48.1 (2019), 61–74; Michael White, 'Carnegie Philanthropy in Australia in the Nineteen Thirties – A Reassessment', *History of Education Review* 26.1 (1997), 1–24; Ellen Lagemann, *The Politics of Knowledge: The Carnegie Corporation, Philanthropy, and Public Policy* (Middletown: Wesleyan University Press, 1989); Edward Berman, *The Ideology of Philanthropy: the Influence of the Carnegie, Ford, and Rockefeller Foundations on American Foreign Policy* (Albany: State University of New York Press, 1983).

[108] 'Private Hospitals Act 1908', *Government Gazette of the State of New South Wales*, 8 September 1909, Issue 120, 4937.

[109] David Green, 'The 1918 Strike of the Medical Profession against the Friendly Societies in Victoria', *Labour History* 46 (1984), 72–87; Gillespie, *Price of Health*.

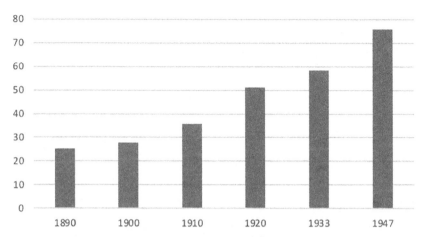

Figure 4.2 Average beds per public hospital in New South Wales
1890–1947. *Data source*: NSW Yearbook

governments across the Anglo world found themselves – often reluc-
tantly – subsidizing growing hospitals.[110] In New South Wales, the
average public hospital grew from twenty-five beds per hospital in
1890 to seventy-six beds per hospital in 1947; see Figure 4.2. Nurses
complained that this growth in public hospital care undermined their
businesses, particularly because it provided healthcare to their own
middle-class market.[111] This was not wholly true at the time they complained: the number of private hospitals, mostly women-owned, continued to grow in New South Wales until the Second World War – see
Figure 4.3. Nevertheless, the expansion of hospital care for the middle
class did not always, as some historians have claimed, push poor and
working-class people out.[112] In many ways this was because of the rise of
almoners/medical social workers, who began the task of systematizing
charity for an industrial world.

---

[110] McPherson, *Bedside Matters*, 135–136; Gillespie, *Price of Health*; Anne Crichton, *Slowly
Taking Control? Australian Governments and Health Care Provision 1788–1988* (Sydney:
Allen & Unwin 1990); Vogel, *Invention of the Modern Hospital*, 120–132; Abel-Smith,
Hospitals; Starr, *Social Transformation of American Medicine*, 27–29; Eugene Vayda,
Robert Evans, and William Mindell, 'Universal Health Insurance in Canada: History,
Problems, Trends', *Journal of Community Health* 4.3 (1979): 217–231.
[111] 'Union for Nurses' (Letter to the Editor), *Australasian Nurses' Journal*, 18 March 1919,
80–81.
[112] George Gosling, *Payment and Philanthropy in British Healthcare 1918–1948*
(Manchester: Manchester University Press, 2017).

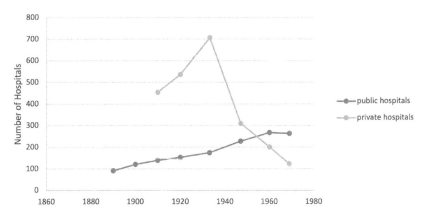

Figure 4.3 Public and private hospitals in New South Wales
1890–1969. *Data source*: NSW Yearbook

Scientific Charity and Industrial Medicine for a Modernizing Economy

Hospital-based social work had its origins in the Charity Organisation Society, which was formed in the mid-nineteenth century to rationalize charitable donation. Their goal was to prevent charity 'dependency' by reducing opportunity to access donations, filtering multiple sources of assistance through one institution.[113] This society established medical social work, appointing what was known as the 'Lady Almoner' to the Royal Free Hospital in London in 1895. Rather than requiring a letter of recommendation from a hospital subscriber, admission to the Royal Free Hospital was based on need, particularly financial need. Miss Mary Stewart, a trusted member of the Charity Organisation Society, was paid a very high annual salary of £125 to be Lady Almoner, assessing the requirements and deservedness of hospital outpatients. The intention

---

[113] Peel, *Miss Cutler and the Case of the Resurrected Horse*; Richard Kennedy, *Charity Warfare: The Charity Organisation Society in Colonial Melbourne* (Melbourne: Hyland House, 1985); Bernard Harris, *The Origins of the British Welfare State: Society, State and Social Welfare in England and Wales, 1800–1945* (Basingstoke: Palgrave Macmillan, 2004), 54–58; Gareth Jones, *Outcast London: A Study of the Relationship between Classes in Victorian Society* (London: Verso, 2013); Peter Mandler, 'Poverty and Charity in the Nineteenth Century Metropolis', in Peter Mandler (ed.), *Uses of Charity* (Philadelphia: University of Pennsylvania Press, 1990), 1–37; Jane Lewis, *The Voluntary Sector, the State, and Social Work in Britain: The Charity Organisation Society/Family Welfare Association Since 1869* (Brookfield: Edward Elgar, 1995).

was that the almoner would act 'as a deterrent to potential abusers of the free treatment available at the hospital'.[114] A training school grew at St Thomas's Hospital, training almoners for British hospitals and acted as the model for medical social work in North America and Australasia.[115]

North American hospitals used the label 'medical social work' over almonry, a description that became preferred everywhere as social workers elsewhere in the Anglo world adapted their North American colleagues' commitment to scientific rationality over charity.[116] The task of distancing themselves from old-fashioned charity work helped expand the scope of hospital almonry. The almoner quickly earned her keep not only by saving the hospital 'unnecessary' expense but by also helping patients become well, sometimes by accessing a range of charities. This, as one *New Zealand Herald* article demonstrated, was not just a result of social work's well-documented shift in scientific consciousness, but it was also a consequence of the centralization of healthcare in larger hospitals. In 1931, the newspaper explained:

The doctor in private practice knows his patient's family and surroundings. He uses this knowledge to assist him in arranging treatment. But the hospital physician cannot know anything of his patients, and very often he realises that it is not entirely medical treatment they need most.[117]

Larger, more impersonal healthcare institutions were matched with increased systematization everywhere. In medical care, this produced a new field of work:

A man wants a splint or a pair of crutches. These are not supplied by the hospital, but the almoner finds means of obtaining them. Perhaps a neurotic woman cannot be cured without a month or two on a farm, with plenty of fresh air and peaceful surroundings. The almoner arranges this. The hospital doctor cannot acquire necessary information as to his patient's home surroundings ... He can

---

[114] Lynsey Cullen, 'The First Lady Almoner: The Appointment, Position and Findings of Miss Mary Stewart at the Royal Free Hospital 1895–99', *Journal of the History of Medicine and Allied Sciences* 68.4 (2013), 551–582.

[115] Bell, *Hospital Almoners*; Kathleen Woodroofe, *From Charity to Social Work in England and the United States* (London: Routledge and Kegan Paul, 1962); Ivey, 'Becoming a Social Worker', 11–29.

[116] Jane Miller and David Nicholls, 'Establishing a Twentieth Century Women's Profession', *Lilith: A Feminist History Journal* 20 (2014): 21–33; Angela Woollacott, 'From Moral to Professional Authority: Secularism, Social Work, and Middle-Class Women's Self-Construction in World War I Britain', *Journal of Women's History* 10.2 (1998), 85–111; Woodroofe, *From Charity to Social Work*; Lawrence, *Professional Social Work in Australia*.

[117] 'Hospital Almoners', *New Zealand Herald*, 31 March 1931, 13.

count on the almoner obtaining it, and thus light may be thrown on the contributory causes of disease.[118]

From a question of the rational management of charity – how to ensure aid reached those whom middle-class assessors deemed *deserving* – arose a field that systematized what home-visiting medical doctors and nurses had been doing as a matter of individual relationship with patients.[119] Like Rainsford's uncluttered desk with fewer pigeonholes and drawers in which to stash the chaos of an array of individual relationships with unique clients, the move of medical care from home visits and home-like institutions to larger, more industrial organizations demanded a more scientific set of techniques for the management of increasingly unfamiliar patients.

For the medical profession, the move to larger institutions was coupled with the growth of a new partnership with capital that sought explicitly to keep working bodies working. The 'hospital problem' in the 1920s was paired with industrial medicine as key signifiers of a rapidly changing healthcare system. Industrial medicine was the logical extension of the medical services that first served empires and then sought systemic changes, such as sanitation, for the improvement of public health.[120] There was significant 'value to the employer and employee,' argued Dr Ivan Blaubaum, 'of an efficient scheme of medical supervision in industrial enterprises.' Blaubaum worked for Barnet Glass's rubber factory in North Melbourne, which made products that included rubber 'baptist trousers' for clergy performing baptisms by immersion.[121] Australian industrial medicine, Blaubaum mourned, was nowhere near as advanced as it was in America. There, medical experts advised on work environment, including 'lighting, ventilation, cleanliness … and prevention and treatment of accidents'. In the Southern Hemisphere, however, 'the smallness of industrial concerns' meant even relatively large companies, like Glass's rubber manufacturing, could employ only a part-time

---

[118] Ibid.

[119] Shurlee Swain, 'Negotiating Poverty: Women and Charity in Nineteenth-Century Melbourne', *Women's History Review* 16.1 (2007), 99–112; Jonathan Reinarz, 'Investigating the "Deserving Poor": Charity and the Voluntary Hospitals in Nineteenth-Century Birmingham', in Anne Borsay and Peter Shapely (eds), *Medicine, Charity and Mutual Aid: The Consumption of Health and Welfare in Britain c.1550–1950* (London: Ashgate, 2007), 111–129.

[120] Starr, *Social Transformation of American Medicine*, 180–197; Gillespie, *Price of Health*, 31–56; Anderson, *The Cultivation of Whiteness*.

[121] Kathleen Thomson, 'Glass, Barnet (1849–1918)', *Australian Dictionary of Biography*, *Volume 9* (Melbourne: Melbourne University Press, 1983).

doctor.[122] Blaubaum visited the factory for an hour each day, he said, treating minor injuries associated with work, advising on sanitation, guiding policy in case of epidemics (the 1918/19 influenza pandemic was a recent memory, though in fact a key problem was diphtheria), examining new applicants to ensure they were physically capable of the work and also examining 'employees who show a falling off in their capacity to work'. Among the advantages that Blaubaum cited was that the manager knew how long a sick employee should be off work, 'removing or minimizing certain causes of lost time' and the 'detection of malingerers'.[123] Industrial nurses were important too, though as Lucy Taksa argues, they introduced gendered power dimensions that opened new possibilities for labour resistance against the 'clinical gaze'.[124]

Industrial medicine thus became an instrument of scientific management.[125] It had some antecedents. British medical practitioners began considering occupational diseases in the eighteenth century, observing the new dangers that emerged in factories and mines.[126] In North America, the expansion of railways made for dangerous work so that railway companies established clinics and hospitals along their lines. Paul Starr says that there were more than 6,000 surgeons who specialized in rail-related injuries.[127] Similarly, in outback Australia, in response to serious mine accidents and respiratory and other diseases resulting from the lead-laden dust released by blasting, Broken Hill Proprietary built a hospital.[128] Employee medical services were integrated into the corporate paternalism that became known as 'welfare capitalism'.[129] In companies and industries that pursued welfare capitalism, medical services

---

[122] Ivan Blaubaum, 'Industrial Medicine', *Medical Journal of Australia*, 26 November 1921, 481.

[123] Ibid.

[124] Lucy Taksa, 'Handmaiden of Industrial Welfare or Armed Combatant Considering the Experience of Industrial Nursing at the Eveleigh Railway Workshops', *Health and History* 1.4 (1999), 298–329.

[125] Maarten Derksen, 'Turning Men into Machines? Scientific Management, Industrial Psychology, and the "Human Factor"', *Journal of the History of the Behavioural Sciences* 50.2 (2014), 148–165.

[126] H. Buess, 'The Beginnings of Industrial Medicine in England', *British Journal of Industrial Medicine* 19.4 (1962), 297–302.

[127] Star, *Social Transformation of American Medicine*, 201.

[128] Forsyth, 'Class, Professional Work, and the History of Capitalism in Broken Hill'.

[129] Gøsta Esping-Anderon, *The Three Worlds of Welfare Capitalism* (Princeton: Princeton University Press, 1990); Stuart Brandes, *American Welfare Capitalism 1880–1920* (Chicago: Chicago University Press, 1976); Charles Fahey and John Lack, 'Silent Forms of Coercion: Welfare Capitalism, State Labour Regulation and Collective Action at the Yarraville Sugar Refinery 1890–1925', *Labour History* 101 (2011), 105–122; Sandford Jacoby, *Modern Manors: Welfare Capitalism since the New Deal* (Princeton: Princeton University Press, 1997).

were just part of constellation of services for workers and their families, which could include company housing, schools, picnic days, and leisure parks. Importantly, these positioned workers as citizens of corporations. This not only reduced industrial unrest; it also likely accelerated the growing belief – especially palpable for veterans of the recent world war – that healthcare was a right of citizenship.[130]

Industrial medicine, 'applied to the purpose of preventing and alleviating sickness and injury among industrial workers in order that they may enjoy the benefits of continuous productive employment', became entangled with new questions about the traditional value medicine placed on rest and leisure for recovery. 'A person's ill-health is often ascribed to overwork when it might as readily be concerned with over indulgence in more harmful pursuits,' argued Regius Professor of Medicine at Oxford University, Sir Edward Farquar Buzzard, whose views were reported across the Anglo world. It was time American medicine re-evaluated 'when and how rest and recreation should be prescribed, and continuance of work advised'. Work, the anonymous conveyer of Buzzard's thesis in Australia claimed, was 'the curse of Adam' but 'the blessing of mankind'.[131]

This logic pertained to the work of medical practitioners as well as industrial workers whose productivity medicine sought to protect. Just as, for accountants, scientific management was to be applied to one's own time-as-capital, so too was the medical practitioner exhorted to prescribe themselves virtuous forms of rest:

The weary medical practitioner at the end of a day of worrying toil is apt to submit to what he imagines are the demands of his body for rest. He should realize that his fatigue is mental rather than physical ... At night the medical practitioner may best relieve his mental fatigue by utilizing fresh avenues for thought.[132]

It further mattered that these avenues of not-rest be suitably virtuous. As medical reporters exhorted readers of newspapers across North America, Farquar Buzzard advised 'the pursuit of art, science or literature', in place of rest.[133]

This was no mere criticism of the long-standing prescription of rest and leisure; it was an exhortation for the medical profession itself to boost

---

[130] Sandford Jacoby, *Employing Bureaucracy: Managers, Unions, and the Transformation of Work in the Twentieth Century* (Mahwah: Lawrence Erlbaum Associates, 2004), 29–48.
[131] 'Rest, Work and Play', *Medical Journal of Australia*, 9 March 1931, 567–568.
[132] Ibid.
[133] For instance, *The Brooklyn Citizen*, 6 August 1932, 4; *The Kingston Daily Freeman*, 1 August 1932, 4; *Evening Star* (Washington), 1 August 1932, 27.

its collective investment in human capital. Such pursuit of professional development was seen, by one author for the *Medical Journal of Australia*, to replenish reserves worn away by work. Just as businesses completed annual stocktakes, so should the medical practitioner take stock of their own human capital:

In his mental stocktaking, in drawing up his profit and loss account, the medical practitioner has to consider his income and expenditure – his income in knowledge of disease, his use of that knowledge to build up reserves of wisdom and his expenditure in the application of knowledge and wisdom to relieve human suffering and add to the common storehouse of medical science.[134]

This investment was taking place during a difficult time for medicine. Diminished incomes during the Great Depression made practice very stressful for many doctors, as it did for everyone else. Such increases in the investment of professional time in the accumulation of rapidly advancing medical knowledge was grounded in the 'potent interrelation', as one medical journal correspondent put it, 'between the body human, the body economic, and the body spiritual'.[135] The professional class answer to the economic slump was harder work offset by purely virtuous leisure, investments they believed to be ultimately profitable to themselves and to society. In time, this would require constant increases in education as professional specialties sought distinction by ever-rising credentials. Such applications of industrial medicine to themselves show, however, that as well as skimming profit from capitalist enterprise, this Taylor-style medicine also promoted a widespread, embodied vision of the professional class's moral order, applied inwardly.

Conclusion

In the late nineteenth and early twentieth centuries, most professional work was performed in traditional bourgeois businesses – small home-based healthcare businesses and schools, small accountancy and legal partnerships, one-man newspapers. As this changed, with growing schools, hospitals, law firms, business enterprises, and media empires, the structure of employment and the management of work changed dramatically. This chapter has showed the ways this transformation was reflected materially in the wide flat desk, neat orderly rows of desks in offices and schools and of beds in larger hospital wards. It was also

---

[134] 'Stocktaking', *Medical Journal of Australia*, 27 June 1931, 787.
[135] MB ChB, 'An Economic Commentary and Diagnosis' (Letter to the Editor), *Medical Journal of Australia*, 18 March 1933, 356; see also Swain, 'Negotiating Poverty', 105.

reflected in increasingly orderly work practices, some inspired by scientific management, which were connected to the entire moral enterprise attached to professional work.

This 'search for order' or 'professional ideal' embodied in scientific management of the professional self and its expansive institutions was not merely rhetorical.[136] 'Idealism', historian Robert H. Wiebe showed, supplied the 'superstructure' of the 'philosopher-kings, the rational public, the social consensus'.[137] This is true, but industrialized expansion of the scale and scope of professional enterprise, not idealism, was the material force that made this happen. This material expansion, shaped by rational efficiencies affected by industrial work habits, transformed the business structures within which professional work was performed. Some professional organizations fought to retain a fee-for-service, rather than salaried form of income, as we will see in Chapter 5, but for the most part professionals supported the growth of enterprises that made them a salaried class. This was because it also enabled professionals to extend their virtuous influence through society and the economy. Professional solutions to the social and economic problems of the Depression era, like auditing, education, welfare, and public health, seemed so moral, so justifiable on rational as well as moral grounds. As a result, virtue capitalism became embedded throughout the economy and permeated the modern state. Their relationship to the state is the subject of Chapter 5.

---

[136] Perkin, *Rise of Professional Society*, 116–170.   [137] Wiebe, *Search for Order*, 162.

Part II

Managing the Global Economy, *c.*1945–1975

5   Angels of the State

'While we have heard a certain amount of ribald laughter about the use of brains in Government,' US president Franklin D. Roosevelt said of his newly established 'brain trust' from Columbia University in 1934, 'it seems to be good practice. It will be continued. We are going to call on trained people. Ability, rather than politics, enters into most of the choices made in our Government.'[1] Across the Atlantic, prioritizing expertise made sense to the former British prime minister, David Lloyd George, too. His 'new deal' for Britain, proposed one year after Roosevelt's, sought to overcome the ravages of war and economic depression, brought about by the forces he summarized as 'Mars', referring to the ancient god of war, and 'Mammon', a biblical term for money. 'In 1914 the God of War sent the world reeling through the gates of hell,' he said. 'The God of Money has since been completing the tragedy.'[2] Lloyd George was unable to persuade even his own party of a rethink of the logics of government and capitalism, but the idea simmered anyway. In 1945, with intellectual support from a report drafted by William Beveridge, Labour prime minister Clement Attlee brought Britain's welfare state into being.[3] The welfare state captured a desire that was felt across the world in the wake of two world wars and the Great Depression, for government based on expertise, directed to collective welfare rather than expressing vested interests.[4] In this welfare state, Mars and Mammon were to be set aside, and the global economy ruled by the rationality of the professional class. The age of experts had arrived.[5]

---

[1] 'President Roosevelt's Brain Trust Address', *Buffalo Evening News*, 21 June 1934, 8.
[2] 'Mr Lloyd George's Speech: Full Report of First Outline of the "New Deal"', *The Guardian*, 18 January 1935, 4.
[3] Asa Briggs, 'The Welfare State in Historical Perspective', *European Journal of Sociology* 2.2 (1961), 221–258.
[4] Briggs, 'The Welfare State in Historical Perspective', 221.
[5] On technocracy, see Timothy Mitchell, *Rule of Experts: Egypt, Techno-Politics, Modernity* (Berkeley: University of California Press, 2002).

The Anglo settler colonies were remarkably influential in shaping this era. Canadian, Aotearoa/New Zealander, and Australian bureaucrats drew on their progressive, 'social laboratory' traditions to negotiate key elements of the agreements built at Hot Springs in 1943, which established the Food and Agriculture Organization, and Bretton Woods in 1944, leading to the International Monetary Fund and the World Bank.[6] The Bretton Woods conference made US dollars the world's currency of trade, which among other things put America in the position of managing global stability. This chapter is not mainly about such influential planners, seen from the top, though we do need to understand the ways in which familiar individuals like Bretton Woods economists John Maynard Keynes (British Delegation), Harry Dexter White (US Treasury Department), Louis Rasminsky (Bank of Canada), and H. C. Coombs (Australian Department of Post-War Reconstruction) fashioned a world that deepened the connection between professional experts and the modern state.[7]

There are three main ways in which I explore the question of professionals and the modern state in this chapter. The first is the lens provided by the 'executive committee' for mid-century capitalism, the technocratic planners of the welfare state.[8] Under the agreements set in motion at Bretton Woods, each segment of the Anglo world facilitated a massive investment in human capital, which underpinned full employment. The Anglo world expanded education in schools and universities in ways that complied with the barely hidden hand of American big capital, often disguised as state aid or philanthropy. This made the welfare state a *working state*, rapidly growing universal human industriousness.

The second part of this chapter focuses on professional objections to state interference. The Saskatchewan doctors' strike helps show the centrality of healthcare to the welfare state, and the profession's resistance to any governmentality but their own. The final perspective I offer

---

[6] They built on traditions commenced after the Great War. See Kate Darian-Smith and James Waghorne, 'Australian Universities, Expertise and Internationalism after World War I', *Journal of Australian Studies* 43.4 (2019), 412–428; Sluga, *Internationalism in the Age of Nationalism*.

[7] Of many, see Benn Steil, *The Battle of Bretton Woods: John Maynard Keynes, Harry Dexter White, and the Making of a New World Order* (Princeton: Princeton University Press, 2013); Helen Thompson, *Might, Right, Prosperity and Consent* (Manchester: Manchester University Press, 2013); Eric Helleiner, *Forgotten Foundations of Bretton Woods* (Ithaca: Cornell University Press, 2018); Bruce Muirhead, *Against the Odds: The Public Life and Times of Louis Rasminsky* (Toronto: University of Toronto Press, 1999); Tim Rowse, *Nugget Coombs: A Reforming Life* (Cambridge: Cambridge University Press, 2002).

[8] This refers abstractly to the executive committee as discussed in Karl Marx and Friedrich Engels, *The Communist Manifesto* (Minneapolis: First Avenue Editions, a division of Lerner Publishing Group, 2018), 9.

here is via the providers of welfare work, especially social workers, who were run off their feet in the wake of post-war reconstruction. These providers of civil services re-gendered the moral regime imagined by men in elite diplomatic roles, bringing it into kitchens, schoolrooms, and shopping baskets. They show that professional class relations were not forged primarily by technocratic central planning, but in the gendered practices of everyday life – practices that also reinforced racist 'colour lines' in social and economic life.

The Executive Committee for an Industrious Working State

In 1944 at Bretton Woods, the US Treasury Department's Harry Dexter White and English economist John Maynard Keynes wrangled over the structure of global finance on behalf of their two powerful economies. At the same time, the less influential segments of the Anglo world's 'executive committee' for capitalist interests found inspiration in the distinct virtue of ending world hunger. To wheat-growing Canada and Australia, the Bretton Woods order was the natural successor to the United Nations Food and Agriculture Conference at Hot Springs in 1943, and they each sought similar advantages to those gained over nutrition. 'Canada, as a great food exporter,' opined E. P. Weeks, recent head of foreign economics in the Canadian Ministry of Information, '... would like to see that the undernourished two-thirds of the world's population reach healthy nutritional levels.'[9] Such goals for nutrition – as for all other aspects of Canadian economic development, according to Weeks – were good for Canadian grain growers. It also instated a 'system of global security', based on centralized management of health, wealth, and food under the rubric of human rights.[10]

Canada was in a good place at the end of the Second World War, having more than doubled its national income due to exports to Britain's war effort. Nevertheless, new pressures were emerging:

The war has, at the same time, created vast problems of domestic reconversion, which in turn can only be solved satisfactorily on the basis of the highest degree of international security and world prosperity.[11]

Canada's continued success, central planners believed, rested on sustained exports. To this end, in a moment of food scarcity internationally

---

[9] E. P. Weeks, 'Canada and Post-War Reconstruction', *Journal of the Royal Society of the Arts* 94.4709 (1946), 113–119, 119.
[10] Weeks, 'Canada and Post-War Reconstruction', 117.   [11] Ibid., 116.

when they could have profited from grain fields unmolested by war, Canada assented to a ceiling on grain prices. This certainly sounded virtuous, but in fact the price ceiling was intended, as Weeks explained to his fellow Canadians, to discourage emerging cconomies from investing in their own agricultural industries while high grain prices made the upfront costs affordable. Combined with a 'far-sighted' policy granting 'export credits', this was intended to embed 'third world' indebtedness to Canadian agricultural interests.[12]

The result, of course, was a system of global dependencies that became governed by debt.[13] The new generation of professional economists, however, did not see all this self-interest as contradictory to the moral goal of feeding the world. As argued in earlier chapters of this book, the kind of virtue that was coming to dominate the global economy could not be divided between the 'heroic' and the 'fake'. The same spirit of virtuous self-interest was now applied by these professional experts to whole national economies, and the centralized plans to end world hunger inspired Australasian economic leaders like their counterparts in Canada. This led them also to seek a policy that they believed was even more central to their economic future than wheat growing: full employment. 'If nutrition policies could be so regulated,' Australian economist H. C. Coombs (known as 'Nugget' because of his small stature) reasoned, 'why not employment?'[14]

As plans began for the new global order, Coombs, who by 1951 was jokingly introduced to Harvard University president James Conant as 'Dictator of Australia', promoted the 'positive approach' at international conferences.[15] The multilateral Bretton Woods agreement threatened Australia and Aotearoa/New Zealand's relatively small southern economies. Both countries, so dependent on northern economies for trade and for wartime credit, really had no choice but to sign.[16] The problem

---

[12] Ibid., 119.
[13] Amy Sayward, *The Birth of Development: How the World Bank, Food and Agriculture Organization and World Health Organization Changed the World, 1945–1965* (Kent: Kent State University Press, 2006); Immanuel Wallerstein, 'The Rise and Future Demise of the World Capitalist System: Concepts for Comparative Analysis', *Comparative Studies in Society and History* 16.4 (1974), 387–415.
[14] Rowse, *Nugget Coombs*, 123.
[15] Stuart Macintyre, *Australia's Boldest Experiment* (Sydney: NewSouth, 2015), 237–270; 'Dictator of Australia' from Craig Campbell, 'Cold War, the Universities and Public Education: The Contexts of J. B. Conant's Mission to Australia and New Zealand, 1951', *History of Education Review* 39.1 (2010), 23–39, 31.
[16] Notes on the Bretton Woods Agreement, for the Minister, 17 January 1946, Monetary, Bretton Woods – Australian Participation, Department of External Affairs Correspondence Series 1946, National Archives of Australia, Canberra, NAA/A1067/ ER46/12/2 PART 1/IID 191413.

was that before the war, a combination of tariffs and preferential trading within the British Empire protected employment. Neither would be available after Bretton Woods. Australasian economists warned that full employment, with every family earning at the minimum Aotearoa/New Zealand and Australian celebrated 'living wage', would increase consumption. Everyone buying more goods, regardless of environmental waste, was seen to be a good thing because it would help drive growth. Whose goods, in a marketplace no longer defined by the British Empire, would they buy, however? Economists believed that Antipodean manufacturing would rarely be competitive, resulting in trade imbalances that would be disastrous under the new system.[17]

There was also the problem of demobilizing the military, which presented a momentous administrative challenge. Hundreds of thousands of military personnel needed to be redeployed in an orderly and productive manner. Simply discharging everyone and hoping that 'total' war economies would change quickly enough risked hard-won political stability. For this reason, Britain was already committed to full employment. In 1944, William Beveridge published a sequel to his welfare-state defining report on social insurance, *Full Employment in a Free Society*. British full employment, as outlined by Beveridge, was grounded in Keynes' 1930s observations about relationships between employment, aggregate demand, and productivity.[18]

Similarly, in 1942, Lyndhurst Giblin, a former government statistician from Tasmania who, by the end of the war, worked towards post-war reconstruction with Nugget Coombs, argued that full employment would be the 'test of democracy' in the post-war world.[19] For Giblin and Coombs, full employment was a moral test with economic implications. Just like demobilization, it could only be achieved with central planning and coordination. For governments which already had a professional workforce administering the war economy, nothing could be more natural than similarly to deploy them for peace.[20] Since Aotearoa/New Zealand and Australia could not afford to opt out of Bretton Woods, Giblin and Coombs sought to persuade the northern economies to also aim for full employment. If the United States especially, alongside Britain, managed their economy with a commitment to full employment, then consumption, they hoped, would find some sort of global

---

[17] Selwyn Cornish and Kurt Schuler, 'Australia's Full-Employment Proposals at Bretton Woods: A Road Only Partly Taken', in Naomi Lamoreaux and Ian Shapiro (eds), *The Bretton Woods Agreements: Together with Scholarly Commentaries and Essential Historical Documents* (New Haven: Yale University Press, 2019), 173–194.
[18] William Beveridge, *Full Employment in a Free Society* (London: Allen & Unwin, 1944).
[19] Macintyre, *Australia's Boldest Experiment*, 237.   [20] Ibid., 122–159.

equilibrium.[21] Not only would Antipodean exports offset their imports, but the world would also establish itself in an upward spiral of growth. Without this, Australasian participation in the Bretton Woods order would quickly collapse. Lyndhurst Giblin said:

> If we were resolute to maintain employment and refuse deflation, we should have to cut down imports, either by direct restriction of imports, or indirectly by depreciations of the currency. Either way would be bad for us, and would tend to lower our standards of living. Besides, either way would invite retaliation from other countries and lead to a cumulative reduction in world trade, such as we got in the 1930s.[22]

Coombs believed that Europe had good reason to share in this 'positive approach'. The profits derived from work on one side and high household consumption on the other would help to rebuild depleted capital stocks.[23]

The United States, by contrast, was initially unsupportive. When another Australian economist, Leslie G. Melville, argued for a global agreement for full employment in 1943, he, along with Coombs, was in regular communication with Keynes.[24] Their correspondence shows that US treasury officials feared the suggestion 'smacked of socialism' but, more fatally, were irritated that an economist from this small southern nation thought he could interfere with US domestic policy.[25] Coombs and Melville persisted, however, arguing at home that full employment and a living wage across the Anglo world (especially) was much more important to Australia than other aspects of the international agreement. Melville's concern was not just parochial. By dismantling Imperial Preference trading and protectionist tariffs to rebuild global capitalism based on an American-centred currency agreement that allowed the free flow of commodities, consumption could not be permitted to falter. Unevenness in employment and wage rates would undermine consumption in some places and thereafter the whole global economic order.[26] Although such advocates of full employment did not get everything they wanted, the US Employment Act of 1946 nevertheless committed the

---

[21] Their imagination of the global excluded the Communist world.
[22] Cited in William Coleman, Selwyn Cornish and Ald Hagger, *Giblin's Platoon* (Canberra: Australian National University Press, 2006), 200.
[23] Rowse, *Nugget Coombs*, 115–151.
[24] Cornish and Schuler, 'Australia's Full Employment Proposals'.
[25] Rowse, *Nugget Coombs*, 123.
[26] Leo Panitch and Sam Gindin, *The Making of Global Capitalism: The Political Economy of American Empire* (London: Verso, 2012).

American federal government to 'creating and maintaining ... conditions under which there will be afforded employment opportunities ... for those able, willing and seeking to work'.[27]

This centralized, expert control of strategy and resources, so obviously the domain of the professional class, had critics.[28] Some doubted the capacity of professional and civil services to implement expert planning. The war, however, had tended to reverse the traditional role of the public service who were largely responsible for the job. Instead of acting as servants of government, civil service bureaucrats were increasingly experts who made decisions and controlled resources. Often as not, they did as they thought right and then explained themselves to elected representatives.[29] This gave them more power to implement expert planning, with little to impede the leap from advice to action. Ideological critics were also becoming progressively boisterous. Conservative politicians suggested that such expert 'blueprints' for society undermined individual liberty and personal responsibility. In the Australian parliament, they began quoting from Friedrich Hayek's then brand-new treatise, *The Road to Serfdom*, equating government central planning with tyranny over individual freedom.[30] Despite their use of Hayekian rhetoric, policy distinctions were often quite subtle.

This was the case in Britain too, where Labour politicians sought an economy driven by 'manpower planning'. Opposing such an approach, Lionel Robbins nevertheless relied on similar economic costings to plan for the 'consciously co-ordinated organization' of higher education.[31] Implementing the Robbins report underpinned British expansion in human capital. It also organized, at least to some degree, British occupation structure. The resulting changes to universities, Robbins further admitted, would result in something that sounded very centrally planned: a 'very extensive transformation of the social and economic picture'.[32]

---

[27] Cited in Michael Bordo and Owen Humpage, 'Federal Reserve Policy and Bretton Woods', National Bureau of Economic Research Working Paper 20656 (2014), 2.
[28] Of many accounts, see Quinn Slobodian, *Globalists: The End of Empire and the Birth of Neoliberalism* (Cambridge, MA: Harvard University Press, 2018).
[29] Macintyre, *Australia's Boldest Experiment*, 266–267.
[30] See objection by Thomas White, including a quote from Hayek: Australian Parliamentary Debates, House of Representatives: Official Hansard, No. 49 (1946), 1004.
[31] Slobodian, *Globalists*, 99–102.
[32] Committee on Higher Education, *Higher Education: Report of the Committee Appointed by the Prime Minister under the Chairmanship of Lord Robbins* (London: Her Majesty's Stationery Office, 1963), 4 and 182.

Not all professional experts were advocates of central planning under-stood narrowly, but these influential professionals nevertheless shared the moral imperative implied in the connection between knowing and doing. By the mid-twentieth century, the 'brains' that Franklin D. Roosevelt reckoned attracted ribald laughter were also the 'hands' of government. Oversight of corporations and market activity produced government Company Acts that fuelled the growth of accountancy, as we saw in earlier chapters. Government of infrastructure – such as roads, highways, railways, airports, bridges, city zoning and planning, water supply, sewerage, and electricity – increasingly brought engineers, sur-veyors, and architects into the business of civil administration. Such public works expanded enormously after the Second World War.

Moreover, full employment extended the ethic that connected expert *knowing* to governmental *doing* to the whole economy. Labour market planners now deployed the whole population towards economic activity in a way that was looser than total war, to be sure, but shared a similar common purpose. In this sense, work was paradoxically the foundation of welfare. In recent decades, welfare has become a loaded term, implying unearned handouts. In the mid-twentieth century, work – or, at least, full employment – was welfare. Work, under the welfare state, was no mere ideal, held by a class who paired labour and virtue. Rather, full employment was the cornerstone of a whole economic apparatus characterized by doing. Having been planned by professional experts, this universal industriousness sought a kind of economic and social well-being consistent with all collective professional ambition. This, the professional executive committee of post-war capitalism seems to have expected, would bring into being strong, stable economies. In turn, especially as the Cold War unfolded, it would demonstrate the value of expert, rational government to populations battered by war and economic depression.

Investors in Massive Human Capital Growth

Full employment led to increases in education, meaning more schooling for children and many adults, for longer. The change was important across the Anglo world, but was arguably most dramatic in Britain. This was because British (and indeed European) education measured by average years of schooling had fallen far behind the settler world. In the United States, Canada, Australia, and Aotearoa/New Zealand, the average years of schooling grew very rapidly in the second half of the nineteenth century (see Chapter 4). British schooling began catching up with the rest of the Anglo world after 1902, though it only began in earnest after the Second World War.[33] The relative slowness of expansions in British education seems odd when many of the *ideas* about education originated there, especially in Scotland. Scottish ideas spread to England as readily as they did to North America and Australasia, but English mass education nevertheless grew relatively slowly.[34] Investment in human capital in the settler world was associated with the flow of money, as Chapter 2 demonstrated. British investment propelled a white-collar workforce in the settler-colonial world, whose reliance on human capital investment also boosted education. In a similar way, after the Second World War, the flow of cash was reversed, and where the money went, so too grew human capital. Now, 13 billion American dollars flowed into Europe, including Britain. Even though a good deal of it flowed back again to pay for American imports, governments also used this Marshall Plan funding to rebuild war-torn infrastructure, to manage businesses and logistics, and medicine and healthcare gained a new priority. British education levels, like the rest of Europe, grew rapidly.[35]

This increased schooling depended entirely on children's industriousness and yet, like full employment, it was considered a central pillar of welfare. The professional class who designed the welfare state stressed their own generosity rather than the free labour of children in producing the world's human capital.[36] Economic historian Claudia Goldin called

[33] Geoffrey Searle, *The Quest for National Efficiency: A Study in British Politics and Political Thought, 1899–1914* (Berkeley: University of California Press, 1971), 207–216; Geoffrey Sherington, *English Education, Social Change and War 1911–20* (Manchester: Manchester University Press, 1981), 62–65; William Richardson, 'The Weight of History: Structures, Patterns and Legacies of Secondary Education in the British Isles, c.1200–c.1980', *London Review of Education* 9.2 (2011), 153–173; Mandler, *Crisis of Meritocracy*.
[34] Geoffrey Sherington, *Alexander Mackie: An Academic Life* (Sydney: University of Sydney Press, 2019), 43–46; Malcolm Prentis, *The Scots in Australia* (Sydney: University of New South Wales Press, 2008); Roderick Macleod, '"In the Hallowed Name of Religion": Scots and Public Education in Nineteenth Century Montreal', in Peter Rider and Heather McNabb (eds), *A Kingdom of the Mind: How the Scots Helped Make Canada* (Montreal: McGill-Queen's University Press, 2006), 227–241; Bruce Curtis, 'The State of Tutelage in Lower Canada, 1835–1851', *History of Education Quarterly* 37.1 (1997), 25–43; Michael Vance, 'A Brief History of Organized Scottishness in Canada', in Celeste Ray (ed), *Transatlantic Scots* (Tuscaloosa: University of Alabama Press, 2010), 96–119; Andrew Hook, 'Troubling Times in the Scottish-American Relationship', in Celeste Ray (ed), *Transatlantic Scots* (Tuscaloosa: University of Alabama Press, 2010), 215–231.
[35] Brad DeLong and Barry Eichengreen, 'The Marshall Plan: History's Most Successful Structural Adjustment Program', National Bureau of Economic Research Working Paper No. 3899 (1991); Scott Newton, 'The Sterling Crisis of 1947 and the British Response to the Marshall Plan', *The Economic History Review* 37.3 (1984), 391–408.
[36] See Mandler, *Crisis of Meritocracy*, 33–36; Ken Jones, *Education in Britain 1944–Present* (Cambridge: Polity Press, 2016).

it the 'human capital century' where profitability, in nearly every sector, was enhanced by increased schooling.[37] Child labour had been gradually prohibited, beginning in the 1830s. It was solidified with compulsory schooling in the 1870s but for some children unfair labour conditions were overthrown as recently as the US Fair Labor Standards Act of 1938. By the end of the Second World War, children were no longer working in factories. Their labour, now unpaid, still contributed to the economy, however much education reformers stressed that schooling was a privilege. It was not just that education was compulsory, either. After 1945, entry to work opportunities depended increasingly on the merit that educators controlled, encouraging children and their parents to invest ever-growing quantities of time and sometimes money in their own human capital. Often enough it also demanded their very their selfhood, as educational merit was internalized, pushing generations of children to continually replenish the global stock of human capital.[38] Scholars increasingly recognize that sometimes children's behaviour that teachers saw as 'deviant' was also a kind of labour resistance.[39]

Human capital investment also went beyond schooling to grow the universities. This too was a moral, as well as economic, decision. 'It is the proper function of higher education,' Lionel Robbins said, 'as of education in schools, to provide in partnership with the family that background of culture and social habit in which a healthy society depends'.[40] This ethic had earlier permeated the settler revolution and was now folding back to reshape Britain itself.[41] Robbins argued that 'a good society desired equality of opportunity for its citizens to become not merely good

---

[37] Goldin, 'Human-Capital Century'.

[38] Jessica Gerrard, 'All That Is Solid Melts into Work: Self-Work, the "Learning Ethic" and the Work Ethic'. *The Sociological Review (Keele)* 62.4 (2014), 862–879; Malcolm Harris, *Kids These Days: Human Capital and the Making of Millennials* (Boston: Little, Brown and Company, 2017); Sharon Gewirtz, 'Give Us a Break! A Sceptical Review of Contemporary Discourses of Lifelong Learning', *European Educational Research Journal* 7.4 (2008): 414–424.

[39] One example of many, Clarissa Carden, 'Managing Moral Reformation: The Case of Queensland's Reformatory for Boys, 1871–1919', *History of Education Review* 50.2 (2021): 226–240.

[40] Committee on Higher Education, *Higher Education* [Robbins Report], 28.

[41] Rebecca Swartz, *Education and Empire: Children, Race and Humanitarianism in the British Settler Colonies, 1833–1880*. Cambridge Imperial and Post-Colonial Studies Series (Cham, Switzerland: Palgrave Macmillan, 2019); John S. Milloy, *A National Crime: The Canadian Government and the Residential School System, 1879–1986*. Manitoba Studies in Native History, 11 (Winnipeg: University of Manitoba Press, 1999); J. R. Miller, *Shingwauk's Vision: A History of Native Residential Schools* (Toronto: University of Toronto Press, 1996); C. Glenn, *American Indian/First Nations Schooling from the Colonial Period to the Present*, 1st ed. (New York: Palgrave Macmillan, 2011).

producers but also good men and women'.[42] Even for Robbins, who in 1937 wrote for the Mont Pelerin Society that 'the principle of international liberalism is decentralization and control by the market', the moral value of education offered good reasons for central planning by government bureaucrats like himself.[43]

'Culture' and 'social habit' were not the only reasons to extend higher education to more students. Demobilization also generated the new trend. Since antiquity, political leaders recognized the social risks if ex-soldiers were not granted opportunities and rewards for their service. Soldier settlement on land, where virtuous yeomanry would occupy time and offer income, was a time-honoured custom which, by the twentieth century, was having mixed results.[44] To assure economic and social stability as each nation demobilized, governments offered education as the grounding of economic and virtuous prospects for veterans, often in place of land. This emerged after the Great War but grew into significant programs by the 1940s. In 1944, what was known as the 'G.I. Bill' was introduced in the United States. There was a 'Canadian GI Bill', also passed in 1944, as was Australia's Commonwealth Reconstruction Training Scheme. Aotearoa/New Zealand's 1941 Rehabilitation Act gave similar educational provision for service personnel.[45]

Governments extended educational opportunity to other citizens who may not have gone to war, but whose sacrifices on the home front were still keenly felt, especially in Britain but also in Australasia. In turn, this expansion transformed higher education to include professional training. This ran into cultural limits, however. In 1939, Robert Menzies, Australia's conservative prime minister, delivered a speech deriding the Master of Salesmanship he had heard was offered by 'an American

---

[42] Committee on Higher Education, *Higher Education*, 33.

[43] Peter Boettke, 'Lionel Robbins, Prophet of International Liberalism', American Institute for Economic Research, 24 September 2018 www.aier.org/article/lionel-robbins-prophet-of-international-liberalism/ Retrieved 23 August 2022; Slobodian *Globalists*, 99–102.

[44] Adrienne Petty, 'I'll Take My Farm: The GI Bill, Agriculture and Veterans in North Carolina', *The Journal of Peasant Studies* 35.4 (2008), 742–769; Marilyn Lake, *The Limits of Hope: Soldier Settlement in Victoria, 1915–1938* (Oxford: Oxford University Press, 1987).

[45] Keith Olson, *The G.I. Bill, the Veterans and the Colleges* (Lexington: University of Kentucky Press, 1974); John Reid and Paul Axelrod, *Youth, University, and Canadian Society: Essays in the Social History of Higher Education* (Kingston: McGill-Queen's University Press, 1989); Thomas Lemieux and David Card, 'Education, Earnings, and the Canadian G.I. Bill', *The Canadian Journal of Economics* 34.2 (2001), 313–344; Philippa Smith, *A Concise History of New Zealand* (Cambridge: Cambridge University Press, 2012), 175–182; Hector Gallagher, *We Got a Fair Go: A History of the Commonwealth Reconstruction Training Scheme 1945–1952* (Melbourne: Hector Gallagher, 2003); Hannah Forsyth, *A History of the Modern Australian University* (Sydney: NewSouth, 2014), 46–66.

University'. A well-known Anglophile, Menzies' subsequent comment was revealing of the ways that he conflated British culture with merit. 'If am to choose between this kind of spurious scholarship and the much laughed at pride of the Indian Babu who puts "Failed BA" after his name,' opined Menzies, extending his anti-Americanism into some white British racism, 'I shall select the Failed BA. Tis better to have loved and lost than never to have loved at all.'[46] While many scholars across the former British Empire would have joined Menzies in preferring to keep universities as they were, the tide of economic and political change nevertheless swept aside such snooty views.[47]

In Britain, the Labour Party promoted the expansion of universities as part of manpower planning.[48] Some Australian state Labor governments did similarly, prioritizing technological universities.[49] Support for expansion was not universal even within the parties: one Western Australian Labor politician, for example, preferred the old style, elite liberal education, declaring in 1957 that 'there is no such thing as a "university of technology". The term is a complete misnomer'.[50] Conservative politicians, though typically less keen on central planning, were nevertheless supportive of university expansion as a part of economic and post-war organization. 'Not only is [expansion of higher education] probably a condition for the maintenance of our material position in the world,' argued Robbins in anticipation of considerable change for the United Kingdom's university system, 'but, much more, it is an essential condition for the realization in the modern age of the ideals for a free and democratic society.'[51] Menzies too, while able to avoid the dreaded Master of Salesmanship for the time being, oversaw massive expansions, especially in science and technology and in scientific research across Australian universities.[52]

The tradition of liberal knowledge was a little overstated if one looked much beyond Oxbridge, but a cabal of America's capitalist elite was nevertheless determined that all Anglophone universities should be redirected to support industry. In this spirit, in 1951, Harvard president James

---

[46] Robert Menzies, *The Place of a University in the Modern Community: An Address* (Melbourne: Melbourne University Press, 1929).

[47] Forsyth, *Modern Australian University*; Mandler, *Crisis of Meritocracy*, 72–95.

[48] William Stewart, *Higher Education in Postwar Britain* (Basingstoke: Macmillan, 1989), 37–38, 46–47.

[49] Hannah Forsyth, 'Expanding Higher Education: Institutional Responses in Australia from the Post-War Era to the 1970s', *Paedagogica Historica* 51.3 (2015), 365–380.

[50] Kim Beazley (Sr), 'Universities Committee Report', Australian Parliamentary Debates, House of Representatives: official Hansard, 28 November 1957, 2694–2723.

[51] Committee on Higher Education, *Higher Education* [Robbins Report], 267.

[52] Menzies, *Place of a University*.

Conant travelled to Australia and Aotearoa/New Zealand. He conducted reconnaissance on behalf of another kind of central planner, the philanthropists.[53] The wealth of nineteenth and early twentieth century's big capital – from Andrew Carnegie's steel, John Rockefeller's oil, and Henry Ford's motor vehicles – was accumulated well beyond that which could safely be reinvested in their corporations. Like others who had encountered this problem, from the Medici in Renaissance Italy to Bill Gates in twenty-first-century America, these capitalists then pursued philanthropy.[54] In the mid-twentieth century, the Carnegie, Ford, and Rockefeller organizations enabled private, well-moneyed groups of men to align higher education with the interests of American capital within the United States and overseas. The Carnegie Corporation in particular used investment in research and education to encourage the Antipodean dominions to separate further from Great Britain and bring their research – now the foundation of American military and industrial dominance – into closer conversation with North America's.[55]

American universities were also changing, in line with transformations to the professional class. Conant was responsible for transformations at Harvard that brought meritocracy closer than family connection to the centre of elite recruitment and – despite considerable evidence of his own anti-Semitism – removed barriers to Jewish students.[56] The role of university scientists in the Manhattan Project helped grow new links between scientific research and American military prowess. The resulting military-academic-industrial complex made research and innovation central to the system of American manufacturing, which became entangled with expansions in the US military.[57] With research so central to American strategic and economic dominance, these capitalist philanthropists sought to ensure the United States was also the world's research bank. Just as central bankers and political leaders at Bretton Woods guaranteed that cash from global trade would pass through US financial

---

[53] James Conant, 'Confidential Report to the Carnegie Corporation on the University Situation in Australia in the Year 1951', *History of Education Review* 39.1 (2010), 8–22; Campbell, 'Cold War, the Universities and Public Education', 23–39; Wayne Urban, 'Australia and New Zealand through American Eyes: The "Eyes" Have It', *History of Education Review* 39.1 (2010): 53–58.
[54] Inderjeet Parmar, *Foundations of the American Century: The Ford, Carnegie, and Rockefeller Foundations in the Rise of American Power* (New York: Columbia University Press, 2012).
[55] Campbell, 'Cold War, the Universities and Public Education'.
[56] Wayne Urban and Marybeth Smith, 'Much Ado About Something?: James Bryant Conant, Harvard University, and Nazi Germany in the 1930s', *Paedagogica Historica* 51.1–2 (2015), 152–165.
[57] Stuart Leslie, *The Cold War and American Science: The Military-Industrial-Academic Complex at MIT and Stanford* (New York: Columbia University Press, 1993).

centres, so too did the leaders of America's industrial-academic complex cause global research to flow through US universities. Achieving this was a collaboration between philanthropy and the US government. Fulbright agreements, for example, leveraged wartime debt accrued via lend-lease arrangements to scoop research from the old British dominions, which previously would have dutifully returned to Oxford and Cambridge, and delivered it instead to the United States.[58]

This research needed, from the perspective of big capital, to be worthwhile. On his mission to Australasia, Conant was scathing about British influence on Antipodean research. 'The continual to-and-fro flow of professors from Oxford and Cambridge to Australian universities', Conant wrote in his confidential report, 'does not help the situation. In my experience, people who have been at Oxford and Cambridge are particularly inept at analysing or suggesting improvements in university organization'.[59] A key problem, Conant believed, was that the Australasian universities were there primarily for the purpose of British cultural and economic coherence. 'There can be no doubt that the Australian universities have served a very important function as outposts of British culture in a new land', Conant explained, referring particularly to Australia (his mission to Aotearoa/New Zealand did not require such a report). 'Continuous connection with Great Britain must have been of the greatest importance in keeping Australia firmly tied into the Commonwealth pattern'.[60]

The Carnegie Corporation sought to disrupt these Imperial ties. Antipodean universities, the corporation's leaders believed, must instead serve industrial interests. The problem, as Conant saw it, was that Australian class interests prevented such efforts. Conant reported that 'the lines between pastoralists' – who were influential in universities 'ownership and management of industry, and labor unions are firmly fixed'.[61] Since industrial money was also the foundation of philanthropic investment in the United States, a lack of support by industry meant that Australasian universities were over-reliant on taxpayer funding. Conant sneered that this 'socialist state without a doctrine' applied to 'the whole British Empire'.[62] Universities that existed for the purpose of

---

[58] Alice Garner and Diane Kirkby, '"Never a Machine for Propaganda"? The Australian-American Fulbright Program and Australia's Cold War', *Australian Historical Studies* 44.1 (2013), 117–133; Walter Johnson and Francis Colligan, *The Fulbright Program: A History* (Chicago: University of Chicago Press, 1965); Sam Lebovic, *A Righteous Smokescreen: Postwar America and the Politics of Cultural Globalization* (Chicago: Chicago University Press, 2022).

[59] Conant, 'Confidential Report', 10–11.   [60] Ibid., 12–13.   [61] Ibid., 16.

[62] Ibid., 12.

maintaining the British Empire 'had withdrawn into themselves, into a cloistered atmosphere', one Australian industrialist told Conant.[63] Conant supported work by the New South Wales Labor Party to redirect university efforts in research and education to heavy industries, which was where most labourers were employed.[64] Labor's interest was clear. As well as propping up coal mining, steel production, manufacturing, and atomic energy, the universities that grew under this pressure provided pathways from working-class trades into university engineering.[65] Conant's mission shows that the expansion of a rapidly transforming higher education sector across the Anglo world helped bring into being the vision that the economic 'executive committee' established at Bretton Woods. This intentionally transformed higher education from a small, rarefied 'ivory tower' to what moral philosopher Percy Partridge considered at the time to be its opposite, institutions that were 'public utilities or instrumentalities', funded by government 'because they carry out public functions, as hospitals and public transport systems do'.[66] Over the two decades following 1960, around 200 new universities were established worldwide. They were 'utopian', as historians Jill Pellew and Miles Taylor have argued, seeking a distinctive purpose that was open to new political and disciplinary experimentation.[67] But they were also – some might say primarily – about feeding the labour market where the professions were continuing to grow rapidly. In 1979, H. C. Coombs called university students 'capitalist fodder'. He was being provocative, hoping governments might seek something rather more virtuous than they had achieved since post-war reconstruction.[68]

Between the enrolments to produce 'capitalist fodder' for professional work, expansions in schooling, and research for military or industrial purposes, investment in human capital – so important to the initial rise of the professional class – was escalating rapidly. It was profoundly shaped by capitalist interests, including philanthropic arms of American capital, but also by the influence of the economic planners who were now at the heart of governments everywhere. The division here was evidently not based in public or private interests, nor in the sense that some schools or

[63] Ibid.   [64] Ibid., 9.

[65] Forsyth, 'Expanding Higher Education'; Forsyth and Pearson, 'Engineers and Social Engineering'.

[66] Percy Partridge, 'Comment on the Social Role of Higher Education by S. Encel', in Edward Wheelwright (ed), *Higher Education in Australia* (Melbourne: F. W. Cheshire, 1965), 34.

[67] Jill Pellew and Miles Taylor, 'Introduction', in Jill Pellew and Miles Taylor (eds), *Utopian Universities* (London: Bloomsbury, 2021), 1–18.

[68] Herbert Coombs, *Science and Technology: For What Purpose?* (Canberra: Australian Academy of Science, 1979), 21–47.

universities were more elite than others. Instead, an alliance of US foreign policy and American capital encouraged the growth and direction of education and research across the Anglosphere and beyond. These changes were needed by US capitalists just like the Antipodean economies needed full employment. Human capital was a key foundation for American wealth. Just as the Bretton Woods agreement sent American surpluses into Europe, Japan, and Australasia as aid, philanthropy, and investment, so now would human capital grow there, recycling back into the US military-industrial complex to grow American capitalism.[69]

Governmental, Even When Anti-State

Healthcare was also human capital investment. Citizens across the Anglo world were particularly conscious of it after the wars. Indeed, wars helped medicine seem a right of citizenship. Since the mid-nineteenth century when Americans waged a Civil War and British soldiers participated in the Crimean War, English-speaking soldiers expected that if they were injured, the state which sent them would also provide medical care.[70] Twentieth-century wars were only different in that more soldiers expected improved treatment, partly because medical science was better, but also because medicine was now a tool of war. By the Second World War, Britain's Royal Army Medical Corp and Army Nursing Service provided what was likely a decisive advantage.[71] They achieved this through preventative techniques, including vaccination and careful hygiene and sanitation, which helped reduce losses from typhoid and other diseases. By keeping mobile hospital services within reach of battle lines, surgical and medical treatment – improving anyway with developing technologies, training, and techniques – could be provided in a timely manner.[72] Medical research also proceeded apace so that by 1944, penicillin helped military personnel recover from burns and infections. It also reduced the effect of the sexually transmitted diseases which had proven so devastating in the previous world war.[73]

---

[69] Evan Schofer and John Meyer, 'The Worldwide Expansion of Higher Education in the Twentieth Century', *American Sociological Review* 70.6 (2005), 898–920; Yanis Varoufakis, *The Global Minotaur: America, Europe and the Future of the Global Economy* (London: Zed Books, 2011); Lebovic, *A Righteous Smokescreen*.

[70] Charles Rosenberg, *The Care of Strangers: The Rise of America's Hospital System* (New York: Basic Books, 1987), 4; John Sweetman, 'Medical Staff Corps', *Journal of the Society for Army Historical Research* 53.214 (1975), 113–119.

[71] Mark Harrison, *Medicine and Victory: British Military Medicine in the Second World War* (Oxford: Oxford University Press, 2004), 1–7.

[72] Harrison, *Medicine and Victory*, 9.   [73] Ibid., 128–130.

When service men and women returned home, they and their families were entitled to the same kind of hospital and medical benefits that were a feature of welfare expenditure in Britain, Canada, Australia, and Aotearoa/New Zealand after the Great War.[74] Just as various GI Bills brought forth the possibility of increased educational rights for citizens, so too was medicine a key part of the new social contract. This made healthcare a key question for the nation state. The possibility of nationalizing medicine was on the cards for some political leaders since the Great Depression. Aotearoa/New Zealand introduced universal health coverage just prior to the Second World War in the 1938 Social Security Act, though like the scheme Australia later implemented, this became a hybrid public-private system.[75] The consolidation of the post-war welfare state across the English-speaking nations gave new opportunities for national healthcare. The United States, as is well known, was left far behind the others in terms of national provision of funded healthcare, looking instead to disparate forms of private insurance, often via employers. This approach linked welfare to full employment more explicitly than elsewhere, but also crucially integrated healthcare with the finance sector.[76] Canada and Britain went furthest in terms of nationalizing healthcare, developing public systems that sought universal medical coverage for all.[77] On the surface, massive increases in public funding would surely have boosted the medical profession. Doctors worldwide, however, were frequently opposed to universal government-funded healthcare, though closer inspection of the evidence, historian Fallon Mody has shown, suggests that the extent of this opposition may have been exaggerated.[78]

Medical resistance to planned healthcare came to a particularly dramatic climax in 1962 in the Canadian province of Saskatchewan. This moment in Canadian history is notorious. The Saskatchewan archives have prepared kits for teaching it to children, perhaps showing how close

[74] Mark Edele and Robert Gerwarth, 'The Limits of Demobilization: Global Perspectives on the Aftermath of the Great War', *Journal of Contemporary History* 50.1 (2015), 3–14; Stephen Garton, 'Demobilization and Empire: Empire Nationalism and Soldier Citizenship in Australia after the First World War – in Dominion Context', *Journal of Contemporary History* 50.1 (2015), 132.

[75] Gillespie, *Price of Health*, 251–279; Smith, *Concise History of New Zealand*, 161.

[76] Colin Gordon, *Dead on Arrival: The Politics of Health Care in Twentieth-Century America* (Princeton: Princeton University Press, 2005).

[77] George Gosling, *Payment and Philanthropy in British Healthcare, 1918–1948* (Manchester: Manchester University Press, 2017); Gregory Marchildon, 'Medicare: Why History Matters', in Gregory Marchildon (ed), *Making Medicare: New Perspectives on the History of Medicare in Canada* (Toronto: University of Toronto Press, 2012), 3–20.

[78] Fallon Mody, 'Revising Post-War British Medical Migration: A Case Study of Bristol Medical Graduates in Australia', *Social History of Medicine* 31.3 (2018), 485–509.

the nation came to a US-style health system that now costs much more than Canada's in the aggregate and is nevertheless much less accessible to those most in need.[79] The Saskatchewan doctors' strike is useful in this book as an emblem of medical resistance to universal healthcare everywhere. Although the policy context was different across the Anglosphere, medical objections to state control were remarkably consistent. This helps to show what was at stake. Many scholars have wryly pointed out that medical practitioners were protective of their incomes, which were typically much higher than almost all other people, including educated professionals.[80] But the problem with centrally planned medicine was also about expert authority, which doctors considered to be intimately entangled with money.

It began in 1960, when a provincial election in Saskatchewan was fought on the issue of universal healthcare. A former Baptist pastor, Tommy Douglas, led the Co-operative Commonwealth Federation to the polls on a platform featuring state-funded health insurance, which was intended to act as a model for the entire country.[81] The Saskatchewan College of Physicians and Surgeons campaigned heavily against it.[82] Not all doctors agreed, producing what was framed as a quarrel between 'salaried' physicians employed in hospitals or larger practices and those whose businesses were based on individual fee-for-service.[83] Dr Alexander Robertson, chair of the salaried section of the College of Physicians and Surgeons, was forced to resign over his support for the government plan. Even among salaried practitioners, he was, he admitted to the press, among 'only a small minority of doctors who disagree with the general attitude of the college in opposing a government-sponsored plan'.[84] Saskatchewan newspapers reported that 'only six' doctors were in favour of state-funded healthcare, with a College survey showing 567 'unalterably opposed to a program of government controlled medicine'.[85]

[79] Patrice Dutil, 'Foreword', in Gregory Marchildon, (ed), *Making Medicare: New Perspectives on the History of Medicare in Canada* (Toronto: University of Toronto Press, 2012), vii–viii; Gregory Marchildon, 'Legacy of the Doctors' Strike and the Saskatoon Agreement', *Canadian Medical Association Journal* 188.9 (2016), 676–677.

[80] Among many others, see James Gillespie, *Price of Health*.

[81] 'Sask. Showing Way to Health', *The Leader-Post* (Regina), 19 April 1960, 2.

[82] '"The Doctors' Position" A Presentation of the Saskatoon and District Medical Society', Presented over CFQC-TV, 1 July 1962, W. G. Davies Papers, Provincial Archives of Saskatchewan, SAB/R-30.1.

[83] 'Doctor Quits Committee', *The Leader-Post* (Regina), 23 June 1960, 5.

[84] 'Robertson Quits Paid Doctors Chairmanship', *The Leader-Post* (Regina), 23 June 1960, 1.

[85] 'Only Six Doctors in Sask. Favor State Health Scheme', *Star-Phoenix* (Saskatoon), 1 June 1960, 3.

Two weeks before the election, Douglas was evidently losing patience. 'I do not object,' he pronounced, 'to people opposing the medical plan, but I do object to them getting in the gutter to do it.'[86] He was particularly incensed by racist opinions that said under his scheme, 'British doctors will pull out of the province *en masse*' and that the profession will be filled with 'the garbage of Europe'.[87] Douglas further considered 'abominable' the claim that the system would undermine religious freedom by compelling Catholic doctors to go against their consciences on birth control.[88] Douglas expressed 'puzzlement' about medical opposition, since in 1948 they had asked for such a plan.[89] As the election inched closer, however, he suggested to the media that doctors were actually worried that if they received a salary rather than fees in exchange for individual services, they would have to pay as much tax as everyone else.[90] Medical doctors denied financial self-interest, arguing that 'if making money was all that concerns us, we would welcome this Act, because under it, we would never again have an unpaid bill'.[91]

Tommy Douglas easily won the election, his party claiming 37 of 54 seats despite a swing against them in the popular vote. Nevertheless, the Saskatchewan College continued to claim that state health insurance would destabilize democracy, bring around Hitler-style controls of personhood, and undermine religious freedom. In their campaign against government funding of medical services, doctors expressed marked reservations about becoming 'civil servants'. A general practitioner from Estevan, Dr M. Rubin, said that 'doctors realize their incomes will not change much' but that 'it's the element of control that doctors dislike':

Most of us spent many years in medical college and doing post-graduate work. If we had wanted to become civil servants, we would have come to Regina and asked for desk jobs. One of my main reasons for going into medicine was to be an individual.[92]

Although Dr Rubin framed this individuality as just reward for his years of dedicated training, for the medical profession internationally, where the same question of state funding and expert independence was also under discussion, professional autonomy was about much more than personal preference.

---

[86] 'Douglas Charges Some Doctors Using "Abominable" Methods', *The Leader-Post* (Regina), 25 May 1960, 9; see also 'Doctors Printing "Trash" – Douglas', *The Leader-Post* (Regina), 2 June 1960, 1.
[87] 'Douglas Charges Some Doctors', 9.   [88] Ibid.   [89] Ibid.
[90] 'CCF Accusations "Foolish" – Doctors', *The Leader-Post* (Regina), 8 June 1960, 23.
[91] 'The Doctors' Position', W. G. Davies Papers, 5.
[92] 'CCF Accusations "Foolish"', 23.

In fearing that state funding would also mean state control, medical practitioners sought to retain their daily decision-making.[93] In their television presentation, Dr Jack Leddy of the Saskatoon and District Medical Society said that the legislation meant government 'may make regulations setting out the terms and conditions under which I practice medicine. That can be anything … they can direct the nature of treatment'.[94] In the same broadcast, Dr A. E. Buckwold argued that 'this puts us in a situation where the practice of medicine and the good of our patients are subject to the whims of politicians, and political expediency'.[95]

Medical practitioners' individual expert judgement was core to the perceived efficacy of their work. This is to say, medical practitioners held a genuine fear that state control would prescribe precise treatments and procedures for every condition rather than rely on their expert assessment of each case.[96] In this way, medical doctors were understandably resisting deskilling, in that they feared being reduced to mere applicators of state-authorized procedures. Deskilling typically had led to reduced incomes, but the issue went much deeper. For medical doctors as for other professionals, control over one's own work was central to professional identity, as Dr Rubin's testimony affirmed. More importantly, it was also central to the performance of expertise – to being a good doctor.

Politicians were aware of the potential problem. This entire debate was taking place in the shadow of Nazi medicine.[97] Tommy Douglas spent considerable effort in 1959 and early 1960 explaining that universal insurance would not be attached to 'compulsion', which was the word least-favoured by the medical profession.[98] Medical doctors in Saskatchewan – and indeed, in Australia and to a certain extent in Britain, not to mention the rest of Canada – believed that the right to choose one's doctor was more important than state-funded healthcare, placing consumer choice at the heart of their vision for democracy.

The Saskatchewan College of Physicians and Surgeons linked their individual freedom as medical experts to patient choice as a matter of

---

[93] It is worth noting that the same fears applied to universities as government funding increased; see Gwilym Croucher and James Waghorne, *Australian Universities: A History of Common Cause* (Sydney: NewSouth, 2020), 78–107.
[94] 'The Doctors' Position', W. G. Davies Papers, 3.   [95] Ibid.
[96] This did happen under private insurance schemes, since, as Paul Starr explained, 'the ability to prescribe is the power to destroy [insurance companies]', Starr *Social Transformation of American Medicine*, 26.
[97] Ulf Schmidt, 'Medical Ethics and Nazism', in Laurence McCullough and Robert Baker (eds), *The Cambridge World History of Medical Ethics* (Cambridge: Cambridge University Press, 2008), 595–608.
[98] 'No Compulsion Upon Doctors', *The Leader-Post* (Regina), 17 December 1959, 3.

democracy. In the manifesto that the College developed in 1960, the right to choose one's own doctor and to bring fee payment with that choice was enshrined in the College standpoint.[99] At this point it is important to recall that medical practitioners did not display the same kind of attachment to consumer choice a few decades earlier when they pushed homeopathy out of the profession and vilified Chinese medicine (see Chapter 3). Self-serving enclosure, licensure, and even monopoly were hardly foreign to the profession. To their evident surprise, the public saw medical insistence on fee-for-service as similarly self-interested.[100]

Overseas, other medical doctors similarly negotiated to self-interested effect, more or less.[101] But in July 1962, Saskatchewan medical practitioners took on the state. Just as the Douglas legislation was about to come into effect under the new Premier Woodrow Lloyd, almost all Saskatchewan doctors went on strike. A skeleton medical crew was available for emergencies at certain hospitals – urgent patients had to be transferred there – but otherwise the profession withdrew their services.[102] Careful to avoid calling it a 'strike', which they rightly thought might undermine public sympathy for wealthy professionals, medical services were made unavailable, and doctors held public demonstrations, with placards that read 'suspend Medicare now', 'government responsible for chaos', 'government ignores us' and 'democracy is threatened' (see Figures 5.1 and 5.2).

Outside of medicine – and certainly outside of Canada – there was little sympathy for the profession's cause.[103] As historian Gregory Marchildon points out, being salaried did not cause a similar crisis for nurses or other healthcare providers, an anomaly that members of the public likely also noticed.[104] Some American newspapers suggested the Saskatchewan doctors were breaking their Hippocratic Oath. Editorials

---

[99] 'Doctors Against Govt Controls', *The Leader-Post* (Regina), 3 November 1959, 3; 'Doctors', *Star-Phoenix* (Saskatoon), 3 March 1960, 12.
[100] This is certainly how Marxist scholars have tended to interpret the history of profession in general and of medicine in particular; see Willis, *Medical Dominance*; Friedson, *Professional Dominance*; Larson, *Rise of Professionalism*.
[101] Medical practitioners achieved concessions under the British NHS, while Australian doctors resisted nationalization; see Gillespie, *Price of Health*.
[102] 'Strike Victim', *The Windsor Star*, 3 July 1962, 1.
[103] Gordon Lawson, 'The Road not Taken: The 1945 Health Services Commission Proposals and Physician Remuneration in Saskatchewan', in Gregory Marchildon (ed), *Making Medicare: New Perspectives on the History of Medicare in Canada* (Toronto: University of Toronto Press, 2012).
[104] Marchildon, 'Legacy of the Doctors' Strike', 676–677.

argued that the strike, rather than garnering support for doctors, was assembling Congress support for US president John F. Kennedy's push for Medicare for the elderly – though this did not eventuate until 1965 under President Lyndon Johnson.[105] In Pittsburgh, former Canadian doctors described the strike as 'unthinkable' and 'very dangerous', views that were reported back in Canada.[106] Six million US union members showed no solidarity at all for the medical strike, with their representative body, the American Federation of Labor and Congress of Industrial Organizations, condemning the 'callous action of Saskatchewan doctors who have left their posts and now refuse to treat the sick'.[107] 'In view of what is happening', argued one editorial in Calgary, Alberta, 'it is not surprising that public sympathy for doctors is rapidly evaporating'.[108] Within days, counter-strike pickets appeared outside offices of the Canadian Medical Association in Toronto and Montreal, led by self-described 'housewives'.[109]

The Saskatchewan doctors' strike ended in late July 1962 with the assistance of British medical practitioner and Labor politician, Stephen Taylor, then a visiting professor in Newfoundland. In a self-congratulatory autobiographical account of his role in managing negotiations, Taylor said that his experience in both politics and medicine helped him. 'I know, from experience, that planning will only work if it is flexible and non-confining', he gloated. This was related to the democratic claims that doctors had made: 'To do his best, man must be free', Taylor argued, 'and he must feel free as well.'[110] This freedom, Taylor argued, worked better under the Saskatchewan 'fee-for-service' model than Britain's National Health Service; for all that, in the end, he supported Canadian Medicare. The language of nineteenth-century charity focused on a 'deserving poor' is evident in his, and in other medical doctors', justification. '[Fees for service] encourages self-reliance' among patients, Taylor argued, while for the doctor 'it rewards industry and energy'. The perceived problem of greedy doctors was easily addressed, he suggested, with similar forms of individual responsibility: 'excessive earnings can be reduced by the simple process of

[105] 'Doctors Strike Aids JFK Program', *The Vancouver Sun*, 4 July 1962, 3; 'Do Doctors Have the Right to Strike?' *Fort Worth Star-Telegram*, 9 September 1962, 131.
[106] 'Different Opinions of Strike', *The Windsor Star*, 3 July 1962, 1.
[107] 'Doctors Strike Effect Seen', *The Windsor Star*, 9 July 1962, 9.
[108] 'Wrong Choice', *Calgary Herald*, 6 July 1962, 4.
[109] 'Housewives Picket CMA in Toronto', *The Vancouver Sun*, 4 July 1962, 3.
[110] Lord Taylor, 'Saskatchewan Adventure: A Personal Record', V. L. Matthew fonds - MG241, University of Saskatchewan Archives, 3.

limiting items of service to a number within the capacity of the honest and efficient doctor'.[111]

Taylor's account echoed a longer history in which medical practitioners sought to enforce personal responsibility in the wider community. Chapter 4 showed that the medical profession became incensed, from a moral as well as self-interested perspective, when those whom they believed could pay for healthcare instead used free hospital services. The profession consistently maintained that if one could pay for medical care, morally they should – a morality doctors sought to police by central evaluation of other peoples' circumstances, as we saw in Chapter 4 about the rise of the almoner/medical social worker. In the same spirit, one of the pamphlets that doctors distributed in 1962 described Saskatchewan's patients as 'you, the self-reliant and responsible citizen'.[112]

Medical practitioners, with some exceptions, tended to adhere to an ethic of personal responsibility, which placed them at odds, on occasion, with the welfare state. The medical profession was, of course, deeply involved with the welfare state, but supported it only insofar as it did not interfere with a transactional model of medical service. Medicine was not alone in this. Law, engineering, and accountancy – all male-dominated professionals, at the time – also preferred individual responsibility over collective insurance. This was even though, in some parts of the English-speaking world, a majority of certain professions were employed by government. For all his moralizing over personal responsibility, 'I am at heart a planner', Taylor said nevertheless in his *Saskatchewan Adventure*.[113] So too were the rest of the professional class – unless of course their own professional expertise was also subjected to planning by others. In the end, medical resistance in Saskatchewan fizzled, bringing the Douglas plan into effect all while Taylor mouthed sentiments that seemed sympathetic to medical individuality. Universal healthcare never stopped medical practitioners insisting on a universal morality grounded in personal responsibility, in fact, but such moral-economic objections were insufficient, at least in this case, to impede state-funded investment in Canadian healthcare.

---

[111] Taylor, 'Saskatchewan Adventure', 13.
[112] 'Political Medicine Is Bad Medicine', Pamphlet. Advisory Planning Committee on Medical Care, Thompson Papers, University of Saskatchewan Archives USask/91 Accessed via Saskatchewan Council for Archives and Archivists, http://digital.scaa.sk .ca/gallery/medicare/en_doc-strike.php, Accessed 4 August 2021.
[113] Taylor, 'Saskatchewan Adventure', 3.

Gendering the Angels of the State

Even universal healthcare could not make everyone perfectly healthy. Injury, chronic sickness, mental illness, and disability were a reality then as now. Indeed, no one was ever more than 'temporarily able-bodied'. As historian Yves Rees has shown, histories of capitalism that focus on labour and capital can inadvertently contribute to disability as labour's 'other'. Historically, disability made people 'unproductive citizens', aligning 'true' citizenship with labour effort, a mistake Rees asks us not to replicate in our histories of capitalism. Many bodies, moreover, were disabled by work accidents, poverty, and by the stress of the very industriousness the era expected, making such bodies 'archives of capitalism'.[114]

They were also archives of war. As post-war reconstruction proceeded, many veterans were unable to participate in the human capital accumulation expected of everyone else. There were those left with permanent disability or mental trauma, and others who never saw a front line, like widowed mothers of young children.[115] Their sacrifice demanded acknowledgement and gave state planners further reason to make welfare central to the changing regime.[116] For this, nation states turned to social work, a profession dominated by women.[117]

While medicine contradictorily fought both for and against central planning in the name of universal personal responsibility, a significant portion of women professionals were scrambling to assist those for whom such personal responsibility was unmanageable. As technocrats planned the welfare state based on full employment, state planners asked leading social workers, women, heading up local professional associations and university departments, to organize resources for those unable to participate in the universal industriousness demanded by full employment and expanding education. In the United States, the number of social workers more than doubled between 1930 and 1940 and continued to grow by an average of 68 per cent each decade until 1980.[118] Growth in Britain was also very strong. In 1931 there were around 9,000 social workers but by

---

[114] Yves Rees, 'Thinking Capitalism from the Bedroom: The Politics of Location and the Uses of (Feminist, Queer, Crip) Theory', *Labour History* 21.1 (2021), 9–31.

[115] Victorian Association of Social Workers, 'Observations on the Proposed Constitution Alteration', Australian Association of Social Workers, Melbourne University Archives, MUA/AASW/1990.0024.16.

[116] Stephen Garton, *The Cost of War* (Oxford: Oxford University Press, 1996).

[117] See Patricia Evans and Gerda Wekerle, *Women and the Canadian Welfare State: Challenges and Change* (Toronto: University of Toronto Press, 1997).

[118] Calculated from US Census Occupation Reports 1930, 1940, 1950, 1960, 1970, and 1980.

1951 there were 25,000. In Australia, where social work only professionalized in the 1930s, numbers almost doubled between 1931 and 1947.
These were still only just over 2,000 social workers, a number that
slightly declined by the 1961 census.[119]

When the Australian Commonwealth government embarked on post-
war reconstruction in 1942, this small group of social workers were
caught off guard. Too few social workers were available to juggle new
central planning demands. As well as implementing Commonwealth-level
reconstruction, they also worked with state governments to establish welfare regimes that supported unemployment relief, child welfare, mental
hygiene, and childcare for working widows.[120] Social workers were considered the experts on welfare, and government bombarded them with
questions, seeking their opinion on a wide range of welfare policies
emerging in response to changing conditions. For example, should
widowed mothers be provided with state-funded childcare? And, if not,
should they be permitted to take their children to work?[121] The archives
and papers of Australia's professional social workers in this period are
frantic in tone. Norma Parker and Jocelyn Hyslop, who led chapters of
the Australian Association of Social Workers in Sydney and Melbourne
respectively, embraced the opportunities that the welfare state presented
for their profession. Embodying the cliché that if you want something
done, you should ask a busy woman, Parker and Hyslop's correspondence
shows the heavy lifting being performed by professional women as central
planning was rolled out. It was a bipartisan task where radical feminists like
Jessie Street joined relatively conservative women like Norma Parker,
combining women's traditional charitable concern with more radical plans
for social and economic change.[122]

Seeking to address the surge in demand for social work services, these
women leaders established new university diplomas in Australasia, but in
doing so they also further narrowed access to the professional association.[123] By 1945, when Eleanor Roosevelt read the *Open Letter to*

---

[119] Australian census 1931, 1947, 1961.
[120] 'Observations on the Proposed Constitution Alteration', Australian Association of
Social Workers.
[121] Government Establishment of Day Nurseries, Australian Association of Social
Workers, Melbourne University Archives, MUA/AASW/1990.0024.16.
[122] Correspondence from National Council of Women of NSW to Jessie Street, president
of Australia Women's Charter Conference, 14 June 1946, Box H2289, Australian
Association of Social Workers, New South Wales Branch - further records,
1932–1979, State Library of New South Wales; Ivey, 'Becoming a Social Worker',
31–41.
[123] Constitution and Rules, Australian Association of Social Workers, Melbourne
University Archives, MUA/AASW/1990.0024.16.

Women of the World at the United Nations asking 'trained women … to assume responsibilities when new opportunities arise', Parker and Hyslop were already run off their feet. Their work, however, was only just beginning.[124] Work demands on professional women, perhaps especially those trained in social science, were very broad. As well as their traditional focus on charity and welfare, educated women were also responsible for transformations in the household economy. Women social scientists strongly influenced post-war reconstruction centred on housing to ensure that even when their work was unpaid, women were nevertheless virtuously industrious.

Housing was part of the post-war social contract for women, just as full employment was for men. 'Mrs Australia', announced Antipodean government propaganda, 'you and I and our three hundred thousand neighbours will get our dream houses'.[125] This dream, like the offices and institutions in which idealized middle-class husbands were employed, was dominated by the modern efficiencies promised by scientific management. Amidst the post-war building boom that dotted suburbs across the English-speaking world with houses and flats that all bore a remarkable resemblance to one another's functionality, governments, and builders were attentive to the scientific kitchen. The scientific kitchen was intended to enable the professional housewife to move efficiently from food preparation to food serving.[126]

Middle-class women's economic lives were grounded in more than a hardening of gender norms that tied them more deeply to the kitchen, irrespective of its scientific design. While assuring returned veterans had paid employment was a key priority, women's household labour was also essential to the global order. Women's unpaid work provided the literal and metaphorical nutrition for male full employment and children's increased schooling, including the responsibility Roosevelt decreed to 'train their sons and daughters to understand world problems and the need for international cooperation'.[127] Most importantly, however, women were largely responsible for consumption.[128] Consumption, as this chapter showed earlier, was the flip side of an economic order

---

[124] Open Letter to the Women of the World, read by Mrs Eleanor Roosevelt to the General Assembly, and subsequent discussion by delegations, at the first session of the General Assembly, A/PV.29, 12 February 1946, United Nations Digital Library, https://digitallibrary.un.org/record/198574?ln=en, Retrieved 3 September 2021.

[125] Cited in Macintyre, *Australia's Boldest Experiment*, 185.

[126] Macintyre, *Australia's Boldest Experiment*, 185–186.

[127] Roosevelt, 'Open Letter to the Women of the World'.

[128] Lizabeth Cohen, *A Consumer's Republic: The Politics of Mass Consumption in Postwar America* (New York: Vintage, 2003), 62–109; McCarthy, *Double Lives*, 232–234; Grimshaw, Warne and Swain, 'Working Mothers'.

founded on full employment. For women, the unpaid labour of consumer desire compounded the effortfulness of growing expectations for
household cleanliness accompanying the 'labour-saving' devices they
purchased.[129] Children were now either too young to help or too busy
building the global stock of human capital at school. Women's unpaid
work became an increasingly solitary business, leading more married
mothers to seek paid work than their representation in 1950s magazines
has led many scholars to suspect.[130]

Women's industriousness in the *trente glorieuses* helps reveal the alliance between capital and the state as both pursued new forms of central
planning. This chapter has already shown the Carnegies, Rockefellers,
and Ford Foundations of the upper echelon of American capitalist
power working to effect change in the flow of scientific research across
the Anglo world. For middle-class women, the efforts that capital
asserted were less coordinated, but they were relentless, nevertheless.
The lawnmower, Mixmaster, and vacuum cleaner constituted the
necessary 'conspicuous consumption' that, as Chapter 6 will show,
marked professional class status. A sparkling home, neat lawn and
polished appearance became essential criteria for middle-class
womanhood.[131]

Even in the midst of a centrally planned welfare state, appropriate
women's consumption was a matter of her 'personal responsibility', for
all that it was also fairly compulsory.[132] Individual responsibility was the
necessary moral foundation, as political philosopher Jessica Whyte has
shown, of the anti-central planning neoliberals of the Mont Pelerin
Society.[133] Rather than technocratic rule, their leading economist
Friedrich Hayek argued, morality would evolve via market preferences.
These preferences would only be reliable, Hayek believed, with an
underlying moral framework grounded in personal responsibility.
Without personal responsibility, how else would market decisions result
in the kind of moral freedom he envisaged; and how else could the
inequalities that it necessarily produced be justified as adequately virtuous?[134] Middle-class women, subject to a regime that required high levels
of consumption to assure their class identity, sometimes performed this
responsibility in collaboration with the highest levels of government, but
they also did so in their homes.

[129] Ruth Cowan, *More Work for Mother: The Ironies of Household Technology from the Open Hearth to the Microwave* (New York: Basic Books, 1983).
[130] McCarthy, *Double Lives*, 227–260. [131] Ehrenreich, *Fear of Falling*, 34–38.
[132] Cohen, *Consumer's Republic*, 112–165.
[133] Whyte, *Morals of the Market*; Slobodian, *Globalists*.
[134] Whyte, *Morals of the Market*, 51–73.

How Governmentality Built Professional Class Consciousness

While members of the professional class subscribed to an ethic of personal responsibility, few were likely worrying very much about whether central planning by nation states might disrupt global capitalism. Professional class interests had almost nothing to do with a global market that, as Hayek and Robbins feared, might be threatened by sovereign states whose responsibility for the well-being of its industrious workforce could lead them to redistribute some wealth away from profiteers on a global scale.[135] The connections between the professional class and global capitalism were about virtue that led to profit – like when seeking an end to world hunger profited wheat-producing Canada and Australia – not about public control of private wealth.

The fact that ending world hunger and similar projects made a profit but failed to stop 'third world' food shortages represented a problem that was also felt on a local and interpersonal scale. At a global level, professional virtue either affirmed a country's status as a member of the 'core' for whom the global order was designed, or it made a nation dependent or peripheral to the global order.[136] That is, the new global order, while perhaps well intentioned in design, nevertheless helped embed some of the hierarchies established by colonialism, into the post-war international and economic relationships.[137] In the same way, in everyday life professional virtue either confirmed one's status as a member of the professional class or imposed forms of governmentality that felt like meddling, or worse.[138] This is what forged professional class relations, remembering, as E. P. Thompson reminded us, that class is a relationship, not a category into which groups of people are slotted automatically.[139]

To see this in action, let us consider three women who had children in the 1950s and 1960s. Two I knew well; they were my grandmothers. It matters that they were women, for perceptions of dependency and welfare were deeply gendered. Male medical doctors, for example, largely saw their professional expertise as a matter of personal freedom and the fees that were paid to them a matter of personal responsibility for their clients. The medical profession not only imposed this personal responsibility on women patients, but it also constituted privileges that were not

---

[135] Slobodian, *Globalists*.   [136] Wallerstein, *Modern World-System III*.

[137] Helleiner, *Forgotten Foundations of Bretton Woods*, 3–4.

[138] See Lucinda Beier, *For Their Own Good: The Transformation of English Working-Class Health Culture, 1880–1970* (Columbus: Ohio State University Press, 2008).

[139] Edward Thompson, *The Making of the English Working Class* (New York: Vintage Books, 1966).

available to the predominantly female professions of nursing or social work. This implicit gendering of the ideological division between central planning and anti-central planning will become important in the remaining chapters of this book, but here it matters because women were typically imagined to be the *recipients* rather than providers of professional services. While not really true, since many women were in fact professionals, the perceived relative level of power is telling. The professions' epistemology of *doingness* relied on an implied passivity among 'the people' who, as historian Tim Rowse argues, were always 'other'.[140] It did not matter if they were other by class, race, or gender, but they were constructed as passively not-expert, nevertheless.

Some women were less 'other' than others, however. Adeline was one. She was my father's mother, living in the eastern suburbs of Sydney. Adeline's upper-middle-class English grandfather met her German grandmother on a ship to Australia in the late nineteenth century. By the end of the Great Depression, the family money was long gone but Adeline remained firmly middle class. When she married at the end of the Second World War, Adeline relinquished her short career as a legal secretary for the full-time work of housewifery.

For Adeline, as for others of her class, the family doctor, family accountant and lawyer, her husband's banking colleagues, and her children's teachers actively bolstered her class status. Each interaction respectfully acknowledged her standing and intelligence. The accountant and lawyer upheld her as a conscientious and prudent woman. Her husband's colleagues expressed appreciation for her dedication to their community, sometimes with engraved gifts that are now in my kitchen. Her children's teachers made her feel a responsible mother, even when they had to respectfully speak to her about her sons' classroom behaviour. And her doctor helped her through three difficult childbirths, and 'fixed her up' when she asked him to so she wouldn't endure another. Unlikely to be belittled in any of these interactions, Adeline's relationship to professionals reinforced all that she believed about school, work and household discipline, financial prudence, and personal and family responsibility.

In the same decades, my other grandmother Beverly was in working-class Tasmania. The daughter of a whaler, she married and settled in a very small mining town where she raised six children. Beverly took paid work when she needed to, at one point proudly working as a dental

---

[140] Tim Rowse, 'The People and Their Experts: A War-Inspired Civics for H.C. Coombs', *Labour History* 74 (1998), 70–87.

nurse. When my mother graduated dux of her tiny local school, Beverly had to give her the disappointing news that the family could not afford for her to go away and complete high school. Decades later as a young mother myself, I asked Beverly how she managed so many children. 'Oh it was easier in those days,' she explained. '[N]o one watched everything you did, tellin' you it was wrong.' For Beverly, interactions with professionals did not reinforce her belief that family came first, including for the children who would be tasked with looking after one another and staying out of the house until teatime. On the contrary, when she did encounter professionals, for the most part Beverly found that they meddled and judged.

Sometimes professional meddling, such as coerced adoption, had consequences lasting generations.[141] Beverly was not white – she was of Samoan descent – but she could 'pass'. Other women of colour were not always so lucky, as shown by accounts of what historian Peter Read labelled the 'Stolen Generations' of Australian Aboriginal and Torres Strait Islander peoples.[142] The Stolen Generations referred to the systematic consequences of forced child removal among Indigenous peoples in Australia. This was a common tool of state-sponsored settler-colonial rule, with child removal and forced adoption also a part of the tragedy of colonization for First Nations North Americans and Métis as well as for Māori and other Native Pacific peoples.[143]

A 1997 report on Australia's Stolen Generations entitled *Bringing Them Home* tells the story of a young woman named Millicent who became a mother at the same time that my grandmothers were each raising children. Millicent lived on a government-run facility in Western Australia. Like many First Nations women across the settler colonies, professionals controlled Millicent's life, strictly regulating her income and restricting her consumption to items they deemed

---

[141] See Denise Cuthbert and Marian Quartly, '"Forced Adoption" in the Australian Story of National Regret and Apology', *The Australian Journal of Politics and History* 58.1 (2012), 82–96.

[142] Read, *The Stolen Generations*.

[143] Margaret Jacobs, 'Remembering the "Forgotten Child": The American Indian Child Welfare Crisis of the 1960s and 1970s', *The American Indian Quarterly* 37.1–2 (2013), 136–159; Shurlee Swain, '"Homes are Sought for These Children": Locating Adoption Within the Australian Stolen Generations Narrative', *The American Indian Quarterly* 37.1–2 (2013), 203–217; Allyson Stevenson, 'Vibrations Across a Continent: The 1978 Indian Child Welfare Act and the Politicization of First Nations Leaders in Saskatchewan', *The American Indian Quarterly* 37.1–2 (2013), 218–236; Erica Newman, 'History of Transracial Adoption: A New Zealand Perspective', *The American Indian Quarterly*, 37.1–2 (2013), 237–257.

adequately virtuous. In 1962, medical professionals forcibly took Millicent's daughter from her, just as professionals had removed Millicent from her own mother twenty years earlier.[144] While the rule of experts deepened gender distinctions, it was also responsible for continued structural racism. Millicent's story shows that in the post-war welfare state, virtue capitalism extended its colonial task of extracting value from those the middle class saw as 'below' them. For generations of parents and their stolen children, the professional class continued to do this well into the post-war period, with horrifying cruelty.

Conclusion

This chapter argues that the global economic order established after the Second World War was a moral order that drew on professional virtue traditions, built by the professional class over the previous seventy years or so. Opponents of central planning, who sought to protect global capitalism from democracy, were the same. Incipient neoliberalism too was a moral order, grounded in a similar commitment to personal responsibility, which in time would also shape the ways nation states structured their economies. For now, the logic of professional virtue embodied in welfare state reforms governed international relations, also shaping global economic hierarchies, and interpersonal class relations. The global order was structured on forms of authority informed by gender and the shifting global colour line. As a result, the class relationships that professional virtue nourished in the mid-twentieth century also reinforced gender and racial inequality.

Governmentality is central to this analysis. The universal industriousness promoted by the age of experts supported profitability, but as a moral regime it also encouraged people to internalize ethics about hard work, individual contributions to their shared economic responsibility, and service to others, especially via family obligations. These attributes informed the welfare state, to be sure, but later they would also help neoliberalism function. Giorgio Agamben's theological framing sits lightly behind this argument to see the professional class as *angels of the state*, regardless of their employer, or even whether they sided with state central planning or the Mont Pelerin Society's idealized global

---

[144] *Bringing Them Home: Report of the National Inquiry into the Separation of Aboriginal and Torres Strait Islander Children from Their Families* (Canberra: Commonwealth of Australia, 1997), https://humanrights.gov.au/our-work/bringing-them-home-report-1997, Retrieved 3 September 2021.

market, free of pesky state democracies with their tendency to redistribute resources.[145]

In part, this is because professionals were central planners in their hearts, shaped as they were by the epistemology of their work, connecting *knowing* and *doing*. But their angelic governmentality was also present in the nature of the modern state, which after the Second World War relied on rational action for its legitimacy. Professional expertise 'glorified' the modern state, in Agamben's terms, even in the moments that professionals rejected state control. By performing their work, the professional class affirmed, demonstrated, and brought rational governmentality into being. This sustained the moral order represented by the welfare state, which in turn became entangled in the practice of everyday life – and in hearts, desires, selfhood, and becoming.

This governmentality, combined as it was with the moral-economic logic of the Bretton Woods agreements, enabled professionals to extract value from those they deemed 'below' them, just as core nations also extracted value from those countries struggling to decolonize. The logic not only profited the professionals as a class but also bolstered the moral authority of the first-world state. It was an alliance of expertise with governmental authority which made this class 'professional-managerial'.[146] And it had real-world effects. It was no coincidence that this set of logics kept the professional class in charge – for now. Decolonization was under way, however, slowly disrupting the logics that informed both the global Bretton Woods–era economic order and professional class relations. By turning the racial and gendered logics of professional virtue upside down, decolonization produced a crisis in the professional class. This is the subject of Chapter 7. First, this book will explore what exactly was 'classy' about this work.

---

[145] Agamben, *The Kingdom and the Glory*, 144–166.
[146] Ehrenreich and Ehrenreich, 'The Professional-Managerial Class'.

6   Classy Work

By the 1950s and 1960s, growing cohorts of young people were conscious that getting a better job was how one moved upwards in class terms, and that more education would help. In 1962, Nancy Fisher of Roosevelt High School in Dayton, Ohio, told her local paper that 'statistics show that a college education is needed if we even want to think about a job in the future'. The first in her family to go to college, Fisher wanted to study history and government, become a teacher for a while, and eventually go into foreign service. Bill Kennedy of Belmont High School told the same reporter he was leaving Dayton to study physics, while Steve Hempelman said he was going to university because he wanted to be a doctor. None were in it just for the job prospects, however, according to the *Dayton Daily News*. The same pathway would also make them better people and build a better America. 'No matter what you're studying to be', Hempelman told the paper, 'an engineer, a teacher, a doctor – you're going to help the rest of society. And a better educated population will mean a better economy, an all-round better nation'.[1]

The *Dayton Daily News* hardy needed to tell its readers that professional work was 'classy', this was obvious. Becoming a professional was how one accrued and maintained class status. As Chapter 5 argued, this class aspiration encouraged the universal investment in human capital that was making the new global economy work. In everyday life, individuals getting an education and seeking a better job, often a professional job, was an important way that technocratic goals would be achieved. Aspiration everywhere was required, in fact, irrespective of technocratic planners' political outlook. While educational opportunity for all was a key plank of the welfare state, the kind of ambition it embodied was also central to the moral economy underpinning F. A. Hayek's neoliberalism, too. Desire for a better job, a better home, and better commodities was

---

[1] *Dayton Daily News*, 3 June 1962, 4.

the moral driver, according to Hayek and his comrades, for a better economy and better society.[2] Both sides of contemporary politics therefore supported the rise and rise of what Harold Perkin called the 'professional society', a system of social organization comprised of priorities and institutions valued by the professional class.[3]

These values are also deeply familiar. Experience can make it difficult in the present to tease out, exactly, what made performing certain occupations such class-making work. Was it the difficulty of the job, the need for a college degree, the place of the work in a hierarchy – or the salary? It could also have been the society the other 'classy' folk – with whom one associated in such workplaces. Or it may have been the virtue attached to serving others, something that young Hempelman from Dayton, Ohio, knew instinctively was connected to the economy and his nation. Each possibility is attached to theories of class, some of them complementary, others wholly incompatible with one another. This chapter interrogates these theories – not abstractly, but in real historical life – to understand what made professionals a class, not just an occupation category.

Issues of class can be difficult to ask historically because the types of sources such questions demand are only intermittently available. How can we really know what people felt and thought about their relationship to one another, and their workplaces? What evidence is there that they were aware of the traits they had in common, or even their own class identity? As well as common characteristics, did they feel and perform solidarity with one another in ways that made them a class 'for themselves'? The 'high burden' of class consciousness, historian Seth Rockman has argued, is sometimes too high to clear with the evidence to hand.[4]

This is particularly troublesome in studying the professional class, who often avoided any discussion of themselves as a class and who sometimes refused to acknowledge the existence of class in society at all.[5] For example, in 1921, Institution of Engineers president William Johnson Newbigen said that while 'an orator may sway a nation to peace or war, no amount of eloquence will lessen the deflection of a loaded beam'.[6] Unlike other forms of power and influence, the beam was banal, its

---

[2] Whyte, *Morals of the Market*.   [3] Perkin, *Rise of Professional Society*.
[4] Seth Rockman, 'The Contours of Class in the Early Republic City', *Labor* 1.4 (2004), 91–108.
[5] See Perkin, *Rise of Professional Society*, 3.
[6] William Johnson Newbigen, 'Presidential Address', *Transactions of the Institution of Engineers* 2 (1921), lxxiii.

displacement under too much load mathematically incontrovertible. The objectivity of the engineer was supposed to be as unassailable as the mathematics that calculated this deflection. The authority over a body of knowledge that Newbigen attributed to such objectivity, as this chapter will discuss, was central to professional class power, though it also actively veiled it.[7]

Despite the distinct interests that the professional class had in hiding their 'classiness', a quirk of the Australasian industrial relations system has left us with records of a case that makes explicit the characteristics of professional class consciousness. Between 1957 and 1961, professional engineers in Australia used formal conciliation and arbitration courts, unique to Australia and Aotearoa/New Zealand, to successfully argue that because their work was professional, this made them members of the professional class and they required a salary commensurate with their status. In what is now stored as more than fifty boxes of argument, lawyers for the professional engineers' union explained exactly what being professional class meant. This chapter uses the *Professional Engineers' Case* to understand the characteristics of the professional class in the mid-twentieth century.

The chapter starts with some background on Australasian arbitration and the place of the *Professional Engineers' Case* in the context of Australia and Aotearoa/New Zealand's unique institutions. I then consider professional class relations via the lenses provided by the case. First, the chapter discusses the material relations engineers had with mid-century industrial capitalism. Then I show the ways that professional class interests were, by this time, inextricable from the national interest. This not only gave professionals another pillar to hide their class interests behind, but it also gave reason for representatives of the nation state to support professional interests as their own. Thirdly, I show their 'class consciousness', meaning engineers' decided association with other established professionals. This, they argued, required them to participate in their own class via consumption standards, which further signalled and facilitated their membership of the professional class. Finally, the chapter explores the ways professional engineers dissociated themselves from the working class. Regardless of their relationship to the means of production, engineers refused the category of 'worker'. In the process, they also pulled up the ladder behind them, reducing worker opportunities for upward mobility.

[7] See Christian Joppke, 'The Cultural Dimensions of Class Formation and Class Struggle: On the Social Theory of Pierre Bourdieu', *Berkeley Journal of Sociology* 31 (1986), 53–78.

Compulsory Arbitration and the Professional Engineers' Case

The *Professional Engineers' Case* was unusual, though it sparked several professional cases like it in the subsequent decades. Soon, professional unions were emerging worldwide, prompting sociologists including Anthony Giddens to anticipate a broad, slow shift by professionals into the working class.[8] The *Professional Engineers' Case* was based in the first instance on some slipperiness in the usage of the word 'engineer'. Engineering traditionally included working-class trades, as well as elite, educated designers of major work. The Amalgamated Engineering Union included engineers in a generic sense, whose specific occupations made them fitters, turners, sheet metal workers, blacksmiths, and boiler-makers. Professional engineers by contrast, like John Whitton who designed the famous zigzag railway over the Blue Mountains from Sydney, long had shared associational space with architects at Science House on Sydney's Macquarie Street. This alone was a marker of professionalism. Macquarie Street was also where the law courts, state parliament, Reserve Bank (and original Sydney mint), state library, and the oldest Sydney Hospital were centred: it was all at once like London's Harley Street, Lombard Street, Bloomsbury, and Lincoln's Inn if they were also squashed next to much smaller Houses of Parliament.

Professional engineering included civil and consulting engineers, as well as the specialties that grew over the past sixty years or so, like mining, chemical, electrical, and aeronautical engineering. Not all of these were university trained; in fact, a majority in 1957 were not.[9] Expanding both engineering and higher education after the Second World War, new universities like the New South Wales University of Technology began building their role in the profession starting with pathways from technical college diplomas to university degrees. This pathway, and its alignment to working-class trades, made engineering a common way for male members of the working class to make their way into professional work.[10] They were useful, moreover. In some specializations, like mining, electrical, or mechanical engineering, there was a productive relationship between trade and professional work: linking on-the-job problem solving connected 'doing' with 'designing', often

---

[8] Giddens, *Class Structure of the Advanced Societies*, 189–209.
[9] Michael Edelstein, 'Professional Engineers in the Australian Economy: Some Quantitative Dimensions, 1866–1980', Working Papers in Economic History (Australian National University), 93 (1987), 16.
[10] Forsyth and Pearson, 'Engineers and Social Engineering'.

facilitating important innovations.[11] Snootier members of the engineering profession periodically railed against their relationship to trades, sometimes suggesting they dissociate themselves by taking the title in French, *ingenieur*.[12]

For the upstanding learned professions of medicine and law, all these qualities made engineers a little less than them. Listen, for example, to court reporter Columb Brennan's sarcasm in 1960 when he asked whether there could be seen 'a more distinguished galaxy of talent than the Association of Professional Engineers?'[13] Writing a column on the 'law courts beat' for the *Law Institute Journal*, Brennan gave a brief account of the legal battle that had 'gone on for years' in which, among other things, there were claims that 'engineers required a higher IQ than doctors and were just as well qualified professionally'.[14] Brennan did not tell his readers in the legal profession that the engineers had also compared themselves similarly to lawyers, though readers were likely aware that if engineers thought they were smarter than doctors, they probably considered themselves superior to lawyers, too. For engineering as for other newer professional occupations, medicine and law were the benchmark professions. Both were not only exemplars for the definition and characteristics of professional organization, but their members were also the yardstick of class identity. In seeking improved working conditions, Australia's engineers were forced to explicitly articulate what in other contexts remained largely unspoken; the foundations on which the professional class rested. The engineers' successful pursuit of status and financial reward underscores the triumph of a new professional social order in which claims of professional virtue and esteem could be confidently made, even by the newer professions. This ensured that they were, eventually, also recognized by their fellow professionals.

The court where the professional engineers made their case was a special consequence of the Australasian 'social laboratory', where both Australia and Aotearoa/New Zealand built economies backed by liberal 'state experiments'.[15] Both countries established similar institutions for arbitration, which consciously sought to avoid the social conflict

[11] Forsyth, 'Class, Professional Work and the History of Capitalism in Broken Hill'; Forsyth and Pearson, 'Engineers and Social Engineering'.
[12] Forsyth and Pearson, 'Engineers and Social Engineering'.
[13] Columb Brennan, 'The Law Courts Beat: Battlers', *Law Institute Journal*, 2 May 1960, 110–111.
[14] Brennan, 'Battlers,' 110.
[15] Stuart Macintyre and Sean Scalmer, 'Class', in Alison Bashford and Stuart Macintyre (eds), *The Cambridge History of Australia* (Cambridge: Cambridge University Press, 2013), 358–376; Smith, *Concise History of New Zealand*, 100.

associated with the rise of the working class in Europe. They achieved this by systems that independently regulated employment conditions and pay rates.[16] Beginning with New Zealand's *Industrial Conciliation and Arbitration Act* of 1894 and a similar Act in Australia in 1904, semi-judicial arbitration tribunals were established when labour parties were in government (in Aotearoa/New Zealand it was a Liberal-Labour coalition) as a response to 1890s reports on 'sweating'. Pember Reeves, who wrote the Aotearoa/New Zealand Act that subsequently shaped Australia's, explicitly argued that arbitration would inhibit class warfare and put an end to strike action. In the spirit of avoiding industrial conflict, arbitration courts developed norms and principles by which judges assessed union and employer claims and disputes.[17]

Conciliation and arbitration tribunals settled all industrial disputes and set minimum pay rates for certain industries. A key principle was the 'living wage'.[18] This had a moral, normative role in establishing the male breadwinner as the relevant economic unit. It was a result of a long-fought campaign, led by government statisticians, who used 'breadwinner' categories in the census as part of the labour movement's campaign for a living wage.[19] The 1871 census of occupations in Queensland went so far as to define male breadwinners against dependent women and children as 'bread eaters'.[20] The system, which as historian Stuart Macintyre argued, grew from 'the sensitivity of the liberal conscience' to sweating and other labour abuses, also consistently protected the 'sanctity of the home'.[21] A wages board, established with arbitration, consisted of representatives of workers and employers, which set

---

[16] Ray Markey, 'Trade Unions, the Labor Party and the Introduction of Arbitration in New South Wales and the Commonwealth', in Stuart Macintyre and Richard Mitchell (eds), *Foundations of Arbitration: The Origin and Effects of State Compulsory Arbitration 1890–1914* (Oxford: Oxford University Press 1989), 156–177.

[17] Gordon Anderson and Michael Quinlan, 'The Changing Role of the State: Regulating Work Arrangements in Australia and New Zealand 1788–2007', *Labour History* 95 (2008), 111–132.

[18] *Commonwealth Arbitration Reports*, 2 (1907), 3–17.

[19] Desley Deacon, 'Political Arithmetic: The Nineteenth-Century Australian Census and the Construction of the Dependent Woman', *Signs: Journal of Women in Culture and Society* 11.1 (1985), 27–47; Deacon, *Managing Gender*.

[20] "The proportion of bread-eaters in the entire population slightly exceeds the bread-winners; but of the males, the bread-winners are more than double the bread-eaters; whilst the female eaters are more than four and a -half times as numerous as the winners', Notes on Table XXVIII, *Census of the Colony of Queensland* 1871, Historical Census and Colonial Data Archive, http://dx.doi.org/10.26193/MP6WRS. Retrieved 28 January 2022.

[21] Stuart Macintyre, 'Neither Capital nor Labour', in Stuart Macintyre and Richard Mitchell (eds), *Foundations of Arbitration: The Origin and Effects of State Compulsory Arbitration 1890–1914* (Oxford: Oxford University Press, 1989), 187.

minimum pay rates under an independent chair.[22] Wages were pegged to economic conditions and adjusted with inflation and deflation. In one instance, during the Great Depression, the basic wage was deflated by 10 per cent. This not only made matters worse, but it also gave the arbitration tribunal the reputation of being a 'bosses' court'.[23]

Arbitration was compulsory for many industries, and the proportion only grew. By the 1970s, most manual and many professional workers were covered by centrally set 'awards' that outlined legally enforceable pay and conditions. Such awards constituted a minimum and did not prohibit voluntary collective bargaining.[24] The system of compulsory arbitration encouraged very strong union membership partly because many awards established preference provisions for union members. Decisions made in arbitration tribunals fell under the authority of the judiciary, a process that legally recognized unions as bureaucratic representatives of industrial workers.[25]

Most wages were indexed against the basic 'living' wage. At the top rate, professional engineers, for example, would eventually be awarded a salary that was 3.5 times the basic wage. Some others were awarded a fraction of the basic wage instead. Women's wage rates since 1950 were set at 75 per cent of the male rate for each award. This was up from 54 per cent and assumed that women were not (or should not be) also supporting a family. Apprentices and other trainees were similarly awarded a wage at a given fraction of the basic level.[26] Unions and employers took cases to the conciliation and arbitration tribunal systematically when award rates expired. They also triggered cases opportunistically when they felt able to push for improved conditions. There were several accepted circumstances that produced such opportunities: one was when new occupations emerged, or old ones became obsolete; another, when technological change affected the skill levels of work processes; and a third was increased educational expectations.[27]

---

[22] Macintyre, 'Neither Capital nor Labour', 188.
[23] Anderson and Quinlan, 'Changing Role of the State', 122. Indeed a key controversy in Australian labour history was once the extent to which the arbitration system was a result of labour advocacy or middle-class liberals; see Macintyre, 'Neither Capital nor Labour', 178–200.
[24] Anderson and Quinlan,' Changing Role of the State'.
[25] Malcolm Rimmer, 'Unions and Arbitration', in Joe Isaac and Stuart Macintyre (eds), *The New Province for Law and Order: 100 years of Australian Conciliation and Arbitration* (Cambridge: Cambridge University Press, 2004), 275–315.
[26] Stuart Macintyre and Richard Mitchell, 'Introduction', in Stuart Macintyre and Richard Mitchell (eds), *Foundations of Arbitration: The Origin and Effects of State Compulsory Arbitration 1890–1914* (Oxford: Oxford University Press, 1989), 13–14; Jack Hutson, *Six Wage Concepts* (Sydney: Amalgamated Engineering Union, 1971).
[27] Forsyth and Pearson, 'Engineers and Social Engineering'.

Skill level was the foundation of the system. Each margin above the basic wage indicated the degree of difficulty in doing the work. In setting wages, however, judges also took social utility into account. This led them to consider the potential social or economic effects of underpayment in certain fields. In the *Professional Officers' Case* of 1918, for example, Justice Henry Higgins, who had also presided over the 1907 Harvester Judgement, found that government-employed office workers needed much higher compensation to assure adequate supply of professional workers to government jobs and to compensate them for what he called the 'drudgery of study'.[28]

On the back of this sense of social utility, some unions argued for *work value*, rather than skill level, as the basis for claims.[29] Several unions looked askance at that type of argument, which they thought reflected a lack of worker solidarity.[30] Indexation against the basic wage was clear and fair, but work value implicitly claimed that some work was better, not just harder. When successful, such arguments tended to cause the union to block entry to the occupation as a condition of success. This was what the professional engineers did, in what was one of the most important work value cases in Australian industrial history.[31] It was significant because it set precedents that enabled other professional-class unions, like the Australian Association of Social Workers, to use the arbitration system to pursue their class interests. My own union, for example, the National Tertiary Education Union, was one of those that was also established as a result.[32]

The *Professional Engineers' Case* took four years, concluding in 1961. There were twenty-three witnesses, around the same number of field inspections by the full bench of the court, fourteen films shown during court and long expositions, filling those fifty or so boxes now held in the archive. Writing in 1971, J. Hutson of the Amalgamated Engineers Union estimated it cost AU$100,000 (AU$1,119,036 in 2020 terms) just

---

[28] Henry Higgins, Judgement: Commonwealth Professional Officers', Case, *Commonwealth Arbitration Reports* 12 (1918), 114; Raymond O'Dea, *Wage Determination in Commonwealth Arbitration* (Sydney: West Publishing Corporation, 1969), 128–135.

[29] O'Dea, *Wage Determination in Commonwealth Arbitration*; Hutson, *Six Wage Concepts*, 132–241.

[30] Sarah Gregson, Michael Quinlan, and Ian Hampson, 'Professionalism or Inter-Union Solidarity?: Organising Licensed Aircraft Maintenance Engineers, 1955–1975', *Labour History* 110 (2016), 35–56; Tom Sheridan, *Mindful Militants: The Amalgamated Engineering Union in Australia, 1920–1972* (Cambridge: Cambridge University Press, 1975), 292; Hutson, *Six Wage Concepts*, 225–229.

[31] Raymond O'Dea, 'Some Features of the Professional Engineers' Case', *The Journal of Industrial Relations* 4.2 (1962), 90–107.

[32] John O'Brien, *National Tertiary Education Union: A Most Unlikely Union* (Sydney: UNSW Press, 2015).

for the claimant organizations, represented by the professional union.[33] It was, as we will see, a risky, high-stakes strategy in which the professional engineers invested considerable resources.

Industrial Capitalism and Professional Work

On the surface, there was no reason at all that these engineers constituted a class of any kind – at least, not together. In 1957 when they launched the *Professional Engineers' Case*, around 60 per cent of engineers worked for one of the three levels of government, especially local councils and state government infrastructure and services.[34] Government engineers did work like ensure road drainage was adequate, oversee road and gutter construction and repair, supervise sewerage contractors, and oversee the construction of electricity substations needed while other groups of electrical engineers concentrated on expanding the grid. Other state engineers worked top to bottom on dam planning and construction, expressways, bridges, telecommunications, electric power stations, and the new nuclear reactor at Lucas Heights, in southern Sydney. Government engineering work was driven by the efficient provision of a public service, not by a profit motive. It was important in the age of experts, for technocratic government focused on providing the infrastructure for the new phase of capitalism, including massive investment in agricultural irrigation, new energy sources like the Snowy Mountains Hydroelectric scheme, and the uranium now mined at Rum Jungle near Darwin. They also worked to improve roads and highways for the growing number of cars driven by suburban families, to roll out vast telephone networks, and invest in television.[35]

Other engineers worked for capitalist enterprises that were strikingly variable. Multinational corporations, like the Anglo-Iranian Oil Company, employed engineers for their refineries. Imperial Chemical Industries (ICI) engaged chemical engineers at their Australian branch. The Olympic Tyre and Bobber Co. Ltd employed engineers for supervising drawing, keeping machines in the workshop maintained, and for construction. Manufacturers hired mechanical engineers to work on industrial plant infrastructure. BHP, now extending far beyond Broken Hill, retained mining engineers for underground works, and chemical and mechanical engineers to manage smelters and steel works. Comeng,

---

[33] Hutson, *Six Wage Concepts*, 227.
[34] 'National Survey Details', *The Professional Engineer* 10.12 (1956), 5.
[35] Work types gained by Trove search 'engineer' through advertising and local government minutes between 1 January 1950 and 1 January 1965; see trove.nla.gov.au.

a popular shortening of Commonwealth Engineering, was a private firm where engineers designed and oversaw construction of locomotives and rolling stock used in mines in Mt Isa, Iron-Ore plants in Western Australia, Steelworks in Port Kembla, and as Sydney's passenger railcars. These organizations were almost wholly driven by profit, though most engineers exchanged their labour for a salary. These corporations were a central feature of the mid-twentieth century, as the technological age brought consumption and increasing automation to the centre of economic life. In arbitration, the union lawyer argued that their profession was responsible for 'the advent of radio, radar and television and, probably before we die, we will see colour television'.[36] The new technologies were powered by Australian fossil fuels extracted, refined, and distributed by engineers to run cars, homes, and the plants and factories of mid-century industrial capitalism.

Not all engineers were employees. Senior engineers had long worked on their own account as consulting engineers. They were often brought in to advise on new public or private projects. By the 1950s, such consultancies were becoming serious concerns, with firms growing to accommodate expansion in demand. The scope of their work was also expanding, so that consulting engineers were often planning and implementing large projects, like new railway line expansions, or mine and drilling exploration. Others worked to construct the 50-metre Olympic-sized public swimming pools that were becoming popular across Australia. Engineers owned companies and partnerships, whose work consulting on logistics and planning for other organizations was becoming important. While most engineers exchanged their labour for government or corporate salaries, this smaller, but significant, group of engineers earned a profit from their own businesses, usually employing labour that included other engineers, but also manual workers.[37] While some corporate board members for Australia's 'big end of town' were also trained engineers, these did not appear in the figures collated by the union.[38]

---

[36] Mr Gillard, the union lawyer, then paused to observe that there was already colour television in America; 'but I was thinking we might not get to America', Transcripts of Proceedings, Professional Engineers' Case Nos 1 & 2 before Conciliation and Arbitration Commission, Association of Professional Engineers, Australia, Noel Butlin Archives Centre, NBAC N4/1, Box 1, 87.

[37] Work types gained by Trove search 'consulting engineer' through advertising and local government minutes between 1 January 1950 and 1 January 1965, see trove.nla.gov.au.

[38] 'National Survey Details', 5; see Claire Wright and Hannah Forsyth, 'Managerial Capitalism and White-Collar Professions: Social Mobility in Australia's Corporate Elite', *Labour History* 121 (2021), 99–127.

With such diverse employment structures, it struck the judges of the arbitration tribunal that this union's members shared no objective relationship to the means of production. Nevertheless, irrespective of public sector, private sector, type, or size of work organization or even profit motive, all the engineers who joined the union and pursued the *Professional Engineers' Case* were persuaded that their interests belonged together. This was no mere theoretical problem. To my knowledge, no dogmatic Marxists marched up to tell the engineering union that what they perceived as a material relationship, shared across a vast range of enterprise types, was not one. It was a problem, however, that challenged the assumptions of the conciliation and arbitration system.

Australia's arbitration system was based on an objective antagonism between capital and labour. Founders of the system hoped they could help labour and capital cooperate, reducing industrial disruptions due to strikes. Initially, this limited the industries that could access arbitration. For example, in hearing the *Insurance Staffs Case* in 1923, Justices Isaacs and Rich argued that 'Industrial disputes occur when, in relation to operations in which capital and labour are contributed in co-operation for the satisfaction of human wants to desires'.[39] This definition was important because there were significant constitutional limits to Australia's Commonwealth-level involvement in industrial disputes.[40] It also potentially limited the court's jurisdiction over certain kinds of work. When it came to white-collar professional work, there was some question about whether the application of expertise could plausibly be considered a confluence of labour and capital in the same sense. Justices Isaacs and Rich thought not:

[Arbitration] excludes, for instance, the legal and medical professions, because they are not carried on in any intelligible sense by the co-operation of capital and labour and do not come within the sphere of industrialism.[41]

In 1923, medical and legal professions were still generally self-employed, with many doctors especially working from their homes to provide services to their local area. State and Friendly Society funding paid many of the medical salaries for those not self-employed, while most lawyers still worked in old-fashioned partnerships. Still, even when such practitioners were employed to work for someone else, capital, as everyone understood it, seemed to have rather little to do with it.

---

[39] Cited in O'Dea, *Wage Determination in Commonwealth Arbitration*, 19.
[40] *Australian Constitution*, Part V, s.51 (xxxv).
[41] Cited in O'Dea, *Wage Determination in Commonwealth Arbitration*, 19.

Engineering was different from medicine and law. For one thing, engineers traditionally had a more obvious affiliation with industrial capitalism. 'No group of men,' pronounced George Julius, inventor of an automatic betting totalizer and president of the Australian engineers in 1925, 'is more vitally interested in industrial development than the Engineers'.[42] The following year, the new president Claude Edward Croker dedicated his address to the most efficient management of labour. 'Many employers are met with so much opposition and discouragement from the employees and labour leaders', Croker argued, 'when making honest attempts [at improved conditions] that they have given up trying'. The 'agitation for shorter hours' among workers, Croker believed, was 'due to a regrettable, or wilful, ignorance of the factor of capital...as part of the cost of production'.[43]

This alliance with industrial capitalism meant that Australian engineers frequently expressed resentment about their links with artisans and tradesmen who smelled of the Trades Hall. They were not alone among the middle-class professions. Although journalists and state-employed teachers were unionized and so were some nurses (in Queensland especially), for most professionals the Australian union movement signified a working-class identity that they generally rejected. So, in 1956, after the professional engineers registered an organization under Australia's Conciliation and Arbitration Act, one prominent editorial pronounced that this professional union was not a 'trade union' because it had nothing to do with 'trades'. Despite this, the first task in progressing the *Professional Engineers' Case* was to establish that engineers were in fact an industry in exactly the sense that Justices Isaacs and Rich had said did not apply to professions.[44] The professional engineers were conscious that their diversity in enterprise structure and alignment (or not) to capitalist profit motives failed to fit the definitions traditionally applied to arbitration. They sought to show that all their work was 'industrial' and that engineering, regardless of sector, was an industry.

Something similar had been raised in the *Professional Officers' Case* of 1918, which was about public service employees. In that case, Henry Higgins maintained that a popular, rather than formal definition of industrial work was required. He said that 'men working see no distinction' between employers, so that it did not matter if their purpose was to make a profit. Turning to the arbitration court's social utility, Higgins

---

[42] George Julius, 'Presidential Address', *Journal of the Institution of Engineers* 7 (1925), xcix.
[43] Claude Edward Croker, 'Presidential Address', *Journal of the Institution of Engineers* 8 (1926), xci.
[44] Cited in Forsyth and Pearson, 'Engineers and Social Engineering', 169.

argued that 'if the labour conditions cannot be regulated for the state as well as for other employers, it is certain – humanly speaking – that there will be trouble'.[45] The *Professional Engineers' Case* relied on Higgins' 1918 argument to include both government and private sector employees together, as part of the same class.

National Interest and Class Interest

If all engineers were employees, this would have suited the court, regardless of the profit motive of employer groups. On the surface this excluded engineers who owned their own business, and the union did not list business owners in their statistics of the employment of engineering union members. Business-owning engineers were not omitted from the case altogether, however, for the coherence of the engineering profession as an industry was more important to their success in arbitration than their status as employees. For the industry to be recognized, this coherence had to include business-owning engineers. Work value was a crucial factor in this respect. Work value was an industrial relations category, but it represented something that was also important to professional class consciousness much more broadly.

Engineering relied, as did all the professions, on their claim to authority over a body of knowledge and its associated practices.[46] This power also rested on the professional class's structural autonomy from other interests. Their 'cold-blooded reason', according to the 1922 engineering president, Robert William Chapman, was inextricable from 'the responsibility and character of his work'.[47] The engineering profession could not be subjected to any other systematic set of interests – neither capital, nor government – or it would compromise that authority. Confidence in engineering judgement could be destabilized just by the idea of bringing material interests to bear on engineering decisions. Several problems could plague public confidence: what if it was cheaper to refine the oil with a technique that made petrol dangerous in the family car? Or if political interests encouraged drilling for oil or gas in places where the work could compromise the family farm's irrigation water – or even the national food supply? If the public did not trust engineering expertise, nor indeed any other kind of professional expertise, they were less likely to call on it. This mattered for all the professions, but in the economy of

---

[45] O'Dea, *Wage Determination in Commonwealth Arbitration*, 28–37.
[46] Abbott, *The System of Professions*.
[47] Robert William Chapman, 'Presidential Address', *Transactions of the Institution of Engineers, Australia* 3 (1922), lxxv.

the 1950s and 1960s, such an absence of trust would cause crippling delays, damaging national interests.[48]

In this sense, the *Professional Engineers' Case* showed that autonomy was a crucial professional virtue. Expert control of a body of knowledge was foundational to their work, but such expertise was for naught without the trust that the community placed in them to wield that expertise correctly. Even if all engineers behaved with integrity, the possibility that other interests might influence engineering could undermine confidence. The union argued that confidence in engineering rested on the profession's solidarity with one another and commitment to their shared body of knowledge, even over other loyalties. It did not matter whether these loyalties were to government employers, big capital, or even their own businesses. It was this virtuous solidarity, much more than their status as employees, that made engineering a profession and an industrial sphere distinct from other sectors.[49]

The arbitration tribunal recognized the social utility of such professional autonomy. It probably helped that the legal profession relied on public trust to a comparable degree. Indeed, the law also shared similarly diverse employment and enterprise structures. As members of an autonomous profession themselves then, Justices Wright, Gallagher, and Mr Arbitrator Galvin who presided over the case were well positioned to understand its moral necessity. In their judgement, they affirmed the union position that '[n]ational interest requires that separate groups of Engineers shall not be regulated piecemeal and haphazardly'. Without autonomous unity, the value of engineering expertise was at risk. If engineering standards were subject to the whims of multiple employers or competing groups of engineers, bridges might not take loads, buildings may not stand, and energy or minerals might not be adequately supplied; the material well-being of the nation was at stake.[50] Similar arguments were made for the other professions: the law must not be subject to political interference, medicine needed to be practiced independently to the production of pharmaceuticals, and university lecturers needed academic freedom. In each case this was a moral position, necessary to assure what the arbitration court now conceptualized as 'national interest' demanding technocratic regulation.[51]

[48] O'Dea, *Wage Determination in Commonwealth Arbitration*, 28–37.
[49] Wright, Gallagher, and Galvin, 'Judgement: Association of Professional Engineers Australia (claimants) v Respondents', *Commonwealth Arbitration Reports* 97(699 and 702) (1958).
[50] Wright, Gallagher and Galvin, 'Judgement', 265.
[51] See Abbott, *The System of Professions*.

For the *Professional Engineers' Case*, this national interest took matters quite a lot further than the court's usual commitment to the social utility of peaceful cooperation between capital and labour. The engineering union and the arbitration tribunal agreed that engineering was something in which society, both government and private sectors, must invest. This was the nature of the *work value* that the union successfully argued. Work value was linked, for the judges who elevated their salaries, to the individual professional's investment in 'the drudgery of study' as for the earlier case overseen by Higgins. But now it went beyond individual investment in education to also tie their worth to the nation.

Achieving this national interest required systems that acknowledged and assured expert autonomy. This meant respecting the right of the profession to control its own standards, to certify entry and career progression, and to discipline deviant members. Such controls, kept in the hands of professionals themselves, were key mechanisms for protecting professional virtue.[52] By connecting professional autonomy to the national interest, the *Professional Engineers' Case* exposed the deep relationship between the foundation of their own class interest – monopoly over the application of a body of knowledge – and national economic structures. This was not only about bringing the power of the state to shelter their market, as Margali Sarfatti Larson has argued. Rather, it shows that the problem was not just a matter of national interest in an economic sense. Instead, the integrity of the state – the state's own virtue – was also entangled with the standing of the professional class. If people could not rely on engineers, they might also see that they could not rely on the state. Legitimacy itself was at stake.[53]

Class Consciousness

In the *Professional Engineers' Case*, union lawyers spent considerable resources arguing that engineering was a profession. The 'galaxy of talent' that journalist Columb Brennan mocked earlier in this chapter comprised many esteemed engineers. Those engineers described their career to the tribunal, in the process also taking care to warn of the disasters that resulted from unqualified or unskilled engineering. Some of these engineers had also previously trained and worked as doctors and

---

[52] Similar discussions were under way in the universities, where the 1957 Murray Review of Australian Universities sought to assure academic freedom as a matter of national interest, see Forsyth, *Modern Australian University*, 57–58.

[53] Larson, *Rise of Professionalism*.

lawyers. This enabled the union's legal team to connect engineering to the two occupations that everyone knew were definitely professional.[54] Veteran of the Second World War, Thomas William Osborne Farrell was one of these. Farrell lived in the popular seaside suburb of Brighton in Melbourne. He had served for some years as an aviation engineer for the military but now worked as a medical doctor at the Royal Melbourne Hospital. His evidence to the arbitration court included a comment on the nature of the body of knowledge, as he had learned it at university. 'A comparison of the medical course and the engineering course,' Farrell testified, shows that the engineering course is based largely on deduction processes whilst the medical course is based primarily on memory.[55] Farrell pointed out that the first year of engineering and medicine degrees were each similarly focused on basic science. They diverged afterwards with engineering focusing first on mathematics, then on practical work. 'Based on my recollection of my various colleagues and students in both medicine and engineering I think the average intelligence quotient is probably higher in engineering,' Farrell told the court. He described the extensive mathematics and administration required of an engineer and the physics and chemistry necessary in both fields – though less so in medicine, he reckoned. The practice of both occupations, he maintained, were strikingly similar:

I consider that the medical practitioner and the qualified professional engineer are both called upon in the normal practice of their respective professions constantly to exercise a wide range of discretion and individual judgement in order to solve the medical or engineering problems which arise ... I believe that generally speaking the responsibility carried by professional engineers is as great as that carried by medical practitioners.[56]

In both professions, as well, professional responsibility was a shared exercise. Farrell said that it was common in both medicine and engineering to 'confer with professional colleagues on difficult or unusual problems'.[57]

As a profession, engineering 'requires similar personal qualities' to medicine and other professions, according to Farrell. These qualities included 'intense interest and enthusiasm', 'logical thought', 'self-reliance, determination, and resourcefulness', 'a desire to achieve tangible results', and a 'capacity to mix with all sorts of men'.[58] The 'considerable mathematical ability' Farrell included required some clarification

---

[54] APEA Exhibit, Transcripts of Proceedings, Professional Engineers' Case Nos 1 & 2 before Conciliation and Arbitration Commission, Association of Professional Engineers, Australia, Noel Butlin Archives Centre, NBAC/N4/51.
[55] APEA Exhibit, NBAC/N4/51, 3.   [56] Ibid., 4.   [57] Ibid.   [58] Ibid., 5.

elsewhere by the union lawyers, as everyone was conscious that computers were coming. These, lawyers for the union argued, would never substitute for professional engineers. Computers were instead imagined to be like unskilled mathematical workers: 'the electronic brain', the union lawyer explained in his opening statement to the case, 'will only do the work of the routine kind'.[59]

The key difference between engineering and medicine, law, dentistry, and architecture, Farrell argued, was that the best of those practitioners were in private practice. Though this was changing already for all those professions, Farrell evidently felt he needed to clarify that engineers were not less committed to their profession than others:

The engineer who is an employee is not a timid man who us unwilling to risk private practice. Because of the nature and the organization of the profession and its work and the structure of our society it is not practicable for professional engineers to go into private practice ... since historically staffs have been built up by big corporations and governmental bodies.[60]

This comparison to other professions was part of the union's work value case. Work value in this sense needed to go beyond the objective national interest that they demonstrated, to also show the equivalence of engineering to other professions in terms of skill level, social value, and personal investment in the performance of the profession.

In the process, the engineers also invoked many other shared aspects of professional work and standing. These were qualitative characteristics that recalled the moral traits long associated with professional work, like dedication, passion, collegial habits, and responsibility. These were necessary to the work that they did to be sure, but it also meant that irrespective of their 'capacity to mix with all sorts of men', engineers *belonged* with other professionals. Moreover, like medicine, accountancy, and law, who continued to ban advertising that might undercut a learned colleague, engineering also had ethics that assured professional solidarity, including that an engineer 'shall not use the advantages of a salaried position to compete unfairly with engineers in private practice'.[61] In describing work value, then, engineers were evidently conscious that they belonged not just to an occupation category, but that they also shared virtuous qualities and habits individually and collegially, and were committed to solidarity with one another's material interests.

---

[59] Opening Speech for Engineers' Case, NBAC/N4/1, 86–87.
[60] APEA Exhibit, NBAC/N4/51, 6.
[61] Code of Ethics (Pamphlet), Supplement to *Journal of the Institution of Engineers* 31 (1959).

Class and Consumption

It was all very well that engineers were well educated, held professional values, and identified with other professionals, but this need not have led to higher pay rates. After all, as Gracchus Babeuf observed during the French Revolution, more education did not make for bigger bellies.[62] Belonging to the professional class was enabled and signalled by a certain 'standard of living', the union argued. 'That in itself might be regarded as a vague statement', the union lawyer conceded. They asked the tribunal to be patient with the problem, for it was central to the case.[63] The union set out the current salaries of engineers, demonstrating their inferiority, on average, to medical doctors, lawyers, and accountants. More importantly for our purposes, they also conducted a survey of members which showed engineers' average levels of spending on a range of items. Segments of this extensive survey, provided for the case, were also published in the union journal *The Professional Engineer* in 1956.

The survey report first catalogued engineers' family homes, long a key signifier of the middle class, alongside other consumer items that offered comfort and demonstrated respectability.[64] This survey showed that engineers were more likely to own (or be paying a mortgage on) their home as they became older and more experienced. This was hardly surprising. More marked was that, on average, 30 per cent of engineers (especially those with the least experience) lived in a home valued in the lowest bracket (less than £3,500). Between 24 and 30 per cent of engineers with fifteen or more years' experience lived in a home in the median bracket (£5,000–£7000). Between 9 and 11 per cent of engineers with twenty or more years' experience lived in homes worth £7,000–£10,000. Seven per cent of those at the peak of their careers (twenty-five to thirty years of practice) lived in homes in the top bracket, valued at more than

---

[62] See Mulholland, *Bourgeois Liberty*, 33–48.

[63] Opening Speech for Engineers' Case, NBAC/N4/1, 226.

[64] Of many, see Michael Winstanley, 'Owners and Occupiers: Property, Politics and Middle-Class Formation in Early Industrial Lancashire', in Alan J. Kidd and David Nicholls (eds), *The Making of the British Middle Class? Studies of Regional and Cultural Diversity Since the Eighteenth Century* (Phoenix Mill: Sutton, 1998), 92–112; Maxine Berg, *Luxury and Pleasure in Eighteenth-Century Britain* (Oxford: Oxford University Press, 2007); Cohen, *Consumer Republic;* Jackson Lears, 'From Salvation to Self-Realization: Advertising and the Therapeutic Roots of the Consumer Culture, 1880–1930', *Advertising and Society Review* 1.1 (2000); William R. Leach, *Land of Desire: Merchants, Power and the Rise of a New American Culture* (New York: Vintage, 2011); Ben Fine, *The World of Consumption* (London: Routledge, 2002).

£10,000, though only 1 per cent of all engineers fell into this top level of home ownership.[65]

Junior engineers tended not to own their own home; indeed, 57 per cent of first-year engineers paid board in a boarding house or a family home, which mostly tells us that they were unmarried. That is not surprising, many were barely twenty years old, though most engineers took out mortgages to purchase what was likely a marital home within four to seven years of starting work. By the time engineers had thirty to forty years' experience, 44 per cent owned their own home outright and 32 per cent were still paying mortgages. Others were renting a home, while a very small number continued to pay board late into their careers.[66] This data demonstrated that few engineers could afford the middle-class lifestyle that would both signal and enable their participation as members of the professional class. If engineering was a profession, then it followed that they must also live in a middle-class home. This was a key element of the union's success in securing a higher pay rate.

In 1956, engineers believed the court would agree that employment of 'domestic help' remained an important metric of class status. Only 11 per cent of engineers regularly employed assistance in the home, including, in the decade in which the motorized lawnmower grew to prominence, in the garden. Most paid less than £100 (AU$3,329 in 2020 terms) per year for all domestic assistance 'suggesting that this help is very limited'.[67] The *Professional Engineers' Case* further enumerated the home 'labour saving' technologies that, in the 1950s, were increasingly expected to act as a substitute for domestic help – for all that they often created more work in the aggregate.[68] Ownership of items such as lawnmowers, refrigerators, and automobiles were catalogued and deemed, for the professional engineers, as inadequate to a middle-class lifestyle.[69]

Vacation expenses were the next important marker of class status. The expansion of white-collar work was largely responsible, in a way not discussed in this book, for the vacation – or 'holidays', as it was mostly

---

[65] In 2020 terms, the lowest bracket was <AU$116.5K, the median bracket was AU$166K–$233K, and the upper bracket was AU$233K–$333K. These equivalences are based on CPI, using the Reserve Bank of Australia inflation calculator. While this gives us a good idea about the value of 1956 Australian pounds in relation to the basket of goods, it is a terrible indicator for house prices which have been subject to far higher levels of asset inflation than CPI. As I write, the current median Sydney house price is AU$1.25M. For more details, see Lisa Adkins, Melinda Cooper, and Martijn Konings, *The Asset Economy: Property Ownership and the New Logic of Inequality* (Medford: Polity Press, 2020).

[66] 'National Survey Results', 8–12.   [67] 'National Survey Results', 9.

[68] Cowan, *More Work for Mother*, 199–201.   [69] APEA Exhibit, 24.

known in some parts of the Anglo world, including Australia.[70] Most engineers spent an upper limit of £50 per year (AU$1,664 in 2020) on vacations. Older engineers on higher incomes typically spent between £50 and £100 (up to AU$3,329 in 2020 terms), 'Even at the highest level,' the union incredulously recounted, 'just 7% of all engineers reported an average expenditure on vacation over £200 per year' (AU $6,658 in 2020 terms).[71] One-fifth of all engineers had travelled overseas 'at some time', though half of these had travelled internationally for work. This too was considered a privilege and was limited to 'engineers in the older age group'.[72]

For engineers, hosting and attending dinner parties with other professionals, sharing sports and other virtuous leisure activities, as well as performing work that was grounded in a shared educational background, all facilitated their participation in the professional class.[73] Engineers often talked about this in relation to professional dress, partly because they were not always terribly good at it. Engineers, who were often working on site, did not always dress 'professionally'. 'On more than one occasion', opined an anonymous 1959 editorial, 'members calling on business at The Institution have been mistaken by junior members of the staff for workmen'.[74]

Engineers did not, however, believe that they could simply consume their way into membership of the professional class, even with more professional attire. The *Professional Engineers' Case* recognized that the work itself was the key substance of value and that this needed to be acknowledged as a professional field. This work, though, was then entwined with middle-class consumption to produce professional identity. The lawyer for the union summarized their claim by the logic that professional identity required consumption levels shared by other professionals. 'First and foremost', he said, 'the organization is a profession'. In recognizing engineering as a profession, 'the only conclusion that this Commission can come to' was a 'wage fixation … whereby they might enjoy a standard of living common to professional men', since 'it is

---

[70] Fred Inglis, *The Delicious History of the Holiday* (London: Routledge, 2000); Cindy Aron, *Working at Play: A History of Vacations in the United States* (New York: Oxford University Press, 2001); Richard White, *On Holidays: A History of Getting Away in Australia* (Melbourne: Pluto Press, 2005).

[71] 'National Survey Results', 8–12.   [72] 'National Survey Results', 9.

[73] See particularly Bourdieu, *Distinction*; Elizabeth Currid-Halkett, *The Sum of Small Things: A Theory of the Aspirational Class* (Princeton: Princeton University Press, 2017), 46–77.

[74] Editorial: To Raise the Status of the Profession of Engineering', *Transactions of the Institution of Engineers* 31 (1959), 58.

submitted one cannot possibly enjoy the status of a professional man on the salaries as set out in Exhibit 24'.[75]

Not Working Class

The union arguments succeeded. In their judgement elevating engineers' salaries, the arbitration commission awarded £1,400 annual salary (2.2 times the basic wage, which was £618 when the judgement was made in 1961) to a first-year post-Diplomate and £1,540 for a second year (2.5 times the basic wage); the latter was also the first-year rate for a university engineering graduate. In the sixth year of work, an engineer's minimum salary was £2,200, which was 3.6 times the basic wage.[76] It was a substantial pay rise that leading engineers thought also reflected a bolstering of their status as professionals.[77]

They also lost a portion of their membership. The trade-off in winning the case was a new commitment to educational barriers. Earlier in the twentieth century, most engineers were trained in workshops, under pupillage systems. Since entry to the profession was by examination and no one worried too much how one came to pass, the profession still had plenty of members who had never been to university. The Diplomates mentioned in the new award had also only studied at technical colleges and in workshops. In the 1950s, universities were only just beginning to train a majority of engineers. Most engineers were qualified via the Diploma, which was held in deep respect and affection across the profession. It was not, however, a qualification equivalent to a medical or law degree, an equivalence that mattered to the union case.[78] Cutting out the Diplomates of Engineering from the profession at that time, however, would have decimated its workforce.

The union argued that after one year of working with other professionals, Diplomates were indistinguishable from someone with a university degree.[79] It likely helped that as engineering faculties were established at new universities like the New South Wales University of Technology (later renamed the University of New South Wales) in 1949 and Monash University in 1958, the Diploma gave advanced standing in engineering

[75] Opening Speech for Engineers' Case, NBAC/N4/1, 226–227.
[76] Wright, Gallagher, and Galvin, 'Judgement', 326.
[77] Brian Lloyd, *Status and Reward: The History of Industrial Representation of Professional Engineers in Australia 1945–1996* (Melbourne: Association of Professional Engineers, 1996).
[78] Edelstein, 'Professional Engineers in the Australian Economy 1866–1980', 15.
[79] Wright, Gallagher, and Galvin, 'Judgement'.

degree programs.[80] The argument was controversial. In the tribunal, the union tried to dazzle the judges with a 'galaxy of talent' on one hand, but on the other hand, they asked them to also include as professionals, members who had not even matriculated from high school.

In the professional association, some members wanted to confine the profession to those who attended university. Many, however, also held opposite views. Dominated as it was by engineers who were deeply suspicious of university training, a vocal group disputed the supposed superiority of those with what they considered inadequate workshop experience. Including Diplomates and considering their standing equivalent to a university degree after one year of experience was a compromise position, struck after considerable acrimony expressed through letters to the professional association journal.

The Diploma was the top rung of the non-university pathway to engineering. The decision excluded many other engineers.[81] As well as pushing some engineers out of the profession, the decision also erected new barriers. Where earlier generations of automotive mechanics, for example, were given opportunity to develop careers in mechanical or aeronautical engineering, this was now unlikely. As historian Michael Pearson has shown, the *Professional Engineers Case* turned car repair into relatively dead-end work, with few opportunities for career progression. The professional engineers likely did not even notice. Their only goal was to show that they were not working class.[82]

Conclusion

In 1962, when Nancy Fisher, Bill Kennedy, and Steve Hempelman decided to go to university, there was no need for them to consider whether they would work for public or private institutions, or start their own business, in the future. Their relationship to the means of production or the profit motive had little bearing on their class status. The evidence outlined in the *Professional Engineers' Case* helps explain why. Irrespective of their employment in public or private sectors, enterprise type or even ownership of a business, the engineers' case shows the ways that professionals recognized each other as members of the same class. As we saw in Chapter 5, there were sometimes conflicts between salaried and sole-trading professionals, as at the beginning of the Saskatchewan

---

[80] Forsyth, "Expanding Higher Education'.
[81] Forsyth and Pearson, 'Engineers and Social Engineering', 169–195.
[82] Michael P. R. Pearson, 'Grease Monkeys: A History of Mechanics in Australia', PhD Dissertation, Australian Catholic University, Sydney, 2021.

doctors' strike. Despite such squabbles, professionals also expressed their solidarity. Ethical bans on advertising, or using the advantages of salaries against colleagues in private practice, acknowledged the structural risks of different relations to profit-making, but assured members prioritized the profession's shared material interests.

In the *Professional Engineers' Case*, this solidarity rested on tools developed by the working class.[83] They formed a union, which gave them strength in a struggle for increased pay by employers. Over the 1960s, professional unions grew across the Anglo world, as more professionals became employees of larger enterprises.[84] The trend to larger enterprise with salaried employees was faster among Australian engineers than other professions, but it was consistent across occupations. In time, most professionals, like the majority of engineers in 1957, were employees, exchanging their labour for a salary. This has made it tempting for some social scientists to see professional employees in the working class. To such scholars, who consider the exchange of labour for wages the class criterion that mattered most, the professional class simply did not exist. Their rejection of working-class status, according to this standpoint, was mere 'false consciousness'.[85]

There is some wishful thinking in this type of analysis. If professionals were workers, they could join with the working class to effect significant structural change.[86] It is evident, however, that professionals did not typically see themselves in this way. If, with E. P. Thompson, we agree that class consciousness is an important way of acknowledging agency, we must take professional rejection of working-class status seriously.[87] Professionals rejected working-class status even when they unionized, for it underpinned their shared 'fear of falling', of losing class standing.[88] The engineers' case shows that professionals' relationship to the working class was not just a matter of clinging to their superior perch; it was a fundamentally antagonistic relationship. For the professional class to gain the substance of 'work value', the 'relation of control which is at

---

[83] They were not alone; see instances of medical professionals adapting working-class techniques of solidarity. Green, 'The 1918 Strike of the Medical Profession'.

[84] Giddens, *Class Structure of the Advanced Societies*, 189–209.

[85] C. Wright Mills argued that most office workers were an exploited working class, whose deskilling, as Harry Braverman recounted the managerial techniques transferred from factory workers to professionals, made them a *lumpen bourgeoisie*; see Mills, *White Collar*; Braverman, *Labor and Monopoly Capital*.

[86] Such politics underpins Erik Olin Wright's attention to the exploitation of assets, which has helped me to see virtue as a material substance. See Erik Wright, *Classes* (London: Verso, 1985).

[87] Thompson, *Making of the English Working Class*.   [88] Ehrenreich, *Fear of Falling*.

the heart of the [professional-managerial class]', they also had to deny it to others.[89]

In this sense, work value was not just an industrial category but a quality by which the professional class made themselves. Their sense of value to society was inextricable from the virtue that is the subject of this book. By the mid-twentieth century, this constellation of virtues cohered into expert autonomy. Professional associations now sought to bolster this autonomy, which legitimized their work by guaranteeing the independence of professional expertise from any interest but their own.

In the *Professional Engineers' Case*, they went so far as to seek state sanction for this independence, but autonomy was a virtue that all professionals shared. Engineers might rely on mathematical accuracy, accountants their probity, and nurses their patience, but the 'work value' in a real, not just industrial, sense was that they all brought the honest application of expertise, unviolated by the interests of capital, labour, or government. Professional associations regulated this honesty in-house with examinations and career pathways that became internalized norms grounded in merit.[90]

This value was realized, as Chapters 1–5 have argued, as a combination of moral and financial profit. The *Professional Engineers' Case* called this 'national interest'. Without engineers who could be trusted to assert their independent judgement, the national economy was at risk, but so too was workplace safety and human well-being. The other professions had a similar role. Probably few teachers, doctors, and journalists were able to calculate the deflection of a loaded beam, but the nation's human capital and democratic legitimacy nevertheless relied on their independent expertise.

It was a precarious position, being professional. Their fear of falling was justified, since the material foundations for their class status resided in little more than their collective virtue. For individual professionals, *displaying* their belonging to the professional class helped shore up that membership.[91] This need for tasteful, respectable consumption was why the engineers needed a pay rise. The case made explicit a longstanding claim that professionals unable to live a middle-class lifestyle due to

---

[89] Ehrenreich and Ehrenreich, 'Professional Managerial Class', 18; also Poulantzas, 'The New Petty Bourgeoisie', 60.

[90] Sennett, *Culture of the New Capitalism*, 131–178. For a discussion of how this affected later generations, see Harris, *Kids These Days*, and Markovits, *Meritocracy Trap*.

[91] This is not the same 'virtue signaling' that the New Right invented in their critique of the 'liberal elite', but it is a kind of virtue signalling in that consumption had a signifying role; see Ehrenreich, *Fear of Falling*, 144–195.

inadequate income might not also be relied upon to bring middle-class virtues to their work.[92]

In this sense, professional class-making was absurdly tautological. Their status was what made the work middle class; and they were middle class because of their work. Having and maintaining a middle-class home, taking appropriate vacations, and purchasing the expected consumer goods, engineers could firmly declare themselves to be members of the professional class. Their work could not be guaranteed to be 'professional' either in a class sense or in the provision of high-standard work, without their ability to perform this level of consumption. This connection between affluence and merit was shared across the professional class. A degree of material superiority – not enough to be obscenely wealthy, but adequate for middle-class standards – contributed to the public's trust in professionals' expertise.[93]

Professional pay rates, in this sense, were not just a reward for the 'drudgery of study', as Higgins had put it, but a way to assure professional work was performed to high standards, and in the national interest. Ironically, this made the drudgery of study more important. The engineers' case informed the court of the immense risks presented by putting uneducated people in charge of the nation's infrastructure. It was no longer sufficient for the engineer to be recognized by the association's exams. Instead, formal recognition by tertiary education systems was key to the protection of the national assets that professionals now became.

This further separated professional experts from the working class. It gave professionals a foundation on which to assert expert authority over those who did not possess such education. To protect the nation, then, the working class ought not only to trust professional experts, but as Chapter 5 argued, they also needed to do what they were told. Professionals often worked in support of the goals of labour, but the *Professional Engineers' Case* shows a willingness to undermine working-class interests if it meant shoring up the moral and economic profit that accrued to the nation. The profit to themselves, professionals kept saying, was only to ensure that they too shared a material interest in this work value.

This was what made them professional-managerial. Professional experts weighed in on decisions that fell in their areas of expertise, but their work relied on other people believing and following their professional judgement. Such obedience was particularly demanded of the working class, but it was also required of capital. Independence from

---

[92] Bourdieu, *Distinction.*   [93] Currid-Halkett, *Sum of Small Things.*

capital was important, even as the value of the professions was *for* capital.[94] This was the deal the professional class struck in the era of settler colonization, establishing moral-economic hierarchies within each occupation and across the economy. Now, in the mid-twentieth century, just as the professional class was ascendant and the professional engineers were able to pin a pay rise to their elevated status, decolonization was poised to expose the moral failings embedded in this hierarchy. This is the subject of Chapter 7.

[94] Ehrenreich and Ehrenreich, 'Professional Managerial Class'.

Part III

The New Class Conflict, *c.*1975–2008

7 Moral Crisis

'Decimal Day' in Britain was 15 February 1971. Suddenly the pound consisted of 100 'new' pennies replacing the 'old' money where there were 12 pennies to the shilling, 20 shillings to the pound, and other combinations of value represented as guineas, half-crowns, and farthings.[1] A trend that began in Europe centuries earlier, the 'new money', was a long time coming. Britain was the last to decimalize in the Anglo world. South Africa disconnected from the British £sd system in 1961, Australia in 1966, and Aotearoa/New Zealand in 1967.[2] Such a transformation in currencies across the former British Empire was hardly the 'shock' produced by the collapse of currency agreements worldwide, as the order established at the 1944 Bretton Woods conference crumbled.[3] For many individuals, however, decimalization of the currency was a shock of another, even better-remembered kind. The new money affected people's everyday lives, transforming the mental arithmetic associated with calculating value, preparing budget forecasts, and paying for milk or bread.[4]

For professionals, a similar kind of currency transformation was also under way. The 'old money', the signifier of value that professionals acquired through their study and experience, was merit. This merit, as Chapters 1–7 showed, was based on who it excluded. The professionalization of nursing, for example, depended on eradicating nurses who, by their class status, resembled 'Sairey Gamp'. Instead, the profession selected young nurses for their middle-class characteristics. In the

---

[1] Michael Lee, 'The Advent of Decimalisation in Britain: 1971', *Historian* 106 (2010), 20–23.
[2] Adrian Tschoegl, 'The International Diffusion of an Innovation: The Spread of Decimal Currency', *The Journal of Socio-Economics* 39.1 (2010), 100–109.
[3] Peter Garber, 'The Collapse of the Bretton Woods Fixed Exchange Rate System', in Michael Bordo and Barry Eichengreen (eds), *A Retrospective on the Bretton Woods System: Lessons for International Monetary Reform* (Chicago: University of Chicago Press, 1993), 461–494.
[4] Lee, 'The Advent of Decimalisation in Britain'.

1970s, this logic was challenged. A moral crisis in each profession demanded professions turn their earlier hierarchies upside down. Teachers began to argue that merit was racist, and that standardized curricula were bad for children. Social workers who worked in the interests of First Nations people exposed the profession's racism when they were reprimanded for not doing the reverse. Medicine was the target of feminist condemnation for its paternalistic control of women's bodies. New journalists became conscious that objectivity failed to expose the corruption embedded in political and social life. Accountants, whose work relied on the mythical objectivity of numbers, were confronted with the vested interests at stake in their interpretation of profits under inflationary conditions. Even engineers, who once thought themselves the literal builders of civilization, were surprized to find that people wanted more of a say in the world they built; undermining, some engineers feared, their expert authority. These crises were not independent from one another. They were, as this chapter will show, all part of the same 'shock' to the economic order.

To understand these new threats to established professional hierarchy, we must see the effect of decolonization on the professional class. The professional class, now global, were some of the original forgers of colonial regimes, especially in the Anglo settler colonies. There and across the colonial world, both the colonized and their colonizers were co-constituted, as historian Achille Mbembe has shown, so that they built a mirrored relationship to one another.[5] Chapters 1–7 of this book showed that the professional class was made from the morality that an older middle class brought to settler-colonization. After 1945, when colonial regimes were dismantling, decolonization held a new mirror up to the professional class, demanding those virtues be reconsidered.

Anti-colonial movements exposed the racial and economic inequalities that hierarchies entrenched, including those based on merit. The moral crisis of the professional class was part of the process where, in international relations, anti-colonial leaders sought reversal of the hierarchies that made African and West Indian nations dependent on dominant economies.[6] These decolonizing countries transformed international institutions. In 1945, when the United Nations formed, there were fifty-one member nations, dominated by the 'white Commonwealth'. By 1974, when the United Nations adopted the anti-colonial New International Economic Order, membership included 138 nations, including members patronisingly referred to as the 'Third

---

[5] Mbembe, *On the Postcolony.*   [6] Getachew, *Worldmaking After Empire.*

World UN'.[7] Such a visible change alerted governmental leaders to anti-colonial efforts. As decolonizing nations sought to transfer the values of the welfare state to the international economic order, they also exposed the exploitative character of hierarchy. Mainstream Anglo world interests became newly conscious of the inequalities on which they had built their institutions.[8] Civil rights activism grew to prominence, leading to other battles for liberation. The civil rights movement was soon joined by those opposing patriarchal institutions and ideas, hoping to further liberate people from oppression based on gender and sexuality.

Such consciousness of moral reformation led scholars to explore the nature of the professional class. Much of the scholarly literature about professional class power emerged in this context, including Harry Braverman's *Labor and Monopoly Capital*, Eliot Friedson's *Professional Dominance*, Terence Johnson's *Professions and Power*, Magali Sarfatti Larson's *Rise of Professionalism*, Nicos Poulantzas' *Classes in Contemporary Capitalism*, and Barbara Ehrenreich and John Ehrenreich's insightful essays on the professional-managerial class.[9] As I discussed in Chapter 1, this body of work continues to influence scholarly understanding of professional power. What those scholars could not see from their moment, however, was that the relationship between virtue and the global economic order was beginning to collapse.

The moral crisis of the professions was also part of the larger economic crisis, which was well under way by the time the New International Economic Order was adopted in 1974. The global currency destabilization triggered by the 1971 'Nixon shock', which ended dollar-gold convertibility, sabotaged the economic order established at Bretton Woods.[10] Already then the 'Great Inflation' that was under way represented problems that philosopher Jürgen Habermas considered part of a 'legitimation crisis', characterized by the decline of public trust in state institutions to manage capitalism.[11] Unemployment rose to dramatic

---

[7] Glenda Sluga, 'The Transformation of International Institutions: Global Shock as Cultural Shock', in Niall Ferguson, Charles Maier, Erez Manela, Daniel Sargent (eds), *The Shock of the Global: The 1970s in Perspective* (Cambridge, MA: Harvard University Press, 2010), 223–236. Samuel Moyn, *Not Enough: Human Rights in an Unequal World* (Cambridge: Cambridge University Press, 2018), 89–118.

[8] Mary Dudziak, *Cold War Civil Rights: Race and the Image of American Democracy* (Princeton: Princeton University Press, 2002).

[9] Braverman, *Labor and Monopoly Capital*; Friedson, *Professional Dominance*; Johnson, *Professions and Power*; Larson, *Rise of Professionalism*; Nicos Poulantzas, *Classes in Contemporary Capitalism* (London: New Left Books, 1975); Ehrenreich and Ehrenreich, 'The Professional-Managerial Class'.

[10] Susan Strange, *Mad Money: When Market Outgrow Governments* (Manchester: Manchester University. Press, 1998).

[11] Habermas, *Legitimation Crisis*.

levels, further undermining trust in the industriousness of the welfare state, and in higher education.[12] The broad sense of 'malaise' grew some potent symbols. An energy crisis triggered by oil shocks and miner strikes produced dramatic lines for fuel in the United States and a three-day workweek to save energy in Britain. These became signifiers of the global transformations underway, resonant as they were with the loss of mid-century stability and the rise of new economic and moral uncertainties.[13]

Civil Rights and Education

Teaching was arguably the first profession to face moral crisis. This was fuelled by the US civil rights movement which grew, as historian Mary Dudziak has shown, in response to the Cold War. As decolonization proceeded in Ethiopia and elsewhere, Jim Crow America hardly offered a shining example of racial inclusion. Fears that this would lead African nations to look to Soviet communism over capitalist democracy encouraged the US government to whittle narratives of progress towards racial justice. In the process, they brought civil rights to the centre of American moral concern. It was by the efforts of people's movements, beginning with the National Association for the Advancement of Colored People, however, rather than government, that real change grew.[14] Schooling, where children's futures were imperilled by racist segregation, was at the centre of this struggle. In 1954, the US Supreme Court found in *Brown* v. *Board of Education* that racial segregation in schools was unconstitutional. The subsequent struggle for school desegregation in Arkansas and elsewhere made international news. In the midst of the human capital investment that characterized the post-war decades, as Chapter 5 discussed, the struggle for desegregation reminded teachers and parents across the English-speaking world that schooling was fundamental to life chances for all children under capitalist systems that relied on human capital.[15]

---

[12] Forsyth, *History of the Modern Australian University*, 100–101.
[13] Charles Maier, 'Malaise', in Niall Ferguson, Charles Maier, Erez Manela, and Daniel Sargent (eds), *The Shock of the Global: The 1970s in Perspective* (Cambridge, MA: Harvard University Press, 2010), 25–48; see further Stefan Eich and Adam Tooze, 'The Great Inflation', in Anselm Doering-Manteuffel, Lutz Raphael, and Thomas Schlemmer (eds), *Vorgeschichte der Gegenwart: Dimensionen des Strukturbruchs Nach den Boom* (Göttingen: Vandenhoeck & Ruprecht, 2016), 173–196; Lawrence Black, Hugh Pemberton, and Pat Thane (eds), *Reassessing 1970s Britain* (Manchester: Manchester University Press, 2016).
[14] Dudziak, *Cold War Civil Rights*.
[15] Gary Orfield, *Public School Desegregation in the United States, 1968–1980* (Washington, DC: Joint Center for Political Studies, 1983).

Desegregating schools was only the beginning. On reading Franz Fanon's anti-colonial classic, *The Wretched of the Earth*, Brazilian educator Paulo Freire argued that the problem with education was not primarily access to schooling. Rather, racism and oppression were built into the bones of curriculum and pedagogy. His book *Pedagogy of the Oppressed*, which was translated into English in 1970, argued that anti-colonial movements required a new system of schooling. This was about liberating the curriculum from Western hegemony, but also about freeing students from paternalistic control. Liberation, Freire said, could not be achieved within paternalistic educational models, which made students passive recipients of colonizing modes of knowledge. Instead, a critical pedagogy should underpin a new, radically student-centred system. This would empower students in oppressed communities to challenge and change the knowledge-foundation of society.[16]

The teaching establishment experienced this new alertness to racism as a crisis for the profession. Opening the 1971 symposium of the professional teachers' association Phi Delta Kappa in Arlington, Virginia, T. M. Stinnet argued that after the past 'decade of an awakening national conscience ... the public was made painfully aware of the plight of certain minority groups and their neglected children'. Now, he said, the teaching profession was under 'intense scrutiny'.[17] At the same symposium, then Dean of Education at the University of Massachusetts, Dwight W. Allen, along with assistant professor Glenn W. Hawks, acknowledged that 'America is a racist society'.[18] Allen and Hawks suggested establishing commissions on racism in the institutions where teachers trained:

Professional trainees, as well as those doing the training, should be encouraged to involve themselves directly in the perplexing problems that permeate American education with respect to matters of racial prejudice ... For example, professionals could be encouraged to consider how language and racism are interrelated, or how children's literature, textbooks, and teaching materials carry the germs of the ugly disease and what might be done to remedy such educationally debilitating processes.[19]

---

[16] Paulo Freire, *Pedagogy of the Oppressed* (New York: Herder and Herder, 1970).

[17] T. M. Stinnet, 'Reordering Goals and Roles', in T. M. Stinnet (ed), *Unfinished Business of the Teaching Profession in the 1970's* (Bloomington, IN: Phi Delta Kappa, 1971), 4, https://files.eric.ed.gov/fulltext/ED073069.pdf, Retrieved 24 March 2022.

[18] Dwight Allen and Glenn Hawks, 'Reconstruction of Teacher Education and Professional Growth Programs (Or How the Third Little Pig Escaped the Wolf)', in T. M. Stinnet (ed), *Unfinished Business of the Teaching Profession in the 1970's* (Bloomington, IN: Phi Delta Kappa, 1971), 19.

[19] Allen and Hawks, 'Reconstruction of Teacher Education', 20.

Teacher training was a key target of reform, with the hope that a new generation of educators might use schooling to build a less-racist society. Similar concerns inspired teachers working with First Nations people across the Anglo world. These educators were newly conscious of education's role in the settler-colonial project. Many recognized that some of this harm amounted to cultural genocide, suppressing Indigenous languages and cultural knowledge as part of what historian Patrick Wolfe would later label the 'logic of elimination'.[20] In pockets of the Anglo world, pioneering teachers sought to reverse the process, particularly by encouraging bilingual education. As Canadian provinces began to close or reform Indian Residential Schools, teachers began teaching children in Cree or Ojibway. 'We think of English and French as the two founding languages,' admitted Dr W. N. Toombs then at the University of Regina. 'But we forget that the Indians were already firmly established here first'.[21] Similarly, in Australia's Northern Territory, bilingual education, teaching in both English and Yolŋu was seen as a way to turn teaching from a colonizing institution to a decolonizing force.[22] In Aotearoa/New Zealand, bilingual education commenced the struggle towards a bicultural society. It was by the growth of bilingual education that we now refer to the country by its Māori name, Aotearoa, as well as by its Pākehā title, New Zealand.[23]

While civil rights and decolonization provided a sharp push for reform in education, other social and cultural changes were also afoot. The crisis in the teaching profession was further fuelled by the cultural and political transformations of the 1950s and 1960s. Paul Goodman's *Growing Up Absurd* described widespread youth alienation from the fundamentally oppressive character of the 'organized system'. When schooling merely promised a future of meaningless, procedural work of the kind C. Wright Mills exposed in *White Collar* and William H. Whyte critiqued in *Organization Man*, was it any wonder young people disengaged? In his sequel, *Compulsory Miseducation*, Goodman further argued that schooling was harmful to children. Education's fundamental failure to nourish the authentic self – authenticity being one of the touchstones of the

[20] Wolfe, *Traces of History*.

[21] Alexis Shields, 'Indian Bilingual Conference Hears of Manitoba Experiment', *The Leader-Post*, 14 March 1978, 4.

[22] Archie Thomas, 'Bilingual Education, Aboriginal Self-Determination and Yolŋu Control at Shepherdson College, 1972–1983', *History of Education Review* 50.2 (2021), 196–211.

[23] Jenny Ritchie and Mere Skerrett, *Early Childhood Education in Aotearoa New Zealand: History, Pedagogy, and Liberation* (New York: Palgrave Macmillan, 2014).

moment – actively taught values that were damaging to children's self-hood and to the society that they would form as adults.[24]

Goodman's critique fell on fertile ground, as the spirit of reform transformed 1960s institutions, including the Catholic Church, which was then responsible for a considerable amount of schooling across the Anglo world. The Catholic education tradition expressed, as historian Robert Orsi has argued, the fervent and fearful ways parents sought to 'pass their religious beliefs and values on to children'. It is also true that parents may have been merely obedient to their bishops, who Orsi argues fell barely short of requiring Catholics to school their children in religious institutions.[25] The Vatican II reforms of the mid-1960s radically altered Catholic education. The rituals and staffing of Catholic schooling were transformed, particularly as the universal call to holiness 'produced a dramatic change in the cost/benefit ratio of religious life and drained Catholic schools of critical human capital'.[26] But the reforms of Vatican II were not primarily economic. Theologian Henri J. M. Nouwen represented some of the new Catholic shift towards inner transformation, which he argued should be made available by teaching. Nouwen sought to reform teaching in the Catholic tradition as a kind of spiritual hospitality. The type of personal becoming Nouwen pursued for all humans required teachers who understood that students could not be 'molded into one special form of the good life'. By contrast to its possibilities for fostering becoming, Nouwen argued that teaching presently tended to be oppressive, so that 'practically every student perceives his education as a long endless row of obligations to be fulfilled'.[27]

Such an emerging role for education as personal growth extended beyond the Catholic system. Many teachers felt that reform was needed for all students, not just those from oppressed or religious communities. For Phi Delta Kappa's Stinnet, who was committed to Progressive-era education, a key problem was that traditional schooling 'reduced the individual [to] a number in the soulless conscience of an error-prone

---

[24] Paul Goodman, *Compulsory Miseducation* (New York: Horizon Press, 1964); Paul Goodman, *Growing Up Absurd* (New York: Random House, 1960).

[25] Robert Orsi, *Between Heaven and Earth: The Religious Worlds People Make and the Scholars Who Study Them* (Princeton: Princeton University Press, 2006), 73–109, quote from 77.

[26] Rania Gihleb and Osea Giuntella, 'Nuns and the Effects of Catholic Schools: Evidence from Vatican II', *Journal of Economic Behaviour and Organization* 137 (2017), 191–213, quote from 192; David Byrne, 'The Construction of Religion as a Subject for Catholic Schools in Western Australia: An Historical Analysis of the Situation from 1929 to 1982', unpublished PhD dissertation, University of Western Australia (2021).

[27] Henri Nouwen, *Reaching Out: The Three Movements of the Spiritual Life* (New York: Doubleday, 1975), 84.

computer'.[28] While Stinnet and others worked to reform mainstream teaching practices, a new wave of alternative schools also emerged, resembling the Fröbel, Steiner, Montessori, and other utopian schools established in the wake of Progressivist education.[29] Growing cohorts of parents now sought student-centred education for their children. In Toronto, for example, the ALPHA (A Lot of People Hoping for an Alternative) commenced in 1972. By 1975, the *Vancouver Sun* reported three alternative high schools in the area: SEED (Shared Experience, Exploration and Discovery), Subway Academy and Contact.[30] Rather than being subjected to a system in which merit was a matter of pass or failure, such schools were self-consciously centred on children's individual becoming.[31]

These alternative schools often looked to the philosopher Ivan Illich. Illich argued that teaching was coercive and controlling, 'schooling' a population into intellectual idleness and political lethargy. In his 1971 blockbuster publication, *Deschooling Society*, Illich maintained that education as it was currently articulated made the world stupider. 'School has become the world religion of a modernized proletariat', Illich argued, making 'futile promises of salvation to the poor'.[32] This book was part of a larger series in which Illich criticized the monopoly power of professionals. 'Helping' professionals made society helpless, stopping them from working collectively to deal with structural problems like poverty, sickness, and ignorance. It was no coincidence, Illich argued, that these were the exact problems that professional experts purported to tackle.[33] This inspired teachers to take a new approach to their students, placing them at the centre of the work.

Teachers also brought the energy of the New Left to their mission. Some joined niche professional associations, often with their own journals. In Australia, the *Radical Education Dossier* (RED) was launched by RED G, the Radical Education Group, in 1976. RED G was an explicitly socialist teachers' organization that aimed to expose the relationships between education and capitalism. This led them to more revolutionary

---

[28] Stinnet, 'Reordering Goals and Roles', 6.
[29] See Susan Semel and Alan Sadovnik, 'The Contemporary Small-School Movement: Lessons from the History of Progressive Education', *Teachers College Record* 110.9 (2008), 1744–1771; Ron Miller, 'Educating the True Self: Spiritual Roots of the Holistic Worldview', *Journal of Humanistic Psychology* 31 (1991), 53–67.
[30] Advertisement, *The Vancouver Sun*, 13 September 1975, 6–7.
[31] Julie McLeod, 'Experimenting with Education: Spaces of Freedom and Alternative Schooling in the 1970s', *History of Education Review* 43.2 (2014), 172–189.
[32] Ivan Illich, *Deschooling Society* (London: Calder and Boyars, 1971), 15.
[33] Ivan Illich, *Limits to Medicine: Medical Nemesis the Expropriation of Health* (London: Marion Boyars, 1976).

conclusions than their reformist colleagues. Contributors to the *Radical Education Dossier* typically saw inclusive education as part of the mythology of the system, rather than a challenge to it. One contributor argued:

There is something much more important to do than working to help disadvantaged groups and I want to go further to claim that merely to work and help disadvantaged groups is not a socially progressive thing to do. In fact, if all you are doing is helping some people to overcome their disadvantage in a system that unfairly disadvantages people, then you are actually helping to reinforce that system. I believe that the most important thing to do is to work towards a society in which there are not disadvantaged groups.[34]

Such professionals believed that their work, even at its most inclusive, was part of a wider system of capitalist exploitation. Like Freire's claim that expanding educational access was not enough to decolonize schooling, radical teachers similarly argued that inclusion was also not sufficient to effect revolution.[35]

Decolonizing Social Work

Like those radical teachers, an emerging generation of social workers shared the view that their work did little to effect real social transformation. Across the Anglo world, many social workers expressed a growing disquiet about their orientation to individuals, especially in case work, which they increasingly felt contradicted the profession's responsibility to promote wider social reform. This was especially perturbing when the practice of social work in the United States was becoming profitable for those now counselling the middle class.[36] Disquiet over the profit motive contributed to a growing suspicion that 'helping' professionals were frequently merely self-serving. In 1957, Marion K. Sanders' 'Social Work: A Profession Chasing Its Tail' was published in *Harper's Magazine* and very widely read. Sanders suggested that social workers were too concerned with their own professionalism to be properly interested in the welfare of others.[37]

---

[34] Trainer cited in Tom Griffiths and Jack Downey, '"What To Do About Schools?": The Australian Radical Education Group (RED G)', *History of Education Review* 44.2 (2015), 170–185, 179; T. Trainer, 'Bandaids or Fundamental Change?', *Radical Education Dossier* (1984) 22, 4–7.
[35] Isobelle Meyering, *Feminism and the Making of a Child Rights Revolution 1969–1979* (Melbourne: Melbourne University Press, 2022), 73–99.
[36] Walkowitz, *Working with Class*, 141–176.
[37] Marion Sanders, 'Social Work: A Profession Chasing Its Tail', *Harper's Magazine*, March 1957, 56–62.

In Australia's Northern Territory, radical social worker John Tomlinson took this further, pointing to professionals' financial stake in the welfare system:

Practitioners in social work, sociology, psychology and many other professions have sought to establish their position in the welfare industry through a process of mystification. Nowhere have the professionals convincingly demonstrated their usefulness in building a better society. They have been particularly irrelevant at the points where they usually claim the greatest expertise, that is, in helping the poor, the 'mentally ill', Aborigines and migrants. The professionals have disregarded the problems of the working class except for quaint studies undertaken intermittently. The professionals have been too busy struggling for a share of the welfare cake to ask themselves what they can contribute, what are their skills. Their greatest fault has been their failure to ask how relevant the current practices of the welfare industry are to welfare problems.[38]

Rather than merely skimming welfare funds for personal gain with little social benefit, however, the problem for social work, as for teaching, was embedded in professional practices.

Tomlinson and other radical social workers argued that the profession was altogether a 'presumptuous business'. 'Social control in an exploitative society,' as John Ehrenreich later similarly wrote, 'could only mean social control of the exploited.'[39] In 1971, John L. Erlich, then an assistant professor at the University of Michigan, argued, 'Those of us who serve the social welfare establishment are in special trouble'. He predicted pushback from social work's client base:

Clients … are throwing off the oppressive role definitions that have been foisted on them for so long. Passive consumers of our largess are disappearing. Finally they have said a resounding no, not only to us, but to the system that in great measure determines what social workers are.[40]

Erlich, alongside the many like him who wrote for *Social Work* in the 1970s, was not concerned that social workers were failing to fulfil their responsibilities. Instead, he suggested that members of the profession were at their most injurious when they were doing their job. Social workers began to pursue new research, exploring the potential injury that they did through race and gender discrimination, and by their treatment of homosexuals. Others criticized the kind of class-based meddling and moral superiority that had long shaped social work's relationship to the

---

[38] John Tomlinson, *Is Band-Aid Social Work Enough?* (Darwin: Wobbly Press, 1977), i.
[39] Ehrenreich, *The Altruistic Imagination*, 200.
[40] John Erlich, 'The "Turned-on" Generation: New Antiestablishment Action Roles', *Social Work* 16.4 (1971), 22–27, quote on 23.

'deserving poor'.[41] A sign of the social and economic divide between social workers and their clients, especially in the United States, was that social workers, unlike their clients, were typically white.[42] The damage that social workers did was particularly obvious in their roles policing the logics of settler colonialism. Working in Australian Aboriginal communities, John Tomlinson was scathing in his criticism of the profession's role in the oppression of Aboriginal people. Social workers, placing First Nations people into housing that facilitated the government's assimilation policy, were a crucial vector of the erasure of Indigenous peoples and culture.[43] They were forced in this way into 'recipient' roles; Tomlinson believed that Aboriginal substance abuse, then endemic in the Top End, was a type of protest against white domination.[44] Even the best welfare workers, Tomlinson argued, who were 'treating' rather than demonizing such social ills only succeeded in 'depoliticizing' this Aboriginal protest. In the process, Tomlinson argued, they also perpetuated racist social stigma.[45]

Community interest in Aboriginal welfare was newly awakened in Australia by the 1965 Freedom Ride, which drew inspiration from the US civil rights movement.[46] In this context, newspapers began reporting the negative effects of 'paternalistic' social work services, including the forced adoption of Aboriginal children. In 1968, for example, the Victorian Director of Aboriginal Welfare spent a week checking his files and was shocked to discover that government social workers were commonly facilitating 'illegal and harmful adoptions'.[47] This practice, which produced the tragedy that became known as the 'Stolen Generations', was the subject of new criticism from radical social workers, including John Tomlinson. They were influenced by international movements that sought self-determination for First Nations peoples across the settler world.[48]

[41] Ehrenreich, *The Altruistic Imagination*, 187–208.
[42] Walkowitz, *Working with Class*, 51.
[43] John Tomlinson, 'Challenging State Aggression against Indigenous Australians', in Deena Mandell and Nilan Yu (eds), *Subversive Action: Extralegal Practices for Social Justice* (Waterloo, Ontario: Wilfrid Laurier University Press, 2015), 27; see Wolfe, 'Settler Colonialism and the Elimination of the Native'.
[44] 'Bandaids for Social Disease', *Tribune (Sydney)*, 22 February 1978, 8.
[45] Tomlinson, *Is Band-Aid Social Work Enough?*, i.
[46] Ann Curthoys, *Freedom Ride: A Freedom Rider Remembers* (Sydney: Allen & Unwin, 2002).
[47] 'Aborigines, Adoption and Assimilation', *Tribune (Sydney)*, 24 July 1968, 11.
[48] Read, *The Stolen Generations*. See of many Coulthard, *Red Skin, White Masks*; Erica-Irene A. Daes, 'An Overview of the History of Indigenous Peoples: Self-Determination and the United Nations', *Cambridge Review of International Affairs* 21.1 (208), 7–26; Laura Rademaker and Tim Rowse, *Indigenous Self-Determination in Australia: Histories and*

Such radicalism was not just talk. In the 1970s, Tomlinson was at the centre of a widely reported case that became known as the 'Nola Affair'. Nola's story helps us see the ways the new criticisms of professional authority were not only changing values applied at work but also producing moral conflicts within the middle class. Nola was a seven-year-old Burarra child who was born in coastal Maningrida in West Arnhem Land, in Australia's Top End.[49] In precarious health because of her premature birth, in 1966 baby Nola spent most of her time in the hospital in the capital city of the Northern Territory, Darwin. A medical social worker there decided it would be better if Nola was fostered with a family in Darwin, still close to medical care, but less institutionalized as she grew.

The social worker hoped Nola would be placed with an Aboriginal family, but the policies of the relevant government department inhibited Aboriginal people from acting as foster carers. When she was eighteen months old, after the period in which Nola would be expected to recover her strength, her parents asked for Nola's return. Complicated bureaucracy was repeatedly invoked so that six years passed without the family seeing Nola. When John Tomlinson was made aware of the case in the early 1970s, he saw from the file that Nola's foster carers had used contacts in the public service to influence the decision to keep Nola from being returned to her family.[50]

In 1973, Tomlinson and other social workers assisted Nola's father Jack to access legal aid – a relatively new institution, informed by a related transformation in values in the law – to lodge a Supreme Court action against the government. At the same time, a visit with Nola was arranged.[51] Jack then took Nola home to Cadell River, under an hour's drive from Maningrida, where her parents lived with their other children. Government lawyers affirmed that Nola's family had rightful custody of their child. However, Nola's white foster carers were outraged by the parents' claim. After Nola returned to Cadell River, they turned to the government, saying that unless the social worker responsible was disciplined, they would launch proceedings

---

Historiography (Canberra: ANU Press, 2020); Audrey Jane Roy, *Sovereignty and Decolonization: Realizing Indigenous Self-Determination at the United Nations and in Canada* (Victoria: University of Victoria, 2001).

[49] She was named Nola Brown in the newspaper reports. This was not her surname, but a name given to the newspapers by foster carers. Out of respect for Nola, I have used her first name, as Tomlinson did in his account of the episode.

[50] Tomlinson, 'Challenging State Aggression'.

[51] The distances in the Northern Territory made this a plane trip.

against the Department of Aboriginal Affairs for abducting Nola from their care.[52] While Tomlinson and other social workers sought to reform social work from a system that consistently imposed settler-colonial logics to one grounded in 'working with the community to solve the issues they identified', other professionals – some social workers, lawyers, and public servants – opposed them.[53] When they caught wind of the case, journalists began to take sides. A story in *The Australian* reported that Nola had been abducted from her white 'parents', no doubt to the consternation of other white adoptive parents of Indigenous children across the settler colonies.[54] Anthropological stereotyping of Native barbarism infused newspaper accounts that spread through the Anglo world. In Florida, for example, the *Miami Herald* reported the story. So too did Canada's *Ottawa Citizen* and *Calgary Herald*.[55] 'White Australians are shocked,' claimed Bill Harcourt in those papers, whose byline at that time listed him with the London Observer Service. Harcourt's words were repeated in newspapers around the world, reporting that Nola was removed by government officials when she was 'promised in marriage to a middle aged aborigine [sic]'. Gesturing to the supposedly excessive 'generosity' of the newly elected Federal Labor government under the leadership of Prime Minister Gough Whitlam and its policy of self-determination, Harcourt recounted 'stories about tribal law and punishment', including grotesque untruths about Aboriginal Elders setting young people on fire as punishment for drinking alcohol. Evidently intended to rouse white indignation, Harcourt wrote that it was 'alleged that Nola Brown has been speared as a punishment and probably already deflowered'.[56]

While Harcourt shamelessly fuelled outrage by invoking such racist images, other journalists reported in favour of Aboriginal self-determination. The *Canberra Times* said that Nola was fitting in with her birth family, including her brothers, and learning to speak Burarra. One said that another professional – a nursing sister, in this case – told the minister that 'Nola is well and happy and is attending school

---

[52] 'Heads May Roll, Says Minister', *Sydney Morning Herald*, 23 September 23, 1973, 28; 'Aboriginal Girl "Happy"', *Canberra Times*, 22 September 1973, 3.
[53] Tomlinson, 'Challenging State Aggression', 27.   [54] Ibid., 31.
[55] William Harcourt, 'Aboriginal Policy to Fuel Racial Strife', *The Miami Herald*, 27 September 1973, 30; William Harcourt, 'Aborigine's Abduction Shock to Australians', *The Ottawa Citizen*, 13 October 1973, 7; William Harcourt, 'Racial Tensions Feared', *Calgary Herald*, 13 November 1973, 4.
[56] Harcourt, 'Aboriginal Policy to Fuel Racial Strife', 30.

regularly'.[57] The *Honolulu Star-Bulletin* said that Nola was happy in her 'bush country home'. They further reported that '[n]o Aboriginal girl these days is forced to marry a man to whom she has been promised'.[58] John Tomlinson was suspended from the public service for his role in the Nola Affair. The following year when he returned to work, he was demoted, leading his colleagues in the small department to take strike action to support him.[59] In an account Tomlinson published in 2015, he said he'd stayed in touch with Nola's family. Nola was able to grow up in her Aboriginal community. Many years later she bore healthy children of her own. In this way, despite the racism of some journalists, the 'Nola Affair' ended well. If Tomlinson was doing his job as it had been laid out for him, Nola's story would likely not have had such a relatively happy ending.[60]

Not all social workers agreed that the kind of criticism that Tomlinson levelled at the profession was productive. They thought, by contrast, that it might undermine their capacity to do good. Refusing the image their colleagues saw in the decolonizing mirror, some social workers, like Harold Weismann from Hunter College School of Social Work in New York, considered traditional middle-class virtues to still present the best path to social progress. In 1972, Weismann argued that the 'mea culpa' of the profession was 'misguided'. He said that radical techniques of reform would fail, and the problem would inevitably return to where it belonged: middle-class aid. Because of this, the middle class needed to be protected from radical criticism:

> [The] basic characteristic of the movement is disdain for the middle class, which is viewed primarily as a constraining factor, if not the enemy. There are two disastrous consequences of this view: the middle class and middle-class oriented are dehumanized and their desire for personal security, economic stability, and self-esteem is denied legitimacy.[61]

Secure, well-paid middle-class employment in the professions was, in his view, the only pathway to 'distributive justice'.

Professional virtue, Weismann believed, required social workers to be able to recognize the contradictions of their role, and band together. The new virtues emerging with decolonization, by contrast, undermined their work:

---

[57] 'Watch Is Being Kept on Girl', *Canberra Times*, 3 October 1973, 15.
[58] 'Abo Girl Happy with Bush Country Home', *Honolulu Star-Bulletin*, 23 September 1973, 3.
[59] 'Appeal against Downgrading', *The Canberra Times*, 17 November 1973, 3.
[60] Tomlinson, 'Challenging State Aggression', 34.
[61] Harold Weissman, 'The Middle Road to Distributive Justice', *Social Work* 17.2 (1972), 88.

The political Left couches its arguments in broad moral terms, and social workers find it difficult to resist these arguments because they cannot accept the moral ambiguity of their profession. However, without such acceptance, social work will never develop a viable moral stance.

Weismann said that instead of allowing themselves to be seduced by stark moral claims, the middle class needed to be pragmatic. In so doing they would protect the institution of social work and 'maintain and promote a set of values for society'. These values were essential, even though 'they will not succeed in the foreseeable future. This is an honorable and consistent position and it may be vindicated in the long run'. This was the opposite of the 'tired scenario of the Left', where professionals and radicals joined to 'press for a better society'.[62] 'Waiting' was the honourable thing to do, he argued, pointing out that 'waiting is considerably more difficult for the service recipients than the service-givers' – though he still thought they should do it.[63]

Women versus Medicine

More than any other profession, medicine was subject to fierce opposition. As Chapter 5 discussed, the medical profession had displayed considerable self-interest as the welfare state took increased responsibility for healthcare. In the shadow of that behaviour, it was now subjected to vociferous criticism from all sides. On the left, Ivan Illich's *Medical Nemesis* argued that medicine actively kept society sick. Moreover, a whole category of illnesses could be attributed to the medical establishment by over-prescription, hospital-borne contagions, and botched treatments.[64] Medicine, other leftist critics of monopolization contended, was an institution that benefited from control of healthcare as a set of ideas and practices. In so doing, this most elite body of professionals hindered society from making themselves healthy.[65] Chicago economist Milton Friedman joined this criticism from the right. In 1962, he argued that professional monopolies inhibited the agency of healthcare clients to choose from a selection of medical services. By contrast to a free market in healthcare, the medical monopoly, he suggested, made medical practice less efficacious.[66]

---

[62] Weissman, 'Middle Road to Distributive Justice', 89.   [63] Ibid., 90.
[64] Illich, *Medical Nemesis*.
[65] Friedson, *Professional Dominance*; Willis, *Medical Dominance*.
[66] Milton Friedman, *Capitalism and Freedom* (Chicago: University of Chicago Press, 1962), 137–160.

Neither left- nor right-wing critics were as strident in their anger at medicine, however, as feminists. The women's liberation movement made medicine a particular target. They saw medical power aligned to patriarchy, a structure that they believed overlapped with ideologies that also repressed people based on class, race, and sexuality. In their 1978 book, Barbara Ehrenreich and Deirdre English noted that as nineteenth-century medicine professionalized, it was only elite women who doctors considered to be 'naturally' frail. Such women, who could pay for medical care, suffered from everything that happened to them, particularly if it had to do with their reproductive system. Wealthier women needed male medical practitioners to attend them when they bled, or when they didn't bleed, from their vaginas, and when they faced childbirth or else when they failed to bear children. By contrast to these fee-paying fragile women, Ehrenreich and English noticed that working-class women and women of colour were conveniently deemed by medical science to be remarkably robust. Such women had little need of medical services, even in childbirth, according to their doctors. This diagnostic pattern served the profession's interests, Ehrenreich and English argued, since such women could not pay for a doctor.[67]

Similar connections between healthcare and patriarchy were also the subject of segments of Germaine Greer's 1970 bestseller *The Female Eunuch*. Here her focus was on sexual health. Greer argued that medical knowledge of women's reproductive systems seemed a little too conveniently daft. While science abounded when it came to the risks to female reproduction if women worked hard in too-senior roles, medicine seemed by contrast utterly incapable of understanding much about women's reproductive health that would offer genuine help when they sought assistance. Certainly, medical understanding of female sexual pleasure was extremely poor.[68] Feminists argued that women's and homosexual sexuality, which they said threatened patriarchal dominance, were actively suppressed by medical science. Such criticisms of the medical establishment became a touchstone of women's and gay liberation movements.[69]

In this way, feminist criticism of patriarchal ideas, rather than just institutions, opened a critical space soon filled by Michel Foucault's *Birth of the Clinic*, translated into English in 1973. This gave critics a

---

[67] Barbara Ehrenreich and Deirdre English, *For Her Own Good: 150 Years of the Experts' Advice to Women* (New York: Anchor Press, 1978).

[68] Germaine Greer, *The Female Eunuch* (London: Paladin, 1971).

[69] Veronica Beechey, 'On Patriarchy', *Feminist Review* 3.1 (1979), 66–82; Ann Ferguson, 'Patriarchy, Sexual Identity, and the Sexual Revolution', *Signs: Journal of Women in Culture and Society* 7.1 (1981), 158–172.

new set of tools with which to point to the authority asserted by the 'medical gaze'. The medical gaze, Foucault argued, gave doctors a kind of priestly power over everyone's bodies.[70] Then in 1978 when his *History of Sexuality* was also translated into English, Foucault gave a new language to the ways that medical and scientific authority over sexuality – especially homosexuality – now substituted for older, religious surveillance via the confessional. The 'truth' about sex in modernity was that it was now science, not religion, that deemed homosexuality 'perverse', with terrible implications for selfhood and becoming.[71]

All these criticisms were experienced as a crisis in medicine. They were accompanied by fierce debates in the letter pages of medical journals across the Anglo world. For some, the solutions seemed straightforward. Certain feminists believed that supporting women medical practitioners was the answer, as women professionals would likely better investigate and support women's sexual and reproductive health. Universities had admitted women to medicine since the nineteenth century, though as a new cohort of women practitioners still understood, they experienced considerable barriers to career progression.[72] Professional leaders saw that many aspects of the medical career ladder needed to be changed to boost women's participation in medical work. These included equal pay for women, childcare and crèche, maternity leave (but not too much so a woman did not fall too far behind), flexible employment, continuing professional development, and a lifting of quotas at university entrance so that the 'wastage' of women not practising did not also contribute to a shortage of doctors.[73]

Progressive medical professionals, particularly younger doctors, were often eager to help transform medicine from a system that controlled sexuality to a profession that supported it. This triggered a range of virtuous transformations in medical practice. Medical journals began to publish work that sought to free bodies from past constraints, especially in the fields of sexual pleasure, homosexuality, and, in some cases,

[70] Michel Foucault, *The Birth of the Clinic: An Archaeology of Medical Perception* (London: Tavistock, 1973).
[71] Michel Foucault, *The History of Sexuality: 1 – The Will to Knowledge* (New York: Random House, 1978).
[72] Rosemary Pringle, *Sex and Medicine: Gender, Power and Authority in the Medical Profession* (Cambridge: Cambridge University Press, 1998); Meghan Scanlan, 'Medical History: First Women in Medicine', *New Zealand Medical Student Journal* 31 (2020), 50–51; Blake, *The Charge of the Parasols*.
[73] R. Holland, 'Comments: Women in Medicine', *Medical Journal of Australia*, 9 January 1971, 54–56.

transgender identities.[74] Reproductive health was a key area of reform since the contraceptive pill, introduced in the 1950s, offered women sexual liberation.[75] In Wellington, Aotearoa/New Zealand, as elsewhere, medical practitioners and nurses established a Women's Health Centre. It was a controversial move. The centre was closed by the city council after just three days. Following ongoing feminist activism, however, centres for women's health, which provided services related to reproductive health, as well as a series of activities that sought to de-medicalize childbirth, spread through Aotearoa/New Zealand.[76]

Reproductive health included abortion, which dominated the sense of crisis among medical practitioners.[77] In the 1950s, many doctors, particularly psychiatrists, supported abortion rights for pregnant women in emotional distress, though this did not necessarily mean that they believed women should decide themselves on whether they should have an abortion: most believed a psychiatrist should use their professional judgement. The Lane Committee, with a majority-women membership, supported an Abortion Act in Britain, which came into effect in 1967.[78] In 1970, the Vancouver Women's Caucus took the 'abortion caravan' to Ottawa, their VW Kombi van topped with a coat hanger–filled coffin that represented women killed during botched illegal abortions.[79] Fears that women were dying due to unprofessional abortion also encouraged

[74] Jennifer Terry, *An American Obsession: Science, Medicine and Homosexuality in Modern Society* (Chicago: University of Chicago Press, 1999); Susan Stryker, *Transgender History* (Berkley CA: Seal Press, 2008); Noah Riseman, *A History of Trans Health Care in Australia* (Melbourne: AusPATH, 2022); Ketil Slagstad and Debra Malina, 'The Political Nature of Sex: Transgender in the History of Medicine', *New England Journal of Medicine* 384 (2021), 1070–1074; James Bennett, 'Keeping the Wolfenden from the Door? Homosexuality and the "Medical Model" in New Zealand', *Social History of Medicine* 23.1 (2010), 134–152. On those medical practitioners who participated in 'cures', see Michael King, Glenn Smith, and Annie Bartlett, 'Treatments of Homosexuality in Britain since the 1950s – An Oral History: The Experience of Professionals', *British Medical Journal* 328.7437 (2004), 429–432.

[75] Elizabeth Watkins, *On the Pill: A Social History of Oral Contraceptives 1950–1970* (Baltimore: Johns Hopkins University Press, 1998); Lara Marks, *Sexual Chemistry: A History of the Contraceptive Pill* (New Haven: Yale University Press, 2001).

[76] Sandra Coney, 'The Women's Health Movement in New Zealand: Past Achievements, Future Challenges', *Reproductive Health Matters* 5.10 (1997), 23–26.

[77] A tiny sample includes Ian Furler, 'On Legal Abortion', *Medical Journal of Australia*, 27 February 1971, 489–495; 'Reasons for Abortion', *British Medical Journal*, 15 August 1970, 362; Esther Greenglass, 'Therapeutic Abortion and Its Psychological Implications: The Canadian Experience', *Canadian Medical Association Journal*, 18 October 1975, 754–757.

[78] Ashley Wivel, 'Abortion Policy and Politics on the Lane Committee of Enquiry, 1971–1974', *Social History of Medicine* 11.1 (1998), 109–135.

[79] Christabelle Sethna and Steve Hewitt, 'Clandestine Operations: The Vancouver Women's Caucus, the Abortion Caravan and the RCMP', *Canadian Historical Review* 90.3 (2009), 463–495.

twelve US states to pass abortion legislation by 1970. The *Roe* v. *Wade* decision was made in 1973, enabling legal abortion in the United States.[80] The prominence of abortion among feminist causes focused the general crisis of *women versus medicine* on the moral choices made by everyday doctors. The letter pages of medical journals across the Anglo world featured doctors objecting to abortion on moral grounds. In January 1971, for example, a medical correspondent with the pen name 'Another Devil's Advocate' wrote to the *Medical Journal of Australia* describing a 'young woman ... [with] an eight-month baby on her knee':

> She told me that she had three children, that she was pregnant again, and that she could not cope with any more children, and asked if I could 'give her something to bring on her periods' – in other words, if I would abort her. I suggested – facetiously – that if she felt she could not manage four children, then on the way home, throw the baby she was nursing into the creek ... About 12 months later she turned up again, this time nursing a baby of four or five months. When I asked her if she was pleased she did not have an abortion, she did not answer me directly. Instead, she looked down, caressed the baby, and said 'Mummy's little Angel.' I did not embarrass her further by referring to the matter again.[81]

While abortion presented a serious set of moral questions for medical practitioners, doctors writing to the medical journal typically took a flippant tone in their letters opposing abortion, as if their moral stance ought to be obvious to the journal's still mostly male readership. For example, 'To aid and abet the mounting of a lethal attack upon a defenceless child is contrary to the Australian concept of a fair go,' quipped Douglas Vann, a medical doctor in Bunbury, Western Australia.[82]

Dr Victor Wallace of Hughesdale, Victoria, was also against abortion, though his concern rested on his belief that Australia needed more future taxpayers. 'I have every confidence in the reproductive capabilities of the Australian people,' he jovially pronounced. Though the White Australia Policy was officially repealed, Wallace did not extend this confidence to the nation's capacity to welcome immigrants: 'There is an absence of racial tension in Australia, and we wish to keep it that way.' Linking medical authority over women's reproductive capacity to border sovereignty, Wallace argued against the possibility that any loss of population via abortion could be regained by immigration. Australia's superiority to

---

[80] Reagan, *When Abortion Was a Crime*, 216–245.

[81] Another Devil's Advocate, 'Psychiatric Indications for the Termination of Pregnancy', *Medical Journal of Australia*, 9 January 1971, 107.

[82] Douglas Vann, 'Psychiatric Indications for the Termination of Pregnancy', *Medical Journal of Australia*, 13 February 1971, 404.

the racial tensions he detected in the mother country was at stake, since 'Great Britain unwisely admitted many coloured people thereby allowing a permanent racial problem to develop'. Perhaps reflecting that his medical colleagues reading might suspect him to be veering too far from the subject of reproductive health, Wallace further gave his view on interracial coupling. 'Intermarriage ... between widely different ethnic groups only accentuates the incompatibilities. Successful adjustment in marriage is difficult enough without introducing disturbing factors,' he opined. For Wallace, continued immigration restriction was a matter of social stability. Both abortion and immigration should be avoided, he thought, because of something that sounded like medical diagnosis: the 'mental health of the community'.[83]

Despite such rhetorical morality, criticisms from Illich and others claimed that medicine ignored the health of the community, though public health seemed to be an exception. Women's reproduction and sexual health were a traditional focus for public health. Women's reproduction was central to the need to populate the settler colonies and to eugenicist interests in protecting the Anglo world from racial 'impurities'.[84] In this context, women (but not heterosexual men, typically) were also feared as the vectors of disease. They were the traditional scapegoat of British public health campaigning. However, in the 1970s, British public health campaigning changed. Rather than the advertising of earlier times, which relentlessly warned of venereal disease, public health institutions began instead to promote generic healthy living. In 1971, Britain's Chief Medical Officer Sir George Godber argued against a focus purely on contagions, suggesting instead that 'health education is most needed to persuade people to do or refrain from doing things for themselves for their long term benefit'.[85] It sought to transfer responsibility for preventative medicine from healthcare authorities to individual Britons. This move, according to medical historian Peder Clark, marked a shift from the kind of welfare state collectivism that once launched the National Health Service to an emerging ethic of individual responsibility, anticipating Thatcher-era neoliberalism.[86]

---

[83] Victor H. Wallace, 'Abortion and Immigration', *Medical Journal of Australia*, 13 February 1971, 404–405.

[84] Jane Carey, 'The Racial Imperatives of Sex: Birth Control and Eugenics in Britain, The United States and Australia in Interwar Years', *Women's History Review* 21.5 (2012), 733–752.

[85] Cited in Peder Clark, '"Problems of Today and Tomorrow": Prevention and the National Health Service in the 1970s', *Social History of Medicine* 33.3 (2019), 984.

[86] Clark, 'Problems of Today and Tomorrow'; see also Emily Robinson, Camilla Schofield, Florence Sutcliffe-Braithwaite, and Natalie Thomlinson, 'Telling Stories About Post-

A similar new commitment to preventative medicine became conspicuous in Australia when in 1975 the Victorian government sponsored a campaign called 'Life. Be in it.', which became one of Australia's most recognized brands. 'Life. Be in it.' promoted healthy living via an animated family man named 'Norm' whose move from beer-bellied couch potato to active living was a model for healthier behaviour than what was then deemed typical for Australian masculinity. The campaign, in historian Manning Clark's words, took a similar stance towards men as the anti-abortion physicians took towards women. Clark said that the 'Life. Be in it.' campaign told 'us how to behave, what to eat and drink and how to spend our time'.[87] It is possible to interpret this as a shift in medical sensibilities towards individual rather than collective responsibility, as Peder Clark argued. It would, however, also be reasonable to suggest that medicine used the moral transformations under way in the 1970s to expand its expert, moral jurisdiction from human bodies and sexual practices to now encompass all of life.[88]

Apolitical Journalism Was Political (and Didn't Sell Very Well)

Journalism was a key vector for public discussion of moral questions like women's reproductive rights, gay liberation, racial inequality, and access to schooling. In this context, journalists reconsidered their tradition of disinterested, factual reporting, recognizing that the choice to be apolitical was political. It was a problem that the profession discussed at length, with new movements within journalism choosing instead to make their moral positions explicit. This produced new approaches to professional virtue, moving away from journalistic neutrality to stress the significance of the media's ethical interventions for important issues of the day. News media was also under intense pressure as economic conditions worsened and media technologies diversified, so that taking a moral stance and making a profit became increasingly conflated.

In 1970, for example, Carey McWilliams, by then editor of *The Nation*, had an eye on TV news, which was changing the ways the profession thought about reporting.[89] In the *Columbia Journalism Review*,

---

War Britain: Popular Individualism and the "Crisis" of the 1970s', *Twentieth Century British History* 28.2 (2017), 268–304.

[87] Cited in National Museum of Australia, Life: Be in It Exhibition, www.nma.gov.au/ defining-moments/resources/life-be-in-it-launch, Retrieved 7 April 2022.

[88] On professional jurisdiction, see Abbott, *The System of Professions*.

[89] Ponce de Leon, Charles, *That's The Way It Is: A History of Television News in America* (Chicago: University of Chicago Press 2015).

McWilliams pointed to 'muckraking', the kind of investigative journalism favoured during the Progressive Era, which was again on the rise. Led by emerging literary luminaries like Norman Mailer and Tom Wolfe, these (new) New Journalists 'rightly sense that newsroom objectivity may result in untruth'.[90] Literary style, a blending of reporting and fiction and first-person 'gonzo' journalism, attracted more readers than boring old news. It also gave journalists the opportunity to consider subjects that could not be explored under older codes of objective reporting.[91] Expanding 'the kind of truths that could be told', the New Journalists used individual stories to tell of larger problems with, for example, US foreign policy. By inserting blunt, overtly moral judgements into news narrative, they explicitly criticized institutions, leaders, and even capitalism itself.[92]

More conservative journalists voiced their own objections to purely objective reporting, though their concern was for the health of the public sphere.[93] In 1970, two years before the Watergate scandal that brought new status to investigative journalism, Gerald Grant from the *Washington Post* wrote that 'the "new journalism" that we need' required professionals who 'wrest meaning from the torrent of events rather than acting as mere transmission belts':[94] 'Journalists work by a code that makes many of them moral eunuchs,' Grant argued. 'The professional, in print at least, generally pretends to be without opinions or convictions'.[95] While agreeing that what previously passed for objectivity may have caused more harm than good, Grant was not persuaded by the literary focus of the New Journalism:

The challenge is to make sense out of the experts and of events. We don't need a whole new breed of novelists in action; we need more cogent journalism that tells us about problems rather than sketching conflict, that gives us the arguments rather than two sets of opposing conclusions. We do not need more passion but more intellect, more understanding.[96]

Gerald Grant attributed part of the problem to the culture of industriousness that characterized the average newsroom. Frantic scurrying, but not considered reading, defined newspaper work. Even long-form journalism was often misinformed, clearly missing key works of

---

[90] Gerald Grant, 'The "New Journalism" That We Need', *Columbia Journalism Review* 9.1 (1970), 13.
[91] James Aucoin, 'Journalistic Moral Engagement: Narrative Strategies in American Muckraking', *Journalism* 8.5 (October 2007), 559–572.
[92] Aucoin, 'Journalistic Moral Engagement'.
[93] Matthew Pressman, 'Remaking the News: The Transformation of American Journalism, 1960–1980', unpublished PhD dissertation, Boston University (2016), 68–99.
[94] Grant, 'The "New Journalism" That We Need', 12.   [95] Ibid., 13.   [96] Ibid.

theory, history, or economics from the journalist's repertoire of ideas. A closer relationship, Grant argued, between journalism and academia would help to deepen public debate, not just make it more readable.[97] Investigative journalism seemed to provide the answer for everyone. With television pilfering advertising revenue from newspapers and magazines, investigative journalism offered a profitable alternative, especially for magazines like *The Nation*.[98] There were some 'fine TV documentaries in the muckraking tradition,' McWilliams conceded, an investigative tradition that 'turned muckraking into dramatic morality plays' on *60 Minutes* since 1968.[99] Such 'authentic' journalism was crucial to coverage of the Vietnam War, including the 'heat of the moment' style adopted by young Australian journalist Arnold Zable in support of the transnational anti-war movement.[100] Nevertheless, for the most part, TV news was a 'segmented commodity', as media scholar John Ellis later described it, which was unable to offer the critical, in-depth reportage of long-form journalism.[101] In the new muckraking tradition, however, it was not the mainstream outlets leading the way:

> The 'underground' press is, to some extent, trying to exploit what it regards as the general press' reluctance to engage in investigative journalism. Many offbeat journals, hard to categorize, belong in the muckraking tradition.[102]

New publications associated with the 1960s and 1970s counterculture were hardly confined to the United States. In Britain, magazines like *IT*, *Oz*, and *Black Dwarf* offered alternative journalism.[103] While in Britain the youthful 'satire boom' was a marker of the end of empire, it was also part of a larger, transnational movement.[104] In Sydney, student magazines like *Tharunka* at the University of New South Wales entered the

---

[97] Ibid.
[98] Carey McWilliams, 'Is Muckraking Coming Back?', *Columbia Journalism Review* 9.3 (1970): 8–15; John Ellis, *Visible Fictions: Cinema, Television, Video* (London: Routledge, 1992).
[99] Mark Feldstein, 'A Muckraking Model: Investigative Reporting Cycles in American History', *Harvard International Journal of Press/Politics* 11.2 (2006), 105–120.
[100] Jon Piccini, *Transnational Protest, Australia and the 1960s: Global Radicals* (London: Palgrave Macmillan, 2016), 106–109.
[101] Ellis, *Visible Fictions*; McWilliams, 'Is Muckraking Coming Back?', 8.
[102] McWilliams, 'Is Muckraking Coming Back?', 13.
[103] Chris Atton and James Hamilton, *Alternative Journalism* (London: SAGE, 2008), 44.
[104] Stuart Ward, '"No Nation Could Be Broker": The Satire Boom and the Demise of Britain's World Role', in Stuart Ward (ed), *British Culture and the End of Empire* (Manchester: Manchester University Press, 2001); Barry York, 'Looking Back at Oz Magazine', *National Library of Australia News*, May 2001, 10–12; Andrew Hannon, '"Hippie" Is a Transnational Identity: Australian and American Countercultures and the London OZ.' *Australasian Journal of American Studies* 35.2 (2016), 39–59.

emerging tradition with verve. Their youthful opposition to media norms landed its editors in court in 1972, charged – like the Australian, London-based editors of *Oz* – with obscenity.[105]

Obscenity perhaps symbolized journalism's moral crisis most dramatically, but the values it represented extended much deeper into the infrastructure of the changing media environment. These youthful, often sexually explicit publications went beyond the destabilization of old systems of cultural deference to hierarchical norms.[106] Their provocatively indecorous work actively sought to challenge, even undermine, the kind of social, religious, and economic rules that traditional morality promoted.[107] Underground journalism and the satire boom placed style, images, and shock tactics at the centre of cultural subversion.[108] Such techniques diverged markedly from the kind of truth telling on which investigative journalism had cut its teeth. Sometimes this playfulness was just for the fun of it, but at other times publications and journalists had explicit political goals. For young people, there were plenty of things to be concerned about, including the Vietnam War, gay rights, and feminism.[109] Underground publications helped journalists turn their work to activism, actively rejecting disinterested objectivity.[110]

Underground counterculture, however, did not have a monopoly on sex. After Australian media mogul Rupert Murdoch bought *The Sun* in 1969, the respectable world of London newspapers gave way to 'sex, sex and more sex' as the new foundation of commercial success. Murdoch added *The Sun* to the *News of the World*, extending his Australian newspaper empire into British tabloids. Murdoch's style was a long way from youth counterculture, but his Australian irreverence bolstered his assault on Fleet Street. Deriding the British newspaper establishment as a bunch of 'snobs', Murdoch took pride in giving people what they wanted, rather than reporting objective truths, a popularity he saw reflected in

---

[105] Anne Coombs, *Sex and Anarchy: The Life and Death of the Sydney Push* (Melbourne: Viking, 1996); Christopher Hilliard, *A Matter of Obscenity: The Politics of Censorship in Modern England* (Princeton: Princeton University Press, 2021), 137–160.

[106] See Florence Sutcliffe-Braithwaite, *Class, Politics, and the Decline of Deference in England, 1968–2000* (Oxford: Oxford University Press, 2018).

[107] Lloyd Ellis, 'The Underground Press in America: 1955–1970', *The Journal of Popular Culture* 24.4 (2000), 379–400; Elizabeth Nelson, *British Counter-Culture 1966–1973: A Study of the Underground Press* (London: Macmillan, 1989).

[108] Hillard, *A Matter of Obscenity*, Ward, 'No Nation Could Be Broker'; Nelson, *British Counter-Culture*.

[109] Nelson, *British Counter-Culture*.

[110] Ellis, 'The Underground Press in America'; James Lewes, 'The Underground Press in America (1964–1968): Outlining an Alternative, the Envisioning of an Underground', *Journal of Communication Inquiry* 24.4 (2000), 379–400.

sales.[111] It was part of what historian Florence Sutcliffe-Braithwaite defined as the 'decline of deference', a reduction in 'the tendency to defer to authority, convention and tradition'. Sutcliffe-Braithwaite argues that more inclusive discourse around democracy perhaps reinforced the trend, but thinks that explanation is insufficient. Rather, she suggests the 'cultural props' of deference, including uniforms and other kinds of dress, reduced their relevance to everyday life at a time that the British Empire, with its ritualized forms of cultural dominance, was being actively dismantled. In newspapers, this decline of deference amounted to less staid and serious news, and more sex.[112]

While Murdoch helped make sex central to the crisis in commercial newspapers, the real problem was money. The economic crisis of the 1970s hit British newspapers hard. The 'quality' British press lost such circulation that the *Times* and the *Sunday Times* stopped printing for a year in the late 1970s, while the *Guardian* and the *Financial Times* struggled to make money. The *Times* had never made a profit, a reality that, by contrast to Murdoch's larrikin commercialism, was a point of pride for those who saw it as a unique cultural institution.[113]

It was to investigative journalism that the quality press pinned their hopes for recovery. In Britain, the big story that reminded the profession of the importance of long-form quality journalism was thalidomide. This drug, prescribed for anxiety, caused hundreds of birth defects in British babies, a scandal that was exposed by investigative reporters at the *Sunday Times* under the leadership of its editor, Harold Evans.[114]

As important as thalidomide was in showing why journalists should pursue moral goals, few stories attracted attention like the 'Watergate scandal', where journalists Carl Bernstein, Bob Woodward, and others at the *Washington Post* exposed a political cover-up within US president Richard Nixon's administration. Their story led to Nixon's resignation in 1974. While investigative journalism was already on the rise, Watergate prompted a widespread 'collective consciousness' of investigative journalism's potential as a watchdog of democracy.[115] In particular, the 1976 film *All the President's Men* helped glamorize journalism as a moral political force. It 'ennobled investigative reporting,' according to

---

[111] Kevin Williams, *Read All About It: A History of the British Newspaper* (London: Routledge, 2010), 200–203, quote about sex: 200.

[112] Sutcliffe-Braithwaite, *Class, Politics, and the Decline of Deference*, 1–13.

[113] Williams, *Read All About It*, 205.

[114] Alfred Balk, 'Britain's Great Thalidomide Cover-up', *Columbia Journalism Review* 14.1 (1975), 24–27.

[115] James Aucoin, 'The Re-Emergence of American Investigative Journalism 1960–1975', *Journalism History* 21.1 (1995): 3–15.

journalism scholar Michael Schudson, and 'made of journalists modern heroes.'[116]

Investigative journalism bourgeoned well beyond the *Washington Post* and American politics. In Britain, Canada, Australia, and Aotearoa/New Zealand, investigative journalism became the pinnacle of journalistic achievement in newspapers and on television.[117] In a recent reassessment of Watergate, Richard Perloff, and Anup Kumar suggest that journalists worldwide grew to focus on the individual morality of political leaders, which displaced their traditionally dispassionate assessment of governmental institutions. Watergate, which Perloff and Kumar describe as a 'refrain, anchor, and focus of comparison' for the profession, pushed investigative journalism toward a more adversarial posture that, at its best, emphasized its role as a 'watchdog of the moral order'.[118]

This marks a new kind of morality that starkly contrasted to the truth telling of the old New Journalism. Professional virtue was now less embodied in journalistic integrity, including a commitment to objectivity. The profession began to measure its success via a test of 'moral indignation'.[119] In the 1970s, such an appetite for moral outrage helped further the relatively new phenomenon of talk radio. Hailed by some 1970s political scientists as a new form of democratic participation, particularly for those they still called 'housewives', talk radio arguably helped weaponize moral indignation. Soon, the virtuous goals that led journalists to discard disinterested objectivity were supplanted by performances of moral outrage, deployed primarily to boost TV or radio audience numbers, news circulation, and advertising revenue.[120]

Accounting for a Legitimation Crisis

While journalists used innovative techniques in the face of dire economic conditions, the Great Inflation presented accountants with an

---

[116] Michael Schudson, *Watergate in American Memory: How We Remember, Forget, and Reconstruct the Past* (New York: Basic Books 1992), 104.

[117] Hugo de Burgh, 'The Emergence of Investigative Journalism', in Hugo de Burgh (ed.), *Investigative Journalism* (London: Routledge: 2008), 32–53; Brian McNair, *News and Journalism in the UK* (London: Routledge, 2003); Wayne Hope, 'A Short History of the Public Sphere in Aotearoa/New Zealand', *Continuum* 10.1 (1996), 12–32; Cecil Rosner, *Behind the Headlines: A History of Investigative Journalism in Canada* (Oxford: Oxford University Press, 2011); Schultz, *Reviving the Fourth Estate*.

[118] Richard Perloff and Anup Kumar, 'The Press and Watergate at 50: Understanding and Reconstructing a Seminal Story', *Journalism Practice* 16.5 (2022), 797–812.

[119] James Ettema and Theodore Glasser, *Custodians of Conscience: Investigative Journalism and Public Virtue* (New York: Columbia University Press, 1998), 12.

[120] Bridget Griffen-Foley, 'From Tit-Bits to Big Brother: A Century of Audience Participation in the Media', *Media, Culture & Society* 26.4 (2004), 533–548.

unprecedented set of problems. In 1966, academic accountant Edward Stamp from Victoria University in Wellington, Aotearoa/New Zealand, expressed the looming existential angst by criticizing the very basis of accounting methodology, observing 'there are over a million sets of mutually exclusive rules, each giving a true and fair view of a company's state of affairs!' It was the job of the individual accountant to choose which of those they would apply in any given instance. The process inevitably required, as Stamp observed, a considerable degree of individual 'judgement'.[121] Accountants, like all other professionals, relied on public trust. Their authority over accounting expertise was based on the neutrality of their work. As a result, the level of judgement accountants used was hidden behind 'a cloak of secrecy'. Stamp pointed out that it was a problem that accountants failed to disclose how they reached their conclusions. For Stamp this produced a contradiction for the profession: the moral authority by which accountancy veiled their individual judgement corrupted the very virtue that granted them such a monopoly in the first place. This problem did not cause a crisis for most accountants until the 1970s, however, when economic conditions produced a massive controversy about the calculation of profit. The crisis that emerged demonstrates the ways that the techniques of accountancy – and the virtue of accountants – were entangled with the global economy.

High inflation was the 'surprise' of the decade, as economist Robert J. Gordon put it in 1977. Official US price indices also showed enormous fluctuations. While inflation was relatively low in 1971–1972 – lower, in fact, than since 1968 – consumer price inflation rose to above 11 per cent in 1974 and was over 12 per cent for nonfarm business. Inflation fell again to single digits in 1975 and returned to low levels comparable to 1971, in 1976.[122] This made business accountancy difficult and roused high passion among those attempting to present accounts in ways that they each considered to be accurate. This was a moment where the Anglo world collaborated. Accountants and economists in Britain led the debate, to which Australians made a substantial contribution. Canadian and Aotearoa/New Zealand accountants had small but important input, while the profession in the United States said they were following the issue while hoping the rest of the English-speaking world would lead the way.[123]

---

[121] 'Auditing Is in "A State of Chaos"', *Sydney Morning Herald*, 7 November 1966, 35.

[122] Robert Gordon, 'Can the Inflation of the 1970s be Explained?', *Brookings Papers on Economic Activity* 1977.1 (1977), 253–279.

[123] Ivan Bull, 'The Conference I Attended', *The Australian Accountant* 46.4 (1976), 219; G. B. Mitchell, 'Current Cost Accounting: Canadian and New Zealand Contributions', *The Australian Accountant* 46.11 (1976), 677–679.

In *The Australian Accountant*, D. R. Rickard sought to summarize the debate and present a way forward. 'By now it must surely be common ground that in real terms "profits" determined by historical cost methods are overstated in times of inflation,' he argued.[124] The kind of problems that emerged if accountants followed their traditional techniques included overestimations of apparent rates of return. This had flow-on effects, like overpayments of bonuses and dividends. It also could affect business-borrowing capacity, wage negotiations, and, in some industries, tariff estimates. In preparing for the coming year, businesses sought to be prepared, with cash available to cover any unexpected price inflation – but how much working capital would they need? Inaccurate calculations in times of inflation, Rickard warned, might cause some businesses to limit or stop operations. Some might even fail. The solution, he suggested, was in a report recently presented to the British parliament.[125]

In 1974, the British Labour government established a Royal Commission, led by Sir Francis Sandilands, to consider the problem of inflation accounting. The Sandilands report recommended that 'current cost accounting' be compulsorily adopted by listed companies and certain other businesses. Current cost accounting was a technique that calculated prices based on replacement, rather than historic, costs. Evaluating assets this way resolved the problem of overestimating profits. When the report was accepted by parliament, Peter Shore, who was then the Labour government's Secretary of State for Trade, said that 'the Government agree that current cost accounting, by bringing out the effects of changes in costs and prices on the fixed assets and stocks used in a business, could lead to a better understanding of the economic performance of companies'.[126] Current cost accounting had fan base in the profession. Emeritus Professor Louis Goldberg of the University of Melbourne described supporters of this technique as 'earnest, eager, what might be called orthodox revolutionaries in danger of becoming doctrinaire'.[127]

Members of the House of Commons were aware that adopting the Sandilands technique of current cost accounting would likely reduce the listed profits of British corporations. Although the measure had broad bipartisan support, it was also the case that no one really liked it.

---

[124] D. R. Richard, 'Current Cost Accounting', *The Australian Accountant* 46.4 (1976), 192–199, quote from p. 192.

[125] Rickard, 'Current Cost Accounting'.

[126] 'Inflation Accounting (Sandilands Report)', British House of Commons Debates Hansard, 26 November 1975, vol. 901, 851–859, quote on p. 851.

[127] Louis Goldberg, 'Some Outlandish Propositions on Inflation and Inflation Accounting', *The Australian Accountant* 46.11 (1976): 659–667.

Conservative MP Terence Higgins, who had been Finance Secretary to the previous government, made it clear that he broadly held to the economics promoted by the New Cambridge School, who wanted substantial revisions to the Sandilands recommendations. John Pardoe, Liberal spokesman for the Treasury, alerted Shore to the reality that this would 'have a substantial effect on the profitability of the private sector of industry'.

A key problem was that when profits declined, so did tax revenue. Bob Cryer from Yorkshire reminded Shore that Sandilands, as CEO of insurance giant Commercial Union was 'no friend of the British Labour movement'. Changing the method of accounting to show lower profits would 'mean handing over hundreds of millions of pounds to the private sector of industry in lost tax revenue'. Labour MP Dennis Skinner too called it a 'scandal', that on the very day that 20,000 workers marched on the house over unemployment, Labour introduced an accounting practice that will 'put even more money into the private sector'. Despite such objections, the recommendations of the Sandilands report were accepted, though the technique was abandoned when inflation reduced.[128]

Once accepted to the House, the Sandilands technique made accountants newly conscious that their professional decisions were also political. The 'true and fair' picture of business performance, which accountants considered their only real goal, was subject not only to 'mutually exclusive rules', as Edward Stamp had argued, but also to partisanship. Rex Thiele, president of the Australian Society of Accountants, was explicit about the implications for Australia. The Australian government was committed to revising company tax in a way that would mean, if accountants did not apply current value accounting, businesses would pay around half of their current tax rate – 'but politically, what would the unions say?' On the other hand, if the profession did apply the technique, which Thiele thought they were morally obligated to do, Australian companies would pay more tax. Then, when 'real profits are shown ... investor confidence could slump, the effect upon the Stock Exchanges, already sensitive, can be imagined'.[129]

In the House of Commons, Pardoe asked, 'Does [Shore] regard the present stated level of profits of this sector to be too high, too low or

---

[128] 'Inflation Accounting (Sandilands Report)', 856; see also John Maloney, 'The Treasury and the New Cambridge School in the 1970s', *Cambridge Journal of Economics* 36 (2012), 995–1017.

[129] Rex Thiele, 'Accounting for the Effects of Inflation', *The Australian Accountant* 46.4 (1976): 200–203, quotes from 202.

about right?', making quantifiable business profits a matter of political opinion.[130] Louis Goldberg thought that such a contingent view of profit might help accountancy acknowledge the ethical questions attached to profit. He said that even the claim that profits were overstated 'implies that somehow there is a "true" or "real" profit'. This was not the case, he argued:

> The concept of profit as a measurement of the result of the activities of people is a man-made concept and not a phenomenon of nature ... It can only be overstated or understated in relation to some other basis of measurement ... None of these is more or less true or real than any other.

People who 'speak or write about profit should search their souls', Goldberg argued. For 'an underlying question', he suggested, 'is whether we are to regard profit as eternally and overwhelmingly a good thing or a bad thing. This is a question of ethics.'

Accountants, Goldberg argued, had come to imagine that 'profit maximization' was the only purpose for business. Older virtues of a 'just price and fair dealing', he suggested, were now reduced to the profit shown on the balance sheet 'not only in the minds of accountants and businessmen, but in their hearts as well'.[131] In this way, the Great Inflation produced an ethical crisis over accounting techniques. This showed objectivity to be impossible, even on the accountant's balance sheet. The 'legitimation crisis' of the Great Inflation had these material foundations. It also had material consequences: 'Suffice it to say,' Rickard concluded in *The Australian Accountant*, 'businesses do not want a true and fair epitaph.'[132]

Losing Control of an Engineered World

The transformations of the 1970s may not have posed the same threat to engineering's revered mathematics as they did to accountancy balance sheets, but the profession entered a state of crisis anyway. Used to a world where their authority was as unquestionable as the deflection of a loaded beam, engineers had previously considered their expertise unassailable. They literally built civilization. And yet, a new environmental consciousness was nevertheless posing a threat to the autonomy that made them professionals. When Rachel Carson's 1962 book *Silent*

---

[130] 'HC Inflation Accounting (Sandilands Report)', 854.
[131] Goldberg, 'Some Outlandish Propositions', 662–663.
[132] Rickard, 'Current Cost Accounting', 198.

Spring brought the dangers of lethal pesticides into public consciousness, this helped grow a more sceptical attitude to the ways scientific expertise shaped the environment.[133] After 'Earth Day' in 1970, where around twenty million people rallied across America to oppose environmental degradation, the people living in the world that engineers constructed now wanted to have a say in the way it was built.

While the environmental movement criticized many aspects of engineering, that was something engineers could work with. In fact, environmental engineering grew rapidly. Without preventing other engineers from increasing carbon outputs, decimating pollinating insects and making some waterways unliveable for fish, a new cohort of environmental engineers promoted technological interventions that sought to reduce air and soil pollution, designed industrial products that were less harmful, produced energy based on renewable sources, and desalinated and recycled clean water supply.[134] By the twenty-first century, environmental catastrophe has become existential for us all. However, for engineers in the 1970s, their chief crisis was about legitimation.

Legitimation affected them because its loss underpinned the general decline in professional authority. In 1975, consulting engineer Peter Miller recognized that professional authority was under threat. He feared that attacks on professionalism, which he connected to broader 1970s shifts in 'values', might displace engineers from the centre of the world they had built.

Professional authority, as discussed in Chapter 6, was bound up with autonomy, which ideally prevented inappropriate influence from capital or government. Miller thought this connected to professionals' experience of power in their workplaces:

The agonising reappraisal of values which is currently disrupting democratic societies has brought many aspects of professionalism under attack ... it is clear that there is a community debate in progress as to whether certain groups (of which medicine, law, engineering and architecture are prime examples) should

---

[133] Rachel Carson, *Silent Spring* (Boston: Houghton Mifflin, 1962).

[134] Consider textbooks and overviews like Richard Flagan and John Seinfeld, *Fundamentals of Air Pollution Engineering.* (Englewood Cliffs, NJ: Prentice-Hall, 1988); Mackenzie Davis and Susan Masten, *Principles of Environmental Engineering* (New York: McGraw-Hill Education, 2013); Frederick Troeh, Arthur Hobbs, and Roy Donahue, *Soil and Water Conservation: Productivity and Environmental Protection* (Englewood Cliffs, NJ: Prentice-Hall, 1980); Isabel Escobar and Andrea Schaefer, *Sustainable Water for the Future: Water Recycling Versus Desalination* (Amsterdam: Elsevier, 2010); Noel Perera, 'Sustainable Energy, Engineering, Materials and Environment: Current Advances and Challenges', *Environmental Science and Pollution Research International* 26.29 (2019), 29507–29508.

be allowed to control the environment in which they work or should have that environment controlled for them by political decision.[135]

Popular dissent posed a threat to what Miller considered to be the engineer's right to control what they did. As democracies reconsidered and sometimes rejected the authority of professional virtue in shaping life, this also diminished engineers' supremacy in decision-making. Miller's fears suggested that they might lose control over the allocation of resources for public infrastructure, the technologies determining industrial priorities and the chemicals selected for use in everything from agriculture to cosmetics. The 'increased public scrutiny' of professional decisions, Miller argued, meant engineers were now pressured to 'take account of more diverse points of view than used to be accepted'.[136]

It was this 'diversity' that Miller saw posed the biggest challenge to the status quo. Engineers and other professionals now performed their work in a world where popular dissent, like the decolonizing mirror, raised questions about the legitimacy of their authority:

The wider diversity of attitude on value judgments means that the likelihood of some people being offended is increased. Offended minorities often become vocal and now have access to powerful communications media to express their dissatisfaction, and so the pressure builds further.[137]

Whether Miller used 'minorities' to refer to race and gender diversity, or whether he referred to the value judgements of a 'minority' of people statistically speaking is not definite. What is certain, however, is that he invoked a type of authority that required engineers to sit unquestioningly atop the hierarchy they had made.

Miller predicted dire consequences if expert authority now included diverse, minority voices. This, he argued, was about money. 'The attack on professions always centres around money', he said, pointing to criticisms of monopoly power. Against such criticisms, Miller argued:

[Imagine if] doctors could not establish their fees but were forced to compete on a monetary basis ... such an environment would lead quite rapidly to the point where the professional, however much he deplored the prospect, would be unable to subjugate his material interests in order to preserve his livelihood, and the standards of medical practice would then fall.[138]

This resembled the arguments engineers successfully used in the Australian Conciliation and Arbitration Tribunal, as discussed in

---

[135] P. O. Miller, 'Professionalism Under Attack', *Transactions of the Institution of Engineers, Australia* 47.1–2 (1975), 3.
[136] Miller, 'Professionalism Under Attack', 3.   [137] Ibid.   [138] Ibid.

Chapter 6. There, the profession's monopoly over their body of knowledge was prized as an asset to the nation, protecting society from substandard work. Now Miller framed this as some sort of threat. 'It is not inconceivable that, faced with such pressures by the community, a profession might consider abandoning its code of ethics … [having] decided that it was an expensive luxury.'

Miller then turned his argument against criticisms of professional monopoly power that were being directed from more conservative angles. 'Submission to [external] pressure,' he argued, 'would be held by some to be 'reacting to the control of the market place' and 'therefore a natural evolution which is likely to be beneficial'. Miller did not believe the market produced virtue this way. Instead, he predicted that market-based competition unregulated by professional monopoly power would diminish standards. This could lead to unsafe buildings, harmful chemical disposal, and ill-advised water management. Milton Friedman, responding to a similar point made by medical doctors, said that '[i]t is extraordinary that leaders of medicine should proclaim publicly that they and their colleagues must be paid to be ethical'.[139] Miller, who acknowledged that engineers had behaved badly in the past with techniques like planned obsolescence, thought this still put them in the best position to assert authority over moral as well as technical decisions.[140]

Miller's opinion article 'Professionalism Under Attack' was the work of just one man, shaking his metaphorical fist at perceived threats to his authority. His ideas are adequately familiar, however, to discern the wider pattern in the challenges to professional authority in the 1970s. This shows that the professional authority that Miller wanted to keep so badly was grounded in a hierarchical schema that connected British 'civilization', whiteness and masculinity with engineers' social standing, and professional expertise.[141] His fears gesture to the logics by which the active dismantling of the type of structure that had previously placed white members of the British Empire at the pinnacle of international relations simultaneously undermined the structure of professional power.[142]

---

[139] Friedman, *Capitalism and Freedom*, 152.
[140] Miller, Professionalism Under Attack', 3.
[141] See Raewyn Connell, *Masculinities* (Berkley: University of California Press, 2005), 193–194.
[142] For discussions of the connections between the whiteness and authority that characterized the old 'white Commonwealth' nations that previously dominated the United Nations and the relationship between whiteness, patriarchal forms of power and professional authority, see Elayne Puzan, 'The Unbearable Whiteness of Being (in Nursing)', *Nursing Inquiry* 10.3 (2003), 193–200; Sonya Aleman, 'Locating Whiteness in Journalism Pedagogy', *Critical Studies in Media Communication* 31.1

Conclusion

The professional class was always entangled with the political-economic regime. It built settler colonialism and came to power under the global order established at Bretton Woods. As that order collapsed and decolonization entered mainstream governance, professional virtue was no longer mirrored back to the professional class in ways that confirmed what they believed about themselves, their work, or the social good. Some professionals were desperate to hold onto the authority they gained when the global economy aligned to their traditional virtues. Others were inspired by anti-colonial movements and sought to invert the hierarchies of the past. For them, new approaches to merit, inclusion, diversity, truth, and selfhood would turn traditional hierarchies upside down, producing a new virtuous purpose that would align to, and maybe even help bring into being, a new decolonizing economy.

While the incompatibilities of these two positions produced tension, they were the symptom, not the cause, of the decade of moral crisis. The 1970s crisis was, as we have always known, economic; I am not seeking to revise our received understanding of the ways collapsing currency agreements, the global oil crisis, and stagflation undermined the global order. The Great Inflation and high unemployment challenged much more than Keynesian economic theories, however. The period of economic shocks also exposed institutions, many of them run by professionals, as unexpectedly fragile. Trust in professional work was built on long-held claims about objectivity and expertise, which the crumbling economic order showed to be dubious. Now, new techniques were needed even to calculate something as fundamental to capitalism as profit. Such challenges to traditional objectivity were materially necessary but they were also experienced as a threat to professional authority.

(2014), 72–88; Alison Bashford, '"Is White Australia Possible?" Race, Colonialism and Tropical Medicine', *Ethnic and Racial Studies* 23.2 (2000), 248–271; Alice Pawley, 'Shifting the "Default": The Case for Making Diversity the Expected Condition for Engineering Education and Making Whiteness and Maleness Visible', *Journal of Engineering Education* 106.4 (2017), 531–533; Anton Lewis, *'Counting Black and White Beans': Critical Race Theory in Accounting* (Bingley, UK: Emerald Publishing, 2020). To fit these into the performance of professional work 'from below', which is the framework of this book, see Sara Ahmed, 'A Phenomenology of Whiteness', *Feminist Theory* 8.2 (2007): 149–168. On race and the United Nations, see Getachew, *Worldmaking After Empire*; Sluga, 'Transformation of International Institutions'; Moyn, *Not Enough*, 89–118; Jon Piccini, *Human Rights in Twentieth Century Australia* (Cambridge: Cambridge University Press, 2019), 119–152. Sonia Tascón and Jim Ife, 'Human Rights and Critical Whiteness: Whose Humanity?', *The International Journal of Human Rights*, 12:3 (2008), 307–327.

The sources of the threat were linked to anti-colonial movements, which presented an alternate set of possibilities. As well as posing a threat to professional authority, decolonization also showed a world that was possible, where the massive profits of the first world were redistributed ` for shared, collective stability and where the dependencies established out of the post-war order were turned to the kind of equalities that would grow genuine self-determination. Such a system also demanded an end to traditional professional authority, which long aligned to assumptions of whiteness, middle-class virtue, and, often enough, patriarchy. This was the link missing from the body of literature that the 1970s produced to explain the professional class. Understandably focused on class-based distinctions between 'hand' and 'brain' work, relations to the means of production, and contradictory ideological roles between labour and capital, scholars failed to see that the substance underpinning professional power – which this book summarizes as virtue – was materially entangled with the global economic order. A moral crisis grew in the 1970s because virtue was not separate from the economic crisis, or from decolonization. Like those changes, it too was material.

This chapter has shown that divisions emerged within the professional class, between the desire to go back to the world where they were in charge and the wish to build a new one based on anti-colonial values. This conflict, such as it was, did not produce revolutionary change. On the contrary, just as environmental engineering did little to impede other professional specializations from accelerating climate damage, so other radical arms of each profession coexisted, albeit in tension, with colleagues seeking to bolster mid-century expert power. Decolonization nevertheless produced shifts in professional virtue. These contributed to an emerging split between the professional and the managerial sides of the professional class. This was divorce of *knowing* from *doing*, which is the subject of Chapter 8.

8   Success Is the Only Virtue

In November 1992, with celebrity culture on the rise, *Vanity Fair* magazine ran a story entitled 'Black Mischief' on a leading figure in British and Canadian journalism, Conrad Black. 'Fabulously wealthy', the article gushed, Black's 'sparkling empire' of newspapers was augmented by his 'new wife, columnist/femme fatale Barbara Amiel'.[1] Black already represented a type. There were other famous, wealthy men, often tending to corpulence, also frequently pictured with glamorous women. These included media bosses like Roger Ailes, who was then soon to establish Fox News, and UK newspaper tycoon George Weidenfeld. Beyond media, business personalities also fit the genre, like Australia's corporate raider, Alan Bond, and the man who, nearly thirty years later, would pardon Conrad Black's crimes in the United States – President Donald J. Trump – who was then a real estate developer.[2] Such convictions were mere possibilities in 1992:

Conrad Black was known in Canada as a highly controversial figure, who had been accused by his critics of everything from hoodwinking rich widows and pillaging pension funds to funneling hundreds of millions of dollars from one company to another. Though he had been the object of minute scrutiny, however, he had never been charged with or found guilty of any wrongdoing.[3]

The whiff of controversy was central to the masculinity Black embodied, which could not be separated from his business activity. By contrast to the earnestness of 1970s virtue, seen in Chapter 7, Black's conservatism seemed subversive. In this, and in the sexualized personal brand they cultivated, Conrad Black and others echoed Hugh Hefner, whose lavish 'Playboy Mansion' lifestyle, established in 1974 with exploited women

---

[1] Edward Klein, 'Black Mischief', *Vanity Fair*, November 1991, www.vanityfair.com/news/1992/11/conrad-black-199211, Retrieved 9 June 2022.
[2] Donald J. Trump, Executive Grant of Clemency to Conrad Moffat Black, 15 May 2019, www.justice.gov/pardon/pardons-granted-president-donald-j-trump-2017-2021, Retrieved 9 June 2022.
[3] Klein, 'Black Mischief'.

workers he called 'Bunnies', produced what R. W. Connell called a 'corporate sexual hero', an answer to the 'male identity crisis' associated with mass working-class unemployment.[4] With his trademark audaciousness, Hefner said, 'Sex is the driving force on the planet. We should embrace it, not see it as the enemy'. For him sex was also about profit and power. Hefner believed embracing sex would 'put the United States back in the position of unquestioned world leadership'.[5] Describing Black's similarly mutinous attachment to capitalism, *Vanity Fair* affectionately likened Black to the fictional character of the 1987 film *Wall Street*, Gordon Gekko. The magazine quoted Black, not Gekko, who said, "Greed ... has been severely underestimated and denigrated – unfairly so, in my opinion."[6]

Such clichés of 1980s capitalist hedonism were sometimes mirrored much further down the occupational hierarchy. The State Library of Victoria holds a self-published, touchingly confessional memoir by Rex Johnson, a Melbourne accountant. In the mid-1980s, the mortgage wholesaler for whom Johnson worked began to show signs of moral disintegration. In Aussie Rules football-mad Melbourne, the directors used company profits to make large donations to their favourite club, Essendon. These donations gave the company bosses access to 'the club's coterie group'. Stretch limousines took them to mid-week footy functions overflowing with champagne. With drinking becoming freshly acceptable to the professional class, the boardroom bar was a feature of the office, which 'even catered for the exotic cocktails preferred by some of the female staff'.[7]

With such excesses, the directors' personal expense accounts began to interfere with company cash flows.[8] Eventually, the company failed under such imprudence. This was the context in which Rex Johnson confessed his own fraudulent downfall. He had a gambling addiction, which began with stock market investment in the 1970s and ended with divorce after he confessed to his wife that he had embezzled clients' trust accounts to fund his habit.[9] Lacking Conrad Black's brazen embrace of the voluminous fruits of capitalist greed, Rex Johnson's story reflects

---

[4] Connell, *Masculinities*, 215; Jonathan Levy, *Ages of American Capitalism: A History of the United States* (New York: Random House, 2021), 549; see also Barbara Ehrenreich on this 'fun morality' in Barbara Ehrenreich, *The Hearts of Men: American Dreams and the Flight from Commitment* (New York: Anchor Books, 2011), 49–58.
[5] Ehrenreich, *Hearts of Men*, 57.   [6] Klein, 'Black Mischief'.
[7] Rex Johnson, *Returning to the Light: The Memoirs of Rex Johnson* (Melbourne: Rex Johnson, 2017), 104; on middle-class drinking, see Julie McIntyre and John Germov, '"Who Wants to Be a Millionaire?" I Do: Postwar Australian Wine, Gendered Culture and Class', *Journal of Australian Studies* 42.1 (2018), 65–84.
[8] Johnson, *Returning to Light*, 104.   [9] Ibid., 131–140.

more traditional moral consequences. Unlike the 'mischief' with which *Vanity Fair* readers were expected to appreciate characters like Conrad Black, Johnson's memoir expressed grief, regret, and loss for his marriage, for the sons for whom the memoir was written and for the family of one of his bosses. Under pressure, perhaps because his father had once been president of the Australian Stock Exchange, the firm's senior partner committed suicide in the face of corporate failure, leaving his widow to care for their four children.[10]

This chapter is about the fall of the professional class from their place of power. Unlike in Rex Johnson's tragic story, this 'fall' was no moral punishment for 1980s excesses. Instead, it marked a split in the professional-managerial class. This divide grew from two related developments, embodied in the transformations to professional virtue seen in both Black's and Johnson's stories. This first was a shift towards an ethic where success was the only virtue that mattered. This new ethic aligned to neoliberal claims that morality was best determined by the market rather than vested interests.[11] Importantly, it was also the way that the rising managerial class believed enterprises would survive globalization. The new ethic applied to all the organizations where professionals worked, whether public or private. This chapter focuses mostly on hospitals, which across the Anglo world could fall into either public or private sectors. Hospitals help move away from the 1980s and 1990s politics of public versus private sectors, which so energized Harold Perkin's history of professions, to instead focus on shared experiences across the professional class.[12]

The second influential development was caused by massive growth in the service-sector economy, as globalization shifted manufacturing off Anglo shores. In this complex environment and in larger enterprises, white-collar labour specialized, separating professional expertise from management, who controlled strategy and resources. Growth was profoundly gendered, as women exponentially entered professions, while men continued to dominate management. When virtue became central to conflicts emerging between the professional and managerial, this too was gendered. The Hugh Hefner ideal connected ruthless managerialism to masculine power, sometimes to a toxic degree.[13] With women swelling the ranks of professional work, professional virtue was depicted as 'weak' and 'feminine' by contrast.

In workplaces, 'effectiveness' became a catch-all virtue that inhibited white-collar dissent against longer, more intense work hours.

[10] Ibid., 106.   [11] Whyte, *Morals of Market*.   [12] Perkin, *Rise of Professional Society*.
[13] Connell, *Masculinities*, 215.

Effectiveness worked this way because it aligned to structures of merit. As professionals internalized merit, they now also absorbed productivity growth into their very selfhood. All this was now done under a managerial gaze, asserted by endless compulsory paperwork.[14] The purpose of this 'audit culture' was managerial control of virtue, now reduced to measures of risk, quality, ethics, and productivity. The result was a kind of moral deskilling, which kept the managerial class in control.[15]

The Virtues of Entrepreneurship

In 1977 a thirty-four-year-old Australian medical doctor, Geoffrey Edelsten, launched a medical start-up in Los Angeles, which the press described as a 'multi-million dollar computer center and medical laboratory'.[16] Using a satellite network, medical doctors from around the world could access a set of diagnostic tools. Doctors who were subscribed to the service were able to get electrocardiogram (ECG) results almost immediately to a terminal, which the newspaper said 'resembles an electric typewriter' on the doctor's desk. A fast courier service returned results via the same device on blood tests and urine samples.[17] This laboratory service was not revolutionary, nor even as ambitious as much of the medical innovation then under way, which included organ transplants, in vitro fertilization (IVF), and DNA sequencing.[18] But Edelsten's publicly commercial stance towards his professional work was melodramatically illustrative of the emerging entrepreneurial ethic. Some hailed him as a 'prophet' for the future of medicine.[19]

In fact, Edelesten's only real innovation was his manipulation of press coverage, enabled by transformations in journalism. Encouraged by some of the more sensational developments of the previous decades,

---

[14] Adapted from Foucault, *Birth of Clinic*.
[15] See Gérard Duménil and Dominique Lévy, *Managerial Capitalism: Ownership, Management and the Coming New Mode of Production* (London, Pluto Press, 2018).
[16] 'Satellites Give this Doctor Around the World Practice', *The Philadelphia Inquirer*, 12 September 1977, 27.
[17] 'Diagnosis and Treatment by Computer', *The Los Angeles Times*, 18 November 1977, 33.
[18] Michael Hopkins, Philippa Crane, Paul Nightingale, and Charles Baden-Fuller, 'Buying Big into Biotech: Scale, Financing and the Industrial Dynamics of UK Biotech, 1980–2009', *Industrial and Corporate Change* 22.4 (2013), 903–952; Lynne Zucker, Michael Darby, and Marilynn Brewer, 'Intellectual Capital and the Birth of US Biotechnology Enterprises', National Bureau of Economic Research Working Paper 4653 (1994); Nobel Prize in 1980. www.nobelprize.org/prizes/chemistry/1980/summary/. Retrieved 31 May 2022.
[19] Chris Masters (Reporter) and Jonathan Holmes (Producer), *Four Corners*, Episode 'Branded', Australian Broadcasting Corporation, 1984. www.abc.net.au/4corners/branded—1984/2832026. Retrieved 20 August 2022.

from the moral outrage that investigative journalism and talk radio encouraged, to Murdoch's 'Page Three girls', celebrity culture grew to take a place that cultural studies scholars likened to religion.[20] Edelsten fed the gossip columnists ostentatious titbits for the stories that now passed for news. They slavishly reported outlandish claims about his work hours (4:00 a.m. – 11:00 p.m., seven days a week), caseload (100 patients a day, delivering 1,000 babies a year), his nine luxury cars with personalized plates like 'sexy' and 'groovy', and a video party invitation recorded in the style of the TV show *Fantasy Island*.[21] As the 'Hugh Hefner of medicine', they also showcased his three splashy marriages to women sometimes more than three decades younger than him; two of these were women known mostly for their own celebrity ambitions and flamboyant, revealing clothing.[22]

Beginning in the late 1970s, Edelsten began cultivating the personal brand that powered this manipulation of celebrity culture. This was purposely subversive. *The Philadelphia Inquirer* told its readers that Edelsten had 'already jarred' the medical profession, with his 'jazzy waiting room where patients are entertained with giant screen television and receptionists in silver jumpsuits serving snacks and coffee'. He was planning to set up a Beverly Hills medical practice, with 'some of the effects from "Star Wars"', which had just screened in May. Such crass commercialism, the press he produced implied, caused a shudder in the prim medical world, where serious, boring science was what made the old elite. Not anymore, if Geoffrey Edelsten had anything to do with it.[23]

After returning to Australia, Edelsten's business interests – which included a tattoo-removing clinic, a glitzy general practice with chandeliers, mink-covered examination tables, a white baby grand piano and a robot receptionist, a Health Maintenance Organization (HMO) that turned out to be illegal in Australia, and ownership of an Aussie Rules football team – were constantly in the news. Through this, Edelsten performed his maxim that 'success is there to be applauded', an idea picked up, the Sydney media gushed, 'in Los Angeles where he lived

---

[20] Graeme Turner, *Understanding Celebrity* (Los Angeles: SAGE, 2014).

[21] For a tiny sample of many, see Mark Metherell, 'The Doctor Who Likes to Do Things That Are New', *The Age*, 12 June 1981, 17; Anna Marie Dell'Oso, 'Sydney's Flying Chain Store GP', *The Sydney Morning Herald*, 21 November 1981, 41; Luke Denehy, 'Geoffrey and Brynne Edelsten: Inside Australia's Most Expensive, Extravagant $3.3 Million Wedding'. www.news.com.au/entertainment/celebrity-life/geoffrey-and-brynne-edelsten-inside-australias-most-expensive-extravagant-33-million-wedding/news-story/fdb85447d322bde51cbb596fcfa4f8a1. Retrieved 31 May 2022.

[22] Frank Bongiorno, *The Eighties: The Decade That Transformed Australia* (Melbourne: Black Inc., 2015), 149–151.

[23] 'Satellites Give This Doctor'.

for a few years mingling with the likes of *Penthouse* publisher Bob Guccione'.[24]

Few professionals pursued celebrity as Edelsten did, but his career marked a wider turn away from virtue. Others who embraced such brazen commercialization often presented their choice as a stark contrast to the ethics of the past where, until recently, some professions were forbidden, in gentlemanly spirit, even to advertise. Such older ethics now seemed to perform class-based superiority, expressing values that entrepreneurial professionals considered elitist.[25] Just as Rupert Murdoch could describe London's quality press as 'snobs who only read papers no one wants', so too could Edelsten take comfort in his lack of pomposity.[26] For those energized by entrepreneurialism, this sense of subverting the old establishment helped make it an exciting time, filled as it was with opportunity. As Conrad Black later explained in an interview with Jordan Peterson, governmental changes like Thatcherism and Reaganomics helped affirm such showy business goals, managerial priorities, and social standing.[27]

Only a few, like Edelsten, were inclined to indulge in an outright rejection of professional ethics: eventually he was stripped of his medical license, imprisoned for employing a Sydney personality known as 'Mr Rent-a-Kill' to deal with one of his business problems, and charged with several types of business misconduct.[28] And yet, even among professionals whose work was both legal and less tacky, the kind of entrepreneurial ideal that Edelsten embraced promoted a broader set of possibilities, where financial success might be the primary virtue that mattered. 'Rebel professors' began to commercialize their findings.[29] Accountants turned from auditors of financial truth to also work as advisers and consultants, building a stake in the business strategies they audited.[30]

---

[24] 'What's It Like to Be Rich? High Living, but Others Beg for Geoffrey to Go Quietly', *The Sydney Morning Herald*, 28 February 1982, 18–19.

[25] Ehrenreich, *Fear of Falling*, 163–165.

[26] Janice Sutherland, *Murdoch*, Episode 1, The Making of a Media Mogul. Special Broadcasting Service, 2012.

[27] Conrad Black to Jordan Peterson, YouTube interview. www.youtube.com/watch?v= lLQZcx_lPzI. Retrieved 20 August 2022.

[28] *Edelsten v. Richmond*, Supreme Court of New South Wales – Court of Appeal (NSWCA), 34 (11 November 1988); Bongiorno, *Eighties*, 149–51; Misconduct was fairly widespread, though generally at the top of corporations, see Claire E. F. Wright, 'Above Board? Interlocked Directories and Corporate Contagion in 1980s Australia', *Australian Economic History Review* 62.3 (2022), 290–312.

[29] Luis M. Garia, '"Ivory Tower" University Men Descend on Rebel Professor', *Sydney Morning Herald*, 31 August 1984, 2.
   Ehrenreich, *Fear of Falling*, 163–165.

[30] Gow and Kells, *Big Four*; Richard Brooks, *Bean Counters: The Triumph of the Accountants and How They Broke Capitalism* (London: Atlantic Books, 2018).

Talk radio influencers began to take cash in exchange for swaying political sentiment – and then took their cue from Murdoch to explain that their commercial success showed that, unlike those elites in the 'quality media', they were merely giving the people what they wanted.[31] What profited professional enterprise, the entrepreneurial logic insisted, if professionals retained their virtue but still lost money?

Working Smarter, Not Harder

Losing money was now the only real sin, and was a problem faced by all enterprises in the chaotic world governed by fluctuating currency prices.[32] Money was difficult for healthcare organizations all over the Anglo world as rapidly emerging technologies increased the cost (and the efficacy) of medical work. Costs were increasing more rapidly in the United States than elsewhere in the Anglo world, arguably due to health insurance that was deregulated under Nixon in 1973.[33] Hospitals, like many other enterprises, were looking for efficiency improvements to survive. In 1985, the Two Rivers Community Hospital in Manitowoc, Wisconsin, employed a consultant to help. Hospital president Willard Sperry told the local press that 'we've got to change in order to compete and survive ... we've got to work smarter, not harder'.[34] The hospital was facing myriad threats, largely because of the changes to funding procedures from insurance companies. The situation needed to be met, he argued, with 'knowledgeable management procedures'. Nursing was the target area, since this was the largest cost.

In this de-industrializing region, working-class women earned or dusted off nursing qualifications to supplement family incomes when factories closed.[35] They now formed a proletarianized nursing workforce who looked anxiously at the external review, where the need for cost-cutting threatened job losses. 'There is just too much paperwork', the consultant – who had yet to arrive – already argued. 'The end result being

---

[31] Catherine Lumby and Elspeth Probyn, 'Interview with Mike Carlton: Money versus Ethics', in Catherine Lumby and Elspeth Probyn (eds), *Remote Control: New Media, New Ethics* (Cambridge: Cambridge University Press, 2003), 100–106.

[32] On the 'age of chaos' see Levy, *Ages of American Capitalism*, 587–732.

[33] OECD (2022), 'Health Spending' (indicator), https://doi.org/10.1787/8643de7e-en, accessed on 7 June 2022,; see Burton Weisbrod, 'The Health Care Quadrilemma: An Essay on Technological Change, Insurance, Quality of Care, and Cost Containment', *Journal of Economic Literature* 29.2 (1991), 523–552.

[34] Denis Hernet, 'Hospital's "Study to Survive" Could Help Fine-Tune Operation,' *Manitowoc Herald-Times*, 17 August 1985, 6.

[35] Gabriel Winant, *The Next Shift: The Fall of Industry and the Rise of Health Care in Rust Belt America* (Cambridge, MA: Harvard University Press, 2021).

the hospital will probably have its staff doing more meaningful work in more logical sequences and not just because "it was always done that way,"' President Sperry explained.[36] This was a typical managerial talking point. As hospitals and other professional enterprises faced funding shortfalls, ever more managers were employed to build productivity. Cost savings were theoretically achieved on efficiencies that were primarily about ensuring professional work was performed within shrinking budgets. Such managers and management consultants were not recognized as costs in the same way as the salaries attached to nurses, doctors, and other professionals. Instead, they were seen as investments reaping profitable rewards in the form of long-term cost savings.[37] The 'smarter', in the phrase that soon became a cliché, largely referred to them.

Management was altogether on the rise as public and private organizations all looked for new ways to cope with the uncertainties they now faced. In the Anglo world's post-industrial economies, all the professions were growing, but none grew like management. The similarity of the pattern between the United States and Australia over the long run (see Figures 8.1 and 8.2) reveals the centrality of management to shared transformations from the end of the Second World War to the early twenty-first century. In both the northern and the southern Anglospheres, management was the main numeric driver of changes in the professional world, especially from the 1980s onwards. Distinctions between the two long-run patterns seem like quibbles compared to their stark similarity. Management grew slightly earlier in the United States, beginning with its entry as a discrete item in the 1940 US census; Australia's census recorded an increase a decade later.[38]

Globalization, fuelled by floating currencies and a massive increase in international trade, boosted this trend by reshaping the context for managerial decision-making. With costs and prices fluctuating in more unexpected ways, managing commercial enterprise became a much more

---

[36] Hernet, 'Hospital's "Study to Survive"'.
[37] The returns on this investment are hotly disputed; see Erin Penno and Robin Gauld, 'The Role, Costs and Value for Money of External Consultancies in the Health Sector: A Study of New Zealand's District Health Boards', *Health Policy* 121.4 (2017), 458–467; Michael Howlett and Andrea Migone, 'Policy Advice through the Market: The Role of External Consultants in Contemporary Policy Advisory Systems', *Policy and Society* 32.3 (2013), 241–254; Julie Froud, Colin Haslam, Sukhdev Johal, and Karel Williams, 'Shareholder Value and Financialization: Consultancy Promises, Management Moves', *Economy and Society* 29.1 (2000), 80–110.
[38] 2901.0 – Occupation, Australian Census of Population and Housing: Census Dictionary, 2016, www.abs.gov.au/ausstats/abs@.nsf/Lookup/2901.0Chapter7602016, Retrieved 9 June 2022.

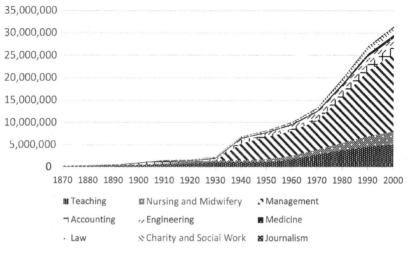

Figure 8.1 Key professions in the United States 1870–2000. *Data Source*: US Census

complex affair. Purchasing materials or equipment was subject to constant change. Decision-makers were needed to make 'flexible accumulation' work: to buy coal, timber, metals, components, casings, tools, and even labour, from wherever they were currently cheapest, whether Australia, Brazil, or Indonesia. By sourcing workers, materials, and components globally, commodities could be made more cheaply. Combined with 'just-in-time' production, minimizing the costs of inventory storage, the number of decision-makers grew.[39]

In public institutions, too, a new breed of manager combined public accountability with cost-minimization regimes.[40] Thatcher's promotion of 'new public management' in government enterprises was part of her determination to drag British business and government institutions alike into a more competitive mode of being based on managerial

[39] C. Rao (ed), *Globalization and Its Managerial Implications* (Westport CN: Quorum Books, 2001); Steven Vallas, 'Rethinking post-Fordism: The Meaning of Workplace Flexibility', *Sociological Theory* 17.1 (1999), 68–101; David Harvey, *The Limits to Capital* (London: Verso, 2018); see also Gabriela Vargas-Cetina, 'Introduction: The Anthropology of Flexible Accumulation', *Urban Anthropology and Studies of Cultural Systems and World Economic Development* 28.3–4 (1999), 193–197; John Urry, *Offshoring* (Hoboken, NJ: Wiley, 2014).

[40] Patrick Dunleavy and Christopher Hood, 'From Old Public Administration to New Public Management', *Public Money and Management* 14.3 (1994), 9–16.

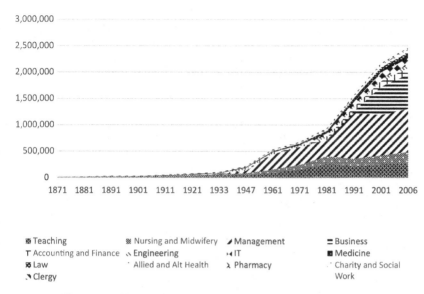

Figure 8.2 Key professions in Australia 1871–2006. *Data Source*:
Australian Census

'idealism'.[41] Somewhat contradictorily, the regulatory state that arose
under neoliberalism also required more public service managers to
respond to government demands for accountability, now subject to relentless metrics.[42] Such managerial decisions were 'tough', compared to
previous decades, since they were often made at the expense of employees,
including professionals. These tough decisions infused the leadership
qualities increasingly valued in hard-hitting managers, enhancing the connections between brazen masculinity and commercial success.[43]

[41] Ronald Kroeze and Sjoerd Keulen, 'The Manager's Moment in Western Politics: The
Popularization of Management and its Effects in the 1980s and 1990s', *Management &
Organization History* 9.4 (2014), 394–413; Christine Cooper, Jonathan Tweedie, Jane
Andrew, and Max Baker, 'From "Business-Like" to Businesses: Agencification,
Corporatization, and Civil Service Reform Under the Thatcher Administration', *Public
Administration* 100.2 (2022), 193–215.
[42] Kanishka Jayasuriya, *Reconstituting the Global Liberal Order: Legitimacy and Regulation*
(London: Routledge, 2005), 95–119.
[43] Raewyn Connell and Julian Wood, 'Globalization and Business Masculinities', *Men and
Masculinities* 7.4 (2005), 347–364; David Collinson and Jeff Hearn, *Men as Managers,
Managers as Men: Critical Perspectives on Men, Masculinities, and Managements* (London:
SAGE, 1996).

Other institutional developments helped foster what became a 'management rush'. Building on the 'visible hand' of management that grew over the previous century, management was now undergoing a new professionalization.[44] In Britain, 'Cassandra-like warnings of accelerated economic decline' led to several reviews of management education. Similar reviews in the Antipodes resulted in new training regimes in higher education settings, seeking a more entrepreneurial business elite.[45] This was not as easy as it sounded. Away from the Master of Business Administration's (MBA) North American heartland, established business elites feared that professionalizing management would separate oversight from the distinctive interests of the enterprises being managed, undermining purpose and reducing the importance of 'character' to business integrity.[46] Despite this, in Britain, Australia, and Aotearoa/New Zealand, the MBA grew rapidly, with what felt like an 'Americanization' of business management and higher education alike.[47] By the early 2000s, around 11,000 MBAs graduated in the United Kingdom each year.[48]

These managers were mostly men, while growth in most other professions was driven by women. Women professionals were growing in the United States for some decades, increasing from 40 per cent in 1970 to 49 per cent in 1980 and reaching 56 per cent of all professionals in 2000, with 50 per cent growth in women professionals just in the 1990s.[49] In Australia, growth in higher education was delayed until the 1990s, but when it did expand, women joined in droves. Professional women in the Australian census grew by a whopping 102 per cent in the 1990s, increasing their share of professional work from 44 per cent of all professionals in 1991 to 54 per cent in 2001.[50] In Canada, though professional work grew altogether by more than 200 per cent, women's share of that work was steady between 1990 and 2000. It was already quite high, at 60 per cent of all professionals.[51] Management as a discrete category did

---

[44] Malcolm Pearse, 'The Management Rush: A History of Management in Australia', unpublished PhD dissertation, Macquarie University (2010).

[45] Chandler, *Visible Hand*; Michael Reed and Peter Anthony, 'Professionalizing Management and Managing Professionalization: British Management in the 1980s', *Journal of Management Studies* 29.5 (1992), 592.

[46] Reed and Anthony, 'Professionalizing Management'; Nick Tiratsoo, 'The "Americanization" of Management Education in Britain', *Journal of Management Inquiry* 13.2 (2004), 122.

[47] Tiratsoo, 'The "Americanization" of Management Education in Britain', 118–126.

[48] Tiratsoo, 'The "Americanization" of Management Education in Britain', 118.

[49] US Census Occupation Statistics, 1970, 1980, 1990, 2000.

[50] Australian Census Occupation Statistics, 1981, 1991, 2001.

[51] Canadian Census, 1981, 1991, 2001.

not make the same gender gains. In Australia, men dominated the field at 72 per cent in both 1991 and 2001 censuses. American managers were not quite so gender imbalanced, but the 58 per cent male share of managerial jobs stayed steady over the 1990s. Only in Canada did women make any real gains in management, increasing their share from 30 to 35 per cent.[52]

Managing Virtue

The rise of managerialism presented a risk to professional virtue. Organizations focused primarily to financial goals jeopardized their reputation when professional work went wrong, which in turn posed financial risks. Since the late nineteenth century, professional character, which embodied the virtues associated with each occupation, was the accepted measure to ensure work was performed to high standards. By the late twentieth century, such a reliance on individual virtue seemed too uncertain, leading to increased managerial control. In healthcare, argued medical historian Paul Starr, 'the insurance companies and hospitals had clear incentives to seek control over physicians'. Hospital managers, like managers of other enterprises, now developed techniques to monitor, punish, and reward the performance of all healthcare workers, including doctors, in ways that would 'exact greater compliance with [the hospital's] own goals'.[53] In so doing, they devised techniques to manage virtue.

Insurance, with its actuarial logic, was an important driver, particularly in the United States since Nixon deregulated health insurance in 1973.[54] The relative financial riskiness of procedures encouraged medical practitioners and institutions to adjust their work practices, using costed liability risk as a guide for quality care. This enabled healthcare workers to assess the cost-benefit of itemized healthcare against any risk, including death or disablement – now understood in financial terms – to themselves or the organization.[55]

Other professionals caring for people, whether small children, women fleeing domestic violence, or elderly residents of nursing homes, were

---

[52] US Census, Canadian Census, Australian Census.
[53] Starr, *Social Transformation of American Medicine*, 26.
[54] Yvonne Doyle, 'Role of Private Sector in United Kingdom Healthcare System', *British Medical Journal*, 2 September 2000, 321.7260, 563–565. www.ncbi.nlm.nih.gov/pmc/articles/PMC1118448/, Retrieved 9 August 2022.
[55] For a contemporary example, see 'What Is Risk Management in Healthcare?' *New England Journal of Medicine Catalyst*, 25 April 2018, https://catalyst.nejm.org/doi/full/10.1056/CAT.18.0197, Retrieved 21 August 2022.

less explicitly guided by monetary value, but were nevertheless subjected to new, carefully audited methods for managing risk. In education, risk management transformed school excursions, set playground safety standards, and helped schools identify students at risk of violence or suicide.[56] Aotearoa/New Zealand developed a risk assessment tool that covered the use of pyrotechnics in school plays.[57] Schools in the United States, where there is a higher incidence of shootings compared to the rest of the Anglo world, have devised risk or threat assessment tools to try to manage firearm violence targeted at children and teachers.[58]

Sociologist Ulrich Beck called it the 'risk society'.[59] He saw this as a process of controlling the condition of anxiety produced by modernity.[60] Risk management, not virtue, was the tool that capital hoped would overcome the uncertainty embedded in the space between capitalist investment and profitable return.[61] When managers explicitly shifted the criterion of success from virtue to profit, they added new risks to these uncertainties. For hospitals, for example, too great a focus on balancing the books presented risks to the efficacy of healthcare. Healthcare failures in turn posed threats to the organization, which managers quantified and monitored. Such risk management arrogated virtues like duty, charity, and temperance into a fantasy of managerial control, transferring what was once trust in each professional's virtuous character to a complex system of processes and checklists.

Few of these risk and quality management systems were opposed by the professional class, largely because their virtues were seeming old-fashioned anyway. The moral crisis of the 1970s, discussed in Chapter 7, exposed 'character' as a function of discriminatory hierarchies which professionals themselves now sought to discard. Nurses, for example, cast off charity, duty, and purity, for example, along with their caps and veils, which they now saw as sexist. Modern nurses still needed virtue,

---

[56] For example: Committee on School Transportation Safety, *The Relative Risks of School Travel a National Perspective and Guidance for Local Community Risk Assessment* (Washington, DC: Transportation Research Board, 2002).

[57] NZ Ministry of Education, Information about fire safety, including fire permits, safety at school sleepovers, and fireworks. www.education.govt.nz/school/property-and-transport/health-and-safety-management/fire-safety/, Retrieved 9 August 2022.

[58] Marisa Reddy, Randy Borum, John Berglund, Bryan Vossekuil, Robert Fein, and William Modzeleski, 'Evaluating Risk for Targeted Violence in Schools: Comparing Risk Assessment, Threat Assessment, and Other Approaches', *Psychology in the Schools* 38.2 (2001), 157–172.

[59] Ulrich Beck, *Risk Society: Towards a New Modernity* (London: SAGE, 1992).

[60] Gabe Mythen, *Ulrich Beck: A Critical Introduction to the Risk Society* (London: Pluto Press, 2004), 1–29.

[61] Jonathan Levy, *Freaks of Fortune: The Emerging World of Capitalism and Risk in America* (Cambridge, MA: Harvard University Press, 2014), 7–20.

but it no longer lived in their exaggeratedly pure womanly bosoms. Instead, by abandoning such gentlewomanly virtues, modern nurses, like other professionals, affirmed that expert work was performed ethically irrespective of class, race, or gender.[62] Quality assurance in nursing and other professional work was no longer about selection into the profession based on a kind of character pre-made with race, class, and gender traits, but about 'quality management'. This turned virtue into 'quality' which, like risk, was a matter of procedural control.[63]

This externalization of virtue from a substance that once resided within professional bodies to become codes and measures of the quality of professional 'outputs' boosted the new managerial regime. Enterprises now sought discretionary, and sometimes autocratic, managerial positions, which gave explicit responsibility to specific managers, rather than diffusing responsibility through professional organizational roles. Work activity was increasingly based on explicit goals and standards, encouraging professionals to focus on results rather than fulfilling responsibilities in a bureaucratic manner.[64]

Quality management became a tool for managers to resist professional autonomy, giving managers discretionary power in exactly the same way as industrial leaders gained power by breaking unions.[65] Public and private sector enterprises worked similarly in this, splitting monolithic, professionally controlled, work areas and moving discretionary management into smaller (but still managed) units. These managers were at the frontline of increased labour force flexibility, compelled to manage contracts and employment based on performance criteria that kept organizations focused on outputs.[66] In addition to this set of changes, public enterprises were also subjected to the austerity, or 'discipline and

[62] Veils and Caps, Royal Australian Nursing Federation, Australian Nursing Federation, NSW Branch deposit Noel Butlin Archives Centre, NBAC/Z486/24; Christina Bates, *A Cultural History of the Nurse's Uniform* (Quebec: Canadian Museum of Civilization, 2012).

[63] Max Travers, *The New Bureaucracy: Quality Assurance and Its Critics* (Bristol: Policy Press, 2007); Francesca Nicosia, 'The Turn Toward Value: An Ethnography of Efficiency and Satisfaction in the American Hospital', unpublished PhD dissertation, University of California, San Francisco (2017); Pauline Barnett and Philip Bagshaw, 'Neoliberalism: What It Is, How It Affects Health and What to Do About It', *New Zealand Medical Journal* 133.1512 (2020), 76–84.

[64] Christopher Hood, 'A Public Management for All Seasons', *Public Administration* 69 (1991), 3–19.

[65] Bob Carter, Andy Danford, Debra Howcroft, Helen Richardson, Andrew Smith, and Phil Taylor, '"All They Lack Is a Chain": Lean and the New Performance Management in the British Civil Service', *New Technology, Work, and Employment* 26.2 (2011): 83–97.

[66] Alfred Chandler, 'The M-form: Industrial Groups, American Style', *European Economic Review* 19.1 (1982), 3–23; Dunleavy and Hood, 'From Old Public Administration to New Public Management'.

parsimony' that characterized the new public management.[67] Employees at one public institution dubbed this austerity 'tolerable sub-optimization', which placed the morals that were still needed to perform professional work – virtues like integrity, compassion, diligence, and equity – in conflict with financial goals.[68]

Moral Deskilling

Management that relied less on individual qualities and more on systems was responding, in part, to growth in the size and complexity of organizations. When multinational corporations brought economies of scale and scope to bear on workplaces – scale by using the same resources to upscale services, often globally; and scope by producing related services, such as consulting, alongside legal, accountancy, or engineering work – large, tentacular enterprises absorbed engineers, pharmacists, and accountants worldwide. To compete, average firm sizes grew everywhere. Legal firms, like US-based Latham & Watkins, grew from partnerships earlier in the century, to large concerns that went multinational in the 1990s. Prominent international accountancy firms, which grew from ordinary local partnerships into the 'big eight' over the twentieth century, became the 'Big Six' in the 1980s and are now the 'Big Four', Deloitte, PWC, EY, and KPMG. Engineering companies like WSP, Arup, 3M, and BAE Systems grew hundreds of offices worldwide, employing thousands of engineers, but also designers, lawyers, IT specialists, accountants, and managers. The new IT giants, like Cisco and Microsoft, were dealt a brief blow by the dot-com crash of 2001, but they soon expanded alongside new players like Google and a revitalized Apple.[69] Healthcare companies – especially pharmaceuticals and diagnostics like Roche, Novartis, Johnson & Johnson, and Pfizer – were also part of the trend, as were insurers like United Health and Cigna.[70]

Even local institutions grew, like schools, universities, and hospitals. For the doctors at the Royal Children's Hospital in Melbourne, this manufactured a newly acrimonious archive. Since the reforms that grew out of Post-War Reconstruction, the senior medical staff produced a

[67] Hood, 'A Public Management for All Seasons'; Dunleavy and Hood, 'From Old Public Administration to New Public Management'.
[68] Laura Hamilton and Kelly Nielsen, *Broke: The Racial Consequences of Underfunding Public Universities* (Chicago: University of Chicago Press, 2021).
[69] Gow and Kells, *Big Four*.
[70] Julio Frenk, Octavio Gómez-Dantés, Orvill Adams, and Emmanuela Gakidou, 'The Globalization of Health Care', in Martin McKee, Paul Garner, and Robin Stotts (eds), *International Co-operation in Health* (Oxford: Oxford Academic, 2001).

bundle of civil correspondence with the hospital's management committee. Doctors raised concerns, though they were relatively affable. For
example, in 1969, Dr Elizabeth K. Turner – who was the first doctor to
administer penicillin in Australia – politely complained to the hospital
about increases in the rent on consulting rooms for private paediatricians.[71] Turner's colleague Dr Murray Clarke, by contrast, wrote that he
accepted that inflation applied to him too and affirmed that private
paediatricians 'are fairly treated'.[72]

These relatively cordial relations deteriorated from 1977, however,
when medical doctors began to complain that they were being frozen
out of hospital administration. 'For some time,' wrote Dr J. F. Connelly
on behalf of the Senior Medical staff, '[we] have been conscious of
problems in communication created by the growth and increasing complexity of the hospital'. By the early 1980s, the senior medical staff faced
conflict on all sides, as control of finances – and therefore the priorities
for professional work – slipped through medical fingers. Doctors were
further troubled by conflict, like their Canadian colleagues of earlier
decades, between medical practitioners who were paid a salary and
private practitioners who worked 'sessions' in the hospital. These two
categories were beginning to merge closer together, they acknowledged,
so that 'unity in this aspect of the medical profession is becoming more a
reality'. This newfound solidarity was largely achieved via their shared
frustration that they no longer had much influence with the hospital's
administration.[73]

The problems for hospital staff and other professionals went beyond
losing control of the priorities that drove resource allocation. The same
systems, as well as removing strategic decision-making from doctors and
other professional experts, also imposed performance schemes that
aligned to institutional metrics like length of stay, bed occupancy rates,
and recovery and readmission rates – a long way from the duty, charity,
courage, and purity of the Nightingale system.[74]

[71] Elizabeth K. Turner to Dr B. W. Neal, 14 January 1969, Minutes and Correspondence
of the Medical Staff Association, Royal Children's Hospital, Melbourne, Public Records
Office of Victoria, PROV/VPRS16804/13. See also https://wmoa.com.au/collection/
herstory-archive/turner-elizabeth.
[72] Murray Clarke to Dr B. W. Neal, 15 January 1969, Minutes and Correspondence of the
Medical Staff Association, Royal Children's Hospital, Melbourne, Public Records Office
of Victoria, PROV/VPRS16804/13.
[73] J. F. Macdonald, Documentation compiled by the Victorian Branch of the Australian
Medical Association, 11 March 1981, Minutes and Correspondence of the Medical Staff
Association, Royal Children's Hospital, Melbourne, Public Records Office of Victoria,
PROV/VPRS16804/14, quotes from Item 6.5, p. 8.
[74] Nicosia, 'The Turn Toward Value'; Barnett and Bagshaw, 'Neoliberalism'.

Similarly, in schools and kindergartens, tools like learning outcomes and standardized testing that were theoretically intended to support educational equity and undermine the 'hidden curriculum' were weaponized to audit teacher performance.[75] In universities, academic work became auditable, with expanding quantities of performance metrics being ever refined to capture nuances of quality and produce what amounted to managerial 'output controls'.[76]

The effect was similar to earlier forms of deskilling. In the past, breaking factory processes into segments meant only the overseer understood the whole. Now professional virtue was broken down and managed piecemeal, usually with relentless forms. Automation, like that which split, in Harry Braverman's assessment, physical labour from managerial 'brain' work, had a similar effect for professionals. In this case, however, digital tracking systems accelerated *moral* deskilling. As managerial imperatives became entangled with the technologies to produce larger amounts of digital data, this 'lively' set of metrics began driving workplace planning and professional performance in the name of assuring quality. Rather than the specific goals that professional experts long sought – such as students whose mathematics improved, families able to access the resources to cope with a terminally ill parent, and annual reports that communicated fairly and accurately to shareholders – these tools enabled managers to specify metrics for generic, abstracted success, even 'excellence'.[77] For professionals now managed by such systems, it produced a 'quantified self', now consisting of automated metrics that captured and, in turn, influenced decisions about individual priorities in the performance of professional work.[78]

---

[75] Raewyn Connell, 'The Neoliberal Cascade and Education: An Essay on the Market Agenda and Its Consequences', *Critical Studies in Education* 54.2 (2013), 99–112; Nicole Mockler, 'Teacher Professional Learning in a Neoliberal Age: Audit, Professionalism and Identity', *Australian Journal of Teacher Education* 38.10 (2013), 35–47; Margaret Sims, 'Neoliberalism and Early Childhood', *Cogent Education*, 4.1 (2017), https://doi.org/10.1080/2331186X.2017.1365411, Retrieved 17 August 2022; Antoni Verger, Clara Fontdevila, and Adrián Zancajo, *The Privatization of Education: A Political Economy of Global Education Reform* (New York: Teachers College Press, 2016).

[76] Guy Redden, 'Publish and Flourish, or Perish: RAE, ERA, RQF and Other Acronyms for Infinite Human Resourcefulness', *Media/Culture Journal*, 11.4 (2008), https://doi.org/10.5204/mcj.44, Retrieved 17 August 2022; Cris Shore and Susan Wright, 'Audit Culture Revisited: Rankings, Ratings, and the Reassembling of Society', *Current Anthropology* 56.3 (2015): 421–444.

[77] See, for example, Bill Readings' characterization of the empty, abstracted 'university of excellence' in Bill Readings, *The University in Ruins* (Cambridge, MA: Harvard University Press, 1996).

[78] Deborah Lupton, *The Quantified Self* (Cambridge: Polity Press, 2016); Deborah Lupton, 'M-Health and Health Promotion: The Digital Cyborg and Surveillance Society', *Social Theory and Health* 10.3 (2012), 229–244; Roger Burrows, 'Living with the h-Index?

From Virtuous Character to Internalized Effectiveness

Professionals began to develop techniques to cope with the ways priorities, values, and metrics developed by the managerial class were imposed on their work performance. Stephen R. Covey's 1989 *The 7 Habits of Highly Effective People* was one of many self-help books that helped professionals internalize the ethics emerging from the new managerialism. Covey referred to this as 'restoring the character ethic'. *The 7 Habits* and other books of its genre offered professionals a way to prioritize success *and* virtue. Covey recalled older virtues, including 'integrity, humility, fidelity, temperance, courage, justice, patience, industry, simplicity, modesty, and the Golden Rule'. In fact, the book repeatedly asked readers to align work habits to their *individual* principles, positing an empty set of generic tools into which individuals could pour their values.[79]

Like many other business self-help books, *The 7 Habits* were laid out mnemonically, helping readers memorize and implement each habit.[80] The first habit was 'be proactive'. Professionals now worked in an environment where they had diminishing control over organizational priorities, their performance was increasingly managed by metrics and machines, and an 'up or out' system of achievement was reducing their 'socially available free time' with much longer hours of work.[81] 'Be proactive' discouraged complaining and offered a vision where proactivity would help professionals regain influence in their organizations.

Metric Assemblages in the Contemporary Academy', *The Sociological Review* 60.2 (2012), 355–372; Ben Williamson, Sian Bayne, and Suellen Shay, 'The Datafication of Teaching in Higher Education: Critical Issues and Perspectives', *Teaching in Higher Education*, 25:4 (2020), 351–365; Phoebe Moore and Andrew Robinson, 'The Quantified Self: What Counts in the Neoliberal Workplace', *New Media and Society* 18.11 (2016), 2774–2792; Minna Ruckenstein and Natasha Dow Schull, 'The Datafication of Health', *Annual Review of Anthropology* 46.1 (*2017*), 261–278; see also Evelyn Ruppert, John Law, and Mike Savage, 'Reassembling Social Science Methods: The Challenge of Digital Devices', *Theory, Culture and Society* 30.4 (2013), 22–46.

[79] Stephen Covey, *The 7 Habits of Highly Effective People* (New York: Simon & Schuster, 1989), 18. Many thanks to Jordana Silverstein for loaning me the copy you had propping open your door.

[80] Melissa Gregg, *Counterproductive: Time Management in the Knowledge Economy* (Durham, NC: Duke University Press, 2018).

[81] On long working hours, see Iain Campbell, 'Long Working Hours in Australia: Working-time Regulation and Employer Pressures', *The Economic and Labour Relations Review* 2 (2007), 37–68; Dora Gicheva, 'Working Long Hours and Early Career Outcomes in the High-End Labor Market', *Journal of Labour Economics*, 31.4 (2013), 785–824; on the connections between long hours and merit, see Markovits, *Meritocracy Trap*; on the 'up or out' ethic, see Louis Hyman, *Temp*, 314–323. Socially available free time is a key concept from Martin Hägglund, *This Life: Why Mortality Makes Us Free* (London: Profile Books, 2019).

Covey's second habit, 'begin with the end in mind', encouraged professionals to focus on goals, outputs, and results. This aligned to the managerial shift, including the new public management, from processes to outputs. This, too, Covey framed as being grounded in 'values', for goals, he said, embodied the reason for doing the work. Boring, time-consuming processes are 'scripts that have already been handed to us', whereas by focusing on goals 'we can proactively begin to rescript ourselves'. For Covey, this helped managers 'empower' individual employees to take personal responsibility for managerial goals, rather than simply doing what they were told. It meant, he explained, that when something goes wrong, employees were more likely to take responsibility to fix the problem, rather than let managers find out later, sometimes too late to apply a remedy themselves.[82]

Habit three, 'put first things first', was also theoretically about virtue, in that it encouraged readers to prioritize tasks that best aligned to their values. This was different to 'eat the frog', from another self-help book, which suggested that performing the most challenging task first would 'have the greatest positive impact on your life'.[83] Covey's habit drew on longstanding time-management techniques to encourage prioritizing results-focused 'high-leverage' activities, which would earn significant rewards. Covey recognized, however, that someone had to do the boring process work. Eight pages were dedicated to the value of delegating. In 1989, chances are this boring, low-reward work was delegated to a woman.[84]

The next habit asked professionals to 'think win-win'. New approaches to management, based on discretionary power and austerity (in wages, at least) rested on disrupting collective action, including union-busting.[85] The 'win-win paradigm', which Covey said was about cooperation, helped professionals internalize these managerial goals. On the surface it posed a threat to hierarchical merit in that 'win-win' discouraged setting up staff to compete for managerial punishment or rewards. Instead, it invited managers to set the parameters for success so that professionals could manage themselves. Such internalization of managerial goals would evidently dismantle class conflict and build

---

[82] Covey, *7 Habits*, 103.
[83] Brian Tracy, *Eat That Frog: Get More Important Things Done – Today!* (Oakland, CA: Berrett-Koehler, 2016).
[84] Gregg, *Counterproductive*.
[85] Brian Towers, 'Running the Gauntlet: British Trade Unions under Thatcher, 1979–1988', *Industrial and Labor Relations Review* 42.2 (1989), 163–188; Jack Barbash, 'Trade Unionism from Roosevelt to Reagan', *The Annals of the American Academy of Political and Social Science* 473 (1984), 11–22.

consequences for staff that were a logical extension of their failure to meet the goal. Those consequences were evidently one's own fault, a structure that in fact aligned perfectly with merit.

The fifth habit, which further undermined the likelihood of class conflict, was deliberately phrased in biblical style: 'seek first to understand, then be understood'. This held out the possibility of convivial workplaces where professional virtue and managerial goals worked in concert, rather than competed for strategy and resources. This, too, was facilitated by habit six, 'synergizing', which had the potential to foster cooperation. For managers, 'synergizing' achieved what the association of mining engineers accomplished early in the twentieth century when they included tradesmen in their profession: they were able to acquire innovations produced as part of the real-world problem solving performed in mines by people with less status. It was another kind of deskilling, appropriating knowledge from below to control labour processes from above.[86]

The final habit was based on a metaphor comparing the time taken to cut down a tree with a blunt tool rather than taking the time to 'sharpen the saw'. Readers of *7 Habits* were invited to draw on the long history of virtuous leisure, where doctors were encouraged to read good literature, but to now link it directly to their professional effectiveness. By instilling discipline into their personal life by exercising and performing self-care, 'effective people' would keep themselves 'sharp'.[87] In this habit, Covey affirmed the class significance of the 'fitness craze' that started in the late 1970s. Barbara Ehrenreich insightfully observed that the craze 'quickly turned fitness – or the effort to achieve it – into another insignia of social rank'. She later showed this was further applied to mindfulness and the 'epidemic of wellness'.[88]

Professionals did not need to actually read Covey or any other self-help book to absorb and perform new expressions of virtue. Carefully curated exercise regimes and other shifting markers of status became part of what social theorist Pierre Bourdieu called 'cultural capital'. By the early twenty-first century, these were beginning to accumulate a new subtlety, as Elizabeth Currid-Halkett has shown. A certain shade of brown leather shoe, a particular stitching for a man's suit, a subtle but recognizable shade of nail polish, and even a body sculpted by purposeful exercise, came to be worn on professional bodies in ways which were visible

---

[86] See Forsyth, 'Class, Professional Work and the History of Capitalism', 39.
[87] Covey, *7 Habits*.
[88] Ehrenreich, *Fear of Falling*, 233; Barbara Ehrenreich, *Natural Causes: Life, Death and the Illusion of Control* (London: Granta, 2018).

mainly to others who did likewise. Such 'inconspicuous consumption' became a secret handshake of sorts, a way to perform one's membership of the professional class – or to be excluded based on subtle signals.[89] Melissa Gregg shows that performing all these personal and professional activities together bore the residue of Frederick Taylor's scientific management, but since the 1980s they also encouraged a performative professional selfhood, whose key virtue was productive success.[90]

A commitment to the relentless acquisition of such markers of professional belonging soon infected children, too. 'Helicopter' parenting, a transference of what Ehrenreich described as a shared 'fear of falling' among the middle class, placed children in baby gyms, swimming classes (even in freezing weather), tutoring regimes, and music lessons in the hope that, alongside expensive schooling, they will grow to be elite at *something*.[91] Middle-class members of the 'millennial' generation that reached adulthood early in the twenty-first century implicitly understood the need to invest every waking moment in their own human capital. Their much-maligned dedication to smartphones and avocado toast were rational investments in this regime of class-signalling, as service-sector productivity growth drove the 'knowledge economy' across the Anglo world.[92] All of these activities – which were, further, notably ableist – amounted to a new kind of virtue, now performed by eating kale, being active, influencing others and organizing one's own work time into efficient success. What Covey's seven habits tell us is that this virtue was about worker productivity. It was no longer the moral *investment* from which older generations of professionals, whose virtues Covey admired, expected to achieve moral and financial returns for themselves and for society. After the 1980s, professional virtue was hollowed into a generic 'effectiveness', reducing what the professional class once hoped for themselves and society to their proficiency at work.[93]

Conclusion

The split of the professional from the managerial side of what, until now, was one class also marked the end of the relationship between virtue and capitalism. The rupture grew from a position of conflict, as an emerging managerial elite saw virtue as their adversary. Virtue was, in fact, a barrier

[89] Currid-Halkett, *Sum of Small Things*, 1–6.   [90] Gregg, *Counterproductive*, 13.
[91] Ehrenreich, *Fear of Falling*; Daniel Rosenblatt, 'Stuff the Professional-Managerial Class Likes: 'Distinction' for an Egalitarian Elite', *Anthropological Quarterly* 86.2 (2013), 589–623.
[92] Harris, *Kids These Days*.
[93] Thanks to Andrew Dunstall (on Twitter) for helping me articulate this.

to the untrammelled pursuit of success promised by the borderless world. Global economic flexibility, where money flowed to where it best produced profits, rested on managers' ability to make tough decisions. Those decisions broke with values cherished by post-war democracies, including universal industriousness, employment stability, and a strong relationship between professional expertise and governmental and organizational priorities. Now expertise became a mere tool for managing organizational success. And success, in turn, became the only virtue that mattered.[94]

Although the rising managerial class benefited most, professionals helped dismantle traditional virtue because it was awful. As Chapter 7 showed, civil rights, decolonization, and women's liberation movements helped expose the ways that virtue was paternalistic, colonialist, and sexist. They showed that the system of merit, the 'currency' that established social and expert value, excluded people based on their race, class, gender, and sexuality. By the 1980s, changes to the global economy also meant that this virtue no longer served professionals. Character traits like duty, loyalty, prudence, and temperance not only seemed old-fashioned, but they also constrained the kind of go-getting encouraged by prioritizing outcomes. Virtues like probity and rectitude were the path to boring work processes, not spectacular results. Through a focus on outcomes, professional effort could align to managerial priorities, putting success first.

This was not wholly successful, however, because professionals still needed virtue. Virtue still underpinned the need to select safe materials for engineering works, taking adequate time to perform work tasks to professional standards, and teaching classes and nursing patients in numbers small enough to be sufficiently attentive. Many professionals, moreover, still wanted to help build a better world. Redirecting this desire into longer work hours and greater 'effectiveness', the professional class now invested virtue not into society, but solely into their own relative status. This included virtuous signals of class position like nutrition choices, exercise, children's music lessons, and performances of self-care. If the professional class was guilty of virtue signalling – a slur thrown by conservatives – it is in this. Instead of a material investment for profitable return, virtue was now a consumer item, which like the lawn mowers and middle-class homes of the 1950s, signalled and facilitated membership of the professional class.

---

[94] I do mean 'mattered' in a material sense: where the professional class earlier made virtue material, managers did the same with success – emptied, now, of its virtuous goals. See Barad, 'Posthumanist Performativity'.

Epilogue
Contours of the New Class Conflict

In the Supreme Court of British Columbia in 1997, Wet'suwet'en Chief Gisday Wa Alfred Joseph argued as follows:

Officials who are not accountable to this land, its laws or its owners have attempted to displace our laws with legislation and regulations. The politicians have consciously blocked each path within their system that we take to assert our title. The courts, until perhaps now, have similarly denied our existence. In your legal system, how will you deal with the idea that the Chiefs own the land? The attempts to quash our laws and extinguish our system have been unsuccessful. Gisday Wa has not been extinguished.[1]

Together the Wet'suwet'en Chief and Delgamuukw Ken Muldoe, Gitksan Chief, argued for the continuation of First Nations laws and peoples in the face of settler colonialism's logic of elimination. It was no isolated case, as native land title also became law in Australia and Aotearoa/New Zealand.[2]

As the British middle class settled on stolen land to administer the empire, colonizers and colonized were co-created.[3] This book has been concerned with the way the mirror of settler colonization forged the professional class and the virtue that made those occupations work, across the Anglo world. As the professions grew in the last quarter of the nineteenth century, this book has shown that professional virtue developed to 'civilize' First Nations land and colonial capitalist expansion alike. Professional work, performing this virtue, helped bring the global colour line into being and used 'merit' to build hierarchies through the global economy based on race, gender, sexuality, and, ultimately, class. The professionals were 'virtue capitalists' in that they

---

[1] Transcript of Proceedings at 65, Delgamuukw, British Columbia [1997] 3 S.C.R. 1010 (No. 23799) cited in Robert Anderson, 'Aboriginal Title in the Canadian Legal System: The Story of Delgamuukw v. British Columbia', in Carole Goldberg, Kevin Washburn, and Philip Frickey (eds), *Indian Law Stories* (New York: Foundation Press, 2011), 591.

[2] Louis Knafla and Haijo Westra, *Aboriginal Title and Indigenous Peoples: Canada, Australia, and New Zealand* (Vancouver: University of British Columbia Press, 2010).

[3] Mbembe, *On the Postcolony*.

invested virtue for social and economic profit, which also accrued to themselves.

But Chief Gisday Wa asked a question that continues to shake the foundations of the global economy that was built from their efforts: 'how will you deal with the idea that the Chiefs own the land?' The settler revolution stole Indigenous land, we know this. And the same revolution also built the twentieth-century global economy. It started with massive human capital investment on the colonial periphery, but within half a century or so, their model conquered the world. The virtue implicit in the human capital century was the foundation of post-war reconstruction. It was the bedrock of the mid-century economic order. It made the *trente glorieuses*, the three glorious decades of growth and income equality.[4]

But it was awful. Not in every respect, for inequality decreased, and virtue was built into economic exchanges in ways that were embodied and had material effects in real peoples' lives. But the same virtues were seeded with forms of harm that cannot be ignored until the children buried in residential schools are all exhumed, physically and metaphorically, across the colonial world. For professional virtue was grounded in a false claim that Chief Gisday Wa's question exposed: you do not own this. Your authority, autonomy, yes even your virtue, is founded on a sleight of hand. It is illegitimate.

We feel this, in the settler-colonial periphery. It is why I have written this book connecting the whole Anglo world, both those parts that have been traditionally peripheral and those that are hegemonic, for the metropole and the periphery are united by this deep colonial scar.

Chief Gisday Wa's question, 'how will you deal with the idea that the Chiefs own the land?', further gestures to the reversal of authority that is at the centre of what passes for class conflict since, at the end of the twentieth century, the managerial class separated from the professional expert. While labour versus capital has been suppressed (but not surpassed, which is important), the logic of decolonization dominates political life.

Let me explain, historically, extending from what I have discussed in this book. When the New Right emerged in the 1970s and 1980s, 'liberal elites' were their key target. Declaring themselves prepared to protect 'plain folks' from the authority professional experts themselves confessed were paternalistic and harmful, the New Right invested in think tanks, journalism, and legal expertise to oppose the decolonizing threat to

---

[4] Piketty, *Capital in the Twenty-First Century*.

established hierarchies. The New Right fought to keep those old colonizing hierarchies, and yet, as Barbara Ehrenreich perspicaciously argued in 1989, this movement also unironically used the 1970s critique of professional hierarchy as the foundation of their superficial, populist alignment to the working class.[5] This was a backlash against the reversal of hierarchies inspired by anti-colonial movements. It has only escalated since Ehrenreich wrote.

At the same time, the professional class faced an assault from another quarter. The rising managerial class, confronted with a new global order that demanded opposition to any virtue that might impede profitable success, began to undermine the autonomy professionals depended on to perform virtuous work. Professionals, now acknowledging the harm that some older virtues did even to themselves, helped dismantle the old procedures. They were inadvertently complicit in their own fall, however, for the virtue professionals still needed to do their work became codified systems of ethics, risk, and quality. The moral deskilling and enhanced managerial control permanently undermined the professional class's ability to capitalize virtue into social and personal profit.

It is perhaps understandable then, between the growth of managerialism and the contemporary rise of the far right, the professional class tends to idealize the mid-twentieth century, as if in doing so they could resurrect it. That deep alienation, the terrible gender, and racial inequalities of the *trente glorieuses* seem less terrible, to the professional class, than their utter loss of power.

There are several problems here, only one of which is the deep self-interest driving nostalgia for the rule of experts. The past cannot be resurrected; the conditions that brought it into being were not, in fact, Roosevelt's 'brain trust', but the rebuilding made possible by the conclusion of catastrophic war. Another brain trust cannot will their own power into being, no matter their vehemence nor even the rationality of their arguments. That time cannot be repeated. And it was not that great in the first place.

The main problem is that while the far right really must be opposed, doing so by buttressing professional technocratic power worsens an already terrible situation. This book has argued that virtue was, and is, used for power. The problem was highlighted for me while I wrote this book through the Covid pandemic. Then, as lockdowns hit the whole world, the lowest-paid workers turned out to be the most essential. What would it have meant if the cleaners, truckers, delivery drivers, postal

---

[5] Ehrenreich, *Fear of Falling*, 193–195.

services, and supermarket shelf stackers declared that their centrality to the proper functioning of our world meant that they should also control it? Would we not have to ask something similar to what Chief Gisday Wa asked, like: 'how will you deal with the idea that essential workers own the managerial decisions?'

This is not what happened. Instead, the new form of class conflict erupted over vaccination and quarantine. 'Trust the science' became emblematic of conflict, for both sides.

In this, as it did throughout the long twentieth century, the professional class behaved as if they – or we, for let us be honest, I am part of this class – they should control the world in ways that their most essential workers have not had the audacity, even at their most vulnerable moment, to claim for themselves. Don't misunderstand me; I too 'trust the science', for science and discovery have added so much value to our world. But the claim that everyone should 'trust the science' has also amounted to 'do what I say', invoking structures of authority that seek a much wider restoration of professional power.

That power – the system of merit and the hierarchies it produced – mirrored the hierarchies established during colonization of Wet'suwet'en, Gitksan and all other First Nations land.

When the professional class invoke such claims to authority, they fail to decolonize. Instead, they reinforce hierarchies that have done us all harm. The brunt of this harm was felt most tragically by Indigenous and enslaved peoples of course. But it is also worn on all the bodies who have invested time, resources, and selfhood in the human capital century.

This situation has left the world, which should have ready access to the best expertise it has ever produced, in a poorer position to confront existential problems like climate catastrophe. Instead, our politics and even often our workplaces are in thrall to a kind of class conflict that consists of two kinds of elites battling for technocratic power. They do this, moreover, while essential workers deliver them their dinners, teach and care for their children, and clean their homes.

It is a system we would do well to turn upside down.

Bibliography

Secondary Sources

Abel, Emily, 'Medicine and Morality: The Health Care Program of the New York Charity Organization Society', *The Social Service Review* 71.4 (1997), 634–651.

Abel-Smith, Brian, *A History of the Nursing Profession* (London: Heinemann, 1960).

The Hospitals 1800–1948 (London: Heinemann, 1964).

Abercrombie, Nicholas and John Urry, *Capital, Labour and the Middle Classes* (London: Routledge, 2015).

Abbott, Andrew, *The System of Professions: An Essay on the Division of Expert Labor* (Chicago: University of Chicago Press, 1988).

Adkins, Lisa, Melinda Cooper, and Martijn Konings, *The Asset Economy: Property Ownership and the New Logic of Inequality* (Cambridge: Polity Press, 2020).

Agamben, Giorgio, *The Kingdom and the Glory: For a Theological Genealogy of Economy and Government* (Stanford: Stanford University Press, 2011).

Ahmed, Sara, 'A Phenomenology of Whiteness', *Feminist Theory* 8.2 (2007), 149–168.

Aleman, Sonya, 'Locating Whiteness in Journalism Pedagogy', *Critical Studies in Media Communication* 31.1 (2014), 72–88.

Allen, Ann, 'Gender, Professionalization, and the Child in the Progressive Era: Patty Smith Hill, 1868–1946', *Journal of Women's History* 23.2 (2011), 112–136.

Althusser, Louis, *On the Reproduction of Capitalism: Ideology and Ideological State Apparatuses* (London: Verso Books, 2014).

Anderson, Gordon and Michael Quinlan, 'The Changing Role of the State: Regulating Work Arrangements in Australia and New Zealand 1788–2007', *Labour History* 95 (2008), 111–132.

Anderson, Robert, 'Aboriginal Title in the Canadian Legal System: The Story of Delgamuukw v. British Columbia', in Carole Goldberg, Kevin Washburn, and Philip Frickey (eds), *Indian Law Stories* (New York: Foundation Press, 2011), 591–603.

Anderson, Warwick, *The Cultivation of Whiteness: Science, Health and Racial Destiny in Australia* (Melbourne: Melbourne University Press, 2002).

Angulo, Alex, *Diploma Mills: How For-Profit Colleges Stiffed Students, Taxpayers, and the American Dream* (Baltimore: Johns Hopkins University Press, 2016).

Aron, Cindy, *Working at Play: A History of Vacations in the United States* (New York: Oxford University Press, 2001).

Arrighi, Giovanni, *The Long Twentieth Century: Money, Power and the Origins of Our Times* (London: Verso, 1994).

Arrow, Kenneth, Samuel Bowles, and Steven Durlauf (eds), *Meritocracy and Economic Inequality* (Princeton: Princeton University Press, 2000).

Ashby, Eric, *Technology and the Academics: An Essay on Universities and the Scientific Revolution* (London: Macmillan, 1958).

Aston, Jennifer and Catherine Bishop (eds), *Female Entrepreneurs in the Long Nineteenth Century: A Global Perspective* (Cham: Palgrave Macmillan, 2020).

Atton, Chris and James Hamilton, *Alternative Journalism* (London: SAGE, 2008).

Aucoin, James, 'Journalistic Moral Engagement: Narrative Strategies in American Muckraking', *Journalism* 8.5 (October 2007), 559–572.

'The Re-emergence of American Investigative Journalism 1960–1975', *Journalism History* 21.1 (1995), 3–15.

Austin, Albert, *Australian Education 1788–1900* (Melbourne: Pitman, 1972).

Axelrod, Paul, *The Promise of Canadian Schooling: Education in Canada 1800–1914* (Toronto: University of Toronto Press, 1997).

Bailkin, Jordanna, *The Afterlife of Empire* (Berkeley: University of California Press, 2012).

Ballantyne, Tony, *Webs of Empire: Locating New Zealand's Colonial Past* (Wellington: Bridget Williams Books, 2012).

Ballantyne, Tony and Antoinette Burton, *Empires and the Reach of the Global 1870–1945* (Cambridge, MA: Harvard University Press, 2012).

Baptist, Edward, *The Half Has Never Been Told: Slavery and the Making of American Capitalism* (New York: Basic Books, 2014).

Barad, Karen, 'Posthumanist Performativity: Toward an Understanding of How Matter Comes to Matter', *Signs: Journal of Women in Culture and Society* 28.3 (2003), 801–831.

Barbalet, Jack, 'Social Closure in Class Analysis: A Critique of Parkin', *Sociology* 16.4 (1982), 484–497.

Barbash, Jack, 'Trade Unionism from Roosevelt to Reagan', *The Annals of the American Academy of Political and Social Science* 473 (1984), 11–22.

Barcan, Alan, *A History of Australian Education* (Oxford: Oxford University Press, 1980).

Barnett, Michael, *The Empire of Humanity: A History of Humanitarianism* (Ithaca: Cornell University Press, 2011).

Barnett, Pauline and Philip Bagshaw, 'Neoliberalism: What It Is, How It Affects Health and What to Do about It', *New Zealand Medical Journal* 133.1512 (2020), 76–84.

Barro, Robert and Jong-Wha Lee, 'A New Data Set of Educational Attainment in the World, 1950–2010', *Journal of Development Economics* 104 (2013), 184–198.

Bashford, Alison, '"Is White Australia Possible?" Race, Colonialism and Tropical Medicine', *Ethnic and Racial Studies* 23.2 (2000), 248–271.

Purity and Pollution: Gender, Embodiment and Victorian Medicine (London: Macmillan, 1998).

Bates, Christina, *A Cultural History of the Nurse's Uniform* (Quebec: Canadian Museum of Civilization, 2012).

Battell, Emma and Adam Barker, *Settler: Identity and Colonialism in Twenty-First Century Canada* (Halifax: Fernwood Publishing, 2015).

Beauman, Katharine, *Women and the Settlement Movement* (London: Radcliffe Press, 1996).

Beck, Andrew, 'The Flexner Report and the Standardization of American Medical Education', *The Journal of the American Medical Association* 291.17 (2004), 2139–2140.

Beck, Ulrich, *Risk Society: Towards a New Modernity* (London: SAGE, 1992).

Beckert, Sven, *Empire of Cotton: A Global History* (New York: Vintage, 2015).

The Monied Metropolis: New York City and the Consolidation of the American Bourgeoisie (Cambridge: Cambridge University Press, 2001).

Beechey, Veronica, 'On Patriarchy', *Feminist Review* 3.1 (1979), 66–82.

Beier, Lucinda McCray, *For Their Own Good: The Transformation of English Working-Class Health Culture, 1880–1970* (Columbus: Ohio State University Press, 2008).

Belich, James, *Replenishing the Earth: The Settler Revolution and the Rise of the Anglo World* (Oxford: Oxford University Press, 2009).

Bell, Enid, *The Story of Hospital Almoners: The Birth of a Profession* (London: Faber and Faber, 1961).

Bellanta, Melissa, *Larrikins: A History* (Brisbane: University of Queensland Press, 2012).

Bennett, James, 'Keeping the Wolfenden from the Door? Homosexuality and the "Medical Model" in New Zealand', *Social History of Medicine* 23.1 (2010), 134–152.

Berman, Edward, *The Ideology of Philanthropy: The Influence of the Carnegie, Ford, and Rockefeller Foundations on American Foreign Policy* (Albany: State University of New York Press, 1983).

Black, Lawrence, Hugh Pemberton, and Pat Thane (eds), *Reassessing 1970s Britain* (Manchester: Manchester University Press, 2016).

Blainey, Geoffrey, 'Herbert Hoover's Forgotten Years', *Business Archives and History* 3.1 (1963), 53–70.

The Rise of Broken Hill (Melbourne: Macmillan 1968).

The Rush That Never Ended: A History of Australian Mining (Melbourne: Melbourne University Press, 1964).

The Tyranny of Distance (Melbourne, Sun Books, 1966).

Blake, Catriona, *The Charge of the Parasols: Women's Entry to the Medical Profession* (London, The Women's Press, 1990).

Boettke, Peter, 'Lionel Robbins, Prophet of International Liberalism', American Institute for Economic Research, 24 September, 2018, www.aier.org/article/lionel-robbins-prophet-of-international-liberalism/

Bongiorno, Frank, *The Eighties: The Decade That Transformed Australia* (Melbourne: Black Inc., 2015).

Bonner, Thomas, *Becoming a Physician: Medical Education in Britain, France, Germany, and the United States, 1750–1945* (Oxford: Oxford University Press, 1995).

Bootcov, Michelle 'Dr George On Lee (葉七秀): Not Just a Medical Practitioner in Colonial Australia', *Chinese Southern Diaspora Studies* 8 (2019) 南方華裔研究雜誌, 第八卷 (2019), 82–101.

Bordo, Michael and Owen Humpage, 'Federal Reserve Policy and Bretton Woods', National Bureau of Economic Research Working Paper 20656 (2014).

Boris, Eileen, *Making the Woman Worker: Precarious Labor and the Fight for Global Standards, 1919–2019* (Oxford: Oxford University Press, 2019).

Bourdieu, Pierre, *Distinction: A Social Critique of the Judgement of Taste* (Cambridge, MA: Harvard University Press, 1984).

Bowler, Kate, *Blessed: A History of American Prosperity Gospel* (Oxford: Oxford University Press, 2018).

Brandes, Stuart, *American Welfare Capitalism 1880–1920* (Chicago: Chicago University Press, 1976).

Brasch, Walter, *Forerunners of Revolution: Muckrakers and the American Social Conscience* (Lanham: University Press of America, 1990).

Braverman, Harry, *Labor and Monopoly Capital* (New York: Monthly Review Press, 1974).

Breen, Richard and John Goldthorpe, 'Class Inequality and Meritocracy: A Critique of Saunders and an Alternative Analysis', *British Journal of Sociology* 50.1 (1999), 1–27.

Brehony, Kevin, 'A New Education for a New Era: The Contribution of the Conferences of the New Education Fellowship to the Disciplinary Field of Education 1921–1938', *Paedagogica Historica* 40.5–6 (2004), 733–755.

Brett, Judith, *Australian Liberals and the Moral Middle Class* (Cambridge: Cambridge University Press, 2003).

The Enigmatic Mr Deakin (Melbourne: Text Publishing, 2018).

Briggs, Asa, 'The Welfare State in Historical Perspective', *European Journal of Sociology* 2.2 (1961), 221–258.

Brown, Sue, 'A Woman's Profession', in Helen Marchant and Betsy Wearing (eds), *Gender Reclaimed: Women in Social Work* (Sydney: Hale & Iremonger, 1986), 223–233.

Brumberg, Joan and Nancy Tomes, 'Women in the Professions: A Research Agenda for American Historians', *Reviews in American History* 10.2 (1982), 275–296

Burnett, Kristin, 'The Healing Work of Aboriginal Women in Indigenous and Newcomer Communities', in Jayne Elliot, Meryn Stuart, and Cynthia Toman (eds), *Place and Practice in Canadian Nursing History* (Vancouver: UBC Press, 2008), 40–52.

Burrows, Roger, 'Living with the h-Index? Metric Assemblages in the Contemporary Academy', *The Sociological Review* 60.2 (2012), 355–372.

Burton, Antoinette, *The Trouble with Empire: Challenges to Modern British Imperialism* (Oxford: Oxford University Press, 2017).

Butler, Judith, 'Performative Acts and Gender Constitution: An Essay in Phenomenology and Feminist Theory', *Theatre Journal* 40.4 (1988), 519–531.

Butler, Leo, *One Hundred Years of Nurse Training at the Royal Women's Hospital* (Melbourne: Royal Women's Hospital, 1963).

Byrne, David, 'The Construction of Religion as a Subject for Catholic Schools in Western Australia: An Historical Analysis of the Situation from 1929 to 1982', Unpublished PhD Dissertation, University of Western Australia (2021).

Cahill, Damien and Martijn Konings, *Neoliberalism* (Cambridge: Polity Press, 2017).

Campbell, Craig, 'Cold War, the Universities and Public Education: The Contexts of J. B. Conant's Mission to Australia and New Zealand, 1951', *History of Education Review* 39.1 (2010), 23–39.

Campbell, Craig and Helen Proctor, *A History of Australian Schooling* (Sydney: Allen and Unwin, 2014).

Campbell, Iain, 'Long Working Hours in Australia: Working-Time Regulation and Employer Pressures', *The Economic and Labour Relations Review* 2 (2007), 37–68.

Cannon, Michael, 'Fink, Benjamin Josman (1874–1909)', *Australian Dictionary of Biography, Volume 4* (Melbourne: Melbourne University Press, 1972).

'Munro, David (1844–1898)', *Australian Dictionary of Biography, Volume 5* (Melbourne: Melbourne University Press, 1974).

The Land Boomers (Melbourne: Melbourne University Press, 1966).

Carden, Clarissa, 'Managing Moral Reformation: The Case of Queensland's Reformatory for Boys, 1871–1919' *History of Education Review* 50.2 (2021): 226–240.

Carey, Jane, 'The Racial Imperatives of Sex: Birth Control and Eugenics in Britain, The United States and Australia in Interwar Years', *Women's History Review* 21.5 (2012), 733–752.

Carnegie, Garry, 'The Development of Accounting Regulation, Education and Literature in Australia 1788–2005', *Australian Economic History Review* 49.3 (2009), 276–301.

Carroll, Mary, 'Republic of the Learned', *History of Education* 38.6 (2009), 809–823.

Carruthers, Barry and Lesley Carruthers, *A History of Britain's Hospitals* (Sussex: Book Guild Publishing, 2005).

Carter, Bob, Andy Danford, Debra Howcroft, Helen Richardson, Andrew Smith, and Phil Taylor, '"All They Lack Is a Chain": Lean and the New Performance Management in the British Civil Service', *New Technology, Work, and Employment* 26.2 (2011): 83–97.

Chakrabarti, Pratik, *Medicine & Empire: 1600–1960* (Basingstoke: Palgrave Macmillan, 2014).

Chakrabarty, Dipesh, *Provincializing Europe: Postcolonial Thought and Historical Difference* (Princeton: Princeton University Press, 2000).

Chandler, Alfred, *Scale and Scope: The Dynamics of Industrial Capitalism* (Cambridge, MA: Harvard University Press, 1994).

'The M-Form: Industrial Groups, American Style', *European Economic Review* 19.1 (1982), 3–23.

The Visible Hand: The Managerial Revolution in American Business (Cambridge, MA: Harvard University Press, 1977).

Christopher, Emma, *Freedom in White and Black: A Lost Story of the Illegal Slave Trade and Its Global Legacy* (Madison: University of Wisconsin Press, 1988).

Clark, Beverly, 'Domesticating the School Story, Regendering a Genre: Alcott's "Little Men"', *New Literary History*, 26.2 (1995), 323–342.

Clark, Peder, '"Problems of Today and Tomorrow": Prevention and the National Health Service in the 1970s', *Social History of Medicine* 33.3 (2019), 981–1000.

Cohen, Lizabeth, *A Consumer's Republic: The Politics of Mass Consumption in Postwar America* (New York: Vintage, 2003).

Coleman, Peter, 'New Zealand Liberalism and the Origin of the American Welfare State', *The Journal of American History* 69 (1982): 372–91

Coleman, William, Selwyn Cornish, and Ald Hagger, *Gilblin's Platoon* (Canberra: Australian National University Press, 2006).

Collini, Stefan, *Public Moralists: Political Thought and Intellectual Life in Britain 1850–1930* (Oxford: Clarendon Press, 1991).

'Snakes and Ladders', *London Review of Books* 43.7 (2021), 15–22.

Collinson, David and Jeff Hearn, *Men as Managers, Managers as Men: Critical Perspectives on Men, Masculinities, and Managements* (London: SAGE, 1996).

Coney, Sandra, 'The Women's Health Movement in New Zealand: Past Achievements, Future Challenges', *Reproductive Health Matters*, 5.10 (1997), 23–26.

Connell, Raewyn, *Masculinities* (Berkley: University of California Press, 2005).

'The Neoliberal Cascade and Education: An Essay on the Market Agenda and its Consequences', *Critical Studies in Education* 54.2 (2013), 99–112.

'Theorizing Intellectuals', *Arena Journal* 45/46 (2016), 12–27.

Connell, Raewyn and Julian Wood, 'Globalization and Business Masculinities', *Men and Masculinities* 7.4 (2005), 347–364.

Conrad, Margaret, *A Concise History of Canada* (Cambridge: Cambridge University Press, 2012).

Cooper, Christine, Jonathan Tweedie, Jane Andrew, and Max Baker, 'From "Business-like" to Businesses: Agencification, Corporatization, and Civil Service Reform Under the Thatcher Administration.' *Public Administration* 100.2 (2022), 193–215.

Cornish, Selwyn and Kurt Schuler, 'Australia's Full-Employment Proposals at Bretton Woods: A Road Only Partly Taken', in Naomi Lamoreaux and Ian Shapiro (eds), *The Bretton Woods Agreements: Together with Scholarly Commentaries and Essential Historical Documents* (New Haven: Yale University Press, 2019), 173–194.

Cott, Nancy, *The Grounding of Modern Feminism* (New Haven: Yale University Press, 1987).

Coulthard, Glen Sean, *Red Skin, White Masks: Rejecting the Colonial Politics of Recognition* (Minneapolis: University of Minnesota Press, 2014).

Cowan, Ruth, *More Work for Mother: The Ironies of Household Technology From the Open Hearth to the Microwave* (New York: Basic Books, 1983).

Cremin, Lawrence, *The Transformation of the School: Progressivism in American Education, 1876–1957* (New York: Knopf, 1961).

Crichton, Anne, *Slowly Taking Control? Australian Governments and Health Care Provision 1788–1988* (Sydney: Allen & Unwin 1990).

Crombie, Annie, 'A Free Hand and Ready Help? The Supervision and Control of Elementary Education in Staffordshire c.1902–1914' *Oxford Review of Education* 28.2–3 (2002), 173–186.

Crompton, Rosemary and Gareth Jones, *White-Collar Proletariat* (London: Palgrave, 1984).

Cronon, William, *Nature's Metropolis: Chicago and the Great West* (New York: W.W. Norton, 1991).

Crouch, Colin, 'Privatized Keynesianism: An Unacknowledged Policy Regime', *The British Journal of Politics and International Relations* 11.3 (2009), 382–399.

The Strange Non-Death of Neo-Liberalism (Cambridge: Polity Press, 2011).

Croucher, Gwilym and James Waghorne, *Australian Universities: A History of Common Cause* (Sydney: NewSouth, 2020).

Cryle, Denis, *The Press in Colonial Queensland: A Social and Political History, 1845–1875* (Brisbane: University of Queensland Press, 1989).

Cuban, Larry, *How Teachers Taught: Constancy and Change in American Classrooms 1890–1980* (New York: Longman, 1984).

Cullen, Lynsey, 'The First Lady Almoner: The Appointment, Position and Findings of Miss Mary Stewart at the Royal Free Hospital 1895–1899', *Journal of the History of Medicine and Allied Sciences* 68.4 (2013), 551–82.

Cumming, Ian and Alan Cumming, *History of State Education in New Zealand 1840–1975* (Melbourne: Pitman Publishing, 1978).

Currid-Halkett, Elizabeth, *The Sum of Small Things: A Theory of the Aspirational Class* (Princeton: Princeton University Press, 2017).

Curthoys, Ann, *Freedom Ride: A Freedom Rider Remembers* (Sydney: Allen & Unwin, 2002).

Curthoys, Ann and Marilyn Lake (eds), *Connected Worlds: History in Transnational Perspective* (Canberra: ANU Press, 2005).

Curtis, Bruce, 'The State of Tutelage in Lower Canada, 1835–1851', *History of Education Quarterly* 37.1 (1997), 25–43.

Cuthbert, Denise and Marian Quartly, '"Forced Adoption" in the Australian Story of National Regret and Apology', *The Australian Journal of Politics and History* 58.1 (2012), 82–96.

Damousi, Joy, Trevor Burnard and Alan Lester (eds), *Humanitarianism, Empire and Transnationalism, 1760–1995* (Manchester: Manchester University Press, 2022).

Dalston, Lorraine and Peter Galison, *Objectivity* (New York: Zone Books, 2007).

Darian-Smith, Kate and James Waghorne, 'Australian Universities, Expertise and Internationalism after World War 1', *Journal of Australian Studies* 43.4 (2019), 412–28.

Daunton, Martin, *Trusting Leviathan: The Politics of Taxation in Britain, 1799–1914* (Cambridge: Cambridge University Press, 2001).

'Michael Young and Meritocracy', *Contemporary British History* 19.3 (2005), 285–291.

Davidoff, Leonore and Catherine Hall, *Family Fortunes: Men and Women of the English Middle Class,1780–1850* (London: Routledge, 2002).

Davies, Owen, 'Cunning-Folk in the Medical Market-Place during the Nineteenth Century', *Medical History* 43 (1999), 55–73.

Davis, Lance and Robert Gallman, *Evolving Financial Markets and International Capital Flows: Britain, the Americas, and Australia, 1865–1914* (New York: Cambridge University Press, 2001).

Davis, Robert, James Conroy, and Julie Clague, 'Schools as Factories: The Limits of a Metaphor', *Journal of Philosophy of Education* 54.5 (2020), 1471–1488.

Davison, Graeme, 'The Rise and Fall of Marvellous Melbourne, 1880–1895,' unpublished PhD Thesis, Australian National University (1969).

The Rise and Fall of Marvellous Melbourne (Melbourne: Melbourne University Press, 1979).

Davison, Graeme and David Dunstan (eds), *The Outcasts of Melbourne* (Sydney: Allen & Unwin, 1985).

Deacon, Desley, *Managing Gender: The State, the New Middle Class and Women Workers 1830–1930.* (Oxford: Oxford University Press, 1989).

'Political Arithmetic: The Nineteenth-Century Australian Census and the Construction of the Dependent Woman', *Signs: Journal of Women in Culture and Society* 11.1 (1985), 27–47.

de Burgh, Hugo, 'The emergence of investigative journalism', in Hugo de Burgh (ed), *Investigative journalism* (London: Routledge: 2008), 32–53.

Daes Erica-Irene 'An overview of the History of Indigenous Peoples: Self-Determination and the United Nations', *Cambridge Review of International Affairs* 21.1 (208), 7–26.

Darwin, John, *The Empire Project: The Rise and Fall of the British World-System 1830–1970* (Cambridge: Cambridge University Press, 2009).

Dejung, Cristof, 'From Global Civilizing Missions to Racial Warfare: Class Conflicts and the Representation of the Colonial World in European Middle-Class Thought', in Christof Dejung, David Motadel, and Jürgen Osterhammel (eds), *The Global Bourgeoisie: The Rise of the Middle Classes in the Age of Empire* (Princeton: Princeton University Press, 2019), 251–272.

DeLong, Brad and Barry Eichengreen, 'The Marshall Plan: History's Most Successful Structural Adjustment Program', National Bureau of Economic Research Working Paper 3899 (1991).

Derksen, Maarten, 'Turning Men into Machines? Scientific Management, Industrial Psychology, and the "Human Factor"', *Journal of the History of the Behavioural Sciences* 50.2 (2014), 148–165.

Detzen, Dominic, 'A "New Deal" for the Profession', *Accounting, Auditing and Accountability*, 31.3 (2018), 970–992.

Digby, Ann, *The Evolution of British General Practice 1850–1948* (Oxford: Oxford University Press, 1999).

Dingwall, Robert, Anne Rafferty, and Charles Webster, *An Introduction to the Social History of Nursing* (London: Routledge, 1988).

Docker, John, *The Nervous Nineties: Australian Cultural Life in the 1890s* (Oxford: Oxford University Press, 1991).

Dodd, Dianne and Deborah Gorham, *Caring and Curing: Historical Perspectives on Women and Healing in Canada* (Ottawa: University of Ottawa Press, 1994).

Doherty, Muriel, *Off the Record – The Life and Times of Muriel Knox Doherty 1896–1988: An Autobiography* (Sydney: New South Wales College of Nursing, 1996).

Dow, Derek, *Safeguarding the Public Health: A History of New Zealand Department of Public Health* (Wellington: Victoria University Press, 1995).

Dow, Sheila, Peter Earl, John Foster, Geoffrey Harcourt, Geoffrey Hodgson, J. Stanley Metcalfe, Paul Ormerod, Bridget Rosewell, Malcolm Sawyer and Andrew Tylecote, 'The GFC and University Economics Education: An Open Letter to the Queen', *Journal of Australian Political Economy* 64 (2009), 233–235.

Dudziak, Mary, *Cold War Civil Rights: Race and the Image of American Democracy* (Princeton: Princeton University Press, 2002).

Duménil, Gérard and Dominique Lévy, *Managerial Capitalism: Ownership, Management and the Coming New Mode of Production* (London, Pluto Press, 2018).

Dunleavy, Patrick and Christopher Hood, 'From Old Public Administration to New Public Management', *Public Money and Management* 14.3 (1994), 9–16.

Durst, Anne, *Women Educators in the Progressive Era the Women Behind Dewey's Laboratory School* (New York: Palgrave Macmillan, 2010).

Dutil, Patrice, 'Foreword', in Gregory Marchildon (ed), *Making Medicare: New Perspectives on the History of Medicare in Canada* (Toronto: University of Toronto Press, 2012), vii–viii.

Edele, Mark, and Robert Gerwarth, 'The Limits of Demobilization: Global Perspectives on the Aftermath of the Great War', *Journal of Contemporary History* 50.1 (2015), 3–14.

Edelstein, Michael, 'Professional Engineers in the Australian Economy: Some Quantitative Dimensions, 1866–1980,' Working Papers in Economic History (Australian National University) 93 (1987).

Edwards, John, *Company Legislation and Changing Patterns of Disclosure in British Company Accounts 1900–1940* (London: Institute of Chartered Accountants in England and Wales, 1981).

Ehrenreich, Barbara, *Fear of Falling: The Inner Life of the Middle Class* (New York: Pantheon Books, 1989).

Natural Causes: Life, Death and the Illusion of Control (London: Granta, 2018).

The Hearts of Men: American Dreams and the Flight from Commitment (New York: Anchor Books, 2011).

Ehrenreich, Barbara and Deirdre English, *For Her Own Good: 150 Years of the Experts' Advice to Women* (New York: Anchor Press, 1978).

Ehrenreich, Barbara and John Ehrenreich, 'The New Left and the Professional-Managerial Class', *Radical America* 11.3 (1976), 7–24.

Ehrenreich, Barbara, and John Ehrenreich, 'The Professional-Managerial Class', *Radical America* 11.2 (1976), 7–32.

Eich, Stefan and Adam Tooze, 'The Great Inflation', in Anselm Doering-Manteuffel, Lutz Raphael, Thomas Schlemmer (eds), *Vorgeschichte der Gegenwart: Dimensionen des Strukturbruchs Nach den Boom* (Göttingen: Vandenhoeck & Ruprecht, 2016), 173–196.

Eley, Geoff, and Kieth Nield, *The Future of Class in History?* (Ann Arbor: University of Michigan Press, 2007).

Ellis, John, *Visible Fictions: Cinema, Television, Video* (London: Routledge, 1992).

Ellis, Lloyd, 'The Underground Press in America: 1955–1970', *The Journal of popular culture* 24.4 (2000), 379–400.

Esping-Anderon, Gøsta, *The Three Worlds of Welfare Capitalism* (Princeton: Princeton University Press, 1990).

Ettema, James and Theodore Glasser, *Custodians of Conscience: Investigative Journalism and Public Virtue* (New York: Columbia University Press, 1998).

Evans, Patricia and Gerda Wekerle *Women and the Canadian Welfare State: Challenges and Change* (Toronto: University of Toronto Press, 1997).

Fahey, Charles and John Lack, 'Silent Forms of Coercion: Welfare Capitalism, State Labour Regulation and Collective action at the Yarravile Sugar Refinery 1890–1925', *Labour History* 101 (2011), 105–22.

Fedders, Barbara, 'The Constant and Expanding Classroom: Surveillance in K-12 Public Schools', *North Carolina Law Review* 97.6 (2019), 1673–1725.

Feldstein, Mark, 'A Muckraking Model: Investigative Reporting Cycles in American History', *Harvard International Journal of Press/Politics* 11.2 (2006), 105–120.

Ferguson, Ann, 'Patriarchy, Sexual Identity, and the Sexual Revolution', *Signs: Journal of Women in Culture and Society* 7.1 (1981), 158–172.

Filler, Louis, *The Muckrakers* (Stanford: Stanford University Press, 1968).

Fitzpatrick, Ellen, *Muckraking: Three Landmark Articles* (Boston: Bedford Books, 1994).

Ford, Lisa, *Settler Sovereignty: Jurisdiction and Indigenous People in America and Australia, 1788–1836* (Cambridge, MA: Harvard University Press, 2010).

Forsyth, Hannah, *A History of the Modern Australian University* (Sydney: NewSouth, 2014).

'Census Data on Universities, Professions and War', in Kate Darian-Smith and James Waghorne (eds), *The First World War, the Universities and the Professions in Australia 1913–1939* (Melbourne: Melbourne University Press, 2019), 10–28.

'Class, Professional Work, and the History of Capitalism in Broken Hill, c. 1880–1910', *Labor* 15.2 (2018), 21–47.

'Expanding Higher Education: Institutional Responses in Australia from the Post-War Era to the 1970s', *Paedagogica Historica* 51.3 (2015), 365–80.

'Reconsidering Women's Role in the Professionalisation of the Economy: Evidence from the Australian Census 1881–1947', *Australian Economic History Review* 59.1 (2019), 55–79.

Forsyth, Hannah and Michael Pearson, 'Engineers and Social Engineering: Professional/Trade Unions and Social Mobility', *Labour History* 120 (2021), 169–195.

Foucault, Michel, *Discipline and Punish: The Birth of the Prison* (Harmondsworth: Penguin, 1979).

The Birth of Biopolitics: Lectures at the College de France, 1978–1979 (London: Palgrave Macmillan, 2008).

The Birth of the Clinic: An Archaeology of Medical Perception (London: Tavistock, 1973).

The History of Sexuality: 1: The Will to Knowledge (New York: Random House, 1978).

Freire, Paulo, *Pedagogy of the Oppressed* (New York: Herder and Herder, 1970).

Frenk, Julio, Octavio Gómez-Dantés, Orvill Adams, and Emmanuela Gakidou 'The Globalization of Health Care', in Martin McKee, Paul Garner, and Robin Stotts (eds), *International Co-operation in Health* (Oxford: Oxford Academic, 2001).

Friedson, Eliot, *Professional Dominance: The Social Structure of Medical Care* (Chicago: Atherton Press, 1970).

Froud, Julie, Colin Haslam, Sukhdev Johal, and Karel Williams, 'Shareholder Value and Financialization: Consultancy Promises, Management Moves', *Economy and Society* 29.1 (2000), 80–110.

Gallagher, Hector, *We Got a Fair Go: A History of the Commonwealth Reconstruction Training Scheme 1945–1952* (Melbourne: Hector Gallagher, 2003).

Garber, Peter, 'The Collapse of the Bretton Woods Fixed Exchange Rate System', in Michael Bordo and Barry Eichengreen (eds), *A retrospective on the Bretton Woods System: Lessons for International Monetary Reform* (Chicago: University of Chicago Press, 1993), 461–494.

Garner, Alice and Diane Kirkby, '"Never a Machine for Propaganda"? The Australian–American Fulbright Program and Australia's Cold War', *Australian Historical Studies* 44.1 (2013), 117–33.

Gidney, R.D. and Millar, W.P.J., *Professional Gentlemen: The Professions in Nineteenth-Century Ontario* (Toronto: Toronto University Press, 1994).

Garton, Stephen, *The Cost of War* (Oxford: Oxford University Press, 1996).

'Demobilization and Empire: Empire Nationalism and Soldier Citizenship in Australia after the First World War – in Dominion Context', *Journal of Contemporary History* 50.1 (2015), 124–143.

Gerrard, Jessica, 'All That Is Solid Melts into Work: Self-Work, the "Learning Ethic" and the Work Ethic', *The Sociological Review (Keele)* 62.4 (2014), 862–79.

Getachew, Adom, *Worldmaking After Empire: The Rise and Fall of Self-Determination* (Princeton: Princeton University Press, 2019).

Gewirtz, Sharon, 'Give Us a Break! A Sceptical Review of Contemporary Discourses of Lifelong Learning', *European Educational Research Journal* 7.4 (2008): 414–424.

Gibb, Phyllis, *Classrooms a World Apart: The Story of the Founding of the Broken Hill School of the Air* (Melbourne: Spectrum, 1986).

Gicheva, Dora, 'Working Long Hours and Early Career Outcomes in the High-End Labor Market', *Journal of Labour Economics*, 31.4 (2013), 785–824.

Giddens, Anthony, *The Class Structure of the Advanced Societies* (London: Hutchinson, 1980).

Gihleb, Rania and Osea Giuntella , 'Nuns and the Effects of Catholic Schools: Evidence from Vatican II', *Journal of Economic Behaviour and Organization* 137 (2017), 191–213.

Gillespie, James, *The Price of Health: Australian Governments and Medical Politics 1910–1960* (Cambridge: Cambridge University Press, 1991).

Goldin, Claudia, 'The Human-Capital Century and American Leadership: Virtues of The Past', *The Journal of Economic History*, 61.2 (2001), 263–292.

Goldthorpe, John and Abigail McKnight, 'The Economic Basis of Social Class', in Stephen Morgan, David Grusky, and Gary Fields (eds), *Mobility and Inequality: Frontiers of Research in Sociology and Economics* (Stanford: Stanford University Press, 2006), 109–136.

Gordon, Colin, *Dead on Arrival the Politics of Health Care in Twentieth-Century America* (Princeton: Princeton University Press, 2005).

Gosling, George, *Payment and Philanthropy in British Healthcare 1918–1948* (Manchester: Manchester University Press, 2017).

Gow, Ian and Stuart Kells, *The Big Four: The Curious Past and Perilous Future of the Global Accounting Monopoly* (Melbourne: La Trobe University Press, 2018).

Graham, Patricia, *Progressive Education from Arcady to Academe: A History of the Progressive Education Association 1919–1955* (New York: Teachers College Press, 1967).

Grant, Donald, 'Hales, Alfred Arthur Greenwood (1860–1936)', *Australian Dictionary of Biography, Volume 9* (Canberra: Australian National University, 1983).

Green, Bill, 'Carnegie in Australia: Philanthropic Power and Public Education in the Early Twentieth Century', *History of Education Review* 48.1 (2019), 61–74.

Green, David, 'The 1918 Strike of the Medical Profession against the Friendly Societies in Victoria', *Labour History* 46 (1984), 72–87.

Greenhalgh, Charlotte, *Aging in Twentieth Century Britain* (Oakland, University of California Press, 2018).

'The Travelling Social Survey: Social Research and its subjects in Britain, Australia and New Zealand, 1930s-1970s' *History Australia* 13.1 (2016), 124–138.

Gregg, Melissa, *Counterproductive: Time Management in the Knowledge Economy* (Durham, NC: Duke University Press, 2018).

Gregson, Sarah, Michael Quinlan, and Ian Hampson, 'Professionalism or Inter-Union Solidarity?: Organising Licensed Aircraft Maintenance Engineers, 1955-75', *Labour History* 110 (2016), 35–56.

Griffen-Foley, Bridget, 'From Tit-Bits to Big Brother: A Century of Audience Participation in the Media', *Media, Culture & Society* 26.4 (2004), 533–548.

'Operating on "an Intelligent Level": Cadet Training at Consolidated Press in the 1940s', in Ann Curthoys and Julianne Schultz (eds), *Journalism: Print, Politics and Popular Culture* (Brisbane: University of Queensland Press, 1999), 142–154.

Griffiths, Tom and Jack Downey. '"What to Do About Schools?": The Australian Radical Education Group (RED G)', *History of Education Review* 44.2 (2015), 170–185.

Habermas, Jürgen, *Legitimation Crisis* (Boston: Beacon Press, 1975).

The Structural Transformation of the Public Sphere: An Inquiry into a Category of Bourgeois Society (Cambridge, MA: MIT Press, 1996).

Haigh, Gideon *The Office: A Hardworking History* (Melbourne: Miegunyah Press, 2012).

Hall, Alan, *The Stock Exchange of Melbourne and the Victorian Economy 1852–1900* (Canberra: Australian National University Press, 1968).

Hall, Catherine, 'Strains in the 'Firm of Wife, Children and Friends'? Middle Class Women and Employment in Early Nineteenth-Century England', in Pat Hudson and William Lee (eds), *Women's Work and the Family Economy in Historical Perspective* (Manchester: Manchester University Press, 1990).

White, Male and Middle Class: Explorations in Feminism and History (Cambridge: Polity Press, 1992).

Hall, Catherine and Sonya Rose (eds), *At Home with the Empire: Metropolitan Culture and the Imperial World* (Cambridge: Cambridge University Press, 2006).

Hall, Catherine, Nicholas Draper, Keith McClelland, Katie Donington, and Rachel Lang, *Legacies of British Slave-Ownership: Colonial Slavery and the Formation of Victorian Britain* (Cambridge: Cambridge University Press, 2014).

Halsey, Albert, *British Social Trends since 1900* (London: Macmillan, 1988).

Hamilton, Laura and Kelly Nielsen, *Broke: The Racial Consequences of Underfunding Public Universities* (Chicago: University of Chicago Press, 2021).

Hancock, Ange-Marie, *Intersectionality: An Intellectual History* (Oxford, Oxford University Press, 2016).

Hannah, Wilma, 'Fink, Theodore (1855–1942)', in *Australian Dictionary of Biography, Volume 8* (Melbourne: Melbourne University Press, 1981).

Hannon, Andrew, '"Hippie" Is a Transnational Identity: Australian and American Countercultures and the London OZ.' *Australasian Journal of American Studies* 35.2 (2016), 39–59.

Harno, Albert, *Legal Education in the United States* (San Francisco: Bancroft-Whitney Company, 1953).

Harris, Bernard, *The Origins of the British Welfare State: Society, State and Social Welfare in England and Wales, 1800–1945* (Basingstoke: Palgrave Macmillan, 2004).

Harris, Cheryl, 'Whiteness as Property', *Harvard Law Review* 106.8 (1993), 1707–1791.

Harris, Malcolm, *Kids These Days: Human Capital and the Making of Millennials* (Boston: Little, Brown and Company, 2017).

Harrison, Mark, *Medicine and Victory: British Military Medicine in the Second World War* (Oxford: Oxford University Press, 2004).

Harvey, David, *The Limits to Capital* (London: Verso, 2018).

Helleiner, Eric, *Forgotten Foundations of Bretton Woods* (Ithaca: Cornell University Press, 2018).

Hilliard, Christopher, *A Matter of Obscenity: The Politics of Censorship in Modern England* (Princeton: Princeton University Press, 2021).

Hine, Darlene, *Black Women in White: Racial Conflict and Cooperation in the Nursing Profession, 1890–1950* (Bloomington: Indiana University Press, 1989).

Histed, Elise, 'Molesworth, Hickman (1842–1907)', in *Australian Dictionary of Biography, Volume 10* (Melbourne: Melbourne University Press 1986).

Hobbins, Peter and Kathryn Hillier, 'Isolated Cases? The History and Historiography of Australian Medical Research', *Health and History* 12.2 (2010), 1–17.

Hood, Christopher, 'A Public Management for All Seasons', *Public Administration* 69 (1991), 3–19.

Hook, Andrew, 'Troubling Times in the Scottish–American Relationship', in Celeste Ray (ed), *Transatlantic Scots* (Tuscaloosa: University of Alabama Press, 2010), 215-231.

Hope, Wayne, 'A Short History of the Public Sphere in Aotearoa/New Zealand', *Continuum* 10.1 (1996), 12–32.

Hopkins, Michael Philippa Crane, Paul Nightingale and Charles Baden-Fuller, 'Buying Big into Biotech: Scale, Financing and the Industrial Dynamics of UK Biotech, 1980–2009', *Industrial and Corporate Change* 22.4 (2013), 903–952.

Horne, Julia, 'The "Knowledge Front", Women, War and Peace', *History of Education Review* 45.2 (2016), 151–167.

Horwitz, Morton, *The Transformation of American Law, 1780–1860* (Cambridge MA: Harvard University Press, 1977).

Howlett, Michael and Andrea Migone, 'Policy Advice through the Market: The Role of External Consultants in Contemporary Policy Advisory Systems', *Policy and Society* 32.3 (2013), 241–254.

Huber, Valeska, Tamson Pietsch and Katherine Rietzler, 'Women's International Thought and the New Professions, 1900–1940' *Modern Intellectual History* 18 (2021), 121–45.

Hyman, Louis, *Temp: How American Work, American Business, and the American Dream Became Temporary* (New York: Viking, 2018).

Im, Yung-Ho, 'Class, Culture, and Newsworkers: Theories of the Labor Process and the Labor History of the Newspaper', Unpublished PhD Dissertation, The University of Iowa, Iowa City (1990).

Inglis, Fred, *The Delicious History of the Holiday* (London: Routledge, 2000).

Irvine, Elizabeth, *Social Work and Human Problems: Casework, Consultation and Other Topics* (Oxford: Pergamon, 1979).

Irving, Terry, 'The Idea of Responsible Government in New South Wales before 1856', *Historical Studies: Australia and New Zealand*, 11.42 (1964), 192–205.

Iriye, Akira, *Global and Transnational History: The Past, Present and Future* (London: Palgrave Macmillan, 2012).

Ivey, Davida, 'Becoming a Social Worker: A History of Women Social Workers in Australia 1929–1965', unpublished Honours Thesis, Australian Catholic University, Sydney (2020).

Jackson, Ben, *Equality and the British Left: A Study in Progressive Political Thought, 1900–64* (Manchester: Manchester University Press, 2014).

Jackson, Michelle, 'Meritocracy, Education and Occupational Attainment: What Do Employers Really See as Merit?', Unpublished DPhil thesis, University of Oxford, Oxford (2002).

Jacobs, Margaret, 'Remembering the "Forgotten Child": The American Indian Child Welfare Crisis of the 1960s and 1970s', *The American Indian Quarterly* 37.1–2 (2013), 136–159.

Jacoby, Sandford, *Employing Bureaucracy: Managers, Unions, and the Transformation of Work in the Twentieth Century* (Mahwah, NJ: Lawrence Erlbaum Associates, 2004).

Modern Manors: Welfare Capitalism since the New Deal (Princeton: Princeton University Press, 1997).

Janak, Edward, 'Education in the Progressive Period (Ca. 1890s–1920s)', in Edward Janak (ed), *A Brief History of Schooling in the United States: From Pre-Colonial Times to the Present* (Cham: Springer, 2019).

Jayasuriya, Kanishka, *Reconstituting the Global Liberal Order: Legitimacy and Regulation* (London: Routledge, 2005).

Jenkins, Celia, 'New Education and Its Emancipatory Interests (1920–1950)', *History of Education: Tavistock* 29.2 (2000), 139–151.

Johnson, Terence, *Professions and Power* (London: Macmillan, 1972).

Johnson, Walter, *River of Dark Dreams* (Cambridge, MA: Harvard University Press, 2013).

Johnson, Walter and Francis Colligan, *The Fulbright Program: A History* (Chicago: University of Chicago Press, 1965).

Jones, Colin and Roy Porter (eds), *Reassessing Foucault: Power, Medicine and the Body* (Psychology Press, 1998).

Jones, Gareth, *Languages of Class: Studies in English Working-Class History 1832–1982* (Cambridge: Cambridge University Press, 1983).

Outcast London: A Study of the Relationship between Classes in Victorian Society (London: Verso, 2013).

Jones, Ken, *Education in Britain 1944–Present* (Cambridge: Polity Press, 2016).

Joppke, Christian, 'The Cultural Dimensions of Class Formation and Class Struggle: On the Social Theory of Pierre Bourdieu', *Berkeley Journal of Sociology* 31 (1986), 53–78.

Josephson Storm and Jason Ānanda, *The Myth of Disenchantment: Magic, Modernity, and the Birth of the Human Sciences* (Chicago: University of Chicago Press, 2017).

Joyce, Patrick, *Visions of the People: Industrial England and the Question of Class* (Cambridge: Cambridge University Press, 1994).

Juillet, Luc, *Defending a Contested Ideal: Merit and the Public Service Commission, 1908–2008* (Ottawa: University of Ottawa Press, 2008).

Kelly, Diana, 'Perceptions of Taylorism and a Marxist Scientific Manager', *Journal of Management History*, 22.3 (2016), 298–319.

Kennedy, Richard, *Charity Warfare: The Charity Organisation Society in Colonial Melbourne* (Melbourne: Hyland House, 1985).

Kett, Joseph, *Merit: The History of a Founding Ideal from the American Revolution to the Twenty-First Century* (Ithaca: Cornell University Press, 2012).

Keynes, John, *Essays in Persuasion* (New York: Norton, 1963).

King, Michael, Glenn Smith, and Annie Bartlett, 'Treatments of Homosexuality in Britain since the 1950s – An Oral History: The Experience of Professionals', *British Medical Journal* 328.7437 (2004), 429–432.

Kirby, Perpetua, 'Children's Agency in the Modern Primary Classroom', *Children & Society* 34.1 (2020), 17–30.

Kmiec, Patricia, '"Take This Normal Class Idea and Carry It Throughout the Land": Sunday School Teacher Training in Late Nineteenth-Century Ontario', *Historical Studies in Education/Revue d'histoire de l'éducation* 24.1 (2012), 195–211.

Knafla, Louis and Haijo Westra, *Aboriginal Title and Indigenous Peoples: Canada, Australia, and New Zealand* (Vancouver: University of British Columbia Press, 2010).

Kocka, Jürgen, 'The Middle Classes in Europe', *The Journal of Modern History* 67.4 (1995), 783–806.

Krauze, Tadeusz and Kazimierz Słomczyński, 'How Far to Meritocracy? Empirical Tests of a Controversial Thesis', *Social Forces* 63.3 (1985), 623–642.

Kroeze, Ronald and Sjoerd Keulen, 'The Manager's Moment in Western Politics: the Popularization of Management and Its Effects in the 1980s and 1990s', *Management & Organization History* 9.4 (2014), 394–413.

Kuznets, Simon and Milton Friedman, *Incomes from Independent Professional Practice* (New York: National Bureau of Economic Research, 1945).

Kwollek-Folland, Angel, *Incorporating Women: A History of Women and Business in the United States* (New York: Palgrave, 2002).

Kynaston, David and David Milner, *City of London: The History* London: Chatto & Windus, 2011.

Labaree, David, 'Progressivism, Schools and Schools of Education: An American Romance', *Paedagogica Historica* 41.1–2 (2005), 275–288.

LaBrèque, Marie-Paule, "Lynch, William Warren," in *Dictionary of Canadian Biography*, Volume 14 (Toronto: University of Toronto/Université Laval, 2003–).

Lagemann, Ellen, *The Politics of Knowledge: The Carnegie Corporation, Philanthropy, and Public Policy* (Middletown, CT: Wesleyan University Press, 1989).

Laidlaw, Zoe, *Colonial Connections, 1815–1845: Patronage, the Information Revolution and Colonial Government* (Manchester, Manchester University Press, 2005).

Lake, Marilyn, *The Limits of Hope : Soldier Settlement in Victoria, 1915–38* (Oxford: Oxford University Press, 1987).

Progressive New World: How Settler Colonialism and Transpacific Exchange Shaped American Reform. (Cambridge, MA: Harvard University Press, 2019).

Lake, Marilyn and Henry Reynolds, *Drawing the Global Colour Line: White Men's Countries and the International Challenge of Racial Inequality* (Cambridge, Cambridge University Press, 2008).

Lambert, David and Alan Lester, *Colonial Lives Across the British Empire: Imperial Careering in the Long Nineteenth Century* (Cambridge: Cambridge University Press, 2006).

'Geographies of Colonial Philanthropy', *Progress in Human Geography* 28.3 (2004), 320–341.

Lampard, Richard. 'Might Britain Be a Meritocracy? A Comment on Saunders', *Sociology* 30.2 (1996), 387–393.

Landahl, Joakim, 'Learning to Listen and Look: The Shift from the Monitorial System of Education to Teacher-Lead Lessons', *The Senses & Society* 14.2 (2019), 194–206.

Larson, Magali, *The Rise of Professionalism: Monopolies of Competence and Sheltered Markets* (New Brunswick, NJ: Transaction Publishers, 2013).

Law, Marc and Sukkoo Kim, 'Specialization and Regulation: The Rise of Professionals and the Emergence of Occupational Licensing Regulation', *The Journal of Economic History*, 65.3 (2005), 723–756.

Lawrence, Robert, *Professional Social Work in Australia* (Canberra: Australian National University Press, 1965).

Lawrence, Susan and Peter Davies 'Melbourne: The Archaeology of a World City', *International Journal of Historical Archaeology* 22.1 (2018), 117–130.

Lawson, Gordon, 'The Road Not Taken: The 1945 Health Services Commission Proposals and Physician Remuneration in Saskatchewan', in Gregory Marchildon (ed), *Making Medicare: New Perspectives on the History of Medicare in Canada* (Toronto: University of Toronto Press, 2012).

Lebovic, Sam, *A Righteous Smokescreen: Postwar America and the Politics of Cultural Globalization* (Chicago: Chicago University Press, 2022).

Leccese, Stephen, 'John D. Rockefeller, Standard Oil, and the Rise of Corporate Public Relations in Progressive America, 1902–1908', *The Journal of the Gilded Age and Progressive Era*, 16.3 (2017), 245–263.

Lee, Gregory and Howard Lee 'Comprehensive Post-Primary Schooling in New Zealand 1935–1975', *History of Education Review* 37.1 (2008), 56–76.

Lee, Jong-Wha and Hanol Lee, 'Human Capital in the Long Run,' *Journal of Development Economics* 122 (2016), 147–169.

Lee, Michael, 'The Advent of Decimalisation in Britain: 1971', *Historian* 106 (2010), 20–23.

Lemieux, Thomas and David Card, 'Education, Earnings, and the Canadian G.I. Bill', *The Canadian Journal of Economics* 34.2 (2001), 313–344.

Leslie, Stuart, *The Cold War and American Science: The Military-Industrial-Academic Complex at MIT and Stanford* (New York: Columbia University Press, 1993).

Lester, Alan, *Imperial Networks: Creating Identities in Nineteenth Century South Africa and Britain* (London: Routledge, 2001).

Levy, Jonathan, *Freaks of Fortune: the Emerging World of Capitalism and Risk in America* (Cambridge, MA: Harvard University Press, 2014).

Ages of American Capitalism: A History of the United States (New York: Random House, 2021).

Lewis, Anton, *'Counting Black and White Beans': Critical Race Theory in Accounting* (Bingley, UK: Emerald Publishing, 2020).

Lewes, James, 'The Underground Press in America (1964–1968): Outlining an Alternative, the Envisioning of an Underground', *Journal of Communication Inquiry* 24.4 (2000), 379–400.

Lewis, Jane, *The Voluntary Sector, the State, and Social Work in Britain: The Charity Organisation Society/Family Welfare Association Since 1869* (Brookfield, VT: Edward Elgar, 1995).

Lewis, Milton and Roy Macleod 'Medical Politics and the Professionalization of Medicine in New South Wales, 1850–1901', *Journal of Australian Studies* 12.22 (1988), 69–82.

Lindert, Peter, *Growing Public: Social Spending and Economic Growth since the Eighteenth Century* (Cambridge: Cambridge University Press, 2004).

Linn, Robert, *Power, Progress & Profit: A history of the Australian Accounting Profession* (Melbourne, Australian Society of Certified Practicing Accountants, 1996).

Lloyd, Brian, *Engineers in Australia* (Melbourne: Macmillan, 1991).

Status and Reward: The History of Industrial Representation of Professional Engineers in Australia 1945–1996 (Melbourne: Association of Professional Engineers, 1996).

Lloyd, Clem, *Profession: Journalist: A History of the Australian Journalists' Association* (Sydney: Hale & Iremonger, 1985).

Love, Peter, *Labour and the Money Power: Australian Labour Populism 1890–1950* (Melbourne: Melbourne University Press, 1984).

Lumby, Catherine and Elspeth Probyn, 'Interview with Mike Carlton: Money versus Ethics', in Catherine Lumby and Elspeth Probyn (eds), *Remote Control: New Media, New Ethics* (Cambridge: Cambridge University Press, 2003), 100–106.

Lundy, Colleen and Therese Jennissen, *One Hundred Years of Social Work: A History of the Profession in English Canada, 1900–2000* (Waterloo: Wilfrid Laurier University Press, 2011).

Lupton, Deborah, *The Quantified Self* (Cambridge: Polity Press, 2016).

'M-Health and Health Promotion: The Digital Cyborg and Surveillance Society', *Social Theory and Health* 10.3 (2012), 229–244.

Lydon, Jane, *Anti-Slavery and Australia: No Slavery in a Free Land?* (London: Routledge, 2021).

Lyotard, Jean-François, *The Postmodern Condition: A Report on Knowledge* (Manchester: Manchester University Press, 1984).

McIntyre, Julie and John Germov, '"Who Wants to Be a Millionaire?" I Do: Postwar Australian Wine, Gendered Culture and Class', *Journal of Australian Studies* 42.1 (2018), 65–84.

Macintyre, Stuart, *Australia's Boldest Experiment* (Sydney: NewSouth, 2015).

Concise History of Australia (Cambridge: Cambridge University Press, 2020).

'Neither Capital nor Labour', in Stuart Macintyre and Richard Mitchell (eds), *Foundations of Arbitration: The Origin and Effects of State Compulsory Arbitration 1890–1914* (Oxford: Oxford University Press 1989).

Macintyre, Stuart and Richard Mitchell, 'Introduction', in Stuart Macintyre and Richard Mitchell (eds), *Foundations of Arbitration: The Origin and Effects of State Compulsory Arbitration 1890–1914* (Oxford: Oxford University Press 1989).

Macintyre, Stuart, and Sean Scalmer, 'Class', in Alison Bashford and Stuart Macintyre (eds), *The Cambridge History of Australia* (Cambridge: Cambridge University Press, 2013), 358–376.

Macleod, Roderick, '"In the Hallowed Name of Religion": Scots and Public Education in Nineteenth Century Montreal', in Peter Rider and Heather

McNabb (eds), *A Kingdom of the Mind: How the Scots Helped Make Canada* (Montreal: McGill-Queen's University Press, 2006), 227–241.

Maier, Charles, 'Malaise', in Niall Ferguson, Charles Maier, Erez Manela, and Daniel Sargent, *The Shock of the Global: The 1970s in Perspective* (Cambridge, MA: Harvard University Press, 2010), 25–48.

Maloney, John, 'The Treasury and the New Cambridge School in the 1970s', *Cambridge Journal of Economics* 36 (2012), 995–1017.

Mandler, Peter, *The Crisis of the Meritocracy: Britain's Transition to Mass Education Since the Second World War* (Oxford, Oxford University Press, 2020).

'Poverty and Charity in the Nineteenth Century Metropolis', in Peter Mandler (ed), *Uses of Charity* (Philadelphia: University of Pennsylvania Press, 1990), 1–37.

Manjapra, Kris, 'The Semi-Peripheral Hand: Middle-Class Service Professionals of Imperial Capitalism', in Christof Dejung, David Motadel, and Jürgen Osterhammel (eds), *The Global Bourgeoisie: The Rise of the Middle Classes in the Age of Empire* (Princeton: Princeton University Press, 2019).

Marchildon, Gregory, 'Legacy of the Doctors' Strike and the Saskatoon Agreement', *Canadian Medical Association journal* 188.9 (2016), 676–77.

'Medicare: Why History Matters', in Gregory Marchildon (ed), *Making Medicare: New Perspectives on the History of Medicare in Canada* (Toronto: University of Toronto Press, 2012), 3–20.

Markey, Ray, 'Trade Unions, the Labor Party and the introduction of Arbitration in New South Wales and the Commonwealth', in Stuart Macintyre and Richard Mitchell (eds), *Foundations of Arbitration: The Origin and Effects of State Compulsory Arbitration 1890–1914* (Oxford, Oxford University Press 1989), 156–177.

Markovits, Daniel, *The Meritocracy Trap: How America's Foundational Myth Feeds Inequality, Dismantles the Middle Class, and Devours the Elite* (London: Penguin, 2020).

Marks, Lara, *Sexual Chemistry: A History of the Contraceptive Pill* (New Haven: Yale University Press, 2001).

Marshall, Gordon and Adam Swift, 'Merit and Mobility: A Reply to Peter Saunders', *Sociology* 30.2 (1996), 375–386.

Martyr, Philippa, 'No Paradise for Quacks? Nineteenth Century Health Care in Tasmania', *Tasmanian Historical Studies* 5.2 (1997), 141–152.

Paradise of Quacks: An Alternative History of Medicine in Australia (Paddington: Macleay Press, 2002).

Marx, Karl, *Capital, Volume. 1* (Harmondsworth: Penguin Books, 1976).

Marx, Karl and Friedrich Engels, *The Communist Manifesto* (Minneapolis, MN: First Avenue Editions, a division of Lerner Publishing Group, 2018).

Theses on Feuerbach, Reproduced from https://www.marxists.org, Retrieved 30 September 2022.

Matthews, Derek, Malcolm Anderson, and John Edwards, *The Priesthood of Industry: The Rise of the Professional Accountant in British Management* (Oxford: Oxford University Press, 1998).

May, Helen, *School Beginnings: A Nineteenth Century Colonial Story* (Wellington, NZ: NZCER Press, 2005).

May, Helen, Kristen Nawrotzki, and Larry Prochner (eds), *Kindergarten Narratives on Froebelian Education: Transnational Investigations* (London, Bloomsbury, 2018).

Mbembe, Achille, *On the Postcolony* (Berkley: University of California Press, 2001).

Mccarthy, Helen, *Double Lives: A History of Working Motherhood* (London: Bloomsbury, 2020).

McCloskey, Deirdre, *The Bourgeois Virtues: Ethics for an Age of Commerce* (Chicago: University of Chicago Press, 2006).

McDonald, Colin and Ruth Teale, 'Knaggs, Samuel Thomas (1842–1921)', in *Australian Dictionary of Biography, Volume 5* (Melbourne: Melbourne University Press 1974).

McKay, Marion, 'Region, Faith and Health: The Development of Winnipeg's Visiting Nursing Agencies 1897–1926', in Jayne Elliott, Meryn Stuart, and Cynthia Toman (eds), *Place and Practice in Canadian Nursing History* (Vancouver: University of British Columbia Press, 2008), 70–90.

Mclean, Ian, *Why Australia Prospered: The Shifting Sources of Economic Growth* (Princeton: Princeton University Press, 2012).

McLear, Patrick, 'Speculation, Promotion, and the Panic of 1837 in Chicago', *Journal of the Illinois State Historical Society* 62.2 (1969), 135–146.

McLeod, Julie, 'Experimenting with Education: Spaces of Freedom and Alternative Schooling in the 1970s', *History of Education Review* 43.2 (2014), 172–189.

Mcnair, Brian, *News and Journalism in the UK* (London: Routledge, 2003).

McPherson, Kathryn, *Bedside Matters: The Transformation of Canadian Nursing, 1900–1990* (Toronto: University of Toronto Press, 2012).

McQueen, Humphrey, *A New Britannia* (Harmondsworth: Penguin, 1970).

Mesquita, Leopoldo, 'The Lancasterian Monitorial System as an Education Industry with a Logic of Capitalist Valorisation', *Paedagogica Historica,* 48.5 (2012), 661–675.

Meyering, Isobelle, *Feminism and the Making of a Child Rights Revolution 1969–1979* (Melbourne: Melbourne University Press, 2022).

Middleton, Sue, 'Schooling the Labouring Classes: Children, Families, and Learning in Wellington, 1840–1845', *International Studies in Sociology of Education* 18.2 (2008), 133–146.

Miller, Jane, 'The Predominance of American Influences on the Establishment of Social Work Education at the University of Melbourne 1920–1960', Unpublished PhD dissertation, University of Melbourne (2015).

Miller, Jane and David Nicholls, 'Establishing a Twentieth Century Women's Profession', *Lilith: A Feminist History Journal* 20 (2014), 21–33.

Miller, Peter and Ted O'Leary, 'Accounting and the Construction of the Governable Person', *Accounting, Organizations and Society* 12.3 (1987), 235–265.

Miller, Peter and Nikolas Rose, 'Governing Economic Life', *Economy and Society,* 19.1 (1990), 1–31.

Miller, Ron, 'Educating the True Self: Spiritual Roots of the Holistic Worldview', *Journal of Humanistic Psychology* 31 (1991), 53–67.

Milloy, John, *A National Crime: The Canadian Government and the Residential School System 1879 to 1986* (Winnipeg: University of Manitoba Press, 2017).

Mills, C. Wright, *White Collar: The American Middle Classes* (Oxford, Oxford University Press, 2002).

Miranti, Paul, *Accountancy Comes of Age: The Development of an American Profession 1886–1940* (Chapel Hill: University of North Carolina Press, 1990).

Mitchell, Timothy, *Rule of Experts Egypt, Techno-Politics, Modernity* (Berkeley: University of California Press, 2002).

Mody, Fallon, 'Revising Post-War British Medical Migration: A Case Study of Bristol Medical Graduates in Australia', *Social History of Medicine* 31.3 (2018), 485–509.

Mockler, Nicole, 'Teacher Professional Learning in a Neoliberal Age: Audit, Professionalism and Identity', *Australian Journal of Teacher Education* 38.10 (2013), 35–47.

Moore, Phoebe and Andrew Robinson, 'The Quantified Self: What Counts in the Neoliberal Workplace', *New Media and Society* 18.11 (2016), 2774–2792.

Morris, Ernest, *A History of the London Hospital* (London: Edward Arnold, 1926).

Moyn, Samuel, *Not Enough: Human Rights in an Unequal World* (Cambridge: Cambridge University Press, 2018).

Muhlmann, Geraldine, *A Political History of Journalism* (Cambridge: Polity Press, 2004).

Muirhead, Bruce, *Against the Odds: the Public Life and Times of Louis Rasminsky* (Toronto: University of Toronto Press, 1999).

Mulholland, Marc, *Bourgeois Liberty and the Politics of Fear: From Absolutism to Neo-conservatism* (Oxford: Oxford University Press, 2012).

Mythen, Gabe, *Ulrich Beck: A Critical Introduction to the Risk Society* (London: Pluto Press, 2004).

Nelson, Elizabeth, *British Counter-Culture 1966–73: A Study of the Underground Press.* (London: Macmillan, 1989).

Newman, Erica, 'History of Transracial Adoption: A New Zealand Perspective', *The American Indian Quarterly* 37.1–2 (2013), 237–257.

Newton, Scott, 'The Sterling Crisis of 1947 and the British Response to the Marshall Plan', *The Economic History Review* 37.3 (1984), 391–408.

Nichols, Robert, *Theft Is Property! Dispossession and Critical Theory* (Durham, NC: Duke University Press, 2020).

Nicosia, Francesca, 'The Turn Toward Value: An Ethnography of Efficiency and Satisfaction in the American Hospital', Unpublished PhD Dissertation, University of California, San Francisco (2017).

Nolan, Melanie, 'The Reality and Myth of New Zealand Egalitarianism: Explaining the Pattern of a Labour Historiography at the Edge Of Empires', *Labour History Review* 72.2 (2007), 113–134.

Núñez, Clara, 'Literacy, Schooling and Economic Modernization: A Historian's Approach', *Paedagogica Historica*, 39.5 (2003), 535–558.

O'Brien, John, *National Tertiary Education Union: A Most Unlikely Union* (Sydney: UNSW Press, 2015).

O'Brien, Laurie and Cynthia Turner, *Establishing Medical Social Work in Victoria* (Melbourne: University of Melbourne Press, 1979).

O'Dea, Raymond, 'Some Features of the Professional Engineers' Case', *The Journal of Industrial Relations* 4.2 (1962), 90–107.

Wage Determination in Commonwealth Arbitration (Sydney: West Publishing Corporation, 1969).

Olson, Keith, *The G.I. Bill, the Veterans and the Colleges* (Lexington: University of Kentucky Press, 1974).

Olssen, Erik and Maureen Hickey, *Class and Occupation: The New Zealand Reality* (Dunedin: Otago University Press, 2005).

Oppenheimer, Martin, 'The Rise and Fall of the Muckrakers', *New Politics* 16.2 (2017), 87–96.

Orfield, Gary, *Public School Desegregation in the United States, 1968–1980* (Washington, DC: Joint Centre for Political Studies, 1983).

Orsi, Robert, *Between Heaven and Earth: the Religious Worlds People Make and the Scholars who Study Them* (Princeton: Princeton University Press, 2006).

Ottewill, Roger, 'Law Breaking in Hampshire as an Expression of Nonconformist Opposition to the Education Act 1902', *Family and Community History* 23.1 (2020), 42–54.

Overy, Richard, *The Morbid Age: Britain and the Crisis of Civilisation 1919–1939* (London: Penguin, 2009).

Paisley, Fiona and Pamela Scully, *Writing Transnational History* (London: Bloomsbury, 2019).

Panitch, Leo and Sam Gindin, *The Making of Global Capitalism: The Political Economy of American Empire* (London: Verso, 2012).

Parker, Lee and Ingrid Jeacle. 'The Construction of the Efficient Office: Scientific Management, Accountability, and the Neo-Liberal State', *Contemporary Accounting Research*, 36.3 (2019), 1883–1926.

Parker, Robert, *Accounting in Australia: Historical Essays* (New York: Routledge, 2014).

Parkin, Frank, *Marxism and Class Theory* (London: Tavistock, 1979).

Parmar, Inderjeet, *Foundations of the American Century: the Ford, Carnegie, and Rockefeller Foundations in the Rise of American Power* (New York: Columbia University Press, 2012).

Pawley, Alice, 'Shifting the "Default": The Case for Making Diversity the Expected Condition for Engineering Education and Making Whiteness and Maleness Visible', *Journal of Engineering Education* 106.4 (2017), 531–533.

Pearse, Malcolm, 'The Management Rush: A History of Management in Australia', Unpublished PhD Dissertation, Macquarie University (2010).

Pearson, Michael P.R., 'Grease Monkeys: A History of Mechanics in Australia'. Unpublished PhD Dissertation, Australian Catholic University (2021).

Peel, Mark, *Miss Cutler & the Case of the Resurrected Horse: Social Work and the Story of Poverty in America, Australia, and Britain* (Chicago: University of Chicago Press, 2012).

Pellew, Jill and Miles Taylor, 'Introduction', in Jill Pellew and Miles Taylor (eds), *Utopian Universities* (London: Bloomsbury, 2021), 1–18.

Penno, Erin and Robin Gauld 'The Role, Costs and Value for Money of External Consultancies in the Health Sector: A Study of New Zealand's District Health Boards', *Health Policy* 121.4 (2017), 458–467.

Pensabene, Tony, *The Rise of the Medical Practitioner in Victoria* (Canberra: Australian National University Press, 1980).

Penrose, Helen, *To Build a Firm: The Maddocks Story* (Melbourne: Maddocks, 2010).

Perkin, Harold, 'History of Universities', in James Forest and Philip Altbach (eds), *International Handbook of Higher Education* (Dordrecht: Springer, 2007), 159–205.

The Rise of Professional Society: England since 1880 (New York: Routledge, 1989).

Perloff, Richard and Anup Kumar, 'The Press and Watergate at 50: Understanding and Reconstructing a Seminal Story', *Journalism Practice* 16.5 (2022), 797–812.

Petty, Adrienne, 'I'll Take My Farm: The GI Bill, Agriculture and Veterans in North Carolina', *The Journal of Peasant Studies*, 35.4 (2008), 742–769.

Phillips, Peter, *Kill or Cure? Lotions, Potions, Characters and Quacks of Early Australia* (Richmond: Greenhouse Publications, 1984).

Piccini, Jon, *Transnational Protest, Australia and the 1960s: Global Radicals* (London: Palgrave Macmillan, 2016).

Human Rights in Twentieth Century Australia (Cambridge: Cambridge University Press, 2019).

Pietsch, Tamson, 'Universities, War and the Professionalization of Dentistry', *History of Education Review* 45.2 (2016), 168–182.

Polanyi, Karl, *The Great Transformation* (Boston: Beacon Press, 1985).

Pollard, Sidney, 'Capital Exports, 1870–1914: Harmful or Beneficial?', *The Economic History Review* 38.4 (1985), 489–514.

Pomeranz, Kenneth, *The Great Divergence: China, Europe, and the Making of the Modern World Economy* (Princeton, NJ: Princeton University Press, 2000).

Ponce de Leon, Charles, *That's The Way It Is: A History of Television News in America* (Chicago: University of Chicago Press 2015).

Poovey, Mary, *Uneven Developments: The Ideological Work of Gender in Mid-Victorian England* (Chicago: University of Chicago Press, 1988).

Popple, Philip, *Social Work Practice and Social Welfare Policy in the United States: A History* (Oxford: Oxford University Press, 2018).

Porter, Roy, *Quacks - Fakers & Charlatans in Medicine* (Charleston: Tempus, 2000).

Poulantzas, Nicos, *Classes in Contemporary Capitalism* (London: New Left Books, 1975).

'The New Petty Bourgeoisie', *Insurgent Sociologist* 9.1 (1979), 56–60.

Poullaos, Chris, 'The Self-Governing Dominions of South Africa, Australia, and Canada and the Evolution of the Imperial Accountancy Arena during the 1920s', in Chris Poullaos and Suki (eds), *Accountancy and Empire the British Legacy of Professional Organization* (London: Routledge, 2010).

Prentice, Allison, *The School Promoters: Education and Social Class in Mid-Nineteenth Century Upper Canada* (Toronto: University of Toronto Press, 2004).

Prentis, Malcolm, *The Scots in Australia* (Sydney: University of New South Wales Press, 2008).

Pressman, Matthew, 'Remaking the News: The Transformation of American Journalism, 1960–1980', Unpublished PhD Dissertation, Boston University (2016).

Pringle, Rosemary, *Sex and Medicine: Gender, Power and Authority in the Medical Profession* (Cambridge: Cambridge University Press, 1998).

Proctor, Helen and Ashleigh Driscoll, 'Bureaucratic Governance, Family Economies and the 1930s NSW Teachers' Marriage Bar, Australia', *Journal of Educational Administration and History* 49.2 (2017), 157–170.

Pugh, D.R., 'English nonconformity, education and passive resistance 1903–6', *History of Education* 19.4 (1990), 355–373.

Pue, Wesley, 'Guild Training vs. Professional Education: The Committee on Legal Education and the Law Department of Queen's College, Birmingham in the 1850s', *The American Journal of Legal History* 33.3 (1989), 241–287.

Puzan, Elayne, 'The Unbearable Whiteness of Being (in Nursing)', *Nursing Inquiry* 10.3 (2003), 193–200.

Quail, John, 'Becoming Fully Functional: The Conceptual Struggle for a New Structure for the Giant Corporation in the US and UK in the First Half of the Twentieth Century', *Business History* 50.2 (2008), 127–146.

Radcliffe, Vaughan, 'Knowing Efficiency: The Enactment of Efficiency in Efficiency Auditing', *Accounting, Organizations and Society*, 24.4 (1999), 333–362.

Rademaker, Laura and Tim Rowse, *Indigenous Self-Determination in Australia: Histories and Historiography* (Canberra: ANU Press, 2020).

Rao, C. (ed), *Globalization and Its Managerial Implications* (Westport, CN: Quorum Books, 2001).

Read, Peter, *The Stolen Generations: The Removal of Aboriginal Children in New South Wales 1883 to 1969* (Sydney: Government Printer, 1981).

Readings, Bill, *The University in Ruins* (Cambridge, MA: Harvard University Press, 1996).

Reagan, Leslie, *When Abortion Was a Crime: Women, Medicine and the Law in the United States 1867–1973* (Berkley: University of California Press, 1997).

Redden, Guy, 'Publish and Flourish, or Perish: RAE, ERA, RQF and Other Acronyms for Infinite Human Resourcefulness', *Media/Culture Journal*, 11.4 (2008), https://doi.org/10.5204/mcj.44.

Redmond, Jennifer and Judith Harford, 'One Man One Job', *Paedagogica Historica* 46.5 (2010), 639–654.

Reed, Michael and Peter Anthony, 'Professionalizing Management and Managing Professionalization: British Management in the 1980s', *Journal of Management Studies* 29.5 (1992), 591–613.

Reddy, Marisa, Randy Borum, John Berglund, Bryan Vossekuil, Robert Fein, and William Modzeleski, 'Evaluating Risk for Targeted Violence in Schools: Comparing Risk Assessment, Threat Assessment, and Other Approaches', *Psychology in the Schools* 38.2 (2001), 157–172.

Rees, Yves, 'A War of Card Indexes: From Political Economy to Economic Science', in Kate Darian-Smith and James Waghorne (eds), *The First*

World War, the Universities and the Professions in Australia 1914–1939 (Melbourne: Melbourne University Press, 2019).

'Thinking Capitalism from the Bedroom: The Politics of Location and the Uses of (Feminist, Queer, Crip) Theory', *Labour History* 21.1 (2021), 9–31.

Reese, Henry, 'Shopgirls as Consumers: Selling Popular Music in 1920s Australia', *Labour History*, 121 (2021), 155–174.

Reid, John and Paul Axelrod, *Youth, University, and Canadian Society: Essays in the Social History of Higher Education* (Kingston: McGill-Queen's University Press, 1989).

Reinarz, Jonathan, 'Investigating the "Deserving Poor": Charity and the Voluntary Hospitals in Nineteenth-Century Birmingham', in Anne Borsay and Peter Shapely (eds), *Medicine, Charity and Mutual Aid: The Consumption of Health and Welfare in Britain c.1550–1950* (London: Ashgate, 2007), 111–129.

Richardson, Alan, 'Merging the Profession: A Social Network Analysis of the Consolidation of the Accounting Profession in Canada', *Accounting Perspectives* 16.2 (2017), 83–104.

Richardson, William, 'The Weight of History: Structures, Patterns and Legacies of Secondary Education in the British Isles, c.1200–c.1980', *London Review of Education* 9.2 (2011), 153–173.

Riseman, Noah, *A History of Trans Health Care in Australia* (Melbourne: AusPATH, 2022).

Rimmer, Malcolm, 'Unions and Arbitration', in Joe Isaac and Stuart Macintyre (eds), *The New Province for Law and Order: One Hundred years of Australian Conciliation and Arbitration* (Cambridge: Cambridge University Press, 2004), 275–315.

Ritchie, Jenny and Mere Skerrett, *Early Childhood Education in Aotearoa New Zealand: History, Pedagogy, and Liberation* (New York: Palgrave Macmillan, 2014).

Robinson, Emily, Camilla Schofield, Florence Sutcliffe-Braithwaite, and Natalie Thomlinson, 'Telling Stories about Post-War Britain: Popular Individualism and the "Crisis" of the 1970s', *Twentieth Century British History* 28.2 (2017), 268–304.

Rockman, Seth, 'The Contours of Class in the Early Republic City', *Labor* 1.4 (2004), 91–108.

Rogan, Tim, *The Moral Economists: R.H. Tawney, Karl Polanyi, E.P. Thompson and the Critique of Capitalism* (Princeton NJ: Princeton University Press, 2017).

Rogers, Daniel, *Atlantic Crossings: Social Politics in a Progressive Age* (Cambridge, MA: Harvard University Press, 1998).

Rosenberg, Charles, *The Care of Strangers: The Rise of America's Hospital System* (New York: Basic Books, 1987).

Rosenberg, Emily, *Spreading the American Dream: American Economic and Cultural Expansion, 1890–1945* (New York: Macmillan, 1982).

Rosenblatt, Daniel, 'Stuff the Professional-Managerial Class Likes: 'Distinction' for an Egalitarian Elite', *Anthropological Quarterly* 86.2 (2013), 589–623.

Rosenthal, Caitlin, *Accounting for Slavery: Masters and Management* (Cambridge, MA: Harvard University Press, 2018).

Rosner, Cecil, *Behind the Headlines: A History of Investigative Journalism in Canada* (Oxford: Oxford University Press, 2011).

Rowse, Tim, *Nugget Coombs: A Reforming Life* (Cambridge: Cambridge University Press, 2002).

'The People and Their Experts: A War-Inspired Civics for H.C. Coombs', *Labour History* 74 (1998), 70–87.

Roy, Audrey Jane, *Sovereignty and Decolonization: Realizing Indigenous Self-Determination at the United Nations and in Canada* (Victoria: University of Victoria, 2001).

Ruckenstein, Minna and Natasha Schull, 'The Datafication of Health', *Annual Review of Anthropology* 46.1 (2017), 261–278.

Ruppert, Evelyn, John Law, and Mike Savage, 'Reassembling Social Science Methods: The Challenge of Digital Devices', *Theory, Culture and Society* 30.4 (2013), 22–46.

Rury, John, *Education and Social Change: contours in the History of American Schooling* (New York: Routledge, 2012).

Russell, Lynette, 'Doherty, Muriel Knox (1896–1988)', *Australian Dictionary of Biography, Volume 17* (Melbourne: Melbourne University Press, 2007).

From Nightingale to Now: Nurse Education in Australia (Sydney, Harcourt Brace Jovanovich, 1990).

Russell, Penny, *A Wish of Distinction: Colonial Gentility and Femininity* (Melbourne: Melbourne University Press, 1994).

Savage or Civilised? (Sydney: NewSouth, 2010).

'A Silly Quarrel about a Sore Knee? Defending Honour in a Professional Dispute, Sydney 1846', *Health and History* 14.2 (2012), 46–73.

Salsbury, Stephen and Kay Sweeney, *The Bull, the Bear, and the Kangaroo: The History of the Sydney Stock Exchange* (Sydney: Allen and Unwin, 1988).

Saunders, Peter, 'Might Britain Be a Meritocracy?' *Sociology* 29.1 (1995), 23–41.

Savage, Mike, *Social Class in the Twenty-first Century* (London: Penguin, 2015).

Identities and Social Change in Britain since 1940: The Politics of Method (Oxford: Oxford University Press, 2010).

Sayward, Amy, *The Birth of Development: How the World Bank, Food and Agriculture Organization and World Health Organization Changed the World, 1945–1965* (Kent, OH: Kent State University Press, 2006).

Scanlan, Meghan, 'Medical History: First Women in Medicine', *New Zealand Medical Student Journal* 31 (2020), 50–51.

Schmidt, Ulf, 'Medical Ethics and Nazism', in Laurence McCullough and Robert Baker (eds), *The Cambridge World History of Medical Ethics* (Cambridge: Cambridge University Press, 2008), 595–608.

Schofer, Evan, and John Meyer, 'The Worldwide Expansion of Higher Education in the Twentieth Century', *American Sociological Review* 70.6 (2005), 898–920.

Schudson, Michael, *Watergate in American Memory: How We Remember, Forget, and Reconstruct the Past* (New York: Basic Books 1992).

Schultz, Julianne, *Reviving the Fourth Estate: Democracy, Accountability, and the Media* (Cambridge: Cambridge University Press, 1998).

Searle, Geoffrey, *The Quest for National Efficiency: a study in British Politics and Political Thought, 1899–1914* (Berkeley: University of California Press, 1971).

Selleck, Richard, *The New Education: The English Background* (London: Pitman, 1968).

Semel, Susan and Alan Sadovnik, 'The Contemporary Small-School Movement: Lessons from the History of Progresive Education', *Teachers College Record* 110.9 (2008), 1744–1771.

Sennett, Richard, *The Culture of the New Capitalism* (New Haven: Yale University Press, 2006).

Serle, Geoffrey, 'Murdoch, Sir Keith Arthur (1885–1952)', in *Australian Dictionary of Biography, Volume 10* (Melbourne: Melbourne University Press, 1986).

The Rush to Be Rich: A History of the Colony of Victoria, 1883–1889 (Melbourne: Melbourne University Press, 1971).

Sethna, Christabelle and Steve Hewitt, 'Clandestine Operations: The Vancouver Women's Caucus, the Abortion Caravan and the RCMP', *Canadian Historical Review* 90.3 (2009), 463–495.

Sewell, William, *Work and Revolution in France: the Language of Labor from the Old Regime to 1848* (Cambridge: Cambridge University Press, 1980).

Shenhav, Yehouda, *Manufacturing Rationality the Engineering Foundations of the Managerial Revolution* (Oxford: Oxford University Press, 2002).

Sheridan, Tom, *Mindful Militants: The Amalgamated Engineering Union in Australia, 1920–1972* (Cambridge: Cambridge University Press, 1975).

Sherington, Geoffrey, *Alexander Mackie: An Academic Life* (Sydney: University of Sydney Press, 2019).

English Education, Social Change and War 1911–1920 (Manchester: Manchester University Press, 1981).

Shore, Cris and Susan Wright, 'Audit Culture Revisited: Rankings, Ratings, and the Reassembling of Society', *Current Anthropology* 56.3 (2015), 421–444.

Sims, Margaret, 'Neoliberalism and Early Childhood', *Cogent Education*, 4:1 (2017), https://doi.org/10.1080/2331186X.2017.1365411.

Slagstad, Ketil and Debra Malina, 'The Political Nature of Sex: Transgender in the History of Medicine', *New England Journal of Medicine* 384 (2021), 1070–1074.

Slobodian, Quinn, *Globalists: The End of Empire and the Birth of Neoliberalism* (Cambridge, MA: Harvard University Press, 2018).

Sluga, Glenda, *Internationalism in the Age of Nationalism* (Philadelphia: University of Pennsylvania Press, 2013).

'The Transformation of International Institutions: Global Shock as Cultural Shock', in Niall Ferguson, Charles Maier, Erez Manela, Daniel Sargent (eds), *The Shock of the Global: The 1970s in Perspective* (Cambridge, MA: Harvard University Press, 2010), 223–236.

Smith, Philippa, *A Concise History of New Zealand* (Cambridge: Cambridge University Press, 2012).

Snyder, Benson, *The Hidden Curriculum* (New York: Knopf, 1971).

Sobicinska, Agnieszka, *Saving the World? Western Volunteers and the Rise of the Humanitarian-Development Complex* (Cambridge: Cambridge University Press, 2021).

Sokoll, Thomas, 'The Moral Foundation of Modern Capitalism: Towards a Historical Reconsideration of Max Weber's 'Protestant Ethic', in Stefan Berger and Alexandra Przyrembel (eds), *Moralizing Capitalism: Agents, Discourses and Practices of Capitalism and Anti-Capitalism in the Modern Age* (London: Palgrave Macmillan, 2019), 79–110.

Starr, Paul, *The Social Transformation of American Medicine* (New York: Basic Books, 1982).

Staubus, George, *Economic Influences on the Development of Accounting in Firms* (New York: Garland, 1996).

Steil, Benn, *The Battle of Bretton Woods: John Maynard Keynes, Harry Dexter White, and the Making of a New World Order* (Princeton: Princeton University Press, 2013).

Stevenson, Allyson, 'Vibrations Across a Continent: the 1978 Indian Child Welfare Act and the Politicization of First Nations Leaders in Saskatchewan', *The American Indian Quarterly* 37.1–2 (2013), 218–236.

Stewart, William, *Higher Education in Postwar Britain* (Basingstoke: Macmillan, 1989).

Strange, Susan, *Mad Money: When Markets Outgrow Governments* (Manchester: Manchester University. Press, 1998).

Streeck, Wolfgang, *Buying Time: The Delayed Crisis of Democratic Capitalism* (London: Verso, 2014).

Stryker, Susan, *Transgender History* (Berkley, CA: Seal Press, 2008).

Sutcliffe-Braithwaite, Florence, *Class, Politics, and the Decline of Deference in England, 1968–2000* (Oxford: Oxford University Press, 2018).

Sutherland, Gillian, *In Search of the New Woman: Middle-Class Women and Work in Britain 1870–1914* (Cambridge: Cambridge University Press, 2015).

Swain, Shurlee, '"Homes Are Sought for These Children": Locating Adoption Within the Australian Stolen Generations Narrative', *The American Indian Quarterly* 37.1–2 (2013), 203–217.

'Negotiating Poverty: Women and Charity in Nineteenth-Century Melbourne', *Women's History Review* 16.1 (2007), 99–112.

Swartz, Rebecca, *Education and Empire: Children, Race and Humanitarianism in the British Settler Colonies, 1833–1880* (Cham: Palgrave Macmillan, 2019).

Sweetman, John, 'Medical Staff Corps', *Journal of the Society for Army Historical Research* 53.214 (1975), 113–119.

Tascón, Sonia and Jim Ife, 'Human Rights and Critical Whiteness: Whose Humanity?', *The International Journal of Human Rights*, 12:3 (2008), 307–327.

Taksa, Lucy, 'Handmaiden of Industrial Welfare or Armed Combatant" Considering the Experience of Industrial Nursing at the Eveleigh Railway Workshops', *Health and History* 1.4 (1999), 298–329.

Tawney, Richard, *Religion and the Rise of Capitalism* (London: Penguin, 1926).

Taylor, Tony, 'Arthur Balfour and Educational Change: The Myth Revisited', *British Journal of Educational Studies* 42.2 (1994), 133–149.

Teese, Richard, *Academic Success and Social Power: Examinations and Inequality* (Melbourne, Melbourne University Press, 2000).

Terry, Jennifer, *An American Obsession: Science, Medicine and Homosexuality in Modern Society* (Chicago: University of Chicago Press, 1999).

Theobald, Marjorie, 'Imagining the Woman Teacher: An International Perspective', *Australian Educational Researcher* 22.3(1995), 87–111.

Knowing Women: Origins of Women's Education in Nineteenth-Century Australia (Cambridge, Cambridge University Press, 1996).

Theobald, Marjorie and Donna Dwyer, 'An Episode in Feminist Politics: The Married Women (Lecturers and Teachers) Act, 1932–47', *Labour History* 76 (1999), 59–77.

Thomas, Archie, 'Bilingual Education, Aboriginal Self-Determination and Yolŋu Control at Shepherdson College, 1972–1983', *History of Education Review* 50. 2 (2021), 196–211.

Thompson, Edward, *The Making of the English Working Class* (New York: Vintage Books, 1966).

Thompson, John, 'American Muckrakers and Western Canadian Reform', *Journal of Popular Culture* 4.4 (1971), 1060–1070.

Thomson, Kathleen, 'Glass, Barnet (1849–1918)', *Australian Dictionary of Biography, Volume 9* (Melbourne: Melbourne University Press, 1983).

Tiratsoo, Nick, 'The "Americanization" of Management Education in Britain', *Journal of Management Inquiry* 13.2 (2004), 118–127.

Tosh, John, *A Man's Place: Masculinity and the Middle-class Home in Victorian England* (New Haven: Yale University Press, 1999).

Towers, Brian, 'Running the Gauntlet: British Trade Unions under Thatcher, 1979–1988', *Industrial and Labor Relations Review* 42.2 (1989), 163–188.

Travers, Max. *The New Bureaucracy: Quality Assurance and Its Critics* (Bristol: Policy Press, 2007).

Trolander, Judith, *Professionalism and Social Change: From the Settlement House Movement to Neighborhood Centers 1886 to the Present* (New York: Colombia University Press, 1987).

Tschoegl, Adrian, 'The International Diffusion of an Innovation: The Spread of Decimal Currency', *The Journal of Socio-Economics* 39.1 (2010), 100–109.

Urban, Wayne, 'Australia and New Zealand through American Eyes: The "Eyes" Have It', *History of Education Review* 39.1 (2010), 53–58.

Urban, Wayne and Marybeth Smith, 'Much Ado about Something?: James Bryant Conant, Harvard University, and Nazi Germany in the 1930s', *Paedagogica historica* 51.1–2 (2015), 152–165.

Urry, John, *Offshoring* (Hoboken, NJ: Wiley, 2014).

Vallas, Steven, 'Rethinking Post-Fordism: The Meaning of Workplace Flexibility', *Sociological Theory* 17.1 (1999), 68–101.

Van Aken, Monica, 'The History of Montessori Education in America, 1909–2004', unpublished EdD Dissertation, University of Virginia (2004).

Vance, Michael, 'A Brief History of Organized Scottishness in Canada', in Celeste Ray (ed), *Transatlantic Scots* (Tuscaloosa: University of Alabama Press, 2010), 96–119.

Vargas-Cetina, Gabriela, 'Introduction: The Anthropology of Flexible Accumulation', *Urban Anthropology and Studies of Cultural Systems and World Economic Development* 28.3–4 (1999), 193–97.

Varoufakis, Yanis, *The Global Minotaur: America, Europe and the Future of the Global Economy* (London: Zed Books, 2011).

Vayda, Eugene, Robert Evans, and William Mindell, 'Universal Health Insurance in Canada: History, Problems, Trends', *Journal of Community Health* 4.3 (1979), 217–231.

Verger, Antoni, Clara Fontdevila, and Adrián Zancajo, *The Privatization of Education: A Political Economy of Global Education Reform* (New York: Teachers College Press, 2016).

Verhoef, Grietjie and Grant Samkin, 'The Accounting Profession and Education', *Accounting, Auditing and Accountability* 30.6 (2017), 1370–1398.

Vogel, Morris, *The Invention of the Modern Hospital: Boston 1870–1930* (Chicago: University of Chicago Press, 1980).

Walker, Stephen and Thomas Lee, *Studies in Early Professionalism: Scottish Chartered Accountants, 1853–1918* (New York: Garland, 1999).

Wallerstein, Immanuel, *Historical Capitalism* (London: Verso, 1983).

The Modern World-System III: The Second Era of Great Expansion of the Capitalist World-Economy, 1730s–1840s (Berkeley: University of California Press, 2011).

'The Rise and Future Demise of the World Capitalist System: Concepts for Comparative Analysis', *Comparative Studies in Society and History* 16.4 (1974), 387–415.

Walkowitz, Daniel, *Working with Class: Social Workers and the Politics of Middle-Class Identity* (Chapel Hill, NC: University of North Carolina Press, 1999).

Ward, Stuart, '"No Nation Could Be Broker": The Satire Boom and the Demise of Britain's World Role', in Stuart. Ward (ed), *British Culture and the End of Empire* (Manchester: Manchester University Press, 2001).

Warne, Ellen, *Agitate, Educate, Organise, Legislate: Protestant Women's Social Action in Post-Suffrage Australia* (Melbourne: Melbourne University Press, 2017).

Watego, Chelsea, *Another Day in the Colony* (Brisbane: University of Queensland Press, 2021).

Watkins, Elizabeth, *On the Pill: A Social History of Oral Contraceptives 1950–1970* (Baltimore: Johns Hopkins University Press, 1998).

Weber, Max, *The Protestant Ethic and the Spirit of Capitalism* (London: Penguin, 2002).

Wiebe, Robert *The Search for Order* (New York: Hill and Wang: 1967).

Weisbrod, Burton, 'The Health Care Quadrilemma: An Essay on Technological Change, Insurance, Quality of Care, and Cost Containment', *Journal of Economic Literature* 29.2 (1991), 523–552.

Wheatley, Steven, *The Politics of Philanthropy: Abraham Flexner and Medical Education* (Madison: University of Wisconsin Press, 1988).

Whelan, Christopher and Richard Layte, 'Late Industrialization and the Increased Merit Selection Hypothesis. Ireland as a Test Case', *European Sociological Review* 18.1 (2002), 35–50.

Whelan, Jean 'Too Many, Too Few: The Supply, Demand, and Distribution of Private Duty Nurses, 1910–1965', unpublished PhD Dissertation, University of Pennsylvania (2000).

White, Michael, 'Carnegie Philanthropy in Australia in the Nineteen Thirties – A Reassessment', *History of Education Review* 26.1 (1997), 1–24.

White, Richard, *On Holidays: A History of Getting away in Australia* (Melbourne: Pluto Press, 2005).

White, Richard, *Railroaded: The Transcontinentals and the Making of Modern America* (New York, Norton, 2011).

Whyte, Jessica, *The Morals of the Market: Human Rights and the Rise of Neoliberalism* (London: Verso, 2019).

The Search for Order 1877–1920 (New York: Hill and Wang, 1967).

Wijffels, Alain and Jonathan Bush, *Learning the Law: Teaching and the Transmission of Law in England, 1150–1900* (London: Hambledon, 1999).

Williams, Kevin, *Read All about It: A History of the British Newspaper* (London: Routledge, 2010).

Williams, Raymond, *Marx and Literature* (Oxford: Oxford University Press, 1977).

Williamson, Ben, Sian Bayne, and Suellen Shay, 'The Datafication of Teaching in Higher Education: Critical Issues and Perspectives', *Teaching in Higher Education* 25:4 (2020), 351–365.

Willis, Evan, *Medical Dominance: The Division of labour in Australian Health Care* (Sydney: Allen & Unwin, 1983).

Willis, Richard, *Testing Times: A History of Vocational, Civil Service and Secondary Examinations in England since 1850* (Boston: Brill, 2013).

Winant, Gabriel, *The Next Shift: The Fall of Industry and the Rise of Health Care in Rust Belt America* (Cambridge, MA: Harvard University Press, 2021).

Winstanley, Michael, 'Owners and Occupiers: Property, Politics and Middle-Class Formation in Early Industrial Lancashire', in Alan J Kidd and David Nicholls (eds), *The Making of the British Middle Class? Studies of Regional and Cultural Diversity Since the Eighteenth Century* (Phoenix Mill: Sutton, 1998), 92–112.

Witz, Anne, *Professions and Patriarchy* (London: Routledge, 1992).

Wivel, Ashley, 'Abortion Policy and Politics on the Lane Committee of Enquiry, 1971–1974', *Social History of Medicine* 11.1 (1998), 109–135.

Wolfe, Patrick, 'History and Imperialism: A Century of Theory, from Marx to Postcolonialism', *The American Historical Review* 102.2 (1997), 388–420.

'Land, Labor and Difference: Elementary Structures of Race', *The American Historical Review* 106.3 (2001), 866–905.

'Nation and Miscegenation: Discursive Continuity in the Post-Mabo Era', *Social Analysis: The International Journal of Social and Cultural Practice* 36 (1994), 93–152.

'Settler Colonialism and the Elimination of the Native', *Journal of Genocide Research* 8.4 (2006), 387–409.

Settler Colonialism and the Transformation of Anthropology: The Politics and Poetics of an Ethnographic Event (London: Cassell, 1999).

Traces of History: Elementary Structures of Race (London: Verso, 2016).

Woodroofe, Kathleen, *From Charity to Social Work in England and the United States* (London: Routledge and Kegan Paul, 1962).

Wright, Erik Olin, *Classes* (London: Verso, 1985).

Wright, Claire, 'Above Board? Interlocked Directorates and Corporate Contagion in 1980s Australia', *Australian Economic History Review* 62.3 (2022), 290–312.

Wright, Claire and Hannah Forsyth, 'Managerial Capitalism and White-Collar Professions: Social Mobility in Australia's Corporate Elite', *Labour History* 121 (2021), 99–127.

Wyhe, Glenn Van, 'A history of US Higher Education in Accounting, Part 1: Situating Accounting within the Academy', *Issues in Accounting Education* 22.2 (2007), 165–181.

York, Barry, 'Looking Back at Oz Magazine', *National Library of Australia News*, May 2001, 10–12.

Young, Sally, *Paper Emperors: The Rise of Australia's Newspaper Empire* (Sydney: NewSouth, 2019).

Yule, Peter, *William Lawrence Baillieu: Founder of Australia's Greatest Business Empire* (Melbourne: Hardie Grant, 2012).

Zakim, Michael, *Accounting for Capitalism: The World the Clerk Made* (Chicago, University of Chicago Press, 2018).

Zucker, Lynne, Michael Darby, and Marilynn Brewer, 'Intellectual Capital and the Birth of US Biotechnology Enterprises', National Bureau of Economic Research Working Paper 4653 (1994).

Primary Sources

Archival Sources

Broken Hill School File, State Records of NSW

William Jamieson papers, University of Melbourne Archives

Law Institute of Victoria, University of Melbourne Archives

Nightingale Papers, British Library

Royal Australian Nursing Federation, Noel Butlin Archive Centre

National association of women lawyers, Schlesinger Library

Papers of Annie Louisa Green, National Library of Australia

Department of External Affairs Correspondence Series 1946, National Archives of Australia, Canberra

W.G. Davies Papers, Provincial Archives of Saskatchewan

V.L. Matthew fonds - MG241, University of Sakatchewan Archives

Thompson Papers, University of Saskatchewan Archives

Australian Association of Social Workers, University of Melbourne Archives

Australian Association of Social Workers, New South Wales Branch - further records, State Library of New South Wales

Association of Professional Engineers, Australia, Noel Butlin Archives Centre.

Australian Nursing Federation, NSW Branch deposit, Noel Butlin Archives Centre

Minutes and Correspondence of the Medical Staff Association, Royal Children's Hospital, Melbourne, Public Records Office of Victoria.

Published Primary Sources

Bringing Them Home: Report of the National Inquiry into the Separation of Aboriginal and Torres Strait Islander Children from Their Families (Canberra: Commonwealth of Australia, 1997).

Beveridge, William, *Full Employment in a Free Society* (London: Allen & Unwin, 1944).

Clunies Ross, Allan, *The People's Money and How They Control it* (Sydney: Sound Finance League of Australia, 1934).

The Workers' Shares under the Companies Act, New South Wales (Hamilton, NZ: Employee Partnership Institute, 1936).

Committee on Higher Education, *Higher Education: Report of the Committee Appointed by the Prime Minister under the Chairmanship of Lord Robbins* (London: Her Majesty's Stationery Office, 1963).

Conant, James, 'Confidential Report to the Carnegie Corporation on the University Situation in Australia in the Year 1951', *History of Education Review* 39.1 (2010), 8–22.

Coombs, Herbert, *Science and Technology: For What Purpose?* (Canberra: Australian Academy of Science, 1979).

Covey, Stephen, *The 7 Habits of Highly Effective People* (New York: Simon & Schuster, 1989).

Davis, Mackenzie and Susan Masten, *Principles of Environmental Engineering* (New York: McGraw-Hill Education, 2013).

Escobar, Isabel and Andrea Schaefer, *Sustainable Water for the Future: Water Recycling versus Desalination* (Amsterdam: Elsevier, 2010).

Flagan, Richard and John Seinfeld, *Fundamentals of Air Pollution Engineering* (Englewood Cliffs, NJ: Prentice-Hall, 1988).

Flexner, Abraham, *Medical Education in the United States and Canada: A Report to the Carnegie Foundation for the Advancement of Teaching* (New York: Carnegie Foundation, 1910).

Friedman, Milton, *Capitalism and Freedom* (Chicago: University of Chicago Press, 1962).

Goodman, Paul, *Compulsory Miseducation* (New York: Horizon Press, 1964).

Growing Up Absurd (New York: Random House, 1960).

Greer, Germaine, *The Female Eunuch* (London : Paladin, 1971).

Hutson, Jack *Six Wage Concepts* (Sydney: Amalgamated Engineering Union, 1971).

Illich, Ivan. *Deschooling Society* (London: Calder and Boyars, 1971).

Limits to Medicine: Medical Nemesis the Expropriation of Health (London: Marion Boyars, 1976).

Johnson, Rex, *Returning to the Light: The Memoirs of Rex Johnson* (Melbourne: Rex Johnson, 2017).

Martineau, Harriet, *Society in America* (New York: Saunders and Otle, 1837).

Menzies, Robert, *The Place of a University in the Modern Community : An Address* (Melbourne: Melbourne University Press, 1929).

Northcote, Stafford and Charles Trevelyan, *Report on the Organization of the Permanent Civil Service* (London: Her Majesty's Stationary Office, 1854).

Nouwen, Henri, *Reaching Out: The Three Movements of the Spiritual Life* (New York: Doubleday, 1975).

Partridge, Percy, 'Comment on the Social Role of Higher Education by S. Encel', in Edward Wheelwright (ed), *Higher Education in Australia* (Melbourne: F.W Cheshire, 1965).

Perera, Noel, 'Sustainable Energy, Engineering, Materials and Environment: Current Advances and Challenges', *Environmental Science and Pollution Research International* 26.29 (2019), 29507–29508.

Stinnet, T. M. (ed), *Unfinished Business of the Teaching Profession in the 1970's* (Bloomington, IN: Phi Delta Kappa, 1971).

Tracy, Brian, *Eat That Frog: Get More Important Things Done – Today!* (Oakland, CA: Berrett-Koehler, 2016).

Trainer, T., 'Bandaids or Fundamental Change?', *Radical Education Dossier* 22 (1984), 4–7.

Troeh, Frederick, Arthur Hobbs, and Roy Donahue, *Soil and Water Conservation: Productivity and Environmental Protection* (Englewood Cliffs, NJ: Prentice-Hall, 1980).

Tomlinson, John, 'Challenging State Aggression against Indigenous Australians', in Deena Mandell, and Nilan Yu (eds), *Subversive Action: Extralegal Practices for Social Justottice* (Waterloo, Ontario: Wilfrid Laurier University Press, 2015), 25–39.

Weeks, E. P., 'Canada and Post-War Reconstruction', *Journal of the Royal Society of the Arts* 94.4709 (1946), 113–119.

Published Government Sources

Australian Colonial Censuses 1871–1901
Australian Census 1911–2001
US Census 1870–2000
Canadian Census 1881–2001
New Zealand Census 1881–1921
Census of England and Wales 1851–1911
Government Gazette of the State of New South Wales
NSW Yearbooks (1890–1969)
Australian Parliamentary Debates, House of Representatives: official Hansard
British House of Commons Debates, Official Hansard
Commonwealth Court of Conciliation and Arbitration, Australia, Commonwealth Arbitration Reports
Constitution of the Commonwealth of Australia

Newspapers, Magazines and Professional Journals

Newspapers

Adelaide Advertiser
Altoona Tribune
Australian Star
Age (Melbourne)
Argus (Melbourne)

Brooklyn Citizen
Bruce Herald
Buffalo Evening News
Calgary Herald
Canberra Times
Cincinnati Enquirer
Dayton Daily News
Decatur Daily Review
Democrat and Chronicle
Evening Post (Wellington)
Evening Star (Washington)
Fort Worth Star-Telegram
Guardian (Manchester)
Gympie Times and Mary River Mining Gazette
Gazette (Montreal)
Glasgow Herald
Glen Innes Examiner
Honolulu Star-Bulletin
Inter Ocean (Chicago)
Kingston Daily Freeman
Leader (Orange)
Leader-Post (Regina)
Los Angeles Times
Mackay Mercury
Manawatu Standard
Manitowoc Herald-Times
Miami Herald
Middletown Times-Press
New Zealand Herald
New Zealand Times
Ottawa Citizen
Portland Guardian
Philadelphia Inquirer
Queensland Times, Ipswich Herald and General Advertiser
Reading Times
San Francisco Examiner
Singleton Argus
South Australian Register
Star (Guernsey)
Star-Phoenix (Saskatoon)
Sydney Morning Herald
Sydney Stock and Station Journal
Tasmanian
Times (London)
Times Union
Tribune (Sydney)
Vancouver Daily World

Vancouver Sun
Victoria Daily Times
Week (Brisbane)
Wellington Times
Windsor Star

Magazines
Harper's Magazine
Vanity Fair

Professional Journals
Australian Medical Gazette
Australasian Nurses' Journal
Australian Nurses' Journal
Australian Journalist
Australasian Accountant and Secretary
Australian Accountant
British Journal of Industrial Medicine
British Medical Journal
Canadian Medical Association Journal
Columbia Journalism Review
Commonwealth Journal of Accountancy
Institution of Engineers Australia, Journal of the
Law Institute Journal
Medical Journal of Australia
Nursing Times
Professional Engineer
Public Accountant
Social Work
Transactions of the Institution of Engineers
Women in Medicine

Index

.

Printed in the United States
by Baker & Taylor Publisher Services